The
Mental
Health
Almanac

The Mental Health Almanac™

Robert D. Allen
EDITOR

Marsha K. Cartier
ASSOCIATE EDITOR

Garland STPM Press
New York & London

Library of Congress Cataloging in Publication Data
Main entry under title:
The Mental health almanac.

Includes Bibliography.
1. Mental health services—United States.
2. Mental health services—Vocational guidance.
3. Mental health services—Information services.
I. Allen, Robert D., 1948–
II. Cartier, Marsha K., 1950–

RA790.6.M39   1978   362.2'0973   77–20599
ISBN 0-8240-7018-6

Printed in the United States of America

To Our Families

Robert D. Allen: to my mother & father (Katherine & Guile) and to my brother & sister (Rick & Renee). Also to Ken Kesey for McMurphy.

Marsha K. Cartier: to my mother—Ida, father—Lee, brother—Gary, grandfather—Elmer, aunt—Agnes, and to my very special friends Merrylee, Pat, LaVerne, Harold & Delores.

Contents

Preface

The *Mental Health Almanac* was born during an investigation of mental health sources at a university library for a therapy research project. It was amazing, at least to us, that there was not a major source book on this field. Instead, information was scattered everywhere. After our research project was completed we discussed the need for such a source book—a book the general public, students, and professionals could use. Having established the need, we tackled the task head on, and the result is the *Mental Health Almanac.*

Interest Levels

The *Almanac* can be used on many different levels, depending on a person's need. The first is just for reading; this will give a comprehensive view of what is taking place topic by topic in the field. The second level is finding information of interest; thereafter, the reader can use public or university libraries, or purchase the material directly. A third level is taking sources of interest (associations, organizations, research centers, books, articles, films, tapes, etc.) and contacting or using them directly for more information. Direct use of the sources will lead far beyond the information given in the *Almanac* since these are fountainheads and need only be approached.

It would have been absurd and impossible to include *all* information, so the *Almanac* is an overview. Nonetheless, it is a complete purview of the mental health field, because it contains all three levels. In this way the *Almanac* is both a resource list and a guide.

Interest Groups

In addition to the usage levels, the *Almanac* appeals to three groups of people who can benefit by it: the general public, students, and professionals. It can be a helpful tool in clarifying the mysteries surrounding

the area of mental health. With this information the public need not feel
confused by or alien to the mental health system. Instead, it can make
appropriate choices according to its interests and needs. This gives
people great power in understanding both the field itself and the options available in it. For example, a mother with a retarded child could
read the *Almanac* and, in gaining knowledge, can help herself and her
child. She could then survey some of the resources at the library or
purchase them directly. Continuing further, she could contact some of
the sources directly and thereby obtain additional information. In
this way she would have a knowledge base to make decisions that
affect her directly; she need not be immobilized by a lack of information or by dependency on an "expert" for answers.

Students can use the *Almanac* in much the same way. It can contribute to their knowledge, aid them in career decisions, and help them
in their studies (research reports, term papers, theses, etc.).

Professionals will find the *Almanac* useful in the approaches already described, in addition to being a refresher, a source list, and an
aid to research and writing.

Classification

Information sources are classified in the *Almanac* according to primary topic areas. However, because of secondary topics, there is considerable overlap in information throughout the book. For example,
sources on children would be located in the primary chapter on children and in others as secondary information. If the source is an organization, even though it is about children, it would also be classified
under Service Organizations. In the latter case, the primary topic area
would be an organization and the secondary topic children. Each
source has one primary topic area, usually with one or more secondary
topics. This means "children" can be found not only in the chapter on
children but throughout the *Almanac* as secondary information. This
pattern holds true throughout the book.

If an address of a source is not listed in the primary area for it, then
look in the Appendix Source List or in the Professional Associations
and Service Organization chapters.

Information

We have checked all the information listed in the *Almanac* thoroughly.
However, in a work of this scope it is impossible for all the informa-

tion to stay viable, and for this we ask your understanding and consideration. The best procedure for further information is to write a source, not sending money until a reply has been received. With this in mind we have tried our best to list all the information on a source. Sometimes the year, price, or some other piece of information was not available, although we would have liked to have included it. Also it should be noted that addresses change, companies and institutions go out of business, and certain materials will no longer be available.

The Future

Preparation of our first edition has been a time of learning and exploration. We hope this work is useful, and we definitely welcome comments and suggestions about it from interested readers. (Please address correspondence to: *The Mental Health Almanac,* P. O. Box 160371, Sacramento, CA 95816.) Tell us what you liked or disliked, what you want more or less of, and what new topics you would like to have included in future editions. *The Mental Health Almanac* will be published biennially, updated and expanded. We would appreciate any help you can give us.

Robert D. Allen—*Editor*

Marsha K. Cartier—*Associate Editor*

Acknowledgments

Without the help of the Mental Health Research Project (California State University—Sacramento, in spring 1976), which provided the leads, this *Almanac* would certainly not have had the range or depth it now enjoys. Our greatest appreciation goes to the following student researchers: Rose Reiwitch, Roger McKee, Ron DeZeeuw, Bonnie Brasher, George Lytal, George (Buddy) McMillan, Jim Landers, Marilyn Bader, Eddie Butler, David Fox, Jeffrey Jones, Les Bowman, Paul Mattiuzzi, Monica Bradley, Charlene Mounts, Kristina Martin, and Vixen Pope.

Special appreciation goes to our typist, Edie Oldfield, for doing an excellent job, as well as putting up with us. Finally, in a work of this scope and size it was necessary to use a vast number of sources, directly and indirectly, and it is impossible to give credit to them all, but we do express blanket appreciation.

Introduction*

An overview of the current mental health care system in America can only be understood within the context of its historical development. This development is characterized by the progression from the establishment of hospitals or asylums for the "insane" to the supplanting of these hospitals by community mental health centers (CMHCs). It is also characterized by the move towards federal control and coordination of the health care system and the trend of general hospitals providing psychiatric services.

It is important to realize that the development of a public mental health care system in America has historically been a reflection of the social, cultural, economic, and philosophical forces affecting a society moving into a complex modern era. The foundations of the system are not necessarily based on scientific or medical facts.

American institutions developed partly from philosophical changes in Europe during the seventeenth and eighteenth centuries. Prior to that, madness or unreason was not viewed within a medical framework as an illness, but instead was tolerated as a natural counterpart to reason or as a religious phenomenon. The development of institutions for the "insane" or the "deviant" was partly a function of the shift away from these conceptualizations and was related to society's shift from a religious to a secular orientation. The development of institutions was influenced to an even greater extent by the nineteenth century phenomena of industrialization and urbanization. Within a rural, agrarian society the landscape had provided room for "lunatics" and "deviants" to wander about harmlessly; informal community and family mechanisms were able to deal with them adequately. In the confines of the new urban society, however, mental hospitals proliferated because there was no room in which to tolerate behavior that was outside of acceptable limits or that was perceived as threatening to the community. Since standards of behavior were defined by middle class

*with Paul Mattiuzzi

values, the populations of institutions have thus traditionally functioned as a means of social control of the urban lower classes.

This development of institutions which emphasized the needs of society more than those of the individual meant that treatment and rehabilitation was of secondary importance in relation to providing custodial care. There were many reform movements during the 1800s aimed at upgrading conditions in mental hospitals and at reorienting them towards "moral therapy" or treatment. The most notable of the reformers was Dorothea Dix who labored for the building of hospitals and the improvement of existing facilities. The efforts at reform were futile for the most part, though, since they attempted to improve and expand mental hospitals and thus perpetuated the system itself.

The development of psychiatry gave additional support to the system, providing a medical and scientific rationale to what was still basically a social institution. The problem becomes clearer in view of current theories which assert that the concept of mental illness is a myth. That is, the mind is a conceptual entity rather than a physical one, such as the brain, and thus cannot be afflicted with an illness which by definition is a physical affliction. The metaphor that someone behaves "as if" he were sick in the mind or "as if" he were mentally ill became accepted as a scientific reality. People are thus labeled mentally ill on the basis of the deviation of their behavior from the norm which, in essence, represents the values and morals of the middle class. Thus the function of mental hospitals as a controlling agent has been obfuscated and legitimized by psychiatric-medical jargon.

This is not to say that there are not large numbers of people who exhibit syndromes of behavior which prevent them from dealing adequately with the problems of living and existing within society. It does imply though that such behavior cannot legitimately be labeled as an illness and that institutions for the "mentally ill" are by their very nature an improper setting for the resolution of such problems. In fact, the evidence is clear that removing a person from his natural environment and placing him in an institution is actually detrimental to his ability to exist and function within society.

World War II brought with it the beginnings of a comprehensive national mental health program in America. The National Mental Health Act was passed by Congress in 1946, authorizing federal aid to the states for mental health services with the intention of improving the treatment and prevention of mental and emotional illness. The impetus for this legislation was the scandalously overcrowded conditions in state mental hospitals, the fact that over one million men were rejected for military service due to psychiatric disorders, and the fact that more men received medical discharges for psychiatric disorders than any other reason. In conjunction with this legislation was the creation of the National Institute of Mental Health in 1949 to implement the National Mental Health Act. These legislative actions focused primarily on granting research funds rather than amending the current system and condition of mental hospitals.

Another trend toward change occurred during the 1950s with the establishment of outpatient clinics in general hospitals in a large number of cities with a result of a corresponding decrease in the number of hospitalized patients. This trend was related to federal funding for the construction of general hospitals with psychiatric services and insurance coverage extended to psychiatric treatment. Of even greater importance was the development of new tranquilizing drugs which facilitated the "maintenance" of the disturbed within the community.

In 1955, Congress passed the Mental Health Study Act in order to obtain an objective analysis of the mental health problem in America. The report resulting from this Act inspired an appeal from President Kennedy for a new federal drive to aid the mentally ill and retarded, resulting in the passage of the Community Mental Health Centers Act in 1963.

The goal of this legislation was to establish care for the disturbed within the community rather than confining them in the isolated, nontherapeutic mental hospitals. The rationale behind this Act may be seen in some of the testimony presented to Congress. HEW Secretary Anthony J. Celebrezze testified that "large state mental hospitals were primarily institutions for quarantining the mentally ill, not for treating them." Senator Lester Hill, floor manager of the Bill, stated that "conditions for the mentally ill have changed very little since the first public mental hospital was opened in 1773." He continued, saying that most mental patients were treated in large public institutions far from home; more than two-thirds of these generally overcrowded hospitals were built before 1900; and more than two-thirds were considered inadequate by a hospital accreditation commission.

The goals of the National Institute of Mental Health in establishing a comprehensive mental health care system are best characterized by this legislation. These goals though are not actually the best representation of the system as it exists.

The National Institute of Mental Health listed 32,000 facilities in the United States that provide psychiatric services. These may be classified primarily by the type of facility and by the types of services provided. The basic types of facilities are: psychiatric hospitals which represent 18.7 percent of the total number of facilities; general hospitals with separate psychiatric services, representing 24.1 percent of all facilities; freestanding outpatient psychiatric clinics, accounting for 35.1 percent of all facilities; community mental health centers which are 9.2 percent of all facilities; residential treatment centers for emotionally disturbed children, 10.8 percent of all facilities; freestanding day hospitals, 1.1 percent of all facilities; and various other multiservice facilities, representing another 1 percent of the total number of facilities. The composition of services provided varies with each facility, but the major types are outpatient treatment, inpatient treatment, and day treatment. Other services that might be provided include diagnosis, day training, special education, work activity, a sheltered workshop, vocational rehabilitation, halfway house service, aftercare, research, consultation to community agencies, and staff training.

REFERENCES

Beigel, A. & Levenson, A. *The Community Mental Health Center: Strategies & Programs*. New York: Basic Books, Inc., 1972.

Brown, B. *A National View of Mental Health*. Washington, D.C.: DHEW, 1974.

Chu, F. & Trotter, S. *The Madness Establishment: Ralph Nader's Study Group Report on the NIMH*. New York: Grossman Publishers, 1974.

Connery, Robert H. *The Politics of Mental Health: Organizing Community Mental Health in Metropolitan Areas*. New York: Columbia University Press, 1968.

Foucault, Michael. *Mental Illness & Psychology*. New York: Harper & Row, Publishers, 1976.

Goffman, E. *Asylums: Essays on the Social Situation of Mental Patients and Other Inmates*. New York: Anchor Books, 1961.

Gottesfelf, H. *The Critical Issues of Community Mental Health*. New York: Behavioral Publications, 1972.

Grob, Gerald N. (ed.). *Mental Illness & Social Processes, 41 Books*. New York: Arno Press, 1973.

Knowles, J. "The Struggle to Stay Healthy." *Time Magazine*, August 9, 1976.

Martin, L.E. *Mental Health - Mental Illness: Revolution in Progress*. New York: McGraw-Hill Book Co., 1970.

Miller, D. *Community Mental Health: A Study of Services & Clients*. Lexington, MA: Lexington Books, 1974.

Ridenour, Nina B. *Mental Health in the United States: A Fifty Year History.* Cambridge, MA: Harvard University Press, 1961.

Sharma, S. *The Medical Model of Mental Illness.* Woodland, CA: Majestic Publishing Co., 1970.

PART I

The
Population

Woman (& Man)*†

1

THE HISTORY OF THE mental health profession's perspectives on women gives clues as to why our society today views women as it does, and why the Women's Liberation Movement has attracted so much attention.

Since written history began, it seems that societies almost universally have held a number of physical and social taboos which pictured the female as inferior to the male, potentially unsanitary, and an object to be used for comfort and enjoyment by the male. Early myths on the psychology of women justified and solidified the inferior position of women in the society. Science held that a functional difference existed between man and woman, that the brain of woman was structured as such to make her less intelligent and more temperamental than man. Darwinism followed in the late 1800's explaining that these sex differences had an evolutionary basis and were necessary to the survival of the human species. Then came Sigmund Freud with his theories on the nature of man, an unfortunate occurrence for the nature of woman.

In the sixteenth century, women could be shut away by dissatisfied husbands indefinitely without their prior knowledge or against their will, or for actions of which society disapproved. In the seventeenth century, women were put into institutions, sometimes indefinitely, for such concerns as prostitution and illegitimate pregnancies. Twentieth century women, who are psychiatrically treated by white, male,

---

*We wanted to have a chapter on WOMAN & MAN; however, in reviewing the information available there turned out to be an abundance on woman, but a scarcity on man, hence the parentheses in the title. Many inferences can be made about this; please draw your own.
†with Kristina Martin

middle–class psychotherapists and then sent to mental institutions, are not necessarily "insane." The most common symptoms that women are hospitalized for are depression, anxiety, sexual frigidity, indecisiveness, guilt, phobia, feelings of powerlessness/hopelessness, aggressiveness, refusal to conform, self-destructiveness and suicidal tendencies. The possibility that the aforementioned are largely the result of societal oppression instead of mental illness has been advocated by many leading authorities.

Research has indicated that what therapists consider their "ideal standard of a healthy human being" is the same sex stereotype of a "healthy man" (competent, assertive, active, intelligent, independent), but different from the sex stereotype of a "healthy woman." Similarly, when asked to diagnose a person, sex unspecified, with the characteristics typically considered female such as nonassertiveness, passivity, dependence, nonaggressiveness, the therapist diagnosed these individuals as mentally unhealthy. This is a double-bind situation for women, created by the traditional perspective of the mental health profession.

According to research, women from industrialized, urbanized cultures, where education is the norm, do have the common desire to combine self-fulfillment outside the home with family orientation; but they feel that men are not receptive to women who stray too far away from family duties. A conflict develops when a woman who wants to pursue a career feels opposition from her family, traditional institutions, employers, or her own conscience. Conflicts involving her sex role can lead to mental health problems. These problems occur at a much higher frequency in married women than in single, divorced, separated or widowed women, and therefore seem to be responses to the stresses faced by married women in today's society.

Mental Health

As a result of cultural pressures from birth, many women accept the dependent character pattern considered "feminine." Although both men and women have conflicts in the areas of self-assertion, aggression, independence, and commitment, men are encouraged and supported from infancy to overcome the anxieties developed in these areas. On the other hand, women are discouraged, often criticized, for being too self-assertive, aggressive, or independent.

Depression is a more common complaint from women than it is

from men. A woman's depression is almost universally accompanied by sexual impairment (dissatisfaction or distaste for sex, but with passive compliance), impairment of marital relationship (the woman is dependent, withdrawn, hostile, and uncommunicative), poor mother-child relationships, and significant inadequacies in work performance (especially if she is a housewife who does not work outside the home).

Symptoms associated with depression include loss of gratification, loss of interest in activities and other people, loss of motivation to live up to responsibilities and accomplish goals, a negative self-concept, exaggerated view of her troubles, low expectations, self-blame, feelings of helplessness, increased dependency, a sense of worthlessness, inadequacy, indecisiveness, fatigue, and insomnia.

Divorce is a common cause of psychological disturbance (related to the stress from the final stages of the marriage and the separation). Three-fourths of women and two-thirds of men who are divorced go through some type of mental treatment.

Depression occurs sometimes as the result of situational causes. Hysterectomies often cause depression, feelings of loss, sexual fears, guilt, anxiety, mourning, aggression, denial, and rationalization. About ten to fifteen percent of women going through menopause become emotionally disturbed excessively by the temporary imbalance of their glandular systems. Menopause symptoms, such as hot flashes, depression and crying, decreased interest in physical appearances, temporarily decreased interest in sexual activities, and aging of the body, can be traumatic experiences for many women; likewise, mastectomy is very emotionally disturbing for some women. In the conditions of hysterectomies, mastectomies, and menopause, women who did not previously have serious mental disturbances, and who have emotional support plus realistic information from their physicians, make it through the situational crisis satisfactorily. Counseling sessions are available for each situation, and are helpful in supporting women and giving them a chance to talk about their feelings.

Slightly more than half of the American population are women. Seventy percent of the prescriptions for mood and consciousness altering drugs are written for women. Of these, thirty- to forty-year-olds are likely to use stimulants; forty- to sixty-year-olds more commonly take tranquilizers; and individuals over sixty use more sedatives. In American society, people have been convinced that there is no such thing as normal or healthy anxiety, and that the magical solution to their problems is to use a drug. The drug industry takes advantage of women's present situation in our society. A typical advertisement in a medical journal, for the tranquilizer Librium, pictures a woman standing behind "jail bars" of broom and mop handles. The caption reads: "You can't set her free, but you can make her feel less anxious."

There are differences between men and women patients in mental institutions. After puberty, more females are admitted to psychiatric hospitals than males, and the women tend to stay longer. There are also more women receiving private treatment. Male patients have a tendency to adopt "feminine" role patterns of behavior, such as passivity or withdrawn and submissive behavior, whereas women patients tend to become hyperactive and aggressive. Psychosomatic disorders in men commonly are peptic ulcers or skin disorders, while women get migraines, headaches, backaches, and experience insomnia. Women patients are more often diagnosed as "hysterical personity" (unstable, overreactive, dependent, egocentric, and self-dramatizing). Men are more often diagnosed as "obsessive-compulsive personality" (rigid, excessive concern with conforming, inhibitions against expressing self and relaxing, overconscientiousness). Women are more often frigid than men are impotent, but men more often have a sexual deviation as their major symptom. Men resort to more violent methods of self-destruction, succeed in suicide three times as often as women, and seem to use the act of suicide as a defensive act against the environment. Women, who attempt suicide four times as often as men, seem to be using the act as a last appeal to the environment for help. An unsuccessful suicide attempt does not mean that the person is not serious. Approximately twelve percent of individuals who make an unsuccessful suicide attempt will succeed within the next two years. Suicide is listed as the tenth leading cause of death in the United States, and third highest for college–age students.

Statistically, more poor, old, black, Latin, and female populations end up in institutions for the mentally "disturbed." Traditionally, the forms of therapy most commonly used were shock treatment, isolation, forced labor, drugs, and an occasional short visit with a professional therapist. Today all these are still used, with the emphasis on chemotherapy (drugs).

Feminist View of the Mental Health Profession

Therapists have an obligation to understand that the female position of social and sexual inequality is real, and is connected with many, valid conflicts. Therapists should help their female patients to explore their particular conflicts and goals, and to find alternate means of resolving conflicts and attaining self–fulfilling goals. The achievement of a positive female identity apart from child-bearer and housewife is crucial for the mental well-being of most women today.

Psychology realizes that activity (not passivity) is a basic human need for a healthy life. The role of passivity is a negative inhibitor of mental health and should no longer be forced upon women. Therapists have an obligation to incorporate the recent findings of psychology into their orientations and practices. They should be knowledgeable about a growing amount of information coming from research on the psychology of women, open to alternate life styles and sex roles, and be community agents of social change, not agents of the status quo who have traditionally oppressed women.

The Women's Liberation Movement is active and effective in changing aspects of our society (morals, institutions, laws, norms, opinions, practices, etc.) that are long out of date. With the liberation of women, men too will realize that they are no longer constricted by the masculine personality and life-style stereotypes.

REFERENCES

Ash, M. "Freud on Feminine Identity and Female Sexuality." *Medical Aspects of Human Sexuality,* 6(7), 1972.

Asken, M.J. "Psychoemotional Aspects of Mastectomy: A Review of Recent Literature." *The American Journal of Psychiatry,* 132(1), 1975.

Boverman, I.K. et al. "Sex Role Stereotypes & Clinical Judgements of Mental Health." *Journal of Consulting & Clinical Psychiatry,* 34(1), 1970.

Brandon, S. "Psychiatric Illness in Women." *Nursing Mirror & Midwives Journal* (London), 134(3), 1972.

Chesler, P. *Women & Madness.* New York: Doubleday & Co., 1972.

Chester, R. "Health & Marriage Breakdown: Experience of a Sample of Divorced Women." *British Journal of Prevention & Social Medicine* (London), 25(4), 1971.

Eastman, P. "Consciousness-Raising as a Resocialization Process for Women." *Smith College Studies in Social Work,* 43(3), 1973.

Freid, E. *Active-Passive: The Crucial Psychological Dimension.* New York: Grune & Stratton, 1970.

Garai, J. "Sex Differences in Breakdown of Mental Health." *Genetic Psychology Monographs,* 81(2), 1970.

Horner, M.S. "Toward an Understanding of Achievement-Related Conflicts in Women." *Journal of Social Issues,* 28(2), 1972.

Mathis, J. "Distorted Views of Women." *Sexual Behavior,* 1(4), 1971.

Miller J. & Mothner, M. "Psychological Consequences of Sexual Inequality" *American Journal of Orthopsychiatry,* 41(5), 1971.

Paykel, E. & Weissman, M. "Marital & Sexual Dysfunction in Depressed Women." *Medical Aspects of Human Sexuality,* 6(6), 1972.

Raphael, B. "The Crisis of Hysterectomy." *Australian & New Zealand Journal of Psychiatry* (Carlton, Australia), 6(2), 1972.

Shafer, N. "Helping Women Through the Change of Life." *Sexology* 36(10), 1970.

Shields, S.A. "Functionalism, Darwinism & the Psychology of Women." *American Psychologist,* 30(7), 1975.

Steinmann, A. "Cultural Values, Female Role Expectancies & Therapeutic Goals: Reseach & Interpretation." In Franks, V. & Burtle, V. (eds.) *Women in Therapy.* New York: Brunner/Mazel Inc., 1974.

Symonds, A. "A Discussion of Dr. Moulton's Article 'Psychoanalytic Reflections on Women's Liberation.'" *Contemporary Psychoanalysis,* 8(2), 1972.

Symonds, A. "The Psychology of the Female Liberation Movement." *Medical Aspects of Human Sexuality,* 5(4), 1971.

Weissman, M. et al. "The Social Role Performance of Depressed Women: Comparisons With the Normal Group." *American Journal of Orthopsychiatry,* 41(3), 1971.

Books

Abortion: A Woman's Guide. *Planned Parenthood of*
New York City
This handbook provides a comprehensive up-to-date outline of how
abortion clinics perform abortions, and precisely what a patient
should expect. The book discusses the many methods of contraception
available. The methods of pregnancy termination are described in detail so that a woman can fully understand the risks and advantages of
each method. $1.50. New York: Ablelard-Schuman, Ltd., 1973.

Booklet for Women Who Wish to Determine Their Own
Names after Marriage
All needed legal information—plus an interesting historical survey.
Compiled by the Center for a Woman's Own Name. $2. Berkeley:
Bookpeople, 1976. 56 pp.

1976 Buyers Guide to Women's Programs and Services.
Kimmel, Ko (Ed.)
This publication lists organizations that offer consulting services, educational programs, films, training, placement, and other services to
employers or individuals interested in the upward mobility of American women. $35. (plus $2 shipping). WTRA, 142 High Street, Portland, ME 04101.

The Inevitability of Patriarchy. *Goldberg, Steven*
A theoretical framework is presented to explain the apparently universal elements of male dominance and high status roles through linkage
of biological and physiological factors to those achievements. Research on cross-cultural studies and hormonal structures is provided to
support the thesis. It is suggested that woman's gratification is
achieved through the roles in which she is biologically unique:
motherhood and nurturance. It is maintained that patriarchy, male
dominance, and male attainment of high status roles are rooted in
human biology and are therefore inevitable. $2.95. New York:
William Morrow, 1973. 318 pp.

Loving Women. *The Nomadic Sisters. Illustrated by*
Victoria Hammond
A sensitively written sex manual by women dealing solely with female
sexual pleasures. The book is intended for women who love women,

women who want more sexual grafification, and anyone else wishing to know more about loving women. $3.50. Berkeley: Bookpeople, 1976. 46 pp.

The Male Dilemma: How to Survive the Sexual Revolution.
Steinmann, Anne; and Fox, David.
The emerging new roles of men and women that have produced dilemmas in relationships between the sexes are examined. Areas discussed include a history of sexual roles, the children of ambivalent parents, an inventory of masculine values, and women in conflict. $12.50. New York: Jason Aronson, 1974. 383 pp.

Masculine/Feminine or Human?: An Overview of the Sociology of Sex Roles.   *Chafetz, Janet Saltzman*
The nature of stereotyped sex roles, how they are reinforced and transmitted, the costs for individuals and for society, the question of who profits and how, and emerging masculine and feminine trends are examined. The differentiation between gender and sex roles is delineated, and it is emphasized that sex roles are learned. $4.95. Itasca, IL: F.E. Peacock Pub., Inc., 1974. 242 pp.

Men and Masculinity.   *Pleck, Joseph H.; and Sawyer, Jack*
Exploitation of the masculine role by institutions to promote their own goals is described. Psychological and sociological studies show how suppression of emotion and anxiety about achievement restrict men's ability to work, play, and love freely. In consciousness raising groups and in their daily lives, men are advised to help one another to understand and to transcend the limitations of the traditional role. The contents include: learning the masculine role; personal and general accounts of how the masculine role has influenced relations with women, children, men, work, and the larger society; descriptions of men who have come together to explore and change themselves. A classified bibliography on men and masculinity is included. $6.95. Englewood Cliffs, NJ: Prentice-Hall, 1974. 184 pp.

On the Psychology of Women: A Survey of Empirical Studies.
Sherman, Julia A.
The psychology of women is explored in light of the domination of male values in the culture. The following areas are examined: the biology of sex differences; psychological sex differences; Freudian theory of feminine development; the female Oedipus complex and its

resolution; moral and sex-role development; adolescence; cyclic
changes; female sexuality; pregnancy; and motherhood and the later
years. A detailed bibliography is included. $13.50. Springfield, IL:
Charles C Thomas, 1971. 304 pp.

Our Bodies, Ourselves: A Book by and for Women.
Boston Women's Health Book Collective
A collection of readings on women and their bodies, written by
women for women, is presented. Chapter topics include: our changing
sense of self; the anatomy and physiology of reproduction and sexuality; sexuality; living with ourselves and others; female homosexuality;
nutrition; exercise; rape and self-defense; venereal disease; birth control; abortion; deciding when to have children; childbearing;
menopause; and women and health care. $2.95. New York: Simon
and Schuster, 1973. 276 pp.

A Practical Guide to the Women's Movement.
Peterson, Deena (Ed.). Foreword by Gloria Steinem
It summarizes the strategies, philosophies, and growth of the movement over the last few years. It also includes a national directory of
groups organized by area with descriptive listings. The reading list
annotates over 500 books on the movement, with a list of women's
periodicals and bookstores. Guidelines provide information on how to
structure a consciousness-raising group and includes topics for discussion (with special sections for young women and black women). $5.
Berkeley: Bookpeople, 1975. 214 pp.

**Psychoanalysis and Women: Contributions to New Theory and
Therapy.**   *Miller, Jean Baker*
A new outlook on the psychology of women and the role that the
suppression of women has played in the conscious and unconscious
life of both women and men is presented through the writings of
psychoanalysts. $12.50. New York: Brunner/Mazel, 1974. 422 pp.

Psychology of Women: A Study of Bio-Cultural Conflicts.
Bardwick, Judith M.
Biocultural conflict and its effects on the psychology of women are
studied. The subjects covered are: a discussion of the contributions of
psychoanalytic theory to ideas about the psychology of women; some
studies on the effects of hormone fluctuations during the menstrual
cycle, pregnancy, and menopause on the behavior of various types of

women; literature dealing with hypothalamic control of reproductive hormones; a review of sex differences in various abilities, and in such personality traits as dependency, passivity, and aggression; and a discussion of the theme that observed psychological differences between men and women are the result of physical differences which directly and indirectly affect personality development. $7.95. New York: Harper and Row, 1971. 242 pp.

Readings on the Psychology of Women.   *Bardwick, Judith M. (Ed.)*
This book is an academic collection of 47 theory and research papers from the professional literature of psychology, sociology, anthropology, endocrinology, obstetrics, and psychosomatics. The papers are organized into seven sections: the development of sex differences; socialization, cultural values, and the development of motives; the traditional role: gratifications, frustrations, and stresses; the Women's Liberation Movement; intercultural comparisons; women in relationship to their bodies; and women and criteria of mental health. $9.95. New York: Harper and Row, 1972. 335 pp.

Rebirth of Feminism.   *Hole, Judith; and Levine, Ellen*
A study of the resurgence of feminism in the United States—a history and analysis of the origins, organizational development, philosophical thinking, issues, and activities of the new women's movement. A brief discussion of the first feminist movement in America in the 19th and early 20th centuries is included to serve as an indication that the contemporary women's movement has a much-ignored historical predecessor. $4.50. New York: Quadrangle Books, Inc., 1971. 488 pp.

Sappho Was a Right-on Woman.   *Abbott, Sidney;*
and Love, Barbara
An examination of the new honesty concerning female homosexuality, written by two self-avowed lesbians. The first part of the book deals with what life was like for lesbians in the past and the second part deals with the hope for a brighter future. $1.95. New York: Stein and Day, 1973. 247 pp.

Sisters in Crime: The Rise of the New Female Criminal.
Adler, Freda
The extent and nature of the changing pattern of crimes committed by women in the United States is examined, and its future course is plot-

ted. It is suggested that as women become increasingly liberated, the means and opportunity for commiting traditionally male crimes become more available to them, and that women are just beginning to emerge as a force capable of impacting a male dominated society with biased laws and unequal opportunity. With the newfound liberation, men and women can be expected to follow parallel criminal careers. $8.95. New York: McGraw-Hill, 1975. 278 pp.

Unbecoming Men
A men's consciousness-raising group writes on oppression and themselves. $2. Berkeley: Bookpeople, 1971. 64 pp.

Vaginal Politics. *Frankfort, Ellen*
The women's health movement is examined. The issues described involve many different levels of awareness. One level concerns the psyche—how a woman perceives her body. Another level concerns external factors—the health facilities, doctors, and drugs. $6.95. New York: Quadrangle, 1972. 250 pp.

Woman, Culture, and Society. *Rosaldo, Michelle Zimbalist; and Lamphere, Louise*
A collection of literature on the nature of women's and men's roles in different societies is presented. The importance of woman's work compared with man's, the beginnings of the idea that woman's work was less important than man's, the status of women, the roles of men and women in the family and in the public world; the use of power; female dominated societies; sexual functions; the historical patterns for male dominance; and sex roles in class societies are discussed. Sexual roles in relation to power and authority over resources, people, and behavior patterns are also explored. $12.50. Stanford, CA: Stanford University Press, 1974. 352 pp.

Woman in Sexist Society. *Gornick, Vivian; and Moran, Barbara K.*
Twenty-nine essays were gathered together to demonstrate that women's condition is the result of a slowly formed, deeply entrenched, extraordinarily pervasive cultural (and therefore political) decision that a woman shall remain a person defined by her childbearing properties and her status as a companion to men. The essayists examine the institutions of sexist marriage; sexuality; the male-female socialization process; psychosexual theory; the cult of beauty; education; work; literature; civil rights. $12.50. New York: Basic Books, 1971. 515 pp.

Women in Therapy: New Psychotherapies for a Changing Society.
Franks, Violet; and Burtle, Vasanti
Current approaches to psychotherapies as they apply to women are
presented in a group of essays on feminine psychodynamics. Clinical
and statistical data representing several viewpoints are included. The
following topics are discussed: a historical view of women and
therapeutic approaches; biological and cultural approaches to
therapy; approaches to problematic behaviors of depression; the
phobic syndrome; alcoholism and homosexuality; views of contemporary psychotherapies; therapies and public agencies; and comments on
the constants and changes seen for the female role. $12.50. New York:
Brunner/Mazel, 1974. 441 pp.

The Women's Movement: Social and Psychological Perspectives.
Wortis, Helen; and Rabinowitz, Clara
It is maintained that the change in women's role is irreversibly
dynamic but not necessarily swift, and that the implications for men,
children, and societal patterns in general are many and must be
worked out slowly. Subjects treated include the evolution of behavior,
sexist mythology, gender role development, the concept of mothering,
Swedish sex-role patterns, changes in the concept of the family,
psychological consequences of sexual inequality, the single woman in
today's society, and the black woman. $10.00. New York: AMS Press,
1975. 168 pp.

Articles

Abortion Counseling.   *Asher, John D.*
The counseling needs of pregnant women seeking an abortion are
discussed. Abortion counseling has three basic aims: (1) to aid the
woman in making a decision about an unwanted pregnancy; (2) to
help her implement the decision; and (3) to assist her in controlling her
future fertility. The single most important function of the counselor is
to help the woman weigh the alternatives and arrive at her own decision. A woman sympathetically counseled and supportively aided in
dealing with an unwanted pregnancy will be able to integrate the
experience into her life. 6 references. *American Journal of Public
Health*, 62(5):686–88, 1972.

Borrowing Basics for Women
This pamphlet tells how to build a credit rating regardless of marital status; how to shop for the best loan; and how to understand the new credit laws that prohibit discrimination based on sex. This pamphlet is free. Write to: Citibank, 399 Park Avenue, New York, NY 10022.

The Contemporary Woman and Crime. *Simon, Rita James*
In an examination of the extent of female criminal activity, recent statistics and trends on arrest rates, court convictions, prison sentences, and parole are analyzed. It is hypothesized that as women assume new roles and participate more widely in the labor force, they will be exposed to greater opportunities to commit certain types of crimes more commonly committed by men in the past; e.g., fraud, embezzlement, larceny, and forgery. It is also hypothesized that as women take on new occupational roles, receive comparable compensation, and experience less of the frustration commonly associated with traditional expectations of women, they will be less driven to commit crimes of violence. 49 references. Rockville, MD: NIMH, 1975. 98 pp.

Early Origins of Envy and Devaluation of Women: Implications for Sex Role Stereotypes. *Lerner, Harriet E.*
Early origins of envy and devaluation of women and implications for sex role stereotypes are discussed. A review of psychoanalytic writings reveals how theorists label active displays of competitiveness, aggression, and intellectual ambitiousness in women as phallic or masculine and similarly label manifestations of passivity, submissiveness, emotionality in men as effeminate or feminine. 22 references. *Bulletin of the Menninger Clinic*, 38(6):538–53, 1974.

Early Papers on Women: Horney to Thompson. *Moulton, Ruth*
The contributions of Karen Horney to the development of psychoanalytic thinking about women are reviewed, and the transition between Horney's early papers and the beginning of later studies of feminine psychology by such pioneers as Clara Thompson is traced. 37 references. *American Journal of Psychoanalysis*, 35(3):207–23, 1975.

Feminism, Psychotherapy and Professionalism. *Tennov, Dorothy*
Professionalism and especially psychotherapy are severely criticized as being antagonistic to feminism. Psychotherapy is an unproven and

expensive tyranny of one individual over another, supposedly to "help" but often to the detriment of the recipient. Professionalism is the banding together in mutual self-protection of an in-group which has managed to gain a monopoly over some kind of service technique. It is argued that all women should forsake the gratifications of psychotherapy and reject professionalism for the cause of sisterhood. 3 references. *Journal of Contemporary Psychotherapy,* 5(2):107–11, 1973.

The Feminist Therapist Roster. *Brodsky, Annette (Ed.)*
This is a national listing of therapists to which one can write requesting information about credentials, services provided, and feminist position held. 40¢. Know, Inc., P.O. Box 86031, Pittsburgh, PA 15221. 1976.

The Hazards of Being a Professional Woman. *Frabian, Judith Janaro*
Problems encountered by women in the professions are outlined and the relationship problems with men on different levels of authority are discussed. A professional woman ends up being a projective device for every man's stereotype of her, independent and exclusive of her behavior; a male's fears and fantasies get intermingled with his perceptions of her in such a way that rather gross distortions inevitably appear. In relationships with subordinates, a woman can supervise males more easily than females; men adapt a passive/aggressive stance when supervised by a woman; women, however, who may have accepted their stereotypes, perceive other women as competitive elements in the fight for attention. In relations with peers, the woman professional may be a scapegoat. In relations with authority figures, women are conditioned to act out the expected role relationship; the woman is expected to embellish, enhance, satisfy, and fulfill the ego need of her superiors. The real tragedy is that women have adopted values complementary to male domination and consequently view themselves as appropriately dealt with when they are being subtly derogated. *Professional Psychology,* 3(4):324–26, 1972.

The History of Psychology Revisited: Or, Up With Our Foremothers. *Bernstein, Maxine D.; and Russo, Nancy Felipe*
The history of psychology is reviewed, with emphasis on contributions made by women. Women's contributions to the theoretical development of psychology have had a major impact on the development of new fields of inquiry, both in psychology and in related social sciences.

Classical texts in all fields of psychology have been written by women, or contributed to by women as second authors. It is suggested that women in psychology be taught their intellectual history and the contributions of contemporary women be preserved. 59 references. *American Psychologist,* 29(2):130–34, 1974.

Men Drive Women Crazy. *Chesler, Phyllis*
The present state of psychotherapy for women is analyzed. It is concluded that some far-reaching changes will have to take place, both in the attitudes of clinicians and in the nature of the therapy they dispense. Therapists must learn to recognize the stereotypes about women that they share. Women patients should seek women clinicians who understand female problems and the broad social conditions that have produced them. *Psychology Today,* 5(2):18, 22, 26–27+, 1971.

Report on the Task Force on Sex Bias and Sex Role Stereotyping in Psychotherapeutic Practice
Incidents of circumstances perceived as indicative of sex bias or sex role stereotyping in psychotherapy with women were described in an open-ended questionnaire completed by 320 female psychologists, assumed to have had experience both as consumers and practitioners of psychotherapy. Four general areas of perceived sex bias and sex role stereotyping which affect women as clients in psychotherapy emerged: (1) fostering traditional sex roles; (2) bias in expectations and devaluations of women; (3) sexist use of psychoanalytic concepts; and (4) responding to women as sex objects, including seduction of female clients. 26 references. *American Psychologist,* 30(12):1169–1175, 1975.

Woman and Man. *Tavris, Carol*
A 109-item questionnaire on attitudes and experiences on the roles of men and women in society was circulated to readers of *Psychology Today.* The questionnaire was designed to explore four broad issues: (1) experiences and beliefs that contribute to a person's support of, or opposition to, the Women's Liberation Movement (WLM); (2) different meanings of women's liberation for men and women; (3) the accuracy of the media's portrayal of women in the movement, and the accuracy of the movement's assessment of nonmembers; and (4) factors that distinguish women who are active in WLM from those who are not. About 20,000 responses were received. Results indicated that WLM has a long way to go, at least by the movement's standards. At

the same time, they are moving toward a reintegration of values that may, in the long run, be the most revolutionary change of all. Charts summarizing the findings are included. *Psychology Today*, 5(10):57–64, 82–85, 1972.

Audio Tapes

Opening Up the Man-Woman Relationship
Guidelines for enhancing and fostering relationship growth are shared and explored. The focus is toward facilitating a synergistic flow between two individuals and the simultaneous augmentation of both the feeling of commitment and the awareness of freedom in the relationship. Marta Vago, Jerry Gillies, Bert Knapp. $9. 90 min. 1972. Big Sur Recordings.

Psychotherapy and Women's Liberation
Stephanie Miller, a psychiatric worker at the Community Center for Mental Health in Dumont, New Jersey, discusses topics relevant to psychotherapy and women's liberation. $6.95. At 1⅞ IPS Cassette. 60 min. 1973. Behavioral Sciences Tape Library.

Selling Women Short
Colette Nijhof of NOW's National Image Committee talks about the image of women in the advertising media; the harmful, long term effects that a continuous projection of a negative image has on women's self-esteem and sense of identity. She clearly draws the relationship between the sexual exploitation of women in the advertising media and the systematic oppression of women in American society. $10. 28 min. Pacifica Tape Library.

Training the Woman to Know Her Place
A lecture about the pervasive effects of sex role conditioning on women in America. Psychologists Darryl and Sandra Bem contend that this conditioning is primarily responsible for the lack of motivation among women to pursue careers other than those which society deems appropriate for them. A fast moving, humorous lecture, complete with role playing games. $14. 60 min. Pacifica Tape Library.

Women as Losers
Members of the Women's Liberation movement expound on what liberation really consists of; status images as part of the mechanism of a society which treats people as commodities; the effect of the media on the image of women; and, the relationship between the Women's Liberation movement and the Black Liberation struggle. $14. 65 min. Pacifica Tape Library.

Films

Assertive Training for Women: Part I
Especially appropriate for high school and college students. Ten vignettes deal with simple interpersonal situations: borrowing class notes; refusing dates; dealing with friends, a physician, and a pushy waitress; and a job interview, as well as more complex situations involving parents who are overly protective and controlling or critical of friends and grades in school. Sale: $250. Rental fee per day of use: $25. 17 min. 16mm. Color and sound. American Personnel and Guidance Association, Washington, DC.

Assertive Training for Women: Part II
Especially appropriate for college age and older. Eleven vignettes begin with simple interpersonal situations: someone cutting into line, dealing with a demanding employer and an unpleasant garage mechanic, being asked to canvass for charity; and conclude with a series of more complex situations involving a passive husband, a flirtatious man, an unreasonably angry friend and a highly opinionated male. Sale: $250. Rental fee per day of use: $25. 18 min. 16mm. Color and sound. American Personnel and Guidance Association, Washington, DC.

Leader's Guide to Assertive Training for Women
This paper-bound booklet provides a brief outline of assertive training techniques and terms as well as a group leader's discussion model. Also included is an elaboration of each vignette shown in Parts 1 and 2 of the Assertive Training film series. Carefully describes the rights involved in each vignette and the suggested assertive response. Joan Pearlman, Karen Coburn and Patricia Jakubowski-Spector. $2.75. 1973. 24 pp. American Personnel and Guidance Association, Washington, DC.

The Black Woman
A discussion is presented by several noted black women, including
Nikki Giovanni, Lena Horne, Bibi Amina Baraka, and others, concerning their roles in contemporary society and the problems they
confront. Focuses on the relationship of black women to black men,
white society, and the liberation struggle. Sale: $265. Rental fee: $14.
52 min. 16mm. Optical, b/w. 1970. University of Indiana, Audiovisual
Center, Bloomington, IN 47401.

Masculine or Feminine: Your Role in Society
What are today's changing attitudes toward the masculine and
feminine role in society. Conflicting viewpoints. Historical backgrounds and development of the roles. Rental: $10.50. 19 min. 16mm.
Color. 1971. Film Library—Oregon.

Virginia Woolf: The Moment Whole
Selected passages from Virginia Woolf's writings are analyzed to convey her concept of woman and to articulate the problems and pressures of being a woman writer. The personality of the artist is also
examined, including her feminist ideas. Rental: $15.00. 10 min.
16mm. Optical, color. 1972. University of California, Extension
Media Center, 2223 Fulton St., Berkeley, CA 94720.

Contacts

NEWSLETTERS AND BULLETINS

Artemis   For the business woman. $12/10 issues. 525 West End Ave.,
New York, NY 10024

Female Liberation Newsletter   National in scope, published bi-
weekly. $3/year. Box 303, Kenmore Square Station, Boston MA
02215

Know News   National in view, excellent articles, also publishes many
pamphlets which are listed. Published monthly. $4. Box 86031,
Pittsburgh, PA 15221

Men Sharing $2/year. Men's consciousness raising newsletter.
Campus Free College, 466 Commonwealth Ave., Boston, MA
02115

The New Feminist $3. Many articles and points of information. Published quarterly. P.O. Box 597, Station "A," Toronto 116, Ontario, Canada

Sisters $5. Varied. Published monthly. 1005 Market St., #208, San Francisco, CA 94103

The Spokeswoman $7. Many different types of articles, lots of contacts and information. Published monthly. 5464 So. Shore Dr., Chicago, IL 60615

The Transitional Woman $5/10 issues. For women facing life changes. 18340 Ventura Blvd., Tarzana, CA 91456

Weal Washington Report $2.50/six months. Summary, latest action in legislation and courts on women. Monthly. 1253 4th St., S.W., Washington, DC 20024

The Woman Activist $5. Political issues and commentary. Published monthly. 2310 Barbour Rd., Falls Church, VA 22043

Womanpower $30. Monthly. Complete information on equal job opportunities. 222 Rawson Road, Brookline, MA 02146

Women's Agenda $10. Excellent resources on all subjects of interest, lots of information and contacts. Monthly. 370 Lexington Ave., New York, NY 10017

Women Today $15. Information on overview of women's issues, groups, etc. Bi-weekly. National Press Building, Washington, DC 20004

WONAAC Newsletter Latest information on abortion issues. Monthly. $3. 150 Fifth Ave., Suite 843, New York, NY 10011

National Organization for Women, 1957 East 73rd St., Chicago, IL 60649

National Women's Political Caucus, Suite 603, 1302 18th St., N.W., Washington, DC 20036

Both **NOW** and **NWPC** publish a Newsletter, also many of their local Chapters do.

JOURNALS

Brother $3/year. A forum for men against sexism. P.O. Box 4387, Berkeley, CA 94704

Feminist Studies $6/year. Varied. Published quarterly. 606 West 116th St., New York, NY 10027

Journal of International Institute of Women's Studies $9/year. Empirical and theoretical articles. Published quarterly. 1615 Myrtle St., N.W., Washington, DC 20012

Lavender Woman $3/year. Varied. Published bi-monthly. 1434 W. Thorne, Chicago, IL

Momma $9/year. For single mothers. Monthly. 928½ Marco Place, Venice, CA 90291

Women and Art $2/year. Published quarterly. 89 E. Broadway, New York, NY 10002

Women's Studies Forum for scholars. Professor Wendy Martin, Dept. of English, Queens College of C.U.N.Y., Flushing, NY 11367

SPECIAL HELP PAMPHLETS

Borrowing Basics for Women Credit, loans, etc. Free. Citibank, 399 Park Ave., New York, NY 10022

Child Care and Disabled Dependent Care Deductions for child care, etc. Free from your local Internal Revenue Service Office

Employment Packet $5.35. 19 articles on job discrimination and how you can fight it and win. Write for free catalog of publications which are extensive and also very inexpensive. Know, Inc., Box 86031, Pittsburgh, PA 15221

Feminist Book Mart Write for free catalog of women's books and nonsexist children's books. P.O. Box 149, Whitestone, NY 11357

The Feminist Economic Alliance Communications network of feminist credit unions and enterprises. Contact: Susan Osborne, FFCU, 170 York St., New Haven, CT 06510

How To Decide $5.95. Workbook to decision making skills, sort out your goals, etc. College Board Publications, Box 2815, Princeton, NJ 08540

SPEAKERS' BUREAUS

Movement Speakers Carole Cullum, 1736 R St., N.W., Washington, DC 20009 (the bureau is not exclusively for Women's Movement speakers)

National Women's Political Caucus Jane McMichael, 1302 18th St., N.W., Room 603, Washington, DC 20036

New Feminist Talent Associates 250 West 57th St., New York, NY 10019

OTHER CONTACTS

The Feminist Psychology Coalition / Therapy Referral Collective c/o Weisberg, #10B, 520 Cathedral Parkway, New York, NY 10025

Women's History Library   Over 4,000 issues of international collection of women's periodicals, as well as books, etc. 2325 Oak St., Berkeley, CA 94708

2

Marriage and Family*

TODAY THERE ARE APPROXIMATELY 70,000,000 households in the United States. In 1950 there were close to 44,000,000. This represents an increase of about 39 percent in only 27 years. The average size of the household has dropped from 3.37 persons in 1950 to 3.01 in 1973. A current study shows that it has now dropped to 2.9 persons per family. This is the first time in history that it has gone below 3 persons. The smaller size is due to couples waiting longer to have their children. Modern birth control methods and better education about the problems of feeding the overcrowded earth, also are contributing factors.

The number of households, as recorded by the type of heads of households, are as follows: out of the present 70,000,000 households, more than 61,000,000 are Caucasian and 8,000,000 are other ethnic groups. In the white households 70.2 percent are husband-wife heads, 9.1 percent are male heads, and 20.7 percent are female heads. In the other ethnic groups 49 percent are husband-wife heads, 13.6 percent are male heads, and an incredible 37.4 percent are female heads.

There are approximately 2,000,000 marriages a year, or 9.9 percent per thousand, down 1.1 percent in 1977. Although the number of marriages has steadily decreased and the divorce rate has increased yearly, marriage does not seem to be going out of style as evidenced by the high number of people who remarry after a first-failed marriage. There are approximately 1,077,000 divorces or annulments annually. In all these, approximately 870,000 children are involved. The average number of children per divorce is 1.22. In the last two decades the number of children from divorced homes has tripled.

Rapid social changes, urbanization, changes in work patterns, in-

*with Eddie Bulter

24

creased mobility, economic changes, the influence of mass media, education, government policies, and the restructuring of the extended family into the nuclear family has greatly affected marriage and the family. It is impossible to find a single cause for the high divorce rates, but it is evident that the family greatly influences their offspring and thus, their families in turn. Studies have found the following variables most likely to contribute positively to a successful marriage: the happiness of the parents' marriage; minimal conflict of offspring with the parents; close relationships of the offspring with parents and siblings; parental openness about sex; firm discipline in childhood; advanced education; and a contented childhood. Therefore, in order to break the unhappy marriage cycle, we have to develop happy and healthy families on which children can model themselves.

The mental health professional has responded to the needs of the family as shown through an increase in services in institutions and private practices throughout the United States. A wide variety of approaches are being used from group therapy, to conjoint therapy, to videotaping. It is difficult to evaluate the success and couples may be happier divorced than married. The increased concern about and study of marriage and family should help the American home to create an environment that promotes mentally healthy and well adjusted individuals.

Some of the current trends in marriage and family are:

1) Today couples are marrying later.
2) American families are highly mobile. Only 57.4 percent lived at the same address between 1970 and 1974. Moving can disrupt both children and parent in their interpersonal relationships, school, and jobs.
3) Divorces are more frequent. In fact, the Census Bureau reports the divorce rate in the last four years has increased as much as it did in the entire, previous decade.
4) Approximately three-fourths of the women and five-sixths of the men who are divorced will remarry within an average time of three years.
5) Recent reports indicate that somewhere between one-half and two-thirds of those who remarry will remain married as long as both partners survive. (U.S. Bureau of Census, 1976.)
6) The total number of children per divorced woman who remarries and then remains married until the end of her reproductive period is similar to the total number for women who remain in their first marriage. (U.S. Bureau of Census, 1973).
7) One-fourth of all Caucasian schoolchildren and more than

one-half of all Black schoolchildren live in one-parent homes, in homes with one or more stepparents, or apart from either parent.

REFERENCES

Aldous, Joan & Dahl, Nancy (eds.). *International Bibliography of Research in Marriage & Family.* Minneapolis, MN: University of Minnesota Press, 1974.

Bell, Robert R. (ed.). *Studies in Marriage & the Family.* New York: Thomas Crowell, 1973.

Fleming, Jennifer B. & Washburne, Carolyn K. *For Better, For Worse: A Feminist Handbook on Marriage & Other Options.* New York: Charles Scribner & Sons, 1977.

Glick, Paul C. "Updating the Life Cycle of the Family." *Journal of Marriage & the Family,* Feburary 1977, pp. 5–13.

Gunter, B.G. "Notes on Divorce Filing as Role Behavior." *Journal of Marriage & the Family,* February 1977, pp. 95–7.

Smith, James R. & Smith, Lynn G. (eds.). *Beyond Monogamy: Recent Studies of Sexual Alternatives in Marriage.* Baltimore: Johns Hopkins Press, 1974.

Sussman, Marvin B. (ed.). *Sourcebook in Marriage & the Family,* 4th ed. New York: Houghton Mifflin Co., 1974.

U.S. Bureau of Census. "Household & Family Characteristics" and "Number, Timing, and Duration of Marriage & Divorces in the U.S." *Current Population Reports.* Washington, DC: US Gov't. Printing Office, 1975.

Books

Family Health Indicators: Annotated Bibliography. *May, Jean T.*
An annotated bibliography keyed to the family and covering the areas of medicine, biostatistics, economics, linguistics, and operational research is presented. 1024 references. Rockville, MD: NIMH, 1974. 212 pp.

A Family Therapy Notebook. *Peck, Bruce B.*
Approach to family therapy is presented which is based on advances made by the previous generation of family therapists and researchers. Five sections are included: (1) the children, mother, and family therapy; (2) married couples and the extended family; (3) divorce and remarriage; (4) extensions of a family philosophy; and (5) postscript. $11.50. Roslyn Heights, NY: Libra Publishers, 1975.

Fatherhood: A Sociological Perspective. *Benson, Leonard*
This book surveys research and theory from sociology, anthropology, and social psychology on the role of the father in family and community life. 700 references. New York: Random House, 1968. 371 pp.

Helping Unmarried Mothers. *Bernstein, Rose*
An analysis is made of potential psychological and social hazards of unmarried mothers and the factors that determine whether they will receive certain services. Specific attention is paid to the adolescent unmarried mother, the unmarried father, and persistent issues of improving and extending services and prevention including crisis intervention. $6.95. New York: Association Press, 1971. 187 pp.

Marital and Family Therapy. *Glick, Ira D.; and Kessler, David R.*
An introduction to marital and family therapy is presented. Topics considered include: some of the core concepts relevant to an understanding of families; a frame of reference for planning and carrying out family therapy strategies; a summary of current research on family process and treatment. Separate sections are devoted to such topics as: seminal ideas in family therapy; seminal theorists of family therapy; a comparison of theorists; family therapy now and in the future. $10. New York: Grune & Stratton, 1974.

Marriage and Family Therapy.   *Nicholas, William C. Jr.*
An anthology of articles on marriage and family therapy is presented. An overview of marriage and family therapy is followed by discussions of parent-child therapy, marital group therapy, and the dynamics of working with the family as a unit. Conjoint therapy is described and praised, but its limitations are recognized. Communications theory and a behavioral exchange model are discussed in relation to a few marriage counseling procedures and several notes on the practice and preparation of training counselors. Editorial comments and updates are also included. $5. Minneapolis: National Council on Family Relations, 1974. 312 pp.

Mother's Day Is Over.   *Radl, Shirley L.*
This book focuses on mothers in average homes, with healthy children, and without financial distress. The author's aim is to show that it is not enough for every child to be wanted at the time of birth, but forever afterward. She deals with mothers' identities and feelings of self-worth and especially mothers' real feelings toward motherhood. The pressures, the frustrations, and the responsibilities of motherhood as well as the joys are discussed. New York: Charterhouse, 1973. 234 pp.

Mothers in Poverty: A Study of Fatherless Families.   *Kriesberg, Louis*
It is contended that there is no comprehensive subculture of poverty which accounts for husbandless mothers choosing to be dependent upon public welfare rather than upon their own employment. Evidence demonstrates the great importance of contemporary situational factors in affecting the choice of financial support for the family. Childrearing patterns that affect the child's later independence and educational achievement are analyzed. $12.50. Chicago: Aldine, 1970. 356 pp.

Sex, Living Together, and the Law.   *Massey, Carmen; and Warner, Ralph*
A legal guide for unmarried couples (and groups). What the authors present here is clear and simple information on sex, housing, property, credit, children, and other practical concerns of people living together. Renting and sharing a home, prior families or starting a family, buying a house, splitting up, death, gay couples, groups, and dealing with laws and lawyers are some of the concerns of this book. $4.95. Berkeley: Bookpeople, 1975. 192 pp.

The Silent Misery: Why Marriages Fail. *Griffin, Gerald G.*
Causes of failure in marriages, or the ways they are socially programmed to fail are discussed. It is estimated that eighty percent of American marriages end in divorce, annulment, desertion, or general misery. The successful marriage is described as one in which both spouses continue or achieve through marriage the psychic balance and harmony of free flowing activation of their unconscious potential, each allowing the other to express this through individuality. Consideration is also given to methods and effectiveness of marriage counseling. $6.95. Springfield, IL: Charles C Thomas, 1974.

Techniques of Family Psychotherapy: A Primer. *Bloch, Donald A.*
A collection of articles dealing with the practice of family therapy as a psychotherapeutic method of treatment is presented. Such topics as the family crisis, the initial interview, the clinical home visit, audiovisual techniques, multiple family therapy, and marriage therapy are discussed. The specific methods utilized in family treatment and the theoretical framework supporting these methods are described. $10.75. New York: Grune & Stratton, 1973. 124 pp.

Violent Home: A Study of Physical Aggression between Husbands and Wives. *Gelles, R.J.*
Research study on the types, incidence, and causes of violent attacks between family members, especially husbands and wives. The social structure and the structure of the violent family suggests that certain positions produce stress that can lead to incidents or patterns of intrafamily violence, a detailed discussion dealing with the interaction between victim and offender that leads to an attack is also presented. In addition, the theory that the family is a "training ground for violence" is proposed, the author contends that role models for family violence presented in early childhood are translated into actual violence in later family life. An extensive list of references is provided along with both subject and author indexes. The appendix contains a demographic profile of the total sample of respondents and their families. $6. Beverly Hills: Sage Publications, Inc., 1972. 230 pp.

We Take This Child: A Candid Look at Modern Adoption.
Berman, Claire
The adoption process is reviewed, with the major focus on the potential parents of an adopted child. The difficult decision-making process that is involved, the numerous problems and stages created by the

waiting period, and basic problems that adoption creates for both the family and the child are examined. Descriptive passages of actual adoptions are interspersed with commentary by agencies and organizations interested in the adoption procedure. Interracial adoptions, older children, handicapped children, single parent adoptions, and intercounty adoptions are discussed. The relationship between parents and agencies, as well as that between parents and the adopted child, is described as a complex dynamic. $5.95. Garden City, NY: Doubleday, 1974. 201 pp.

Articles

Alternatives in Child Rearing in the 1970s. *Eiduson, Bernice T.; Cohen, Jerome; and Alexander, Jannette*
The child rearing practices, values, and beliefs of counter culture groups are examined and compared with those of two parent nuclear families of the 1970s. 69 references. *American Journal of Orthopsychiatry,* 43(5): 720–31, 1973.

A Consumer's Guide to Therapy for Couples. *Koch, Joanne; and Koch, Lew*
Different techniques of couples counseling are described and evaluated. New social problems that have caused marital problems are outlined, and sex therapy is emphasized because of its high success rate and to illustrate a number of recent trends in marital therapy. Couples are urged to check out therapists' credentials and to clearly define their goals in therapy. *Psychology Today,* 9(10):33–38, 40, 1976.

Dialogue: What It Is Like To Be a Divorcee. *Schimel, John L.*
A discussion among three women who compare their sexual experiences and problems during and after marriage is presented. All of the women experienced sexual problems in their marriages and after divorce experienced a period of promiscuity. The role of children in the divorcee's life and their influence on sexual behavior are examined. Among other topics discussed are: the image of the divorcee as fair game; the position of the divorcee in society; lesbianism as an option; and future relationships, including remarriage. *Sexual Behavior,* 2(8):26–30, 1972.

Grandparents and Intergenerational Family Therapy.
Spark, Geraldine M.
The role of grandparents in intergenerational family therapy is discussed. Unresolved loyalty conflicts and unsettled accounts between first and second generation family members are often projected onto, or lived out, in the marital or parental relationship. It is felt that an intergenerational treatment focus may yield greater possibilities for constructive and fundamental change in a family system. Five references. *Family Process,* 13(2):225–37, 1974.

The Lesbian Mother. *Goodman, Bernice*
In a paper presented at the 50th Annual Meeting of the American Orthopsychiatric Association, the lifestyle of the lesbian mother, with all of its problems and rewards, was studied. Specific attention was focused on the mother-child relationship and on the development of the child. Consideration was also given to similarities and differences between lesbian and nonlesbian mothers. Data was based on two years of individual and group therapy. *American Journal of Orthopsychiatry,* 43(2):283–84, 1973.

Marital Therapy: Emerging Trends in Research and Practice.
Gurman, Alan S.
Trends in the research and clinical practice of marital therapists were examined. Implications of these emerging trends in research and practice are discussed in terms of the future of marital therapy. Thirteen references. *Family Process,* 12(1):45–54, 1973.

Mismating. *Scanzoni, Letha; and Scanzoni, John*
Problems of mismating in marriage are analyzed. Realistic marriage counseling involves an awareness that the phenomenon of mismating exists, that it exists in two forms (initial and subsequent) and that the best solution is prevention. Six references. *Medical Aspects of Human Sexuality,* 8(4):9–10, 12, 16, 18, 23–24, 26, 28, 1974.

The Missing Partner: Men as Clients in Marriage Counseling.
Asarnow, Claire
The observation that men are harder to involve in marriage counseling than women was examined. Study of the preferred type of modality employed revealed that men preferred individual to joint interviews. (M.S.W. Thesis). *Smith College Studies in Social Work* 43(1):25–26, 1972.

On the Question of Compulsory Marriage Counseling as a Part of Divorce Proceedings. *Sonne, John C.*
The question of compulsory marriage counseling as a part of divorce proceedings is discussed. It is concluded that only voluntarily received therapy has a chance for success. *Family Coordinator,* 23(3):303–05, 1974.

Outline (Alphabet) of 26 Techniques of Family and Marital Therapy: A Through Z. *Friedman, Philip H.*
A guide to the beginning family and marital therapist in his endeavors to intervene into the intricacies of dysfunctional family systems. Techniques are outlined for the benefit of psychiatric residents, psychology interns, social work students, psychiatric nurses, and aides to provide some structure to their search for specific techniques to use in family therapy. References sample the literature on techniques in family and marital therapy. 56 references. *Psychotherapy: Theory, Research and Practice,* 11(3):259–64, 1974.

Psychological Testing in Marital Dysfunction. *Boyarsky, Rose E.*
General outlines to the types of information needed by marital and sexual counselors for dealing with marital dysfunction are presented. Five areas of interest provide crucial information for the counselor: a measurement of individual psychopathology, measurement of sexual attitudes and value systems, masculine/feminine role identification, role expectations and interpersonal interaction style. Specific standardized tests are named for each of the general areas. It is noted that very few tests are valid for garnering information for marital dysfunction, because most tests are designed to measure individual qualities, whereas marital counseling involves dealing with a relationship. It is further suggested that a new look at tests within a framework of psychosituational assessment may be most useful. 21 references. *Marriage and Family Counselors Quarterly,* 9(2):31–40, 1975.

Research Findings on the Outcomes of Marital Counseling.
Beck, Dorothy Fahs
A review of studies on marital counseling from a variety of disciplines and treatment perspectives which reports generally positive outcomes and suggests future research directions as presented. 43 references. *Social Casework,* 56(3):153–81, 1975.

Sex Differences in Happiness and Unhappiness. *Garai, Josef E.*
The marital relationship is more critical for the happiness of the woman than it is for the man. Women express dissatisfaction with marriage and blame their husbands much more frequently for marital problems than husbands blame wives. As a result of greater emotional invesment in a marriage, women as a group report that they are less happy than men. *Genetic Psychology Monographs,* 81(2):130, 1970.

Till Divorce Do You Part. *Greene, Roberta*
This handbook provides information on divorce problems from the perspective of women. It deals with the do's and don'ts of divorce, the pitfalls of separation, violence, choosing a lawyer, grounds for divorce, support and alimony, custody and visitation, insurance, taxes, property, etc. Pittsburgh: Know, Inc., 1972. 37 pp.

The Undeclared War between Child and Family Therapy.
McDermott, John F., Jr.; and Char, Walter F.
Family therapy is examined historically and the forces which influenced and shaped its present form are considered. The historical discussion includes a review of the theories of Nathan Ackerman, the founder of family therapy. The problems of children often exist independently of parent-child problems, and should be examined independently. The cognitive and emotional levels of children must be considered before attempts to improve family "communication" push the child out of the therapeutic picture. Child psychotherapists need to reassociate themselves with family therapy in order to treat children and not merely use them as scapegoats for their parent's problems. 17 references. *Journal of the American Academy of Child Psychiatry,* 13(3):422–36, 1974.

The Wrong Reasons for Motherhood. *Silverman, Anna;*
and Silverman, Arnold
The most frequently encountered wrong reasons for motherhood are discussed. The reasons for childbearing are: (1) ego satisfaction through the child's accomplishments; (2) to save a marriage; (3) to justify an unhappy childhood; (4) as a symbol of maturity; (5) as a symbol of sexual maturity; (6) as insurance in old age; (7) as an occupation. The following motives deal with the state of pregnancy: (1) as an attention-getting device; (2) as atonement for the "sin" of intercourse; (3) as proof of existence. The final reasons reflect the need

for social acceptance: (4) to provide grandchildren; (5) for religious reasons; (6) to fit in the peer group. Any woman who has children with the intention of using the child to overcome personal, marital, or social problems should not become a mother. *Sexual Behavior,* 2(5):58–64, 1972.

Audio Tapes

Children and Divorce
Dr. Richard A. Gardner gives advice to children of divorced parents. The fact that children of divorced parents are often referred to as coming from a "broken" home indicates our society's fears and expectations for these children. A home that remains unhappily intact is usually worse than one broken by divorce, provided that the children are given the right information about their situation. $14.95. 30 min. Center for Casette Studies.

Children in the One-Parent Home
Presents suggestions for the single parent, stressing some of the advantages of the one parent home. $11. At 1⅞ IPS Cassette, 21 min., 1970. New Media Marketing Manager, College and University Division, McGraw-Hill.

Conjoint Family Therapy.   *Virginia Satir*
A workshop series of psychodrama and encounter approaches which help people to outgrow the destructive "games" played in families. $90. (10 tapes). 14 hours. 1968. Big Sur Recordings.

Family Communication and Growth.   *Virginia Satir*
A discussion of a number of family therapy techniques. $9. 60 min. 1967. Big Sur Recordings.

Marital and Family Therapy
The multiple facets of marital and family therapy are presented in a factual and theoretical context essential for an effective therapeutic approach. James L. Framo of Temple University describes family systems concepts, examines pathological symptoms from a family transactional viewpoint, and explores the types and dynamics of marriage and marital therapy. The individual tape titles are: (1) Introduction to

Family Systems Concepts and Historical Development of Family Therapy; (2) Symptoms from a Family Transactional Viewpoint, Part 1; (3) Symptoms from a Family Transactional Viewpoint Part 2; (4) The Family Life Cycle: Impressions; (5) Some Family Therapy Techniques: Early Phases; (6) Dynamics of Marriage and Marital Therapy; (7) Sexual Problems in Marital Therapy, and Husbands' Reactions to Wives' Infidelity; (8) Marriage Therapy in a Couples Group; (9) Divorce Therapy; (10) Therapy Involving Adults with their Family of Origin: You Can Go Home Again; (11) My Families, My Family, On Working with One's Marital Partner as Cotherapist; and (12) Personal Reflections of a Family Therapist. $7.95 each. At 1⅞ IPS Cassette. 60 min. each. 1974. Behavioral Sciences Tape Library.

Marital and Sexual Counseling

Underlying considerations involved in marital and sexual counseling are discussed in 12 parts. Topics include: (1) an introduction to marital and sexual counseling and the intake interview; (2) a psychiatrist and a marriage counselor collaborate in the treatment of couples with marital problems; (3) a marriage counselor consults a psychiatrist about treatment of infidelity: a heterosexual, a bisexual and a marriage counselor consult a psychiatrist about involvement in treatment, the abreactive experience and traumatic psychic injury; (4) sexual disorders in marriage; (5) therapy for sexual maladjustment and sensate-focused sexual therapy: an adaptation of the Masters and Johnson technique; (6) alcoholism: the nature of the problem and the alcoholic marriage; (7) the use of psychological testing in marriage counseling; (8) the control of fertility: considerations pertinent to marriage counselors and uncontrolled fertility; (9) premenstrual tension, menopause, hysterectomy: considerations pertinent to marriage counselors and practical suggestions for marriage counseling; (10) divorce counseling: general questions about divorce and some answers and differences in the lawyer-client and the marriage counselor-client relationship during a divorce; (11) remarriage; and (12) premarital counseling and training in and referrals for marriage counseling. $6.95 each. At 1⅞ IPS. Cassette. 60 min. each. 1973. Behavioral Sciences Tape Library.

Principles and Techniques of Family Therapy

A comprehensive guide for evaluating and treating families is presented by Rodney J. Shapiro of the University of Rochester. Methods are illustrated that have proven consistently effective in treating families. The emphasis is on the actual practice of family therapy and a

variety of techniques are described in detail. The individual tape titles
are: (1) Principles and Characteristics of Family Therapy; (2) Evaluating the Family—Part 1; (3) Evaluating the Family—Part 2; (4) Treatment of the Family—Part 1; (5) Treatment of the Family—Part 2; and
(6) Working with Children, Adolescents, and Couples. $7.95 each. At
1⅞ IPS. Cassette. 60 min. each. 1974. Behavioral Sciences Tape Library.

Films

Carl Rogers on Marriage: Persons as Partners
Dr. Rogers answers the question of whether there are any factors in
partnerships between men and women which distinguish between
those which are satisfying, enriching, growing, and permanent from
those relationships which are unenhancing and do not work, ending in
unhappiness, separation, or divorce. Sale: $250. Rental fee per day of
use: $25. 28 min. 16mm. Color and sound. American Personnel and
Guidance Association.

Dark at the Top of the Stairs
Set in a small Oklahoma town in the 1920s, this film is a poignant
drama of a couple whose struggle against economic difficulties and the
imminent breakup of their marriage is reflected in the uncertainties of
their two children. Robert Preston, Dorothy McGuire, Eve Arden,
Angela Lansbury, Shirley Knight. Rental: $37.50. 124 min. 16mm.
Color. 1960. International Film Bureau, Inc.

East of Eden
This is a story that intimately searches into the hearts of men and
women as a modern reworking of the Biblical story of Cain and Abel,
and also as a close study of the generation gap between a father and his
two very different sons. James Dean, Julie Harris, Raymond Massey.
Rental: $35. 115 min. 16 mm. Color. 1955. International Film
Bureau, Inc.

Families Get Angry
Families Get Angry permits children to gain insight into frustrations
that arise from family quarrels. The quarrel depicted begins as the
father in a black, low-income family is trying to stretch too little

money to pay too many bills. Equally frustrated in her reciprocal position, the mother sharply defends her spending as absolutely minimal. Rental: $7.75. 9 min. 16mm. Color. 1972. Film Library— Oregon.

On Being an Effective Parent
The parent effectiveness training (PET) program, developed by Dr. Gordon, applies basic counseling skills and human relations techniques to parent-child relationships. Dr. Gordon teaches parents the skill of active listening, a technique used when it is the child who has a problem. He also teaches parents how to accurately communicate their own concerns and needs. Sale: $300. Rental fee per day of use: $30. 45 min. (two reels). 16mm. Color and sound. American Personnel and Guidance Association.

Story of Sarah and Paul: Marital Therapy Techniques: Tapes I & II
Marital therapy techniques used with a middle-class black couple with one baby, who sought treatment in a time of crisis precipitated by the wife's need for major heart surgery, are presented in two videotapes designed to be used as independent teaching presentations. The first tape includes edited portions of the initial evaluation session, with voice over comments. Narration deals with the therapist's techniques of defining the major problems, obtaining information, selecting the agenda for the session, gauging responses to interpretations, engaging the couple in therapy, and guiding the negotiation process from concrete proposals through repetition and response to closure. The second tape contains critiques of several subsequent therapy sessions. The narration explains methods of relating to young children to gain information about the family, summarizing major issues, selecting an agenda, negotiation, clarifying and teaching. The evolution of a new and more satisfying relationship between the couple as a result of therapy is noted. The videotapes, which can also be used independently, are recommended for restricted use only. Rental: $15. ½ inch videotape b/w. Tape I: 45 min. Tape II: 60 min. 1972. Continuing Education Media, Eastern Pennsylvania Psychiatric Institute, Henry Ave. & Abbottsford Rd., Philadelphia, PA 19129.

Violent Family
Two evaluation sessions of the initial stage of family therapy, which can be used either independently or together, are presented. The first videotape, entitled "Motherhood and Marriage—Session I," features

the initial evaluation of a family, in which the husband was ordered by his parole board to seek family therapy because of multiple violent behavior. The therapist approaches the family through the youngest son. In the second evaluation session, entitled "Christmas Pain— Session II," the development of the theme of deprivation is illustrated, and this theme is linked to the intrafamily violence. The videotape is recommended for restricted use only. Rental: $15. ½ inch videotape, b/w. 60 min. each. 1973. Continuing Education Media Division, Eastern Pennsylvania Psychiatric Institute, Henry Ave. and Abbottsford Rd., Philadelphia, PA 19129.

Children

3

TILL THE TWENTIETH CENTURY children were considered the property of their parents in most cultures. In ancient Rome a man could sell, abandon, or kill his child if he pleased. When a Roman citizen was in his father's house, his rights regressed to those of family chattel.

Parents and schoolmasters, from the ancient philosophers to the American colonists, believed that sparing the rod led to the spoiling of children. Whippings and floggings have been acceptable means of disciplining children in many cultures. American colonists even enacted laws that demanded the obedience of children. In Massachusetts and Connecticut, for example, filial disobedience was punishable by death. The Massachusetts Stubborn Child Law, enacted in 1654, was reaffirmed in 1971 by the state's highest court, which ruled that children have no right of dissent against the reasonable and lawful commands of their parents or legal guardians. The law was finally repealed in 1973.

Even today standards of normal and acceptable child care vary by culture and subculture. Practices considered to be mild abuse in one subculture in others would be normal, desirable patterns of child rearing, everyday discipline, or legitimate folk medicine.

Despite cultural variations, however, there are norms of acceptable child care in this country. Since the 1960s, all 50 states, the Virgin Islands, and Guam have enacted laws to protect children whose parents fail to meet minimal standards of care. In 1974, Congress passed the Child Abuse Prevention and Treatment Act, Public Law 93–247, which defines child abuse and neglect as "the physical or mental injury, sexual abuse, negligent treatment, or maltreatment of a child under the age of eighteen by a person who is responsible for the child's

39

welfare under circumstances which indicate that the child's health or welfare is harmed or threatened thereby."

Most psychologists believe childhood helps shape the emotional development, personality, and intelligence of the adult. That is one reason for the current trend toward preschool education and the emphasis on early educational and social skills. Unfortunately, the emotional development of children has not had as much attention.

More than half the United States population is now under 25 years of age, and it is estimated that more than 10 percent of this precious resource, about ten million youths, require mental health services. Their needs range from hospitalization for treatment and reversal of serious psychopathology, to the early intervention of doctors, teachers, counselors, and parents in handling mild, transient problems to prevent later developmental crises.

The factors affecting the mental health of children are vast and complex. Mental health problems make themselves felt in virtually every aspect of a child's life: at home, at school, in social settings. Their solution, therefore, requires the contributions of agencies with varied functions and programs, each emphasizing different dimensions of the child's world.

The mental health of children rests, ultimately, on the health of our total society, from the smallest unit to the largest. The stability of the home and the well being of the family, the compassion of the surrounding community, and the social conscience and action of the government and its citizens are all crucial.

Child Abuse

One grave and perhaps the largest contributing factor affecting and damaging the mental health of thousands of children is child abuse. The incidence of child abuse in the United States is alarming. Estimates of actual cases range from 500,000 to 4,000,000 incidents of child abuse annually. The reason for the discrepancy between these estimates is the large gap between the reported cases and the actual incidence of maltreatment. Despite the discrepancy, it is obvious that thousands of children in this country are victims of abuse and neglect each year.

Children are abused and neglected in families from all socioeconomic levels, races, nationalities, and religious groups. The problem is not limited to racial minorities nor to the poor, even though these groups account for proportionately large figures in reported statistics. In 1968, for example, the nationwide rate of reported incidence of child abuse was 6.7 per 100,000 for white children, compared to 21.0 per 100,000 for nonwhites.

Poor families and nonwhite families are reported more frequently than middle– and upper–class whites for several reasons. Members of lower socioeconomic groups are the clients of welfare agencies, municipal hospitals, and outpatient clinics. Compared to middle– and upper–class families, they not only have more contacts with many different types of community agents, but their homes, lives, and problems are also more open to professional scrutiny. These facts, however, do not deny the profound effects of social and economic deprivation, housing problems, unemployment, and subcultural and racial pressures on the lives and behavior of parents who maltreat their children. Any stress can make life more difficult, and the ramifications of poverty and discrimination can aggravate any problem. Such factors are involved to some degree in many cases of abuse and neglect. But no matter how necessary and useful it might be to improve the socioeconomic status of a family, this should not be confused with treating the more deeply rooted character problems involved in abusive behavior. Individual acts of abuse may occur when parents are faced with a crisis involving finances, employment, illness, or various other matters, but such crises cannot be considered justification for abuse. Crises are common in the lives of many parents who do not maltreat their children; and on the other hand, maltreatment does occur in families that are wealthy, well educated, and well housed.

Two other misconceptions about child abuse are that the parents, unaware of their own strength, unwittingly injure their children while disciplining them; and that the parents are possibly psychotic. It is incorrect to believe that abuse is caused by parents who simply "don't know their strength." Abusive or neglectful behavior is a complete pattern of parenting behavior. Its cause generally involves the childhood experience of the parent, parental misconceptions of the child, and crises in the life of the family which can precipitate incidents of abuse. Studies have found that parents who abuse or neglect their children show an incidence of psychoses, neuroses, and character disorders similar to that in the general population; only 10 percent of the parents exhibit serious psychiatric disorders. Given the necessary combination of circumstances, anyone could abuse or neglect a child.

Maltreatment can leave children with physical, emotional, and psychological scars, or even result in death. Estimates of the mortality rate range from 5 to 27 percent.

Physical injury resulting from abuse can include cuts, burns, bruises, abrasions, contusions, shock, laceration of internal organs, hemorrhage, subdural hematoma, and fractures. Because of their exceedingly fragile tissues, infants are particularly susceptible to physical injuries resulting from even mild abuse. Depending on the type and severity of maltreatment, long term physical effects can include mental retardation, loss of hearing or sight, lack of motor control, and speech defects.

Child victims of abuse and neglect have also been found to have learning behavior and habit disorders. Some maltreated children experience problems such as drug abuse, obesity, teenage pregnancy, and delinquency in later life. Many appear to pattern their adult lives on their past, abusing their own children and sometimes others as well. Among the most infamous adults who were maltreated as children are Arthur Bremmer, Sirhan Sirhan, James Earl Ray, Lee Harvey Oswald, and John Wilkes Booth.

Although it is not known whether criminal behavior is a rare or common outcome of maltreatment, it is clear that both maltreated children and their parents are in need of help. Human suffering of both children and adults will decrease with increased awareness of the high incidence of child abuse and increased availability of such services as parent hotlines, and Mother's Emergency Stress Service.

REFERENCES

Aries, P. *Centuries of Childhood.* New York: Alfred A. Knopf, 1962.

Child Abuse and Neglect—The Problem and Its Management. Washington: DHEW, Publication No. (OHD) 75–30073, 1975.

Davids, Anthony (ed.). *Child Personality & Psychopathology: Current Topics.* New York: John Wiley & Sons, 1976.

Davis, Glenn. *Childhood and History in America.* New York: Psychohistory Press, 1977.

Fontana, Vincent J. *Somewhere a Child Is Crying: Maltreatment—Cause and Prevention.* New York: Macmillan, 1973.

Gottlieb, David (ed.). *Children's Liberation.* Englewood Cliffs, NJ: Prentice-Hall, 1973.

Helfer, Ray E. and Kempe, C. Henry (eds.). *Battered Child.* Chicago: University of Chicago Press, 1974.

Jersild, Arthur. *Child Psychology.* Englewood Cliffs, NJ: Prentice-Hall, 1975.

Joint Commission on Mental Health of Children. *Mental Health from Infancy through Adolescence.* New York: Harper & Row, 1973.

Kempe, C. Henry and Helfer, Ray E. (eds.). *Helping the Battered Child and His Family.* Philadelphia: J.B. Lippincott, 1972.

Mussen, Paul H., Conger, John J. and Kagan, Jerome. *Child Development and Personality.* New York: Harper & Row, 1974.

Schmitt, Barton D. (ed.). *Child Protection Team Handbook.* New York: Garland Publishing Inc., 1977.

Books

Advocacy for Child Mental Health. *Berlin, Irving N.*
Ten basic rights essential to the well-being of children are outlined, and the field of child development and its significance for child health professionals are reviewed. Such factors as nutrition, infant rhythms, effects of maternal deprivation, child abuse, daycare, developmental delay, preschool and school age stress, sexual maturation, and high-risk registers are covered. $13.50. New York: Brunner/Mazel, 1975. 352 pp.

Annotated Bibliography on Child Abuse.
Listing of 114 books, journal articles, and other documents covering the sources of abusing behavior and community and legal intervention (dated 1958 through 1975) with subject, author, and title indexes. NCJRS Microfiche Program, P.O. Box 24036, Washington, DC 20024, 1975. 250 pp.

Baby and Child Care. *Spock, Benjamin*
This is an updated version of the handbook to childcare that parents have used faithfully for the last two decades. In this edition Spock adds the need to teach a child the social and moral obligations and updates the sexual terminology. 95¢. New York: Pocket Books, 1968.

Behavior Therapy with Children. *Graziano, A.M.*
The implications of behavior modification for the delivery of contemporary child mental health services are examined, and a comparison of its impact with traditional clinical models is provided. $9.50. Chicago: Aldine-Atherton, 1971. 458 pp.

Child Mental Health in International Perspective. *David, Henry P.*
Mental health services for children throughout the world are described in this book from the Joint Commission on Mental Health of Children. Sections on emotionally disturbed youth, culturally disadvantaged and retarded youth, delinquent youth, manpower, and prevention and group care are included. Many of the articles reflect the emphasis on a rational approach to planning which allows many programs to be unified. It is apparent that the United States lacks a system of care for children which integrates children's services with other

health, welfare, and educational systems. $10. New York: Harper &
Row, 1972. 432 pp.

Child Welfare League of America:
Standards for Child Protective Service.
The standards for child protective service developed by the Child Welfare League of America are presented. The standards are intended to
be goals for continuous improvement of services to children, and represent practices that are considered most desirable in providing the
social services that the community offers through various agencies, to
help them and their parents with problems affecting childrearing.
Areas considered include: protective service as a child welfare service;
intake; social work in protective service; protective service and the
court; organization and administration of protective service; protective service and the community. 95 references. $2.50. New York:
Child Welfare League of America, 1973. 85 pp.

Children in Play Therapy. *Moustakas, Clark E.*
Examples of the process of therapeutic play are presented with normal
children and children with emotional problems. Transcriptions of
children's dialogue in play therapy are included. Discussion areas include preventive play therapy, attitudes in play therapy, situational
play therapy with disturbed children, and implications of play therapy
outside the playroom. $10. New York: Jason Aronson, 1973. 256 pp.

Choosing Child Care: A Guide for Parents. *Auerbach, Stevanne;*
and Freedman, Linda
Finding good, dependable child care is a problem many parents face.
Choosing Child Care leads parents through a clear, step-by-step process for locating the kind of quality child care situation they want and
enables them to make informed choices from among the alternatives.
$3. Berkeley: Bookpeople. 80 pp.

Day Care. *Evans, E.B.; Shub, Beth; and Winsteine, Marlene*
How to plan, develop, and operate a day care center is discussed.
There are four basic categories: (1) mechanisms for starting a center,
rules, regulations, whom the center will serve, and how the program
will be directed; (2) developing a site, teaching a staff, setting up a
health and social service, and caring for the children; (3) the necessary
components of a classroom and curriculum; and (4) planning a budget
and raising funds. $6.95. Boston: Beacon Press, 1971. 337 pp.

Emergencies in Child Psychiatry: Emotional Crises of Children, Youth, and Their Families. *Morrison, Gilbert C.*
In a collection of contributions by authorities in child psychology and psychiatry, urgent emotional problems are detailed, clinical problems and findings are described, treatment approaches defined, and theoretical concepts outlined. Research methodologies are provided or proposed for emotional crises in children and youth. Selection and use of various psychotherapeutic approaches are explained, school and community involvement discussed, and possible need for hospitalization and use of medication considered. Emotional problems discussed include suicide attempts and threats, acute anxiety accompanied by physical symptoms, conversion and dissociative reactions, sexual promiscuity and precocious pregnancy, acute school phobia, runaways, homicidal threats and attacks, drug abuse and intoxication, fire setting, incestuous relationships and sexual assault on children. $24.50. Springfield, IL: Charles C Thomas, 1975. 482 pp.

An Introduction to Art Therapy: Studies of the "Free" Art Expression of Behavior Problem Children and Adolescents as a Means of Diagnosis and Therapy. *Naumburg, Margaret*
The problems of using art therapy in dealing with emotionally disturbed children are discussed. The life history and case studies of six maladjusted children from 4–17 years old are given; art therapy was adapted to the special needs and sexual fears of each youngster. The release of dreams, fantasies, and conflicts is converted into images by the patient in order to facilitate verbal communication. Therapists and special educators are instructed how to encourage the release of the unconscious into spontaneous painting. Color reproductions of original drawings by behavior problem children are included. $10. New York: Teachers College Press, 1973. 225 pp.

Mental Health Programs for Preschool Children: A Field Study. *Glasscote, Raymond M.; and Fishman, Michael E.*
The delivery of mental health services to young children is discussed in two sections: an overview of issues in the development and care of young children, and a description of seven model preschool mental health programs. More than 20 programs ranging from nursery and outreach programs through consultation, parent education, and advocacy are described in detail. The services described consist primarily of psychoeducational or therapeutic programs serving emotionally dis-

turbed, autistic, and other handicapped children. $7. Washington, DC: Joint Information Service, 1974. 182 pp.

The Mental Health of Children: Services, Research and Manpower. *Joint Commission on Mental Health of Children*
Subjects dealing with services and research in child mental health are examined. Programs of prevention and rehabilitation research and its uses in manpower utilization are discussed and recommendations for defining goals for the utilization of manpower in child mental health services and for age appropriate prevention approaches are offered. The organization, administration and financing of services are also considered, proposing a more responsive system of services to children emphasizing health, cognition, and development of interpersonal relationships. Finally, the clinical issues of child mental health are analyzed, presenting a panorama of development and biopsychosocial processes. $15. New York: Harper & Row, 1973. 446 pp.

A Primer of Child Psychotherapy. *Adams, Paul L.*
An informal guide to child psychotherapy for the beginning therapist is presented. The therapist is reminded that both the child and his surrounding environment need changing. The child's inner world is described as a world apart from the adult's, and it is considered a separate way of life. Topics discussed are the child's family and how the family can be involved in therapy, the child himself, the referral source, the child mental health team, and the human service agencies of the whole community. Suggestions are offered on how to conduct the initial interview with the child, the conduct of sessions, and ways of terminating therapy when the therapist's goals have been reached. Special approaches of therapy with the adolescent are included. $9.95. Boston: Little, Brown & Co., 1974. 207 pp.

The Psychology of the Elementary School Child.
Binter, Alfred; and Frey, Sherman
Research on the psychology of the elementary school child is reviewed in six major areas. The areas concern: (1) the study of human growth by following total child growth; (2) the systematic observation of the child; (3) the cognitive domain of children; (4) the child's concept of death; (5) the childhood concept of sexuality and sexual learning; and (6) the cultural forces that influence child psychology. The counselor's role is examined in each area of discussion. Chicago: Rand McNally, 1972.

Theories of Child Development. *Baldwin, Alfred*
This book explores six theories of development: (1) Jean Piaget; (2) Carl Hull (S-R Theory); (3) Kurt Lewin (field theory); (4) Sigmund Freud; (5) Heinz Werner (organismic approach); and (6) Talcott Parsons and Robert Bales (sociological approach). Baldwin supports the "common sense" approach to child rearing which Fritz Heider advocates. $10.95. New York: John Wiley & Sons, 1967.

U.S. Facilities and Programs for Children with Severe Mental Illnesses—A Directory.
Service programs for children with severe mental illness are cataloged. Programs and facilities listed include those which serve children diagnosed as autistic, schizophrenic, or as having any of the other childhood psychoses or severe mental disorders. Programs are listed by state. Rockville, MD: NIMH, 1974. 448 pp.

We Can Change It! *Shargel, Susan; and Kane, Irene*
A bibliography of nonsexist books for children and suggestions on how to select and present books to young people. Illustrated with photos and drawings. $1.50. Berkeley: Bookpeople. 24 pp.

Who's Minding the Children? The History and Politics of Day Care in America. *Steinfels, Margaret O'Brien*
The history of day care programs in America is traced from 1854, when a New York hospital established nursery school programs for the children of poor women, and the issue of whether or not day care is a threat to the family is examined. Five major conclusions concerning the need to develop day care programs carefully and gradually are given. $8.95. New York: Simon and Schuster, 1973. 281 pp.

Articles

Child Abuse and Neglect Activities
Child abuse and neglect activities that come under the federal government's jurisdiction are reported. Projects undertaken by various agencies are summarized. Washington, DC: U.S. Dept. of Health, Education and Welfare, 1975. 16 pp.

Child Protective Services and the Law. *Becker, T.T.*
Some of the questions which the author discusses include how due process can be assured for both parent and child in a neglect hearing, whether such hearings will be adversary proceedings, who should represent the child, and how conflicts of interest can be resolved. In addition, the author advises protective agencies to provide legal consultation to help their staff prepare cases for court processing. American Humane Association, P.O. Box 1266, Denver, CO 80201, 1968. 24 pp.

Developing a Collaborative Model for Mental Health Professionals Working in the Schools. *Cohen, Raquel E.*
Framework, objectives, and principles underlying the development of a collaborative model for mental health professionals and teachers in the school setting are discussed. Techniques which mental health professionals can employ within the collaborative role include: (1) promoting teacher understanding of mental health principles; (2) working with specific children; (3) consultation; and (4) coordinating a range of services to the child which encompasses the school and other community agencies. 31 references. Final Report, NIMH Grant MH–9214, 1973. 20 pp.

From "I" to "We." *Murphy, Lois B.; and Leeper, Ethel M.*
Important aspects in personality development and childhood socialization experiences are discussed, and the role of the child care center in promoting healthy child development is explored. It is concluded that good total development in childhood can provide prerequisites for further growth and can help to prevent the beginnings of retardation, disorganized behavior, early delinquency, and emotional disturbance. 60¢. Caring for Children, No. 8, Washington, DC: Supt. of Documents, Government Printing Office, 1974. 28 pp.

Protecting the Sexually Abused Child. *McKerrow, Wilson D.*
Sexual abuse of children and the role of children's protective services in helping sexually abused children and their families are discussed. Differences in cases where the offender is a stranger and those in which the offender is a relative or friend are reviewed. An interdisciplinary approach through in-depth studies is recommended. 3 references. In: *American Humane Association,* Second National Symposium on Child Abuse. pp. 38–44. Denver, CO: American Humane Association, 1973.

Selected References on the Abused and Battered Child
Bibliographical references to domestic and foreign sources, including
journal articles, books, and newspaper reports. References are provided by year for the period 1968 to 1973. Superintendent of Documents, Government Printing Office, Washington, DC 20402, 1973. 23
pp.

Audio Tapes

Children and Evil
Many of our ideas of evil are formed in early childhood. The program
examines both fairy tales and child psychology to find out what some
of the most important influences are in the development of one's first
ideas about good and evil. $12.95. 30 min. Center for Cassette Studies.

The Impact of Stress on Children
Concepts and techniques applicable to early childhood crises are dis-
cussed in a symposium presented by the Center for Preventive
Psychiatry. The discussions center on helping children deal with ill-
ness, accident, hospitalization, death, and parental separation. Indi-
vidual discussions are presented by Ann S. Kliman, Dr. Richard A.
Gardner, Dr. Arthur Zelman, Doris Ronald, Dr. Myron Stein, and Dr.
Gilbert Kliman. The individual tape titles are: (1) Do We Hear—Can
We Help; (2) When Parents Separate; (3) Helping Young Children
Cope with Accident, Illness, and Hospitalization; (4) The Children
Know . . . But Should We Talk About It in Class; and (5) The Impact
of Death on Young Children. $7.95 each. At 1 7⁄8 IPS Cassette. 60 min.
each. 1974. Behavioral Sciences Tape Library.

Films

Behavior Modification: Teaching Language to Psychotic Children
This film, based on the work of Ivar Lovaas at UCLA, demonstrates
reinforcement and stimulus fading techniques used in teaching language skills to psychotic children. Frequent use of graphs and charts
illustrates effects of the treatment program and rates of improvement.

Sale: $580. Rental: $50/day. 42 min. 16mm. Color/sound. 1969.
Prentice-Hall Film Library.

Children in Peril
This is a documentary film on the subject of child abuse in America. It
describes the problem and its scope, and provides information for an
audience of the general public. This is a good, general visual essay on
the overall national problem of child abuse, its victims, and the type of
programs seeking to remedy the syndrome. Sale: $325. Rental: Write
for information. 22 min. 16 mm. Color. 1972. Xerox Films, P.O. Box
444, Columbus, OH 43216.

Childhood: The Enchanted Years
This film series looks at children in their first few years of life. It points
out that a baby is born without any of the characteristics that are
man's—a logical mind, a language, an erect posture, highly coordinated and specialized hands which make tool use possible—and that
he develops all of these in his first few years of life. An infant's progress from complete dependency to a determined will of his own with
discernable adult characteristics, is rapid. Captured in this film series
are these first four years. Sale: $575. Rental: $35. 52 min. 16 mm.
Color. Psychological Films, Inc.

The Epileptic Child
The epileptic child is discussed. Problems are defined, methods of
managing them are illustrated, and positive ways in which the general
public can help are suggested. Useful for orienting or instructing new
employees in institutions or services for children with mental handi-
caps, or in community education programs for the general public.
Sale: $125. Rental: $5.25. 30 min. 16mm. b/w. 1969. Net Film Service, Audio-Visual Center, Indiana University, Bloomington, IN
47401.

Free To Be ... You and Me
Involves young people in the endless possibilities of their own uniqueness as they explore such life-enhancing concepts as independence,
peer and sibling cooperation and self-fulfillment. Based on the nation-
ally best selling record and book and produced by Marlo Thomas and
Carole Hart for the Ms. Foundation, Inc. Rental: $15.25. 1974. Film
Library–Oregon.

Help for Mark
This film is directed toward parents and teachers of trainable retarded
children as well as students in special education, educational psychology, child development, clinical child psychology, and behavior
modification. Application of behavior modification principles and
techniques which can be applied in the home environment receive the
most attention. By Victor L. Baldwin and H.D. Bud Fredericks. Sale:
$250. Rental: $25/day. 17 min. 16mm. Color/sound. 1970. Prentice-
Hall Film Library.

In a Class . . . All by Himself
One child in twenty is affected by minimal brain dysfunction. These
children are hyperactive and have visual and audio perception problems. If they are not helped, they fail in the classroom. As they grow
up many go to prison, become alcoholics, and 75 percent of them must
be institutionalized temporarily or permanently. This film focuses on
the ways—medication, special education, and psychology—that these
hyperkinetic children can be helped to become self-sufficient adults.
Sale: $500. Rental: $36. 50 min. Color. 1972. Films Incorporated.

It Feels Like You're Left Out of the World
A central theme here is that the self-esteem of a child with a learning
disability is in severe jeopardy and that withdrawal from learning or
active aggression are frequently the visible manifestations of low opinion of self. In the film, children and their parents speak openly of their
frustration. Several guidelines for a sensible approach to the children
are given. Rental: $4.25. 28 min. 16mm. Film Library–Oregon.

The Neglected
This is a portrayal of families whose children have come under the
protection of community authorities as a result of abuse or neglect. It
demonstrates that skilled techniques can change patterns of dangerous
and unhealthy family relationships and help unstable human beings
achieve acceptable standards of parenthood. The operation of the
Child Protective Services is shown. Sale: $225. Rental: $15. 30 min.
16mm. b/w. 1965. International Film Bureau, Inc.

This Child Is Rated X
White paper series. The inequities of juvenile justice and the abuse of
children's rights. How the court system, detention facilities, and training schools are used to punish children for minor offenses, such as

53

truancy and running away. Interviews with children from four institutions and with penal authorities. Need for "attention" rather than "detention" homes. Rental: $26.50. 52 min. 16mm. Color. 1971. Film Library–Oregon.

Contacts

American Academy for Cerebral
 Palsy
University Hospital School
Iowa City, IO 52240

American Academy of Pediatrics
1891 Hinman Ave.
Evanston, IL 60201

American Association for Health,
 Physical Education and Recreation
1201 16th St., N.W.
Washington, DC 20036

American Association of
 Elementary–Kindergarten–Nursery
 Educators
NEA Center
1201 16th St., N.W.
Washington, DC 20036

American Association of Workers for
 the Blind, Inc.
Suite 637
1151 K St., N.W.
Washington, DC 20005

American Corrective Therapy
 Association, Inc.
811 St. Margaret's Rd.
Chillicothe, OH 45601

American Foundation for the Blind
15 W. 16th St.
New York, NY 10011

American Home Economics
 Association
2010 Massachusetts Ave., N.W.
Washington, DC 20036

American Humane Association
Children's Division
P.O. Box 1266
Denver, CO 80201

American Physical Therapy
 Association
1740 Broadway
New York, NY 10019

American Rehabilitation Counseling
 Association of the American
 Personnel and Guidance
 Association
1607 New Hampshire Ave., N.W.
Washington, DC 20009

The American Speech and Hearing
 Association
9030 Old Georgetown Rd.
Washington, DC 20014

Association for Childhood Education
 International
3615 Wisconsin Ave., N.W.
Washington, DC 20016

Association for Children with
 Learning Disabilities
2200 Brownsville Road
Pittsburgh, PA 15210

Association for Education of the
 Visually Handicapped
711 14th St., N.W.
Washington, DC 20005

The Association of Rehabilitation
   Centers, Inc.
7979 Old Georgetown Rd.
Washington, DC 20014

Bureau of Education for the
   Handicapped
U.S. Office of Education
400 Maryland Ave., N.W.
Washington, DC 20202

Children's Advocates, Inc.
21 James St.
Boston, MA 02118

Child Study Association of
   America—Wel-Met, Inc.
50 Madison Ave.
New York, NY 10010

Child Welfare League of America,
   Inc.
67 Irving Place
New York, NY 10003

Closer Look
Dorothy Dean, Project Director
National Special Information
   Education Center
Suite 610-E
1201 16th St., N.W.
Washington, DC 20036

Council of Organizations Serving the
   Deaf
Suite 210
4201 Connecticut Ave., N.W.
Washington, DC 20008

Day Care and Child Development
   Council of America, Inc.
1401 K St., N.W.
Washington, DC 20005

Education Commission of the
   States
Suite 300
1860 Lincoln St.
Denver, CO 80203

The ERIC Clearinghouse on
   Handicapped and Gifted Children
The Council for Exceptional
   Children
1920 Association Drive
Reston, VA 22091

ERIC (Educational Resource
   Information Center/Early
   Childhood Education)
University of Illinois at
   Urbana-Champaign
805 West Pennsylvania Ave.
Urbana, IL 61801

ERIC Information Retrieval Center
   on the Disadvantaged
Teachers College
Columbia University
New York, NY 10027

Joseph P. Kennedy, Jr. Foundation
Suite 510
719 13th St., N.W.
Washington, DC 20005

Lawyer's Committee for Civil Rights
   Under Law
Suite 520
733 15th St., N.W.
Washington, DC 20005

Mental Health Law Project
1751 N St., N.W.
Washington, DC 20031

Muscular Dystrophy Association of
   America, Inc.
1790 Broadway
New York, NY 10019

National Association for Black Child
   Development
Black Child Development Education
   Centers
1028 Connecticut Ave., N.W.
Suite 514
Washington, DC 20036

National Association for the
Education of Young Children
1834 Connecticut Ave., N.W.
Washington, DC 20009

The National Association for Gifted
Children
8080 Springvalley Drive
Cincinnati, OH 45236

National Association for Mental
Health
1800 North Kent St., Rosslyn Station
Arlington, VA 22209

National Association for Retarded
Children
420 Lexington Ave.
New York, NY 10017

National Association of the Deaf
Suite 321
2025 I St., N.W.
Washington, DC 20006

National Association of State
Directors of Special Education
Suite 610-E, NEA Building
1201 16th St., N.W.
Washington, DC 20036

National Center for Law and the
Handicapped
1235 N. Eddy St.
South Bend, IN 46617

National Center for the Prevention
and Treatment of Child Abuse and
Neglect
1001 Jasmine Street
Denver, CO 80220

National Center on Child Abuse and
Neglect
Children's Bureau
Office of Child Development, DHEW
P.O. Box 1182
Washington, DC 20013

National Committee for Prevention
of Child Abuse
Suite 510
111 East Wacker Drive
Chicago, IL 60601

National Congress of Parents and
Teachers
700 North Rush St.
Chicago, IL 60611

National Council for the Gifted
700 Prospect Ave.
West Orange, NJ 07052

The National Easter Seal Society for
Crippled Children and Adults
2023 W. Ogden Ave.
Chicago, IL 60612

National Epilepsy League, Inc.
Room 2200
203 N. Wabash Ave.
Chicago, IL 60601

The National Foundation—March of
Dimes
800 2nd Ave.
New York, NY 10017

National/State Leadership Training
Institute on the Gifted and
Talented
Suite 708
316 W. Second St.
Los Angeles, CA 90012

Office of the Gifted and Talented
U.S. Office of Education
Washington, DC 20202

Parents Anonymous
National Office
2810 Artesia Boulevard
Redondo Beach, CA 90278

Parent Cooperative Preschool
International
P.O. Box 40123
Indianapolis, IN 46240

Play Schools Association
120 West 57th St.
New York, NY 10019

The President's Committee on
  Employment of the Handicapped
U.S. Department of Labor
Washington, DC 20210

President's Committee on Mental
  Retardation
Washington, DC 20201

State/Federal Information
  Clearinghouse for Exceptional
  Children
Council for Exceptional Children
1920 Association Drive
Reston, VA 22091

United Cerebral Palsy Association,
  Inc.
66 E. 34th St.
New York, NY 10016

U.S. Department of Health,
  Education and Welfare
Office of Education
400 Maryland Ave., S.W.
Washington, DC 20202

U.S. Office of Education
Bureau of Education for the
  Handicapped
7th and D Sts., S.W.
Washington, DC 20202

Adolescence

4

ADOLESCENCE IS A VERY TURBULENT PERIOD, involving changes, both physical and emotional, that many times lead to alienation, insecurity, and identity crisis. Puberty causes many physiological changes, such as an increase in sex hormones and new developments in the body structure and functions. Puberty for the female involves menstruation and the development of breasts and pubic hair; and for the male, the development of pubic hair, increased musculature and a deep voice. Sexual maturation results in a new sexual awareness which can create many fears and painful experiences.

The adolescent is extremely self-critical and self-conscious to the point of appearing egocentric. Along this same line, adolescents become more introspective and analytical and are constantly questioning: "Who am I?" The psychoanalyst, Eric Erikson, labeled the adolescent period as "adolescent 'identity crisis'" because the adolescent is trying to develop his/her own identity as a person. Adolescents are seeking to clarify who they are and what role they will perform in society. The adolescent is on the threshold of adulthood, which means he/she has to begin to think about a career, college, leaving home, and possibly, marriage.

From this brief sketch of the adolescent experience, it is easy to understand why this is such a critical time in human development. The high rate of adolescent suicides, trouble with the law and school, drug and alcohol abuse, pregnancies, and runaways indicates that adolescence is a critical period for both adolescents and society.

In the last eight years peer counseling, hotlines, walk-in services, and help with adolescent problems, such as venereal diseases and pregnancy, have been developed by various outreach agencies throughout the nation. However, most of these agencies are on the periphery of

traditional mental health services because most of their funding originally came from drug prevention programs. These agencies have been
able to communicate with adolescents; they have expanded their services to nondrug problems and are filling the gap for unsuccessful,
traditional programs. Mental health services in the past have been
extremely unsuccessful in dealing with adolescents because of several
factors: the services were mistrusted by adolescents; treatment was
made available only to very disturbed individuals; and the services
only used traditional therapy procedures. Perhaps outreach services
that have been extremely successful in dealing with adolescents in the
future will be asked to coordinate their services with mental health
agencies in helping to solve adolescent problems.

The information and statistics concerning four major areas in
which adolescents' needs and problems appear to be alarmingly high
are presented below.

Runaways

Estimates of how many adolescents run away from home each year in
the United States range from 500,000 to 1,000,000, ages 10 to 17
years old. Of the runaways, it is speculated that nearly one-half are
girls, and the average age is about 15 years old. If there are 500,000
one-time runaways per year, then approximately 1½ percent of the
total United States population (ages 10–17) runs away each year. Fur-
thermore, this means that approximately 2.7 percent of all families
with at least one youth, ages 10–17, will have at least one runaway per
year.

At least one-half of all youth who run away from home stay within
the town or general vicinity in which they live. Most runaways go to a
friend's or relative's house. In general, the length of time away from
home increases with age. The repeater–runaway is definitely in the
minority, the majority do so only once. Most runaway episodes seem
to be poorly planned and reflect impulsive behavior. The current data
on runaways has found a slight seasonal and monthly variation, with
more episodes tending to occur in summer and fall and near vacation
times.

Most of the literature on runaways attributes the cause to various
situational factors, rather than psychopathological ones, as once was
thought. Another trend is that runaways most often have inadequate
parent-child relationships and unhappy, stressful home environments.

Alcohol Abuse

In the last few years there has been a shift from drugs to alcohol by adolescents. This could be due to the availability of alcohol and the less severe consequence for its use than for illegal drugs. By conservative estimates, approximately 5 percent of the adolescents in the United States have a drinking problem; however, other estimates go as high as 23 percent.

Arrests of persons under the age of 18 for driving while under the influence of alcohol increased by more than 400 percent between 1960 and 1974.

One study on fatal car crashes found that adolescent drinkers were more likely than adults to be responsible for these crashes, and that they tended to have more crashes with less alcohol in their blood than adults. Because of adolescents' small size and their inexperience with alcohol, adolescents may feel the effects of alcohol more quickly and more strongly than adults do with similar amounts.

The two recurring reasons adolescents drink are: sociability and self-expression. The first reason is due to peer pressure; the second reason is due to the need to be a part of the normal adult identity. They consider drinking a kind of rite of passage into adulthood. Why some adolescents develop drinking problems and others do not is not known. Most likely, there is a combination of psychological, physiological, sociological, and environmental factors in the adolescent's life which causes him/her to go beyond the norm.

Drug Abuse

Among adolescents (12 to 17 years old) more than one in five (22.4 percent) report having used marihuana and more than half (12.3 percent) report current use. Among adolescents, .5 percent have used heroin, .9 percent have used hallucinogens and 5.3 percent have used other opiates.

The second largest category of drug use (second to marihuana) falls into the nonmedical use of psychotherapeutic drugs. One in ten adolescents have reported the use of tranquilizers, stimulants, or sedatives.

Although alcohol is becoming more of a problem than drugs, it still has a destructive effect on adolescents, and as the usage figures show, it is still a problem.

Studies have found that drug education is of little value in prevention. Prevention is most effective by the reinforcement of social networks of extraparental adults and stable peer groups.

Motivational studies of drug users indicate family breakdown, lack of identity, insecurity and sexual confusion as primary causes for emotional and social escape through drugs.

Outreach programs throughout the country have provided drop–in centers, peer group counseling, homes for runaways, and help for various adolescent problems. These have helped to solve the drug problem as well as to prevent it.

Crime

Homicides committed by youths under the age of 18 have increased 225 percent from 1960 to 1974.

From 1960 to 1974 robbery has increased 300 percent, burglary 139 percent, and aggravated assault 212 percent by youths under the age of 18.

Between 1960 and 1974 the violations of drug laws has increased an incredible 3,777.7 percent.

Another shocking increase has been in violent crimes. From 1960 to 1974, violent crimes by adolescents have increased 254 percent.

The statistics above are staggering. The high unemployment rate among youths may be one of the contributing factors in the increase of robberies and burglaries. The increase in violence could be a reflection of the violent trend in society as a whole.

Whatever the cause, it is evident that the adolescent period should be of concern to everyone.

REFERENCES

Adams, James F. *Understanding Adolescence: Current Developments in Adolescent Psychology.* Boston: Allyn & Bacon Inc., 1976.

Esman, Aaron H. (ed.). *The Psychology of Adolescence: Essential Readings.* New York: International Universities Press, 1975.

Gersh, Marvin J. & Litt, Iris S. *The Handbook of Adolescence.* New York: Dell Pub. Co., 1974.

Hicks, James T. *Adolescent Growth in Groups: A Look at Group Counseling on the High School Level.* Master's Thesis. California State University-Sacramento, 1976.

Kett, Joseph F. *Rites of Passage: Adolescence in America, 1790 to the Present.* New York: Basic Books, 1977.

Miller, Derek. "The Medical and Psychological Therapy of Adolescent Drug Abuse." *International Journal of Child Psychotherapy*, Vol. 2, No. 3, 1973, pp. 309–30.

Mussen, Paul H., Conger, John J. & Kagan, Jerome. *Child Development & Personality*. New York: Harper & Row, 1974.

Nuttall, Ena V., Nuttall, Ronald L., Polit, Denise & Clark, Karen. "Assessing Adolescent Mental Health Needs: The Views of Consumers, Providers, and Others." *Adolescence*, Vol. 12, No. 46, 1977, pp. 277–85.

Runaway Youth: Annotated Bibliography & Literature Overview. Washington, DC: DHEW, 1975.

Sourcebook of Criminal Justice Statistics of 1976. Washington, DC: U.S. Dept. of Justice, Law Enforcement Assistance Admin., 1977.

Books

The Adolescent Experience. *Semmens, James P.; and Krantz, Kermit E.*
A guide for the professional and the lay person dealing with counseling, treating, teaching, and understanding the adolescent is presented. The authors feel that this is a new world of and for young people and that older generations must change ideas, values, and priorities if they wish to remain relevant. The following subjects are examined: societal changes which have contributed to the new counterculture; questions of concern to adolescents about anatomy and physiology; issues of masturbation, homosexuality, contraception and premarital sexual intercourse; issues of pregnancy, abortion, venereal disease and drug abuse; premarital and marital counseling; and various approaches and techniques of counseling and intervention into teenage problems. $10. New York: Macmillan, 1970. 384 pp.

The Adolescent in Group and Family Therapy. *Sugar, Max*
Specific uses of group or family therapy with the adolescent are described. Specific problem areas explored include adolescent narcissism, structure and setting of adolescent groups, therapy for pubescent boys with absent fathers, organization of an adolescent unit in a state hospital, office network therapy, and the use of an open forum to defuse a high school critical mass. Other topic areas include the role of family therapy in adolescent psychiatry, the process of intergenerational reconciliation, use of cotherapists as advocates in family therapy, and multiple family therapy groups with adolescent drug addicts. $13.50. New York: Brunner/Mazel, 1975. 304 pp.

Adolescent Psychiatry: Volume II—Developmental and Clinical Studies. *Feinstein, Sherman C.; and Giovacchini, Peter*
Papers on the broad cultural aspects of adolescence are presented in the second volume of a series sponsored by the American Society for Adolescent Psychiatry. The 27 chapters range from a preoccupation with how the mind of the adolescent works, to the function of ideologies on the impact of culture. The volume is divided into five parts: Adolescence; General Considerations; Sexuality in Adolescence; Psychopathological Aspects of States of Adolescent Development; Psychotherapy of Adolescence; and the Adolescent in the World. $15. New York: Basic Books, 1973. 461 pp.

The Adolescent Years. *Wattenberg, W.W.*
Social and psychological problems of adolescence are discussed according to the multi-causality principle of behavior. Suggested solutions to adolescent problems include greater availability of psychological aid, ranging from counseling to behavior therapy. Family therapy and the provision of better school and recreation facilities are also considered. 2nd Ed. $12.50. New York: Harcourt Brace Jovanovich, 1973. 458 pp.

Adolescents Grow in Groups: Experiences in Adolescent Group Psychotherapy. *Berkovitz, Irving H.*
Experiences in adolescent group psychotherapy are described, and examples are provided from inpatient and outpatient settings. Thirty psychiatrists, psychologists, and social workers provide clinical examples of the group process in adolescent psychotherapy. Discussions of therapeutic techniques and theories are included. $10. New York: Brunner/Mazel, 1972. 250 pp.

Delinquents and Criminals: Their Social World. *Hughes, H.M.*
Collection of readings geared toward student interests, and aimed at providing them with an understanding of sociological concepts and methods. The first selection discusses the sociologists' view on delinquency, crime and deviance and describes the research methods used in the remainder of the book. Other readings concern analyzations of delinquent behavior, socioeconomic status and delinquency recidivism, organized crime, and deviant behavior which is socially condemned, though not illegal. The final selection reports upon alcohol and drugs in relation to delinquency and crime. Boston: Holbrook Press, 1970. 211 pp.

Juvenile Rights since 1967: An Annotated, Indexed Bibliography of Selected Articles and Books. *Von Pfeil, H.P.*
Alphabetical listing of 1073 periodical references and 343 books on the rights of children and the law relating to the juvenile court. $15. South Hackensack, NJ: Fred B. Rothman, 1974. 216 pp.

Problems of Adolescents: Social and Psychological Approaches. *Hardy, R.E.; and Cull, J.G.*
This collection of fifteen articles presents a broad overview of the problems and behavior of delinquent boys and girls and reviews the therapeutic and rehabilitative options available for these youths.

Among the specific topics addressed in these selections are the causes
of delinquent behavior, the relationship of family environment to delinquency, indices of prediction of delinquent behavior, and the delinquent's relations with his family, school, and peer group. Several articles are provided on drug related concerns, including types of drugs
and the relationship of drug abuse to juvenile delinquency. The articles
dealing with rehabilitative approaches offer information on youth as
volunteers, peer group approaches to rehabilitating the youthful drug
offender, the role of vocational rehabilitation with the youthful offender and the development of meaningful job opportunities. $14.75.
Springfield, IL: Charles C Thomas, 1974. 294 pp.

Psychological Disturbance in Adolescence.   *Weiner, Irving B.*
A probing examination of those patterns of psychological disturbance
which account for the vast majority of problems in adolescent patients
is presented. The disturbances include schizophrenia, depression and
suicide, school phobia, academic underachievement and delinquent
behavior. Descriptions and procedures for assessing the presence and
severity of disturbances, as well as psychotherapeutic techniques for
treating them, are included. Details on the goals and strategy of adolescent psychotherapy and methods of initiating, building and terminating the treatment relationship are discussed. $14.95. New York:
John Wiley and Sons, 1974.

Readings in Adolescent Psychology.   *Powell, Marvin;*
and Frerichs, Allen H.
A collection of readings is presented in an attempt to give the students
the opportunity to explore in depth studies, modern studies, and
studies spanning the major areas of adolescence, especially in the area
of self-concept. The 10 areas presented are covered in most current
adolescent psychology textbooks. A cross reference chart correlating
these articles to major text books is included. $4.95. Minneapolis:
Burgess Publishing Co., 1971. 331 pp.

The Teenage Pregnant Girl.   *Zackler, Jack; and Brandstadt, Wayne*
Statistics for the rise in teenage pregnancy, its causes, its relation to
poverty, and prospects for change are presented in a collection of 19
studies. Medical complications and obstetrical, nutritional, and
psychological problems of the pregnant teenager are discussed. The
role of the community health nurse is outlined and the importance of
providing continuing education for teenage mothers is emphasized.

Guidelines are provided for evaluating the efficacy of programs in contraception and help to unwed mothers. $12.95. Springfield, IL: Charles C Thomas, 1975. 336 pp.

Thorns & Thistles: Juvenile Delinquents in the United States, 1825–1940. *Mennel, Robert M.*
Juvenile delinquency in the United States from 1825–1940 is reviewed in an analysis of informed opinion. Theories and feelings of men and women who cared for delinquents and helped prevent delinquency are discussed. Recollections of delinquents themselves are included. Major topics covered deal with: houses of refuge, 1825–1860; preventive agencies and reform schools, 1850–1890; scientific explanations of delinquency, 1880–1910; crises and changes in institutional care, 1880–1910; the juvenile court, 1899–1940; and modern theories of juvenile delinquency, 1900–1940. $10. Hanover, NH: University Press of New England, 1973. 231 pp.

Where Do I Go To Buy Happiness? Insights of a Christian Counselor. *Skoglund, E.*
Suggestions to help seeking, lonely and alienated teenagers find the caring and self-esteem prerequisite to human development are presented. Self-esteem should be sought and developed in the context of constructive human interaction. $3.95. Downers Grove, IL: Inter-Varsity Press, 1972. 157 pp.

Articles

The Dissonant Context and the Adolescent Self-Concept.
Rosenberg, Morris
The diversity of contexts to which the individual, particularly the adolescent, may be exposed in his social life are analyzed, stressing some of the self-concept consequences of dissonance or consonance. Three specific aspects of self-concept are considered: self-esteem, stability of the self-concept, and group identification. 53 references. Bethesda, MD: NIMH, 1973. 44 pp.

Family Therapy with Adolescents and the Process of Intergenerational Reconciliation. *Stierlin, Helm (Unpublished paper)*
The process of intergenerational reconciliation is discussed in terms of family therapy with adolescents. Three tasks of reconciliation are out-

lined: integrative reconciliation; adaptive reconciliation; and reparative reconciliation. An adolescent can accept his sexuality only to the
extent that his parents have accepted their own sexuality. Within the
task of adaptive reconciliation occurs a problem area that encompasses the adolescent's quest for autonomy. The task of reparative
reconciliation becomes a task for the whole family and affects
psychotherapeutic interventions. Case histories are presented. 15 references. Bethesda, MD: NIMH, 1973. 17 pp.

Trained Local Youth as Community Mental Health Aides.
Mitchell, Lonnie E.
A new approach to the prevention and treatment of mental health
problems of youth from disadvantaged backgrounds by using trained
local youths from similar backgrounds as community mental health
aides is evaluated. The 17 steps taken in the project action and eight
results are given. The results indicate that the youth have the ability to
perform the duties demanded of them with varying degrees of efficiency. The model has been adopted by the Washington, D.C. Health
Department for its adolescent programs in mental health. The program has attracted attention as a mechanism providing "new careers"
for disadvantaged youths excluded from the mainstream of society. 30
references. Final Report, NIMH Grant MH-14837, 1969. 17 pp.

The Unmarried Adolescent Parent. *Juhasz, Anne McCreary*
Factors leading to illegitimate pregnancy and birth among adolescents
are discussed, as well as the extent of the problem among the various
socioeconomic levels. The literature indicates that in general unwed
mothers are characterized by lack of self-esteem and by too little basic
faith in their own ability to win loyal affection or sustained respect
from others. Both the mother and father of such adolescents are influ-
ential on their ideas about sexual relationships and their ability to
handle them successfully. Too little attention has been paid to the
problems of the unwed father and the psychological effects of his
parenthood. Wide social attitudes exist regarding acceptance of the
unwed mother, especially for those who keep their babies rather than
relinquish them for adoption. Considerable financial difficulties also
face those who decide to raise their own children, as well as psychological and physical complications affecting their health. The solution to
the problem appears to be education of young women and provision
of methods of contraception with parental consent. 22 references.
Adolescence, 9(34):263–72, 1974.

Audio Tapes

Adolescent Group Psychotherapy
The rationale for group psychotherapeutic treatment of youth is
analyzed. Included is a detailed list of criteria for selecting members of
a group, and specific examples of actual group conferences. Dr. Nor-
man S. Brandes is lecturer. The individual tape titles are: (1)
Paraanalytic Treatment Approaches to Outpatient Group Psychother-
apy of Adolescents and Young Adults; (2) Paraanalytic Treatment
Approaches—Group; and (3) Paraanalytic Treatment Approaches—
Group. $6.95 each. At 1⅞ IPS cassette 45 min. each, 1974. Behavioral
Sciences Tape Library.

Adolescents in Crisis
The adolescent's normal development, significant external influences,
fantasies and feelings, his visible habits and behaviors, and relationship to the family structures are explored. The influence of life crisis in
adolescent deviancy, including drug addiction, criminality, suicide,
and homosexuality, is examined. The need for stronger guidelines and
parental involvement in changing danger into opportunity is probed
through the outcomes of crisis intervention clinics. Dr. Jacob Christ of
McClain Hospital, Belmont, Mass., is lecturer. The individual tape
titles are: (1) Adolescent Development; (2) Case History; and (3) Individual and Family Crisis. $7.95 each. At 1⅞ IPS cassette 60 min each,
1974. Behavioral Sciences Tape Library.

Normal and Abnormal Behavior of Adolescence.
Normal and abnormal behavior of adolescence is examined in 12
parts. Emphasis is on the etiology, diagnosis, and treatment of developmental disorders, as well as analysis of current trends in the adolescent subculture. Topics include: (1) Developmental Crises in Black
Adolescents; (2) Patterns of Drug Abuse Among Middle-Class Adolescents; (3) The Hospital Management of Disturbed Adolescents (in two
parts); (4) Psychological Development During Adolescence; (5) Adolescents and Adults; (6) Sociologic Perspectives of the Marihuana Controversy; (7) The Management of Drug Abuse in the Outpatient
Psychotherapy of Adolescents; (8) The Severely Neurotic and the
Psychotic Adolescent; (9) Psychological Functions of the Counterculture; (10) The Adolescent with a Communication Disorder; (11) In-

novative Services for Youth. $6.95 each. At 1⅞ IPS cassette 60 min. each, 1972. Behavioral Sciences Tape Library.

Psychotherapy of Adolescents
Technical problems unique in the psychoanalytic treatment of adolescents are discussed in 12 parts. Emphasis is on transference difficulties, rebellion, the problem of confidentiality versus responsibility, and conflicting loyalties within the therapist himself. Topics include: (1) The Initial Evaluation; (2) The Diagnostic Process and the Planning of Treatment; (3) The Therapeutic Alliance and the Early Stages of Treatment; (4) Transference Manifestations and Their Management; (5) Transference and Countertransference; (6) Regression and its Prevention; (7) Management of the Dependent Adolescent; (8) The Adolescent and His Parents; (9) Depression and Suicide; (10) Learning Disabilities—Psychotherapy and Adolescent Subcultures; (11) Delinquent and Promiscuous Homosexual Behavior; (12) Termination of the Treatment of Adolescents. $6.95 each. At 1⅞ IPS cassette 60 min. each, 1973. Behavioral Sciences Tape Library.

Films

Cry for Help
The alarming amount of mental illness among adolescents. Focuses on three teenagers—Debbie, Gloria, and Jim—patients at the State Mental Hospital at Napa, California. Their common background of unpleasant experiences and their diagnosis and treatment at the hospital. Rental: $26.50. 33 min. 16mm. Color. 1970. Youth. Film Library–Oregon.

Guidance for the 70s: Self-esteem
Teenagers are shown learning about self-esteem and how to build it. The group discovers that communication gaps with parents, rivalry between brothers and sisters and friends, and fear of not being accepted as worthwhile or important contribute to lower self-esteem. They find that, while others' opinions certainly are a factor, the biggest put down of all is one given by oneself. The group works on changing negative self-talk to positive in order to increase self-esteem. Rental: $15. Sale: $260. 17¾ min. Filmstrip. Color. 1971. BFA Educational Media, 2211 Michigan Ave., Santa Monica, CA 90404.

Invention of the Adolescent
History and development of the concept and designation of "adolescent." Status and difficulties of this group between childhood and adulthood. Drastic change in society's placement of the adolescent in today's world. Rental: $8.75. 28 min. 16 mm. 1968. Film Library–Oregon.

Rebel without a Cause
The boy here is from a "good" family; he is neither deprived nor neglected where material things are concerned. Lack of communication and imbalance of parental authority account for the boy's instability and violent behavior. James Dean, Natalie Wood, Sal Mineo, Jim Backus. Rental: $42. 111 min. 16mm. Color. 1955. International Film Bureau, Inc.

Who Cops Out?
Raises the question of the choices today's adolescents make when faced with the confusion and uncertainty of the teen-age years. The film focuses on five adolescents who have made five different choices: a pregnant girl who may be asked to leave school; a school dropout working at a gas station; a high school football star; a scholastic achiever; and a runaway drug user. Each of these young people describes his feelings and attempts to explain the reasons for his choice. Counterpointing these interviews, a narrator presents the critical alternatives which confront the adolescent at this time in his life and stresses that the choice must always be his. Presented in the teen-agers' own language, this open-ended film does not lecture, but tries to motivate youth to analyze their own decisions. Sponsored by the State Mental Health Authorities of California, South Carolina and Maryland. Produced by the Mental Health Film Board; written and directed by Irving Jacoby, with Richard L. Frank, M.D., as psychiatric consultant. Rental: $10. Sale: $150. 11 min. 16mm. Color. 1970. International Film Bureau, Inc.

5

Elderly*

Population

ONE OUT OF TEN PERSONS in the United States is 65 or more years of age, or 21.8 million men and women. The proportion of "65 plus" to the general population varies by race and ethnic origin: 11 percent whites, 7 percent blacks, and 4 percent persons of Spanish origin. The life expectancy for the black male is 60 years as compared to 67.5 years for the white male. The American Indian has a much lower life expectancy of 45.0 years. By the year 2000, the estimated population of older Americans will be 31 million.

Residence

Approximately one-half (45.4 percent) of "65 plus" lives in California, Illinois, New York, Ohio, Pennsylvania, Texas, and Florida.

Eight states have more than 12 percent of their total populations in the "65 plus" group: Florida 15.5 percent, Arkansas 12.8 percent, Iowa 12.8 percent, Missouri 12.6 percent, Nebraska and Kansas 12.4 percent each, South Dakota 12.3 percent and Oklahoma 12.1 percent. Most older Americans live in a family setting. About one-third of older people live alone. Close to 5 percent or approximately 1 million older people live in institutions.

Income

Approximately 1.6 million couples have $5,000.00 yearly incomes; 1.1 million couples have an annual income of $3,000.00, and 1.5

*with G.W. McMillan

70

million older persons living alone have incomes of under $1,500.00 a year. More than 2.9 million or 14 percent of older people are in the labor force either working or actively seeking work.

Statistics by nationality indicate that 50 percent of older blacks live in poverty as compared to 23 percent of elderly whites. White men receive about twice the amount of social security as black men. The Mexican-American is the second largest minority in the United States and most have been employed in factories, on farms, in mines, or on construction jobs where often no money was paid into social security deductions.

Institutional Living

Old age is a time of life when chronic illness becomes commonplace in human existence. Yet often there is no one available for sharing the intimate concerns and fears that are provoked by physical and mental incapacities. In fact, a combination of old age, low socioeconomic status and terminal illness can result in a person being removed to an institution which then becomes a hiding place in which he/she dies.

There are two reasons why people are institutionalized. First is their disabling chronic condition and second is their lack of psychological, social or economic means to deal with the outside world.

Many studies have been conducted on institutionalized elderly, most reaching the same alarming conclusions. Patients have in common the characteristics of poor adjustment, depression and unhappiness, intellectual ineffectiveness due to increased rigidity and low energy, negative self–image, feelings of personal insignificance and impotence, and a view of the self as old. Residents tend to be docile and submissive, to show a low range of interests in activities, and to live in the past rather than the present, and are withdrawn and unresponsive in relationships to others. Some suggest that they have increased anxiety which at times focuses on their feelings about death. There are marked increases in mortality rates for aged persons entering mental hospitals and homes for the aged.

Before placing an elderly person in a nursing home or related institution, make a thorough check on the reputation of the establishment. This is easily done by making a spot check, talking to residents, and contacting organizations concerned with the elderly, such as those listed in this Almanac. Organizations can help to check a place out and can give referrals to other establishments with proven, excellent reputations. Many places are excellent, but others are horrible, so beware.

Social Problems

Ask the aged what problems trouble them and they will tell you: un-availability of health services, lack of transportation, social isolation, lack of meaningful participation, and lack of being part of a real community.

Older people's needs are varied but interrelated and urgent. Income and transportation for access to services are related to health. Health, transportation, information and income are related to opportunities for activity. Isolation and loneliness are related to nutrition. Nutrition, of course, is related to health. It is a network of related needs.

The elderly are extremely vulnerable in that their lives are marked by experiences of multiple losses. Traumatic loss, the death of a spouse, or severe debilitation of health come at a time when many elderly cannot cope effectively because they have previously lost social, personal, and economic resources.

Many older people worry about violence, crime, and civil disturbances that have been increasing yearly. Because of this, many elderly are reluctant to get out in the community for fear of being robbed, attacked, or injured. This reluctance prevents them from walking, taking buses and taxis, visiting friends and relatives, shopping for food and other necessities, keeping medical appointments and attending social gatherings. It is difficult to measure the effects of these fears. However, there is no doubt that these problems exist and something must be done to make it possible for the aged to participate in activities of everyday life. The aged population, particularly males, have very high suicide rates. The maximum rate occurs in the 75 to 84 year age group. Sucide rates among females in the 45-and-over age group are considerably lower than the corresponding rates for males. However, female rates in the 45 to 74 year age groups have shown an increase in suicides for many years.

American society excludes older people from many roles and activities that are extremely valuable. The result is an increase in the rate of serious mental disturbances for elderly persons, five times as high as in the rest of the population (without physical causes). Depression is very prevalent in elderly people.

Successful Aging

Society views aging as a hopeless, unremitting downward drift into despair, deprivation, and desolation. The images of aging which have been presented in the public media have focused on disease, poverty, and social isolation.

Successfully aging persons are those who have maintained extensive contacts with other citizens in their community, are still participating in the life of the community either in business, volunteer work, or social or recreational activities. They are, moreover, people who are having a good time in the later years. Many of these people are not only personally and socially attractive, but many of them are physically beautiful. As Eric Pfeiffer put it: "The sun setting is no less beautiful than the sun rising."

REFERENCES

Birren, James. *Handbooks of Aging Series,* 3 Vols. New York: Van Nostrand Reinhold, 1977.

Brody, E.M. and Gottesman, L. "Issues of Institutional Care." *A Social Work Guide for Long Term Care Facilities.* Washington: DHEW, 1975.

Facts About Older Americans. Washington: DHEW, 1975.

Gottesman, L. and Hutchinson, E. "Characteristics of Institutionalized Elderly." *A Social Work Guide for Long Term Care Facilities.* Washington: DHEW, 1975.

Gubrium, Jaber F. *The Myth of the Golden Years: A Socio-Environmental Theory of Aging.* Springfield, IL: Charles C Thomas, 1973.

"The Income Situation." *Foundation News,* July/August 1974, p. 36.

Kart, Cary S. and Manard, Barbara (eds.). *Aging in America: Readings in Social Gerontology.* Sherman Oaks, CA: Alfred Publishing Co., 1976.

Maurus, J. *Growing Old Gracefully.* Canfield, OH: Alba Books, 1977.

"New Outlook for the Aged." *Time Magazine,* June 2, 1975, cover story.

Partnership for Older Americans. Washington: DHEW, 1973.

Pfeiffer, Eric. "Successful Aging." *Third Annual Congress on Improving the Quality of Life in Later Years.* Chicago: American Medical Association, April 1974.

Smith, Bert K. *Aging in America.* Boston: Beacon Press, 1973.

Smith, Elliott D. *Handbook of Aging.* Scranton, PA: Barnes and Noble Books, 1977.

Books

Aging and Mental Health. Positive Psychosocial Approaches.
Butler, Robert N.; and Lewis, Myrna I.
Although this book deals with the nature and problems of old age as well as evaluation, treatment, and prevention programs for the elderly, it specifically describes the twin prejudices of sexism and ageism directed toward older women. A profile of the elderly woman is presented which includes income, employment, marriage, living arrangements, health, and emotional results of prejudices against older women. $7.95. St. Louis: C.V. Mosby Co., 1973. 306 pp.

Aging Better.   *Cowdry, E.V.*
The broad scope of gerontology in a multidisciplinary perspective is examined. The roles of one's medical, sociological, and spiritual advisors in relation to the needs of older people are discussed. A series of chapters deal with disorders of the various organ systems, containing advice on how to avoid or delay these disorders; graphs and charts are included. The disorders include not only those which are aging linked, but many others which may constitute obstacles on the road to old age. Concluding chapters discuss the philosophy of life, attitude toward death, extraordinary means of prolonging life, and euthanasia. $15.50. Springfield, IL: Charles C Thomas, 1972. 481 pp.

Aging: Its Challenge to the Individual and to Society.
Bier, William C.
In the eighth volume of the Fordham University Pastoral Psychology Series, the phenomenon of aging is viewed from a predominantly religious perspective. Topics covered include: historical, cultural and religious views of aging; demographic, physiologic and sociologic dimensions; the psychology and psychopathology of aging; the challenge of retirement; individual concerns such as marriage, family, career, and the prospect of death; and societal organizations and services for the aging. $12.50. Bronx, NY: Fordham University Press, 1974. 292 pp.

Creative Programming for Older Adults.   *Vickery, Florence E.*
A guide book for professionals and paraprofessionals who work with older adults in multiservice centers, housing projects, and residential care institutions is presented. Consideration is given to: (1) older Americans in a technological society; (2) effects of the aging process in

social functioning; and (3) development and administration of social programs for older adults. Recent research findings regarding the social, economic, biological and psychological aspects of aging are summarized in an attempt to suggest potential leadership and involvement roles for the elderly. $12.95. New York: Association Press, 1972. 320 pp.

Directory: National Organizations with Programs in the Field of Aging, 1971.   *National Council on the Aging*
The Directory was assembled to serve as a useful and effective technical assistance tool for community action agencies; voluntary agencies; civic, fraternal, religious, and union organizations, and all other groups concerned with the needs of elderly people on local, state and national levels. Community action agencies should find its contents helpful in their efforts to mobilize community resources on behalf of the elderly poor. $4.85. Washington, DC: National Council on the Aging, 1971. 93 pp.

Facts About Aging.   *Liang, Daniel S.*
Medical, social, and psychological aspects of aging are examined. The subjects range from physical changes with age and how to deal with them, problems of retirement, diets for the aged, sex and the aging, skin conditions, and emotional problems to the medical illnesses of cancer, heart attack, arthritis, strokes, and digestive problems. Also covered are medicare and social service agencies, medical quacks, medical care nursing homes, hospitals and the problem of dying. $3.95. Springfield, IL: Charles C Thomas, 1973. 114 pp.

Gomer's Guide.   *Lewis, Gomer*
A guidebook aimed at the estimated 25-million elderly people who travel in the USA. The publication lists hotels and motels in 25 states east of the Mississippi that offer rates of $15.00 a night or less. It also lists those that extend an additional discount to persons aged 55 or over. The book is in large type to aid those with impaired vision and includes road maps of the 25 states. $3.95. Maplewood, NJ: Hammond, Inc., 1976. 192 pp.

Growing Old in the Country of the Young.   *Percy, Charles H.*
The problems of the aged in America, described as an unusually young country, are discussed from the perspective of a member of the Senate Committee on Aging. The problems encountered in the United States

by the aged minority are described, including: an inadequate Social Security System; dehumanizing welfare programs; discrimination against older workers; forced, arbitrary, sometimes early retirement; and substandard economic means. It is suggested that the U.S. Congress establish an interim goal of assuring retirees an income above the poverty line, and a long range goal of a moderate assured income appropriate to the previous incomes of the retirees. Rewriting of Federal Income Tax laws to ease their burden on the elderly is recommended. Other programs of interest to the aged are discussed, including nutrition and health care. A list of public and private agencies offering services to the aged is provided. $7.95. New York: McGraw-Hill, 1974. 214 pp.

The Neglected Older American: Social and Rehabilitation Services. *Cull, John G.; and Hardy, Richard E.*
Some of the characteristic problems of the senior citizens in the U.S. are explored, including health, disability, poverty, transportation, and religion. The psychological aspects of aging, perspectives on aging in rural America, the rehabilitation needs of older Americans, and how work helps fill some of these needs are discussed. $12.75. Springfield, IL: Charles C Thomas, 1973. 275 pp.

The Psychological Aspects of the Aging Process: With Sociological Implications. *Geist, Harold*
An overview of the entire aging process with emphasis on geriatric psychology, sociology, and counseling is presented. Topics discussed include psychology, demography, personality theory, psychopathology of aging, research, and social and cultural factors. Psychological aspects of aging considered include: cognitive function, creativity, learning, problem-solving, motivation, interests, attitudes, values, psychological tests, sensory and perceptual processes, vision, audition, taste, smell, touch, pain, temperature, psychomotor skills, and pathology. 142 references. $8.50. St. Louis: Warren H. Green, 1975. 178 pp.

The Psychology of Adult Development and Aging.
Eisdorfer, Carl; and Lawton, M. Powell
The state of psychological knowledge about aging is summarized in this book representing the work of the American Psychological Association's task force on aging. Papers presented cover five categories: (1) Foundations of Gerontology; (2) Experimental Psychology; (3) Developmental Psychology of Aging; (4) Clinical Psychology of Old

Age; and (5) Social Environment of Aging. Topical coverage ranges from animal research and psychophysiological studies to problems of housing and transportation. The need for a problem-centered, inter-disciplinary approach is emphasized. $11. Washington, DC: American Psychological Association, 1973. 718 pp.

The Social Forces in Later Life: An Introduction to Social Gerontology. *Atchley, Robert C.*
An introductory text into the study of aging and social gerontology. $8.95. Belmont, CA: Wadsworth Publishing Co., 1972. 400 pp.

Articles

Hearing Our Elderly. *Brooks, Esther L.*
A special service for the elderly, the Jewish Social Service Agency of the metropolitan Washington, DC area, is described. The service is for people over 62 and was initiated in 1968. Special problems of the elderly, such as the stress of retirement, reaction to a change in eco-nomic status with the impact of considerably reduced income, and anxiety involved with the physical changes of becoming older are discussed. Along with professional counseling, a series of supportive services to meet the ongoing casework, crisis intervention, and out-reach programs have been developed. One of the more general spinoffs of the service has been the more positive attitudes toward the elderly by housing managers and nursing staff directors, professionals and paraprofessionals who have been contacted in relation to social therapy groups. It is felt that the elderly have special needs as a group due to where they are in their life cycle as well as to the way in which society has avoided facing up to retirement and aging. *Journal of Jewish Communal Service,* 50(2):189–94, 1973.

Helping Elderly Couples Become Sexually Liberated: Psycho-Social Issues. *Sviland, Mary Ann P.*
Some of society's negative social attitudes towards elderly sexuality are discussed, valuable information about the sexual capacities and activities of the elderly is provided, and a discussion on how counsel-ing for the elderly must take into account cultural and physiological factors which affect sexuality among older persons is given. Specific treatment approaches and special considerations which are critical to

effective sex therapy with the aged are discussed. 20 references. *Counseling Psychologist,* 5(1):67–72, 1975.

Innovations in Programs of Care for the Elderly.   *Kobrynski, Borys*
The profound changes in treatment approaches to psychogeriatric patients is reported. Labels such as senility have been discarded in favor of identical principles for all patients. New therapeutic modalities have been developed that have proved successful in the restoration of the functional state of many elderly patients suffering from organic brain syndromes and social deprivation. The modern approach is away from custodial care in favor of thorough diagnostic investigations and an appropriate therapeutic plan molded for each individual. The patient's environment is also being restructured. Therapeutic programs in mental hospitals and nursing homes for the aged are evaluated. Geriatric rehabilitation techniques have been applied in New York State hospitals with some success. Modern restorative therapy has given rise to some cautious optimism concerning the aged. Reality orientation, sensory training, and remotivation are also briefly described. 8 references. *Gerontologist,* 13(1):50–53, 1973.

The Mental Health System and the Future Aged.   *Kahn, Robert L.*
Patterns of mental health care for the aged in the past and for the future are discussed. The patterns of psychiatric care for the aged can be explained on the basis of a reciprocal aversiveness between the mental health establishment and older persons, based on such factors as mental health ideology (custodialism), social class characteristics, and considerations of age appropriateness. Suggestions for better care for future elderly persons who will have different needs than today's elderly are proposed. 28 references. *Gerontologist,* 15(1):24–31, 1975.

Notes on the Negative Implications of Being Competent in a Home for the Aged.   *Posner, Judith*
Following 2 years of observation in a home for the aged, it is concluded that the assumption in such institutions that the inmates are incompetent and abnormal actually discriminates against those who are most competent. The ironic implications of this fact are discussed, and it is maintained that geriatric centers are, in practice, oriented toward the least competent. The ways in which the "atypical" behavior of competent residents works against them are considered.

Seven references. *International Journal of Aging and Human Development,* 5(4):357–64, 1974.

The Role of a Community Mental Health Center in Developing Services to the Aging: The Older Adult Project. *Santore, Anthony F.; and Diamond, Herbert*
The role of a community mental health center in developing services to the aging was studied. A multifaceted program for an aging population developed by an urban community mental health center (CMHC) in collaboration with a group of local clergymen and their churches is described. The project recruited and trained a cadre of older case aides, who then developed active outreach and casework services as foundations for meeting needs through crisis and intervention, counseling, transportation, nutrition, and socialization. Data are presented summarizing the project's case load and service experience. It is suggested that CMHCs can amplify the new political power of the elderly with their own advocacy and significantly help to surmount the omnipresent bureaucratic, legislative, and funding barriers to essential services for the aging. Nine references. *Gerontologist,* 14(3):201–06, 1974.

Who's Working for Whom? A Proposal for Further Study of Nursing Home Resident–Staff Relations. *McClain, Gary R.; Moss, Miriam; and Gottesman, Leonard E.*
Resident and staff relations were observed and analyzed during summers and weekends of a two year period, in three nursing homes of varying size and administration in Michigan and Pennsylvania. Similar conclusions were formulated in each setting. Instrumental care was more than adequate in all settings; yet, rather than the institution being a home with staff working *for* the residents, the residents must learn to please the staff, and behave according to staff expectations, forcing the resident to focus his emotional energy on handling individual staff personalities, with the staff's conception of the resident based upon how easy he or she is to manage. *Gerontologist,* 15(5):77, 1975.

Audio Tapes

Aging and Quality of Life
A look at the quality of life in the later years as it may be associated with social, environmental, and behavioral variables, and the relationship of these variables to survival into the later years. $12. 1 session, no. 191–75. American Association for the Advancement of Science.

Retirement Counseling
Dr. Harold Geist addresses a group of government retirement counselors on the problems of demography, necessity for early planning, financial resources, specific suggestions for retirees, retirement communities, sources of information on retirement, and the symptoms and psychological implications of aging. $10. including script. Extra scripts $1.50. Cassette. 60 min. AAP Tape Library.

Films

Aging in America
Clinical pictures of problems of the elderly, both outside and within institutional settings, are presented. Vignettes are provided as the focus for brainstorming and problem-solving by the viewer. Different interviewing approaches applicable to patients with varying degrees of cognitive impairment are derivable from the broad range of clinical pictures provided. Problems considered include: retirement, grief, sexuality, senile dementia, economics, concept of aging, psychosomatic complaints, loneliness, and concerns with mental impairment associated with aging. Rental: $25. Sale: $100. ½ inch videotape (Sony). b/w. 30 min. 1973. Continuing Psychiatric Education, University of Washington, Dept. of Psychiatry and Behavioral Sciences, Seattle, WA 98105.

Art Therapy with the Aging
The art therapy program at the Muskingum (OH) county home is documented, presenting a moving account of the aged and the problems they face in this society. The film clearly demonstrates that lone-

liness as well as loss of dignity and integrity often accompany old age. Art therapy is demonstrated as a means to come to terms with the present. Various techniques are demonstrated in which art materials are used in a therapeutic manner. It is concluded that more research into the problems of aging is necessary, as are improved facilities for and care of old people. Rental: $20. 20 min. 16mm. Optical color. 1973. Good Samaritan Medical Center, 800 Forest Ave., Zanesville, OH 43701.

Step Aside—Step Down
The major problems of aging in the United States (such as income, housing, nutrition, and transportation) and the private and government programs successful in solving them are documented. Sale: $80. 20 min. 16mm. Optical color. 1971. National Audiovisual Center, National Archives and Record Service, General Services Administration, Washington, DC 20409.

The Steps of Age
Contrasts the emotional weakness of Jimmy Potter, who goes into a depression and dies soon after his retirement, and the strength of his wife who is able to adjust to old age. A Mental Health Film Board film. Rental: $90. Sale: $175. 25 min. 16mm. b/w. 1953. International Film Bureau, Inc.

Two Worlds to Remember
The discrepancy between predictions, planning, and actual rehabilitation of geriatric patients is explored in the cases of two women, aged 81 and 89, as they are seen in the three months before and three months after they are admitted to the Jewish Home and Hospital for Aged in New York City. The staff makes preliminary evaluations, plans programs for the social adjustment of the two women, and discovers their predictions are often wrong. Rental: $30. Sale: $400. 39 min. 16mm. Optical color. 1970. Jewish Home for the Aged, 120 West 106th St., New York, NY 10025.

What You Do Speaks So Loud
The personal satisfaction of senior citizens who participate in the retired senior volunteer program and the warmth and gratitude of the persons who receive services and attention from senior volunteers are portrayed. The social and psychological aspects of aging are illus-

trated. Free. 15 min. 16mm. Optical color. 1975. Action, 806 Connecticut Ave., N.W., Washington DC 20525.

Contacts

Action Cooperative Volunteers. 806 Connecticut Ave., N.W., Washington, DC 20525. One year of service to local projects which help communities tackle problems of education, poverty and the environment.

Foster Grandparent Program/Action. 806 Connecticut Ave., N.W., Washington, DC 20525. People who want to provide love, attention and help to physically, emotionally, and mentally handicapped children.

Green Thumb, Inc. 1012 14th St., N.W., Washington, DC 20005. Conservation, beautification, and community improvement projects.

Operation Mainstream. U.S. Dept. of Agriculture—Forest Service, Washington, DC 20250. Part-time work in conservation and beautification projects.

Peace Corps/Action. 806 Connecticut Ave., N.W., Washington, DC 20525. Actively recruits older people to serve overseas helping developing nations.

Retired Senior Volunteer Program/Action. 806 Connecticut Ave., N.W., Washington, DC 20525. Retired persons may serve as volunteers in a number of agencies, organizations and institutions.

Score/Action. 806 Connecticut Ave., N.W., Washington, DC 20525. Volunteer program of retired business people who help those in need of their skills (small business, community groups, etc.).

Senior Aides. National Council of Senior Citizens, 1511 K St., N.W., Washington, DC 20005. Aides work in community service organizations performing a wide variety of jobs.

Senior Community Aides Program. 1909 K St., N.W., Washington DC 20006. This program recruits, trains and finds part-time work in public and private nonprofit service programs.

Senior Community Service Project. National Council on the Aging, 1828 L St., N.W., Washington, DC 20036. Part-time work in a variety of community services, from public housing to nutrition programs.

Senior Companion Program/Action. 806 Connecticut Ave., N.W.,

Washington, DC 20525. Help those with special needs, in their own homes, nursing homes, and other institutions.

Teacher Corps. Office of Education, Washington, DC 20202. Serve as tutors or instructional assistants for disadvantaged children.

Vista/Action. 806 Connecticut Ave., N.W., Washington DC 20525. Volunteers in Service to America, people who work for one year in impoverished urban and rural areas helping those involved.

Administration on Aging
U.S. Department of Health,
  Education and Welfare
Washington, DC
The federal focal point, working
  closely with other federal agencies
  and national organizations

American Association of Retired
  Persons
1909 K St., N.W.
Washington, DC 20006
Over 6 million members, 1700
  chapters

The Ethel Percy Gerontology Center
University of Southern California
Los Angeles, CA
Major teaching and research center
  on all aspects of gerontology

Every state has an agency on aging to
  act as an advocate and central
  focus for programs for older
  citizens

National Clearinghouse on Aging
Washington, DC 20201
Extensive information, research, and
  publications (many free)

Office of Older Persons Programs
Office of Economic Opportunity
1200 19th St., N.W.
Washington, DC 20506

Retirement Jobs, Inc.
211 S. First St.
San Jose, CA 95113

Senate Special Committee on Aging
Room G-225
Dirksen Office Building
Washington, DC 20510

Serve: Community Service Society
105 East 22nd St.
New York, NY 10010

PART II

The Concern

Therapy

6

THERE ARE SO MANY DIFFERENT TYPES of psychotherapeutic models (over three hundred identified at present) that a large book is needed for only a summary of them, let alone a thorough explanation. With this in mind we have tried to give an overview of the field by listing the popular, major processes as well as those that are less frequently used but representative of some philosophical position in the spectrum. Just like a bell curve most are in the middle (most popular), but those at the ends must also be recognized in order to get a true picture of what is being practiced today.

Therapy Models

The following is not a summary or an explanation but rather a guide that only gives the simple characteristics of each process. Those of interest should be explored further in order to gain a true understanding of them.

Active Analytic Psychotherapy   Developed by Wilhelm Stekel. The therapist is very active, directive, and challenges the patient in an authoritarian approach. Believes many people can be helped by not having to go into the past, by confronting issues now; tries to find a resolution as quickly as possible instead of long term therapy.

Active Psychotherapy   Developed by Alexander Herzberg. The therapist directs the patient in a series of progressive assignments designed to alter the patient's neurosis.

Activity Group Therapy   Restructuring of emotional and social patterns, mostly used with children, by participation in group activities.

Adlerian Therapy   Developed by Alfred Adler (1870–1937). The therapist develops a close relationship with the client, then helps the client construct a positive life style and plan. Emphasis is on working out this individual life style and plan, not on past events or unconscious forces. The therapist actively makes suggestions and points out self-defeating tendencies.

Analytic Therapy   From Freud's method in the psychoanalytic process where the patient lies on a couch, helping to create a situation of infancy for the patient. This "situational infancy" and dependency on the analyst is designed to bring the patient back to infancy in order to examine feelings and experiences that have blocked natural development.

Antabuse Therapy   Used to treat alcoholics to stop drinking in conjunction with psychotherapy. The drug disulfiram makes a person very ill if alcohol is ingested within twelve hours after taking the drug. This is only to stop the drinking cycle long enough for the alcoholic to get a grip on himself, so he can continue with on-going psychotherapy.

Art Therapy   The use of painting and drawing to help a client express himself, aid resocialization, and to help contact the unconscious basis of emotional problems.

Assertion Structured Therapy   Developed by E. Lakin Phillips. The therapist actively points out "insights" to the patient and helps the patient recognize defective assumptions and expectations that lead to self-defeating experiences, then helps correct this by developing positive approaches.

Behavior Therapy   Based on conditioning, the goal is to substitute negative behavior patterns with positive ones. There is no attempt to change personality, increase insight, or to explore the unconscious. There are many forms of conditioning, some of the most common are: operant (reward positive behavior), aversion (punish negative behavior), and desensitization (elimination of an anxiety by removing sensitivity to it by relaxation, familiarity, etc.).

Bibliotherapy   An approach in which the client is given an assigned "prescription" of selected reading material that will support the regular therapy process and help with the client's problems and conflicts.

Biofeedback Training   Developed by Norbert Wiener, the goal of this sensory feedback (biofeedback) is to become aware of and self-regulate internal bodily processes such as heart rate, brain waves, blood pressure, muscular tension, etc. This is learned through an instrument, of which there are several types.

Carbon Dioxide Therapy   Developed by Ladislas Meduna in 1946, this therapy advocates inhalation of a 70 percent oxygen/30 percent carbon dioxide mixture till the patient reaches a brief coma. Meduna thought this obstructed pathological brain circuits; many consider this approach very dangerous.

Chemotherapy   The use of psychochemical drugs to calm (tranquilizers) or energize (antidepressants) patients is the most widely used therapy today. Proponents hail it as miraculous, others claim it is drugged bondage—the procedure promises to be under much greater attack in the future.

Client-Centered Therapy   Developed by Carl Rogers. Decision and responsibility come from the client, the therapist is nondirective and empathic. Essentially the therapist is like a mirror, helping the client to see himself and develop positive feelings and behavior.

Crisis Counseling   Used with people who are undergoing an immediate crisis (divorce, death of a loved one, loss of employment, etc.) that is disturbing their life. This is a very intensive short term process that concentrates on helping the person deal with the immediate crisis situation. If longer psychotherapy is needed, the person is referred to another form of therapy. Crisis counseling is a part of most county mental health resources and is a major part of suicide prevention, drug and/or alcohol abuse centers.

Dance Therapy   Developed by Marion Chace in 1942. The use of rhythmic movement helps people become active, release their tensions and feelings, serves as an opening to other people, and is a valuable supplement to psychotherapy.

Descriptive Approach   Emphasis is on consciousness, observable behavior, and symptoms, as contrasted to the Dynamic Approach which examines underlying forces of motivation and traces behavior to its origins in experience.

Directive Psychotherapy   Developed by Frederick C. Thorne. At first the therapist is very directive, becoming less so as the client learns to direct his behavior positively. This educational psychotherapeutic process is based on discussion and training situations.

Eastern Way   Many people have turned to eastern approaches rather than use western psychotherapy. Transcendental meditation, Zen Buddhism and yoga are some of the more popular approaches. These appeal to many people because they are concerned with the meaning of life, not to learn but to become. It is a highly direct intuitive way as compared to psychotherapy which is basically a logical scientific process concerned with learning and social adjustment. Many have attacked the eastern way as only working with fairly well integrated individuals, but then too, this criticism has also been leveled at psychotherapy itself. The eastern way has given many people not only relief from tension but also deep personal meaning.

Ego Psychotherapy   Developed by Paul Federn. This approach strengthens or redirects the "ego" (as the integrating force) to maintain a boundary between itself and the id (acceptable expression of these impulses) and between itself and external reality (distinguish between oneself and the outside world). This approach is used mainly with schizoid and psychotic disorders. In direct contrast to Freud, this therapy reinforces resistance to unconscious material—Federn believed too much of that was already being released. Other important aspects are working with a patient's environment and family and having the help of a skilled woman therapist, because Federn believed the mother was the initial source of support for the patient's ego.

Electroshock Therapy (ECT)   In 1935 Ladislas J. Meduna first used convulsion therapy by injection. He thought epilepsy and schizophrenia were mutually exclusive (disproved). This procedure was soon halted because of the high number of fatalities and fractures. Then in 1938 L. Bini and C. Cerletti began using electricity to produce convulsions; a technique used continually ever since. ECT is used for a wide variety of mental disorders, however those who claim it to be effective can not explain how it works. There are many proponents and opponents of this method, and it is increasingly under attack. It should be noted that many institutions and individuals who use this method deny doing so because they are keenly aware of the intensity of feeling against its use. ECT's effects on the brain and memory are not really known, but there are strong indications of memory loss and mental retardation.

Emergency Psychotherapy   Developed during World War II, this therapy is now used for traumas from accidents, floods, death of a relative, etc. It was found that most people in extreme trauma revert to infantile behavior (shock or going beserk); therefore, a parental figure was needed to guide them through the crisis and allow them to release their fear and hostility.

Encounter Groups   Originally developed by Kurt Lewin as a process to train community employees specially assigned to handle interracial conflicts. Now it is primarily a part of the human potential movement. It is not usually meant as psychotherapy but is used to help people discover their potential by interacting with each other. It encourages personality growth and awareness of self and others. Interaction deals with the present, not the past.

Existential Therapy   The goal is not to bring about more socially acceptable behavior or explore the past for sources of conflicts, rather it is to recognize the uniqueness of your own experience, be aware of your potentialities and to keep your freedom of decision. The therapist is empathic, communicative, and helps the client recognize these points by discussion.

Experiential Therapy   Developed by Karl Whitaker and Thomas Malone. The therapist acts as a parent, at the emotional level rather than the analytical, by trying to communicate with the patient's id. The patient is encouraged to "mature," become independent, and finally to reject the therapist.

Family Therapy   Usually one member is seen by the others as "abnormal" but, in reality, he is just the scapegoat; it is the family itself that is in trouble and is, therefore, treated as a unit. The therapist helps them communicate, explore interactions and conflicts, and seek solutions together.

Gestalt Therapy Developed by Frederick S. Perls, this holistic approach strives to make the client aware of his feelings, thoughts, and actions—not by explanation or analysis but by direct immediate experience. The client must be aware of what he is thinking, feeling, and doing and take the final responsibility for himself. This process may be applied individually or in groups.

Group Psychotherapy Using the principles of psychotherapy with a group of people this therapy helps each person to express himself and be aware of others; and to share ideas, feelings, and experiences. Group psychotherapy has a wide variety of approaches and levels on which it can be used.

Health Therapy Increasing in popularity as a supportive process or as a complete alternative to psychotherapy. The goal is prevention or removal of problems through proper nutrition and exercise (see chapter on Health).

Horney Method Developed by Karen Horney (1885–1952). Although she accepted most of the Freudian method she did make major changes by rejecting his primary emphasis on sex and aggression, instead placing major emphasis on the need for emotional security. The patient is made aware of: his erroneous strategies and their consequences; his defense system created to perpetuate them; the discord that maintains his strategies. The therapist is more direct and active than the Freudian analyst.

Hydrotherapy The use of water to control apprehension, tension, and excitement dates back to classical Greece. Some of the major avenues of use are: tubs, footbaths, showers, and swimming pools.

Hypnotherapy The use of hypnosis to alleviate certain physical symptoms (obesity, peptic ulcers, skin diseases, etc.), relieve anxiety and reduce tension. There are many forms and applications of hypnosis in psychotherapy.

Insulin Shock Therapy Developed by Manfred Sakel. For very serious mental disorders, heavy doses of insulin are used to produce prolonged periods of coma depriving the brain of its primary fuel, glucose. Although chemotherapy and electric shock therapy have almost replaced this method (which is considered ineffective and dangerous by many) it is still used by some psychiatrists today.

Jungian Therapy   Developed by Carl Jung (1875–1961). Jung thought disharmony of the psyche produced emotional disorders. The aim of treatment is to integrate the personality by soliciting unconscious resources that will strengthen the individual. The therapist is active, helps direct the process, and helps the individual be aware of and face present conflicts. Jung rejected the Freudian couch method and free association; instead he concentrated on dreams, drawings, symbols, and discussion.

Lobotomy   Psychosurgery is a brain operation that severs nerve pathways between the hypothalamus (emotion centers) and the prefrontal lobe (thinking process centers). After the operation many show more marked symptoms, but most become shy, smiling, immature individuals who only live in the present. Even though its use has been curtailed it is still used as a last resort with severe and chronically disturbed patients. *Cuckoo's Nest* by Ken Kesey, very dramatically showed the destruction of "McMurphy" by psychosurgery.

Logotherapy   Developed by Viktor Frankl. This existential method is based on the "will to meaning." The therapist helps the client find his own individual meaning in life by examining three sets of values: creative, experiential, and attitudinal.

Marriage Therapy   Used with couples to deal with situations and problems disrupting their relationship. The relationship may be varied (married, living together, premarital, and divorce) as well as the approach (successive, simultaneous, conjoint, collaborative, couples group, etc.).

Milieu Therapy   Also known as environmental therapy and the therapeutic community. A "living school" is created by taking the social and physical aspects of the environment into account to help the patient. The positive is emphasized, focusing on the "healthy" part of the patient. Every type of supportive therapy is used, patients are involved in decision making, and the total twenty-four hours a day environment is used rather than a specific therapy time. Milieu therapy has a wide range of use for many different people and is used in many different settings (hospitals, halfway houses, rehabilitation centers, adolescent treatment centers, etc.).

Multiple Therapy   Two or more therapists involved in any form of psychotherapy. Advocates claim it helps each therapist reexamine his approach, tends to complement each other, makes it easier to avoid or dissolve impasses, and finally increases the intensity of the therapeutic relationship for the client.

Music Therapy   Used as a supportive psychotherapeutic treatment, music therapy helps people express themselves nonverbally, release tensions and emotions, and share experiences with others. It encourages self-confidence, relaxation and spontaneity. There are many approaches, from music appreciation and concerts to individual practice.

Narcotherapy   The patient is under the influence of a narcotic drug that increases the acceptance of suggestions made by the therapist.

Objective Psychotherapy   Developed by Benjamin Karpman, this process is carried out in writing in order to avoid the subjective personal relationship in therapy between patient and therapist. Several series of questions are given to the patient over a period of time, bibliotherapy is also used, then at the end the therapist gives the patient a written summarization of the insights gained in the process.

Occupational Therapy   Primarily used to further the recovery of mental patients by activities involving skill (woodworking, painting, crafts, etc.). Each patient's individual plan is carefully worked out by the occupational therapist to promote self-confidence, personal relationships, and to give a sense of accomplishment.

Orgone Therapy   Developed by Wilhelm Reich (1897–1957). The key to psychological well-being, according to Reich, is full orgastic potency since orgasm is the emotional energy regulator of the body. Without orgasm, or if sexual tensions are higher than orgasm released, then these tensions are expressed neurotically. He believed most people have a set of resistances against unconscious sexual tendencies ("character armor") of which the patient must be made aware, their origin must be found and, finally, they must be swept away.

Pastoral Counseling   Conducted by a pastor or religious worker who combines spiritual values with psychotherapy. Concern is with the person's present emotional and spiritual needs, not with the past or the unconscious.

Play Therapy   The use of play activities in psychotherapy with children is the most widely used technique of child therapists. Play therapy has great benefits; it involves those who cannot adequately express themselves verbally; it serves as a mirror to the child's emotional life; it allows testing of approaches and relationships as well as the release of tension; and also allows them to do and be what they want.

Primal Therapy   Developed by Arthur Janov. According to this process parental rejection is the cause of all neurosis and personality disorders, defense against primal pain is the single cause of all symptoms, and the only cure is the reenactment or reliving the traumatic experiences. The therapist helps the patient uncover these experiences, then relive them (resulting in crying, screaming, etc.), after which is a "rebirth." Sometimes props like baby bottles, diapers, and large pictures of parents are used. The process may be used with individuals or groups, and it should be noted that it is extremely controversial.

Projective Psychotherapy   Developed by Molly Harrower. The therapist gives the patient a series of tests (literally hundreds to choose from) then selects the information considered to be most important to deal with during therapy. It is mostly used in conjunction with another form of therapy as a foundation base for gathering information and measuring changes. There are no special tests or sequences employed, and it is not considered to be effective with very disturbed patients.

Psychoanalysis   Developed by Sigmund Freud. The patient's unconscious processes and contents are brought forth and analyzed, plus a transference therapeutic relationship between analyst and client is established. Sessions are usually five times a week over a period of many years. The analyst has the patient lie on a couch (infant stage) in order to "open up" with free association (anything that comes to mind) the unconscious. In order to allow transference to occur the analyst keeps himself "concealed" from the patient; this blankness enables the patient to project feelings from the unconscious on to the analyst. The analyst represents a parent figure or some other very significant person(s) to the patient. The goal is to free the patient from destructive effects of the past by having the patient recognize them, and the transference, and work both through. This process is becoming less used and more criticized today because of the length of time required for therapy (years), the high cost, the fact that only very few people can take part (2 percent of all psychiatric patients) and because the whole process is based on very few cases and unproven theories.

Psychodrama   Developed by J.L. Moreno. The therapist is the director, the patient is the protagonist (actor), and trained individuals as "auxiliary egos" (play different roles) all join together to simulate the patient's life situations. The therapist may be directive, or may just serve as a catalyst. There are a large number of techniques from which to choose, depending on the client and the situation.

Psychotheatrics (PT)   Originated by Robert D. Allen and developed in conjunction with Nina Krebs. The client serves as director with the therapist helping to guide and clarify. PT is based on theories and techniques from theatre and psychotherapy; is action oriented; focuses on individual responsibility; enhances the discovery of options; and helps the individual create a design for behavior change. PT is adaptable for many purposes in a wide variety of settings with people of different levels of sophistication; it may be used as a therapy modality, educational process, theatre technique, or for personal awareness.

Rational Psychotherapy   Developed by Albert Ellis. Emotional problems are considered to be related to erroneous, illogical attitudes that may be restructured by awareness and control. The therapist helps the client be aware of these attitudes and how they are causing problems. Then the client is shown how to exchange them for positive approaches and, finally, to put them into action.

Reality Therapy   Developed by William Glasser. Glasser rejects the psychoanalytic approach which, he says, sees the person as sick, weakening the patient's responsibility. Instead, he sees the client as a weak person needing a therapeutic relationship to strengthen him and encourage his taking responsibility for himself and finding better approaches for handling life situations.

Recreational Therapy   Used as a therapeutic measure to help provide self confidence, stop inertia, and facilitate social contacts. Many different types of recreation may be used (sports, games, field trips, crafts, etc.) in a variety of settings (hospitals, day treatment centers, centers for the mentally retarded, etc.).

Relaxation Therapy   Therapeutic muscle relaxation is used to reduce emotional tension in a number of conditions (insomnia, asthma, peptic ulcers, stuttering, etc.). There are a number of approaches, from massage to cassette tape exercises; the key is for the client to learn the process and use it to relax himself.

Release Therapy   Developed by David M. Levy. Mostly used with children who have anxiety symptoms associated with past events (divorce of parents, death of a family member, frightening experience, etc.). The child is given toys, which he uses to act out the situation; through these he works (plays) out his solution. The therapist, by being sympathetic and permissive, helps the child gain insight and master the problem.

Sector Therapy   Developed by Felix Deutsch (1884–1964). The primary emphasis is on the present, focusing on specific problem-causing areas (sectors). The therapist helps the client cut associative links to old experiences and to establish new, positive ones. There is no attempt in this process to reconstruct the client's personality.

Sex Therapy   Mostly treating sexual dysfunctions, individually, or in groups that share similar problems. Usually, however, this is done with couples, since the relationship is recognized as a unit. Sexological disorders are treated as psychological *and* somatic. In the broadest sense sex therapy includes not only sexual dysfunctions but sexual deviation as well; however, the vast amount is done with couples having sexual problems.

Sheltered Workshop   Run by a team of mental health specialists and is designed to simulate work conditions as closely as possible. It helps patients learn work conditions, helps them cope with "reality" and it enables them to be independent and finally self sufficient. This method has a wide variety of applications and can be used with many different kinds of patients, in or outside the hospital.

Sleep Therapy   Induced by drugs, for about twenty hours a day, from three to seventy days for patients who have schizophrenia, manic-depressive psychosis, and anxiety reactions. It is believed by some that sleep breaks the cycle of mental disorders, but there is little agreement on its effects. There is a high relapse rate and a rise of physical complications, however it is still used when other methods fail. This process is widely used in Europe and the Soviet Union, but little used in the United States.

Sociodrama   Involves role playing: the individual acts out new roles for himself or social roles for others. It is mostly used in clinical and industrial settings for practical purposes (sales problems, staff relationships, applying for a job, group psychotherapy, etc.). The process helps an individual see himself in a more objective way, while at the same time gaining insight into other people.

Sociotherapy   A supportive process, most frequently used by a psychiatric social worker. The point is to modify and use the environment to help the client. There are many ways this can be done, from working with the parents of a disturbed adolescent to making institutional settings more pleasant for patients.

Sullivan Method   Developed by Harry Sullivan (1892–1949). This is based on the premise that our emotional security and what we are, is determined by our relationships with people. Interpersonal theory emphasizes human interactions in life and in therapy. The therapist is a participant observer in the therapeutic relationship and helps the client understand his anxiety, how he has formed intimate relationships, what he has revealed about his interpersonal relationships, and what the future holds for him as a result of his altered attitudes.

Supportive Therapy   Approval, reassurance, and encouragement of positive behavior through therapy modalities that operate on the conscious level. Supportive therapy is in contrast to reconstructive therapy (altering the client's basic personality structure to relieve anxiety) and reeducative therapy (change client's attitudes by allowing him to try and learn new desirable behavior). Although there are many therapy methods in each of these three areas, most of them overlap. Some examples are: reconstructive therapy—psychoanalysis, the approaches of Jung, Adler, Sullivan, Horney, Rogers; reeducative therapy—milieu therapy, behavior therapy, sociotherapy, relaxation therapy, total push therapy; supportive therapy—music therapy, art therapy, bibliotherapy, religious therapy, hypnotherapy.

Total Push Therapy   Developed by Abraham Myerson. Used primarily with patients confined to mental institutions; however, it can also be applied in a wide variety of other settings. This method totally involves patients in continual activities (walks, massage, crafts, sports, etc.) creating a stimulating environment to constantly motivate them. This not only obviously helps morale and institutional conditions, but also prevents deterioration and apathy, enhances self-esteem and self-confidence, and helps build relationships between people.

Transactional Analysis (TA) Developed by Eric Berne. This is a form of group psychotherapy that emphasizes interactions between people and the "games" (customary and sometimes dishonest transactions) they play. Berne holds that we learn our "scripts" early in life and then simply continue them. He says that social responses reveal three ego states, parent, adult and child. The object of TA is to make the client aware of these ego states, the games and scripts that he uses, and then help him consciously choose positive ways to enhance his life.

Vocational Counseling Guidance for a choice of occupation, taking into account the skills and education needed, and the opportunities available in that field. The counselor shows the client as many options as possible, then helps narrow them down by identifying areas in which the client is most interested. The client's needs, goals, values, background, and characteristics are identified in the process. This may be a long or short term process.

REFERENCES

Ard, Ben N. (ed.). *Counseling & Psychotherapy: Classics on Theories & Issues.* Palo Alto, CA: Science and Behavior Books, 1975.

Arieti, Silvano (ed.). *World Biennial of Psychiatry & Psychotherapy,* 2 Vols. New York: Basic Books, 1970.

Banet, Anthony G. Jr. (ed.). *Creative Psychotherapy: A Sourcebook.* LaJolla, CA: University Associates, 1976.

Ehrenwald, J. (ed.). *The History of Psychotherapy: From Healing Magic to Encounter.* New York: Jason Aronson Inc., 1976.

Goldenson, Robert M. *The Encyclopedia of Human Behavior.* New York: Dell Publishing Co., 1975.

Kiernan, Thomas. *Shrinks, Etc: A Consumer's Guide to Psychotherapies.* New York: Dial, 1974.

Kovel, Joel. *A Complete Guide to Therapy: From Psychotherapy to Behavior Modification.* New York: Pantheon Books, 1977.

Mishara, Brian and Patterson, Robert A. *A Consumer's Guide to Mental Health.* New York: Quadrangle, 1977.

Tennov, Dorothy. *Psychotherapy: The Hazardous Cure.* New York: Doubleday & Co., 1976.

Books

The Abnormal Personality.   *White, Robert W.; and Watt, Norman F.*
Freudian theory and behavior theory are integrated in an overview of
abnormal psychology. Learning theory, and behavior and family
therapy are discussed. Community mental health material is oriented
toward the nonprofessional. Schizophrenia is seen as a disease, and
psychosomatic disorders are given a physiological treatment. 4th Ed.
$12.75. New York: Ronald Press, 1973. 628 pp.

**Abstracts of the Standard Edition of the Complete Psychological
Works of Sigmund Freud.**   *Ruthgeb, Carrie Lee (Ed.)*
Available from the Superintendent of Documents, U.S. Government
Printing Office, Washington, DC 20402. $1.75. DHEW Pub. No.
(HSM) 72-9001. 1971.

Applications of Behavior Modification.   *Thompson, Travis;
and Dockens, William S., III*
A range of topics in the field of applied behavior modification is
discussed. The papers apply behavior modification principles to reme-
dial education, marriage and sex counseling, drug abuse, childrearing,
and various psychiatric problems. Ethical and social issues in behavior
modification are debated from the viewpoint of biologists, political
scientists, and psychologists. $28.50. New York: Academic Press,
1975. 554 pp.

Betrayal of the Body.   *Lowen, Alexander*
The use of bioenergetics in therapy, which is the acting out of one's
emotional problems through the use of the body. $1.50. New York:
Macmillan, 1969.

Brief Encounters (Brief Psychotherapy).   *Lewin, Karl Kay*
Theoretical and clinical material considered instructive for brief
psychotherapy encounters is presented. The method of psychotherapy
described is characterized by interpretation of negative transference
and separation anxiety. Theory and technique are amplified by clinical
material, including actual mechanisms and pathological development,
and symptomatology is discussed in relation to classical theories in
these areas. Special emphasis is placed on pathological introjection
and psychic masochism as major determinants of illness, and on the

use of brief psychotherapy in family therapy and counseling. 442 references. $15. St. Louis: Warren H. Green, 1975. 288 pp.

Casebook for School Counselors.   *Morgan, Lewis B.*
This self-teaching text provides a series of simulated counseling incidents and encounters. Each "case" is followed by four questions which test the reader's ability to handle the situation, suggest solutions and predict outcomes. The author lists five suggested responses which for each case are evaluative, interpretative, supportive, probing, and understanding. $4.50 to APGA members. $5.50 to nonmembers. Washington, DC: American Personnel and Guidance Association, 1974. 96 pp.

Client-Centered Therapy.   *Rogers, Carl*
In client-centered therapy, the therapist is non-directive and demonstrates his/her total acceptance of the client. This book has become a classic. $5.95. Boston: Houghton Mifflin, 1951.

The Counselor and the Law.   *Burgum, Thomas; and Anderson, Scott*
This book examines the law as it relates to counseling. Whether the problem is possible malpractice relating to birth control, abortion, drugs or illegal search; whether the issue involves confidentiality, civil disobedience, libel, testing or outright criminality, counselors can refer to a text written by lawyers who understand counseling. $9.00 to APGA members. $10.00 to nonmembers. Washington, DC: American Personnel and Guidance Association, 1975.

Counseling Techniques that Work.   *Dyer, Wayne; and Vriend, John*
This book presents techniques that have "worked" before—and it presents them in a clear fashion. $6.50 to APGA members. $7.50 to nonmembers. Washington, DC: American Personnel and Guidance Association, 1975. 270 pp.

An Elementary Textbook of Psychoanalysis.   *Brenner, Charles*
Fundamental hypotheses of psychic determination and the dynamic unconscious are presented in an explanatory textbook on psychoanalysis. Structural theory is accompanied by clinical findings on human personality. Psychoanalytic findings are related to normal human development, psychopathology, dreams and other aspects of human experience. $2.50. Long Island, NY: Doubleday, 1974.

The First Psychodramatic Family.   *Moreno, J.L.*
The author is the originator of psychodrama. Explains psychodrama,
with personal anecdotes. $4.00. Boston: Beacon Press, 1964.

Games People Play: The Psychology of Human Relationships.
Berne, Eric
This is the classic book on transactional analysis. Easy for everyone to
read because it is written in layman terms. $5. $1.25 (pb). New York:
Grove Press, 1964.

General Introduction to Psychoanalysis.   *Freud, Sigmund*
For layman and professional. $2.95. New York: Simon & Schuster,
1969.

Gestalt Therapy Verbatim.   *Perls, Federick*
This book contains case studies of Perls. $3.50. Lafayette: Real People
Press, 1969.

Great Cases in Psychoanalysis.   *Greenwald, Harold*
The history of the development of psychoanalysis is presented through
a review of case histories. Two clinical studies of Freud are included.
Contributors include Adler, Jung, Klein, Sullivan, and Rogers. Freud,
his followers and his dissenters are discussed, and specialized
psychoanalytic techniques are outlined. $10. New York: Jason Aron-
son, 1973. 256 pp.

**Handbook of Psychotherapy and Behavior Change: An Empirical
Analysis.**   *Bergin, Allen; and Garfield, Sol. (Eds.)*
This is an extensive reference book. Bergin analyzes Eysenck's data
and concludes that he is not entirely right. He said that psychotherapy
has some good aspects to it. But Bergin still views most therapists as
ineffective and possibly harmful. Bergin suggests that we try to find
out why and how the few therapists are effective. $18.95. New York:
John Wiley & Sons, 1971.

**The History of Psychiatry: An Evaluation of Psychiatric Thought and
Practice from Prehistoric Time to the Present.**   *Alexander, Franz G.;
and Selesnick, Sheldon T.*
This book explores the 5000 years of psychiatry. The trends throughout the history of psychiatry, such as magic, organic, and psychologi-

cal approaches are discussed. $11.95 (hb). $1.50 (pb). New York: Harper and Row, 1966.

Humanistic Psychotherapy: The Rational-Emotive Approach.
Ellis, Albert
Defines the responsibilities of the psychotherapist and outlines processes which yield affirmative therapeutic results and lead the patient to levels of personal growth and fulfillment. $2.95. New York: McGraw-Hill, 1974. 288 pp.

I Can If I Want To. *Lazarus, A.; and Fay, A.*
A source book of bibliotherapeutics is presented which emphasizes a multimodal conceptualization of treatment. Twenty common mistakes are identified; a brief case example is given to illustrate the mistake; for each mistake, four or five faulty underlying assumptions are listed; and a program for change is outlined. Some of the problem areas include anxiety, depression, compulsions, marital discord, obesity, and inhibition. $5.95. New York: William Morrow, 1975. 118 pp.

Madness and Civilization: A History of Insanity in the Age of Reason. *Foucault, Michael*
Historical picture of mental institutes in Europe during the 17th and 18th centuries. $2.45. New York: Random House, 1973.

The Manufacture of Madness. *Szasz, Thomas*
The origin of institutional psychiatry through its transition to present-day medical model approach is traced. The use of witch hunts and labeling people insane are compared with sound reasoning. $3.45. New York: Dell, 1971.

Overview of the Psychotherapies. *Usdin, Gene*
A synopsis is presented of the major issues in psychotherapy and of practical methods of application of varied systems of helping distressed people, including behavioral modification, pharmacotherapy, psychoanalysis, group therapy, and marital therapy. The last essay, Zubin's "A Biometric Approach to Diagnosis and Evaluation of Therapeutic Intervention in Schizophrenia" covers 40 years of laboratory and clinical research. $8.50. New York: Brunner/Mazel, 1975. 204 pp.

The Politics of Therapy. *Halleck, Seymour*
The book discusses the political relationship of the therapeutic situation and how it can never be a neutral relationship. Therapy either
oppresses or liberates the client according to Halleck. $10. New York:
Science House, 1971.

The Practice of Mental Health Nursing: A Community
Approach. *Morgan, Arthur James; and Moreno, Judith Wilson*
Practical aspects of psychiatric nursing are presented in an experiential, community based approach. Various treatment modalities, including crisis intervention, individual, group and family therapy,
psychopharmacology, and partial hospitalization are reviewed in
terms of principles and techniques, and are illustrated by case studies.
Consideration is given to medical problems that may present symptoms that mimic those of emotional problems, special problems of the
older patient and the addict, and social aspects of mental health. Factors in relating to the patients are outlined in terms of life experiences
which will help the nurse develop empathy, sensitivity and competence. $7.25. Philadelphia: J.B. Lippincott, 1973. 211 pp.

The Primal Scream: A Revolutionary Cure for Neurosis. *Janov,*
Arthur
The author is the founder of Primal Scream therapy. $7.95. $2.95
(pb). New York: Putnam, 1970.

Psychiatric Dictionary—4th Ed. *Hinsie, L.E.; and Campbell, R.J.*
(Eds.)
This is a one volume reference book on a diverse range of psychiatric
terms and information. $22.50. New York: Oxford University Press,
1970.

Psychoanalysis and Psychotherapy: Selected Papers of Frieda
Fromm-Reichmann. *Bullard, Dexter M.*
Selected papers of Dr. Frieda Fromm-Reichmann on a multitude of
psychoanalytical and psychotherapeutic topics are presented. The
theory and philosophy of psychoanalysis and psychotherapy are discussed, as are personal experiences in the management of schizophrenia, manic-depressive psychosis, and general psychiatric disorders.
The thrust of Fromm-Reichmann's technique is in her encouragement
of the constructive and rewarding aspects of her clients' personalities.

Theoretical perspectives on the etiology and psychodynamics of anxiety are included. $3.95. Chicago: University of Chicago Press, 1974. 339 pp.

Psychopathology. *Buss, Arnold H.*
This is a clearly written view of abnormal psychology. It also has a large list of classifications and definitions of abnormal terms. $10.95. New York: Wiley, 1966.

Psychotheatrics: The New Art of Self Transformation. *Allen, Robert D.; and Krebs, Nina*
Psychotheatrics, a new, efficient, high-impact behavior-therapy based on theories and techniques from theater and the practice of psychotherapy for use in therapy, awareness, education, and theater. It focuses on individual responsibility and provides persons with options and means for structuring and restructuring behavior patterns. This book, by the originators of psychotheatrics, discusses the history of the development of psychotheatrics; its complements; the types of psychotheatrics (e.g., playwright, spectator, and environmental psychotheatrics); the therapy, education, theater, and awareness models of psychotheatrics. It is a valuable working tool for professionals in the mental health field, clinical psychology, psychotherapy, counseling, theater, education, and also for anyone interested in "self-improvement." $17.50. New York: Garland STPM Press, 1978. 250 pp.

Shock Treatment Is Not Good for Your Brain. *Friedberg, John*
A collection of penetrating and often painful firsthand accounts by patients who have experienced shock treatment—a fate narrowly escaped by the author himself. Traditional psychiatric definitions of "mental illness" are challenged by the personal testimonies in *Shock Treatment*. $6.95. Berkeley: Bookpeople, 1976. 244 pp.

Short-Term Treatment: An Annotated Bibliography (1945–1974). *Wells, Richard A.*
Short term treatment and its antecedents are considered in a bibliography covering the major journals in psychology, psychiatry, and social work during the period from 1945 to 1974. A total of 243 articles were located and categorized. $8.00. $4. (pb). Washington, DC: APA Documents in Psychology, 1976. 107 pp.

Social Work Treatment: Interlocking Theoretical Approaches.
Turner, Francis J.
Current theoretical perspectives on clinical social work practice are reviewed and discussed; psychoanalytic, ego psychology, psychosocial, problem-solving, functional, client centered, cognitive, existential, role, general systems, communication, behavior modification, crisis intervention, and family therapy approaches are covered. A series of review chapters is provided. $13.95. New York: Free Press, 1974. 542 pp.

Strategic Intervention in Schizophrenia: Current Developments in Treatment. *Cancro, Robert; Fox, Norma; and Shapiro, Lester*
A variety of new treatment strategies which are proving highly effective in treating schizophrenia are presented. An attempt is made to familiarize clinicians with the array of therapeutic skills that have recently been developed, so that they can selectively utilize specific techniques which are most successful in treating the various manifestations of this heterogeneous disorder. Different strategies for intervention are discussed, including current trends in individual psychotherapy, group and family therapy, extramedical treatment, somatic and pharmacologic treatments, experimental-behavioral approaches, short term hospitalization and aftercare, rehabilitative modalities, and special education techniques applicable to childhood schizophrenia. $12.95. New York: Behavioral Publications, 1974.

The Technique and Practice of Intensive Psychotherapy.
Chessick, Richard D.
A broad range of topics is covered in an examination of the technique and practice of intensive psychotherapy. Office management procedures and a history of psychiatry are included. Psychoanalytic theory is presented from both the individual, or Freudian, and the interpersonal, or Sullivanian, viewpoints. The value of tranquilizers as adjuvants to the therapeutic process is assayed. Specific chapters deal with: Freud's contradictory theories of narcissism, Balint's concept of primary object love, the relationship of theory to the psychoanalytic treatment of narcissistic personality disorders, and metapsychiatry. $12.50. New York: Jason Aronson, 1974. 369 pp.

Through the Mental Health Maze. *Adams, Sallie*
This is a publication of Ralph Nader's Health Research Group (1976). Excellent for the mental health consumer, a must to have if you are

thinking of therapy or are in therapy. Contents include: finding the correct therapist for you; your rights; how to establish a contract with a therapist; what to expect from a relationship with a good therapist; what questions to ask therapists to find out about them and if you really want to engage them; definitions of different types of therapy; and many more areas. $2.50. $4 (including a directory of Washington, DC therapists). Health Research Group, 2000 P St., N.W., Washington, DC 20036. 89 pp.

What is Psychotherapy? Parts I and II. Proceedings of the 9th International Congress of Psychotherapy. *Mogstad, T.E.; and Magnussen, F.*
Papers on the meaning and inadequacies of psychotherapy offered at the 9th International Congress on Psychotherapy in Oslo, Norway, are presented. Psychoanalytic therapy is classified as a pseudoscience, and the individual dynamic model is dismissed as bankrupt. It is concluded that psychotherapy today has refused to be limited to conventional interviews but has spilled over into activities beyond the individual patient. The Freudian meaning of psychotherapy is expanded to include the goals of reaching a consensus, attaining greater efficiency, and providing greater adaptability to various social situations. Contributions cover such issues as family therapy, systems theory, behavior therapy, philosophy, treatment of children, and social psychiatry. Autogenic training, Zen, and the roles of the shaman and the folkhealer in Africa and India are also considered. $67.50. New York: S. Karger, 1975. 617 pp.

Your Perfect Right. *Alberti, R.E.; and Emmons, Michael*
This book on assertive training shows techniques on how to be assertive. These techniques originate from behavioral theories such as desensitization and use of models and successive approximation. It is a good practical guide. $3. ($2.50 prepaid.) Impact, P.O. Box 1094, San Luis Obispo, CA 93401. 1970.

Articles

Changing Society and Psychotherapy. *London, Perry*
Psychotherapy's three stages of development in this century are discussed. Each one occurred in response to a different psychological

motif dominating western society. Stage one was the psychoanalysis which developed at the turn of the century. Stage two was behavior modification and crisis intervention which began developing in the 1950's. These methods share the qualities of speed, a direct attack on presenting symptoms and the promise of a more purely technological basis for treatment than psychoanalysis. Stage three, called therapeutic games, developed as a result of new life styles and an emphasis on personal fulfillment. It is predicted that in the future old treatments will be streamlined, experimental treatments will become more popular and the entire therapy business will continue to expand. *Current,* 164:42–47, 1974.

Current Adlerian Therapies. *Nikelly, Arthur G.*
A review is presented of the use of Adlerian methods of psychotherapy. These techniques range from individual to group methods and are used in mental hospitals, clinics, institutions, and especially in schools. The Adlerian approach is essentially didactic and reeducational and can be learned and applied by nonprofessionals. 22 references. *Comprehensive Psychiatry,* 14(1):41–48, 1973.

Dropout Rates in Mental Health Centers. *Lorber, Judith; and Satow, Roberta*
Staff dissatisfaction with services rather than patient dissatisfaction with treatment is proposed as a cause for the high dropout rate among patients at community mental health centers. Organizational conflicts which contribute to staff dissatisfaction include conflict between training of residents and direct treatment services, effective control of a professional who offers a client service, organizational innovations which represent threats to the autonomy or status of particular persons or groups, and the competition for programs by the various services offered. Stratification of preferred treatment and ideological conflicts are considered to leave community mental health therapists frustrated; in particular, the commonly used long term psychoanalytic approach is seen as misunderstood and rejected by the middle-class patient. It is concluded that as long as long term psychoanalytic therapy is the preferred treatment in mental health centers, patients will continue to drop out. Crisis intervention with its rapid amelioration of symptoms is suggested as a valid alternative therapeutic effort which can alleviate the dropout problem. 39 references. *Social Work,* 20(4):308–12, 1975.

Jungian Analysis Today.   *Whitmont, Edward C.*
A review of Jungian analysis today recalls the basic beliefs of Carl Jung
and how they differ from Freudian theory. The idea that dreams
satisfy a need for spiritual significance is reviewed through the interpretation of a patient's three dreams. It is suggested that Jung's
analytical psychology offers a practical way, through symbolic realiza-
tion, to renew contact with a creative source ground of direction
within each individual. *Psychology Today,* 6(7):63–72, 1972.

Psychiatry and Ideology.   *Paris, J.*
The shaping of psychiatric ideas by prevailing ideological frameworks
is discussed. The development of psychiatric theory and practice has
not been a simple progression, but has oscillated with each change in
the cultural climate. Contemporary psychiatry is divided into a
number of ideological camps, each reflecting aspects of the fragmented
modern "spirit of the times." Allegiance to any one system carries the
danger of sacrificing the care of patients to attain theoretical consis-
tency. Psychiatrists must accept the uncertainties of the eclectic position and abandon utopian attempts to resolve the ambiguities of the
human condition. Eight references. *Canadian Psychiatric Association
Journal* (Ottawa), 18(2):147–51, 1973.

Schizophrenia?   *Ferlemann, Mimi*
A dialogue on schizophrenia is presented. It is concluded that success
in treatment depends upon many factors, but the final and most important factor is the degree to which the patient's family is willing to
participate in treatment. *Menninger Perspective,* 4(3):4–11, 1973. The
Menninger Foundation, P.O. Box 829, Topeka, KS 66601.

Audio Tapes

The Basic Encounter Group
Dr. Carl Rogers discusses the basic encounter group as an instrument
for constructive personal growth, organizational change, resolution of
inter-group tension, and as a new philosophy of science and education.
$54. 6 tapes. 6 hours. 1967. Big Sur Recordings.

Behavior Therapy
Dr. Joseph Wolpe demonstrates behavior therapy including the use of relaxation and reciprocal inhibition with a phobic girl during a university psychiatry colloquium. The demonstration is followed by a question-and-answer session between the audience and the girl. $12. including script. Extra scripts $1. 65 min. AAP Tape Library.

Beyond Freedom What?
B. F. Skinner answers questions from three critics. On this cassette Professor Michael Novak, a theologian; Professor Fred Warner Neal, a political scientist; and Arvid Pardo, a diplomat, confront B.F. Skinner with their misgivings about the theoretical implications and practical limitations of operant conditioning. In response, Dr. Skinner insists that his theory "maximizes individuality," and suggests that if it is not used by us it could be used against us by our enemies. $14.95. 26 min. Center for Cassette Studies.

Bioenergetic Analysis: Concepts and Techniques (I)
Dr. Alexander Lowen explains the basis of bioenergetic theory. $15.95. 35 min.

Bioenergetic Analysis: Concepts and Techniques (II)
Dr. Alexander Lowen talks about learning to respect the body. $15.95. 34 min. Center for Cassette Studies.

Comparative Views of Freud, Adler and Jung
Dr. Gerd Cryns discusses the contributions of Freud, Adler and Jung to the psychoanalytic movement and to his personal growth and development. Freud's ideas, although taken for granted today, were revolutionary and shocking to the Victorian world in which he lived. Adler was the first of the humanistic psychologists, whose contributions to contemporary psychology have largely been ignored. Jung demonstrated that the spiritual search and the truths of psychiatry are not incompatible with each other. $9. 90 min. 1973. Big Sur Recordings.

The Complex Theory of Schizophrenia
Dr. John Perry analyzes a psychosis in Jungian terms. $16.95. 53 min. Center for Casette Studies.

Depression: The Shadowed Valley
Doctors discuss America's number one mental health problem. Some 19 million Americans today suffer from depressive disorders of some kind. In this program 11 doctors concerned with mental health examine the various causes and effects of depression, and consider certain psychotherapeutic and chemical ways of treating it. $16.95. 51 min. Center for Cassette Studies.

An Encounter Group Horror Story
The Leadership Dynamics Institute, established by cosmetics tycoon William Penn Patrick, promised to provide Gene Church with a new approach to his business career. Instead, he entered a class which incorporated physical abuse and torture to promote personal honesty and truth. This account illustrates a bizarre blending of extreme techniques in business training and psychology. $12.95. 30 min. Center for Cassette Studies.

Existential Psychotherapy. *Series of six lectures.*
In these lectures Dr. Rollo May explains what the movement is and its debt to philosophers who followed on from Kierkegaard. No longer is the analyst a distant, almost unseen figure, but one who encounters his patient as a total being whose access to will and decision, freedom and responsibility, is crucial. $79.95. 30 min. each. Center for Cassette Studies.

Existential Psychotherapy (I)
Dr. Viktor Frankl on existential psychoanalysis and logotherapy. $14.95. 40 min.

Existential Psychotherapy (II)
Dr. Viktor Frankl continues his lecture on existential frustration. $14.95. 37 min. Center for Cassette Studies.

Exploring Awareness Through Movement: Lecture-Demonstration
During this informal lecture, with 150 people sitting on the floor, Moshe Feldenkrais leads his audience through a surprising demonstration of increase in ease and range of movement when certain principles of differentiation, reversibility and the resulting inner awareness are brought into play in body functioning. He then describes some of the philosophy and practice on which he has based his work and ends with asking a member of the audience to read an unpublished description of

what "awareness through movement" is all about. $9. 90 min. 1972. Big Sur Recordings.

Farther Reaches of Human Nature
Dr. Abraham Maslow's first public statement of his own expanding vision of man and the human sciences, now elaborated in his book: *Farther Reaches of Human Nature* (Viking-Esalen Series, 1971). $18. 2 tapes. 2 hours. 1967. Big Sur Recordings.

Focus on Karl Menninger
Karl Menninger, founder of the world-famous Menninger Clinic discusses the positive role of psychiatry in redefining what illness really is and how much it is influenced by internal motives. Menninger's philosophy of mental illness is similar to R. D. Laing's. Both psychiatrists see the matrix of mental illness in the total context of a society which can be most charitably described as sick. It is not so much the patient as the environment which is sick. With quiet forcefulness, Menninger asserts that love can overcome hate, man can understand his fellow man, and hope is man's most important ally. $14.95. 28 min. Center for Cassette Studies.

The Freudian Mythology
George Steiner sets out to show that Freudianism has more in common with religion than with science. Dr. Steiner goes so far as to suggest that such concepts as the id, ego, and superego may be understood as analogues of the cellar, living quarters, and attic of any middle-class Viennese house at the turn of the century. $14.95. 26 min. Center for Cassette Studies.

Gestalt Expressive Therapy
Dr. Eugene Sagan illustrates Gestalt expressive therapy with a woman who states as her presenting problem an inability to express and/or inhibit anger. $10 including script. Extra scripts $1. 44 min. AAP Tape Library.

Group Relations and Psychotherapy
The process of discovery and decision in group psychotherapy is examined, along with problems of professionals and nonprofessionals working in the field, methods of teaching and training students in psychotherapy, and the group supervision of psychotherapy. $6.95 each. 60 min each. 1973. Behavioral Sciences Tape Library.

Guidelines for Group Encounters
Dr. William Schutz discusses 19 guidelines for successful group experiences, covering such aspects as achieving complete honesty within the group; how to maintain concentration; why it is important to be physical, rather than verbal, whenever possible; techniques for overcoming blockages in individuals; how the group should be physically arranged; and why getting to know one's own body is perhaps the most important key to self-knowledge. $16.95. 54 min. Center for Cassette Studies.

Human Uses for Behavioral Research
Most therapies seek to bring one back to accepted norms, says Sidney Jourard. They serve as handmaiden to the status quo. They should instead aim to free the individual so that he can achieve maturity. Independence from, rather than dependence on, cultural control, should be the goal of not only therapy, but psychological studies and all education as well. $9. 60 min. 1966. Big Sur Recordings.

Implosive Therapy
Dr. Robert Hogan dramatically demonstrates implosive deconditioning by extinction using as examples snake and rat phobias. The snake tape has been used experimentally in the treatment of frigidity. $15 including script and material. Extra scripts $2. Reel. 52, 46 min. AAP Tape Library.

Individual Gestalt Therapy Interview with Dr. Frederick Perls
On Track One Dr. James Simkin illustrates Gestalt therapy—emphasis on the present, nonverbal communications leading to production of genetic material, use of the fantasy dialogue—with a 34-year-old actor. On Track Two Dr. Simkin interviews Dr. Frederick Perls, who contributes historical and biographical material connected with the development of Gestalt therapy and relates anecdotes of his contacts with Freud, Marie Bonaparte, Karen Horney, Erich Fromm, and others. $12 including script. Extra scripts $1.50. Reel. 34, 48 min. AAP Tape Library.

Interview with Dr. Albert Ellis
Dr. Robert Harper interviews Dr. Albert Ellis on his shift from psychoanalysis to the development of rational-emotive therapy and its theory and practice. $10 including script. Extra copies $1. Cassette. 22, 22 min. AAP Tape Library.

Interview with J.L. Moreno
Dr. James Sacks interviews Dr. J. L. Moreno on his early life and training; the roots of psychodrama and its relation to the theater, psychodrama as a function of the encounter and the development of sociometrics and group therapy. $10 including script. Extra scripts $1.50. Cassette. 27, 27 min. AAP Tape Library.

An Interview with Virginia Satir
Virginia Satir interviewed by Dr. Ernest Kramer on "personhood," conjoint family therapy, problems with graduate education, relationships in therapy, etc. $12 including script. Extra scripts $1.50. Cassette. 21, 18 min. AAP Tape Library.

Introduction to Psychodrama
Dr. James Sacks demonstrates with a group basic techniques of psychodrama including the empty chair, use of the double, etc. $10 including script. Extra scripts $1. Cassette. 30 min. AAP Tape Library.

The Journey Back to the Self
According to R. D. Laing, we tend to try to cure schizophrenics "like we cure bacon—so that we can eat them." We ought instead, he says, to help the schizophrenic find out who he really is by taking him back to the point where he lost himself, even if it means going all the way back to the womb. In this stimulating discussion Dr. Laing outlines the "re-search" necessary in order for a fragmented personality to be reconstituted. $16.95. 52 min. Center for Cassette Studies.

Journey to the Center of Self
Carl Rogers, a student of Freud and innovator of many group techniques, describes the mechanics and interaction of the intensive group process, its merits and dangers. He discusses the "optimal person," the possibility of significant self-knowledge, and the sexual implications of encounter relationships. $16.95. 57 min. Center for Cassette Studies.

The Oedipus Complex
On this cassette, Dr. Fromm and a panel of scholars and psychologists examine nonsexual aspects of the mother-child relationships. $14.95. 28 min. Center for Cassette Studies.

Personality Theory and Psychic Energy
This is an introduction to Jungian theory by Thomas Parker. Highlights include: the conscious and unconscious structure of the personality,

the ego, archetypes, symbols, energy and will. $9. 60 min. 1971. Big Sur Recordings.

The Philosophy and Psychology of C. G. Jung (I)
Dr. Crittenden Brookes examines the work of Carl Jung. $15.95. 45 min.

The Philosophy and Psychology of C. G. Jung (II)
An analysis of Jungian symbology and archetypes. $15.95. 45 min. Center for Cassette Studies.

Psycho-Imagination Therapy
Joseph E. Shorr introduces us to the use of imagination in the realm of psychology. He explains the theoretical framework, methods and effectiveness of his innovative psycho-imagination therapy—the integration of phenomenology and imagination. $16.95. 60 min. Center for Cassette Studies.

Psychological Types I
Breaking away from Freud's emphasis on psychopathology, Jung concentrated on psychotherapy's potential for enhancing individual growth and development. The basic structure of Jung's theory was not a set of complexes and psychological ills, but a grid of personality types whose poles were intuition-sensation, on the one hand, and introversion-extroversion, on the other. Dr. Wheelwright developed the test identifying psychological types, and on this program he introduces Jung's revolutionary concept—its origins and basic definitions. $14.95. 40 min.

Psychological Types II
In part two of his lecture on Jungian psychology types, Dr. Wheelwright describes the four basic personality types: "the sensate extrovert," a Hemingway figure who is best able to adapt to his or her environment; "the sensate introvert," a sensual, abstract person; "the intuitive extrovert," the pioneer who is pragmatic and often stoical; and "the introverted intuitive," the thinker who is the type most closely in touch with his or her unconscious, and who often has artistic impulses. $14.95. 36 min. Center for Cassette Studies.

Rogers–Skinner Dialogue
"Education and the Control of Human Behavior" is the topic in the culmination of the debate between Dr. Carl Rogers and Dr. B. F. Skin-

ner which began in 1956. $15 including script. Extra scripts $2. AAP Tape Library.

Therapy
Leading proponents of modern therapy discuss pros and cons of their methods. Alan Watts advocates Zen, while other therapists involved in the discussion propound theories from Freudian to existentialist based psychotherapy. $18.95. 55 min. Center for Cassette Studies.

Toward Self-Actualization
There are, according to Dr. Abraham Maslow, no less than 14 values or "eternal verities" which can be considered basic human needs. When they are fulfilled, we are self-actualizing. When we are deprived of them, we develop "metapathologies" and often become physically ill. Here Dr. Maslow identifies these values and shows how each of them is fully definable in terms of all the others. $16.95. 58 min. Center for Cassette Studies.

What Is Schizophrenia?
R. D. Laing challenges the traditional interpretations. R. D. Laing has concluded that "maybe schizophrenia is the name we have for an outbreak of health" in a society that is itself sick. He feels we should drop such psychopathological concepts altogether. In this lecture Dr. Laing examines both "the music and the dance of human relationships," and shows how breakdowns in paralinguistic communication lead to all forms of madness. $16.95. 59 min. Center for Cassette Studies.

Wilhelm Reich
Freud angrily broke with his brilliant protege, Wilhelm Reich, when the latter dared to release Freud's "eros" from its clinical definitions. Later, Reich's experiments in America with another life force, what he called "orgone," were met with equal displeasure, and he was finally imprisoned, where, as Edward Mann relates in his interview, Reich was forgotten and eventually died. The author of *Orgone, Reich and Eros,* Mann details the career of this extraordinary pioneer and explores his theories of life and energy forces. $15.95. 59 min. Center for Cassette Studies.

The Will to Power Re-examined
A discussion of the psychological importance of the power drive, the feeling of being in control of a situation and able to do something. The

phrase "will to power" of course comes from Nietzsche, and has been in disrepute because of its misuse by the Nazis. But Walter Kaufmann of Princeton University—the leading interpreter of Nietzsche—argues that in fact Nietzsche was a brilliant psychologist, among his many other talents, and that the will to power is the most basic human motivation. He outlined his views at a Washington symposium during a meeting of the Association of Humanistic Psychologists. Other participants are Heinz Ansbacher, a leading interpreter of Adler, and Helene Papanek, an Adlerian psychotherapist from New York, who gives us Adler's view of power. Animated debate follows. $16.95. 60 min. Center for Cassette Studies.

Films

Albert Ellis: Rational Emotive Psychotherapy Applied to Groups
Marathon weekends of rational encounter, marital counseling, and group psychotherapy are discussed by Albert Ellis. He explains his therapeutic approach and defines the role and training of the leader, the use of exercises, and elaborates on rational emotive psychotherapy applied to group settings. Sale: $250. Rental: $25. 30 min. 16mm. Color. 1972. American Personnel and Guidance Association.

Battle of East St. Louis
CBS documentary production covering the use of encounter group techniques for the resolution and change in racial conflict in East St. Louis. Focus is on confrontation between police and black militant groups through sensitivity group methods. $12.50 rental. 46 min. 16mm. b/w. 1970. Penn State University, Psychology Cinema.

Behavioral Counseling—A Multi-Film Package
Dr. Ray Hosford's film package, consisting of eight films, will engage the counselor, teacher and student alike. The creator of this audiovisual aid shows counselors how to use behavioral techniques to explore and resolve client problems. The desensitization film is available for sale at $250. Rental fee per day of use is $30. All other films in the package are for sale at $200 each; rental fee per day of use, $25 each. Complete package price for sale is $1,650. 8 films. American Personnel and Guidance Association.

Counseling Techniques: Assertive Training
A behavioral counselor helps a client learn to be more assertive with his boss. 14 min.

Counseling Techniques: Desensitization
A client's fear of snakes and how the counselor helps to dispel the phobia make a lucid model for desensitization techniques. Part 1, 25 min.—Part 2, 16 min.

Counseling Techniques: Self-As-A-Model
Demonstrates a new approach to counseling being employed at the University of California, Santa Barbara. 12 min.

Counseling Techniques: Social Modeling
The counselor models the behavior that the client must learn while the client observes closely, noting specific cues that he can use. 15 min.

Counseling Techniques: Reinforcement Procedures
Counselor shows how to use verbal and nonverbal reinforcement techniques with client, and also shows client how to use several self-modification techniques. 13 min.

Identifying the Problem
Demonstrates how a behavioral counselor translates a problem into behavioral terms and helps a client express his feelings. 21 min.

Formulating the Counseling Goal
How a behavioral counselor helps a client consider a variety of counseling goals before selecting the specific behavioral goal that the client wants to learn. 19 min.

Observing and Recording Behavior
The counselor helps a teacher learn how to observe and record so that she can tell if a student is changing his behavior in response to her efforts. 17 min.

Behavior Modification: Teaching Language to Psychotic Children
The use of reinforcement and stimulus-fading techniques in the teaching of speech to psychotic children. The need for correction of self-stimulation and destructive behavior before learning can begin. Importance of eye-to-face contact in initial training. Examples of trainers

working with disturbed children. Based on research of Ivar Lovaas. Rental: $15.25. 42 min. 16mm. Color. 1969. Film Library–Oregon.

Behavior Theory in Practice, Part 1: Respondent and Operant Behavior
Basic research in Skinnerian behavior theory. A salivating dog and a begging baby robin as examples of respondent behavior. Operant conditioning—pecking by a pigeon—established and extinguished. Describes the factors of motivation, preparation, adaptation, and shaping a relation to the pigeon. Rental: $10.50. 21 min. 16mm. Color. 1965.

Behavior Theory in Practice, Part 2: Shaping Various Operants, Various Species
Basic research in Skinnerian behavior theory. The shaping of operants in various species, with detailed attention to lever-pressing in rats. Fixed and variable schedules of reinforcement. The application of behavior theory to human learning as illustrated by the development of programmed instruction, B. F. Skinner describing his handwriting program. Rental: $10.50. 1965. 22 min. 16mm. Color.

Behavior Theory in Practice, Part 3: Generalization, Discrimination, and Motivation
Basic research in Skinnerian behavior theory. Illustrates generalization and discrimination in various responses of a pigeon. Examples of final performances and positive, conditioned and negative reinforcement in several species. Rental: $10.50. 22 min. 16mm. Color. 1965. Film Library–Oregon.

Behavioral Therapy Demonstration.   *Joseph Wolpe*
This film shows how a behavioral therapist helps a client through teaching her muscle relaxation and having her imagine fear-provoking situations in order to desensitize her constant nervousness and high levels of anxiety. Sale: $420. Rental: $18. 32 min. 16mm. Color. 1969. Penn State University, Psychology Cinema.

Broad Spectrum Behavior Therapy in a Group
Highlights of some of the methods involving activity which Dr. Arnold Lazarus uses in groups are shown and discussed. A comparison of group behavior therapy and conventional group therapy is made. Four separate sequences employing different techniques are presented.

Rental: $10.50. Sale: $190. 30 min. 16mm. b/w. Sound. 1969. Penn State University, Psychology Cinema.

A Conversation with Carl Rogers

This is a film interview featuring psychologist and educator, Dr. Carl Rogers. The material covered provides introduction to the work of Dr. Rogers. In this film series Dr. Rogers, founder of client-centered therapy, comments on a variety of subjects including his current thinking on client-centered therapy, on humanistic psychology and his close affinity for a phenomenological approach to human beings. He also talks about the relevance of the education we are offering students and the dilemma of our educational institutions. Among other subjects covered, he discusses the worth of encounter or sensitivity groups, our technologically advanced society, and the scientific approach of providing security in individuals to accommodate to rapid change. Sale: $300. Rental: $30. Used copies may be purchased when available for $175. Transcript: $5 each booklet. Two film series. 30 min. each. 16mm. b/w. Psychological Films, Inc.

A Demonstration of Behavioral Processes by B. F. Skinner

In this documentary, B.F. Skinner offers an introduction to operant conditioning—an area especially important to students in psychology, teacher training, and adult education classes. In a classroom setting, Skinner reviews the history of operant conditioning and explains experimental apparatus. He demonstrates differential reinforcement, and "shaping" techniques used on a pigeon, while showing how pigeons shape their own behavior. In conclusion, Skinner applies principles of operant conditioning to human behavior. Sale: $400. Rental: $40/day. 28 min. 16mm. Color/sound. 1971. Prentice-Hall Film Library.

Fighting Fear with Fear

This CBS-TV film demonstrates the implosion technique. The technique is the opposite of desensitization. In this technique the client imagines the most terrifying situation possible, the logic being that since no danger was involved, the client can unlearn his fear. Sale: $325. Rental: $18. 26 min. 16mm. Color. 1968. McGraw-Hill.

The Fragile Mind

Different therapy approaches are shown clearly by demonstrating each mode through a separate individual's experience. Group therapy, family therapy, encounter group, and other systems are briefly touched on. Comments by patients on changes effected are made. Quite suitable for general distribution as a primer on current methods of therapy for the emotionally disturbed. Sale: $600. Rental: $200. 55 min. 16mm. Color. 1974. Allan Lansburg Prod., 12912 Woodbridge Ave., Studio City, CA 91604.

Frankl and the Search for Meaning
Dr. Viktor E. Frankl is the originator of the school of logotherapy, often referred to as the "third Viennese school of psychotherapy." In this film, Dr. Frankl describes man's search for meaning as a form of "height" psychology as opposed to the Freudian theory, which is described as "depth" psychology. In man's continuous growth upward toward self-actualization, he discovers new meanings for himself. Frankl describes meaning as a form of personalized valuing that each man must have in order to make his life meaningful. Sale: $300. Rental: $30. 30 min. 16mm. Color. Psychological Films, Inc.

Frederick Perls and Gestalt Therapy

Film No. 1
The first film presents the essence of Gestalt therapy. He discusses the "Now and How" as legs on which Gestalt therapy stands. 39 min.

Film No. 2
The second film is a demonstration of actual technique in practice. Dr. Perls discusses his dream theory and describes a dream as an existential message in which man's existence is clarified to him. He then illustrates by an interpretation of two patient's dreams. 36 min. Sale: $400. Rental: $30. Used copies may be purchased for $200. when available. 2 film series. 16mm. b/w. Psychological Films, Inc.

Games People Play—The Practice
This is a portion of a NET documentary made in 1967 and is an interview with Dr. Eric Berne in which he describes the various concepts and terms of transactional analysis. In a session in his home he describes further a patient with a problem and the use of fairy tale conceptualization. Rental: $10. 30 min. 16mm. b/w.

Games People Play—The Theory
Interviews with Dr. Eric Berne by NET documentary staff describes in further detail the theory of transactional analysis, the relationship to

psychoanalysis and discusses game theory in transactional terms. Rental: $10. 30 min. 16mm. b/w. Penn State University, Psychology Cinema.

Guidance for the 70s: Blame Game
Four teenagers working with counselor Daniel Whiteside, learn to translate their blame-messages into "I"-language. Rental: $10.50. 20 min. 16mm. Color. 1974. Film Library—Oregon.

The Humanistic Revolution: Pioneers in Perspective
Carl Rogers talks about his contributions to psychology as a combination of the tough-minded scientist with the sensitive work of the therapist. Rollo May describes his journey from being a psychoanalyst to becoming an existentialist or humanist. Paul Tillich discusses the main points of the humanistic goal for man—the courage to be. Frederick Perls tells of the journey from deadness to aliveness which must be the journey for every humanistically oriented person. Viktor Frankl speaks of *Man's Search for Meaning* which has had such an effect on American psychology. Alan Watts talks of man's search for identity and gives new meanings to the term "unconscious." To conclude the film, Dr. Abraham Maslow discusses his hopes for the future of self-actualization and humanistic psychology. Sale: $250. Rental: $20. 32 min. 16mm. b/w. Psychological Films, Inc.

Journey Into Self
Journey Into Self is a documentary of an intensive basic encounter group. Eight total strangers from various parts of the country meet for the first time in front of the cameras to share some of the most intimate aspects of their lives. The group is lead by Drs. Carl Rogers and Richard Farson. The film focuses on four group members and contains highlights of the most emotional moments of their interaction. Awarded Best Feature Lenth Documentary by The Academy of Motion Picture Arts and Sciences in 1968. Sale: $250. Rental: $60— includes shipping cost, applicable to purchase price. 47 min. 16mm. b/w. Optical sound. 1968. LRC, 7594 Eads Ave., LaJolla, CA 92037.

Leona Tyler on Counseling
Dr. Leona Tyler, former President of the American Psychological Association, addresses herself to a series of significant issues in counseling. In reel one she discusses: the role of the counselor in helping the client transform potentialities into actualities . . . confusion and isola-

tion as two of the basic problems facing young people ... how a counselor goes about choosing a counseling theory ... and why she does not see changing human behavior as the whole objective of counseling. In reel two she continues her discussion with the importance of client feelings in the counseling process ... why she believes there is a greater need for counseling now than ever before ... the reasons why school counselors have not been as effective as they could be ... the changes in the women's movement and the central issues facing women today. Sale: $250. Rental fee: $25/day. 50 min. (two reels). 16mm. Color and sound. American Personnel and Guidance Association.

Lowen and Bioenergetic Therapy
In this two part film series, Dr. Alexander Lowen describes his key ideas of bioenergetic therapy and demonstrates them in his work with a young female patient. Lowen's theory is that the "unconscious" really exists in the muscle constrictions of the body. His view is that therapy requires working with the body as opposed to the "mind." His work represents a totally new dimension of psychotherapy. Sale: $450. Rental: $35. 48 min. 16mm. Color. Psychological Films, Inc.

Maslow and Self-Actualization
Dr. Maslow, founder of the concept of self-actualization, discusses the dimensions of self-actualization and elaborates on recent research and theory related to each dimension. Sale: $500—series. Rental: $35—series. Two film series—30 min. each. 16mm. Color. Psychological Films, Inc.

Rollo May and Human Encounter
Film No. 1: Self-Self Encounter and Self-Other Encounter
The first section of this film is entitled the "Self-Self Encounter." In this part, Dr. May describes man's dilemma as having to see himself as both subject and object in life. As an object, he is manipulated and used; and as a subject, he has freedom and choice. Part Two of the film has to do with "Self-Other Encounter." Here Dr. May discusses the four elements of human encounter—Empathy–Eros–Friendship–Agape. He maintains that if any of the four elements is absent, human encounter does not exist.

Film No. 2: Manipulation and Human Encounter—Exploitation of Sex
The third part of this series deals with the subject of "Manipulation and Human Encounter." Dr. May discusses how man is manipulated

when any of the foregoing elements discussed in Part Two is missing. He also talks about the problem of transference in psychotherapy and sees it as a distortion of human encounter. In this last part of the film, Part Four, Dr. May discusses the exploitation of Eros. He describes modern man's fixation on sexuality and relates it to man's fear of death. He states that man's preoccupation with sex, in reality, is man's unconscious attempt to immortalize himself. Sale: $500. Rental: $35. Used copies may be purchased for $250 when available. 2 film series—30 min. each. 16mm. Color. Psychological Films, Inc.

A Nude Marathon
A documentary film on the role of nudity in group therapy presents Dr. Paul Brindrim and his work. In the film he works with an adult group clothed and in the nude; he discusses briefly his concepts. Rental $12.50. 25 min. 16mm. Sound. b/w. 1968. Penn State University, Psychology Cinema.

Operant Conditioning—Token Economy (Follow the Green Line)
Produced to show what it is like to be a part of the operant conditioning economy program to parents, nursing staff and psychiatric aides of the Camarillo (California) State Hospital. The philosophy that each individual should learn to make decisions and to live with his decisions provoked this experiment. Within an environment engineered for success, the performance criteria are steadily increased, but always within the capacity of each patient (mentally retarded and mentally ill). The token economy system is used to purchase privileges and goods within the institution. Three levels of dormitories and life styles are a constant reminder that appropriate behavior and sufficient tokens provide life's luxuries. At Level A, the patients are gradually weaned from tokens to prepare for life outside the institution. Considerable emphasis is placed on the roles of physical training and sensory-motor training as well as self-help and community skills within one hospital. Rental: $4.25. 39 min. 16mm. Color. Film Library–Oregon.

Reaching Back for Change: A Day of Transactional Analysis
This film shows excerpts from a one-day group therapy session. Pat is followed from her initial treatment contract through her day's work. During this process basic transactional analysis concepts are shown and described as well as some Gestalt and bioenergetic techniques. Sale: $5. Rental: $50. 55 min. 16mm. Color. 1973. Stanley Woollams, M.D., 3443 Daleview Dr., Ann Arbor, MI 38103.

Target Five

Part I

In this first section of the film series, Virginia Satir, family therapist, in cooperation with Dr. Everett L. Shostrom, Director of the Institute of Therapeutic Psychology, demonstrates the four manipulative response forms. Each of the four forms are illustrated by a simulated family wherein Mrs. Satir describes the manipulative response form and it is then demonstrated by a family situation. They conclude this film with a family actualizing together, which is described as "Target Five." 26 min.

Part II

In the second reel, Mrs. Satir and Dr. Shostrom again combine to describe the three essential qualities of an actualizing relationship. The first of these is hearing and listening, the second is understanding, and the third is mutual meaning. Each of these three dimensions of the actualizing relationship are discussed in detail and then demonstrated on film. The development of the actualizing relationship, or "Target Five," is the key goal of this film. Sale: $450. Rental: $35. 2 film series. 48 min. 16mm. Color. Psychological Films, Inc.

Three Approaches to Psychotherapy

Part I: Dr. Carl Rogers

Part I includes: a general introduction to the Film Series; a description of client-centered therapy; the interview by Dr. Rogers with patient—"Gloria;" and the summation of the interview by Dr. Rogers. 48 min.

Part II: Dr. Frederick Perls

Part II includes: a description of Gestalt therapy; the interview by Dr. Perls with patient—"Gloria;" and the summation of the interview by Dr. Perls. 32 min.

Part III: Dr. Albert Ellis

Part III includes: a description of rational-emotive psychotherapy; the interview by Dr. Ellis with patient—"Gloria;" the summation of the interview by Dr. Ellis; and an evaluation by Gloria of her experiences with the three therapists. Sale: Color—$375. each. Black & White—$250 each. Rental: 1 showing of series (3 films)—color: $75. Black & White: $60. Each part separately: black & white: $25. Used series may be purchased when available for $400 plus shipping. Three film series. 16mm. Color and b/w. Psychological Films, Inc.

Together

Filmed in two parts, *Together* features psycholgists Fred S. Keller and B. F. Skinner in an informal discussion of their personal memories and careers. Their conversation gives insight into these men, their professional colleagues, and their work in behavioral psychology. A complementary study kit, free with purchase or rental of the film, was prepared by Keller. Sale: $750. Sale: $400 each reel. Rental: $42 per day, each reel. Part I: 33 min. Part II: 28 min. 16mm. Color. Sound. 1972. Prentice-Hall Film Library.

Health*

7

THE TERM "ORTHOMOLECULAR" has been introduced by Linus Pauling to refer to the concept that by optimizing the levels of concentration of particular substances normally present in the human body certain vital metabolic processes can be influenced advantageously.

One of the great mysteries of biology is why and how cells differentiate at a certain point in the development of the fertilized egg; but when the components are analyzed, the same kind of metabolic machinery is encountered. Be they cells of single-celled organisms such as yeast and bacteria, or groups of billions of differentiated cells of plants and animals, the same amino acids, minerals, vitamins, lipids, nucleotides, and other substances are encountered. Many of these vital substances can be wholly or partially synthesized by the various cells, but there are certain items that must be introduced from the outer environment. For example, minerals cannot be synthesized, but some vitamins and amino acids can be constructed out of simpler compounds by some cells.

In the human organism, this synthesizing ability is limited. A certain number of amino acids must be supplied from food sources; all the vitamins must come from food.

It is common knowledge that the fluid nutrients that bathe the cells are circulated in the blood stream. It is not fully understood exactly how cell reproduction is regulated but it may very well have to do with the permeability of vessel walls and/or the number of cells per unit of nutrient fluid. Thus, controlling the concentration of vital substances in the molecular environment of the cells may be one important means of controlling cell function and growth.

*with James Landers

This concept of orthomolecularity has been introduced in connection with psychiatry to open up a new field of psychotherapy. Orthomolecular psychiatry is defined as the treatment of mental disease by providing the optimum molecular environment for the mind, especially the optimum concentration of those substances normally present in the human body.

The tissues of the human brain are regarded here as the molecular environment of the mind. Mental functioning is therefore dependent upon its composition and structure as well as the levels of certain important chemical reactions. If any upset occurs in this molecular environment, certain reactions may be altered or cease altogether, in some cases effecting profound psychic and physiological changes.

Our genetic inheritance is not only manifested in our physical bodies, but also in our individual biochemistry. This leads to a second fundamental concept. Genetotrophic conditions are those predisposed by heredity and precipitated by nutritional factors. One form of mental retardation, known as phenylketonuria, comes under this heading of genetotrophic diseases. Babies born with this affliction are highly sensitive to phenylalanine, one of the nutritionally essential amino acids. If the diet contains too much phenylalanine, the biochemical mechanisms produce poisonous amounts of a substance which damages brain cells and makes healthy development impossible. When this essential amino acid is limited in the child's diet, the malady disappears. Obviously this problem is a result of the inherited peculiarities in the child's metabolism.

A multitude of inheritance peculiarities exists in the general population. It is reasonable to assume that variations in susceptibility and resistance to *all* types of diseases are the results of peculiarities in inheritance. Newborn babies differ tremendously in sizes of internal organs; circulatory, muscular and neurological systems; brain structures; and breathing and heart rate patterns. Anatomical differences may run into the millions, while more obscure variations in hormone levels and the ability to make certain biochemical transformations (which are probably basic to innate disease resistance) increase the degree of potential variability to astronomical proportions. Based upon these premises, it is not unrealistic to suggest that one's production of necessary chemical substances as well as individual requirements for essential food items may vary similarly. In order to apply the concept of nutrition to physical and mental health, it is necessary to take the hereditary factor into account. Nutrition cannot be consid-

ered without including the individual's specific needs and potentialities.

Pauling advances the hypothesis that mental disease is for the most
part caused by abnormal reaction rates as determined by genetic constitution, diet, and by abnormal concentrations of essential substances.
The functioning of the brain and nervous tissue is more sensitively
dependent on the rate of chemical reactions than the functioning of
other organs or tissues. As a result, for example, symptoms of vitamin
deficiencies may be evident as mental problems long before any physical symptoms appear. A slight variation of a vital substance in the
muscles or an organ, however, may not cause much of a problem. The
same variation of the same substance in the brain or cerebrospinal
fluid may produce profound effects. Certain substances may be normal in blood and lymphatic systems and pathologically low in the
brain tissue. A certain enzyme may have a higher concentration in one
organ than anywhere else, thereby requiring more of the other substances necessary for that organ to function adequately than similar
reactions elsewhere. Ability to synthesize a vital substance may be lost,
or some pathological condition may cause the vessel walls or blood
brain membranes to be affected causing a decrease in permeability.

Although many continue to hold the notion that mental disease is
primarily psychological and nonphysical in origin, an increasing
number of people subscribe to the idea that mental (as well as physical) disease is fundamentally biochemical. Actually, these are not
mutually exclusive propositions. It is commonly known that strong
emotional states such as love, hate, fear, anger, and stress induce
biochemical changes in the human organism, primarily through the
endocrine system. Brain cells can be most definitely affected through
hormonal level changes. Even if one believes that mental illness is
solely biochemical in origin, this does not rule out the role that
psychotherapy can play in alleviating psychochemical reactions to
stress. Nevertheless, it is reasonable to conclude that providing the
molecular environment of the mind with all that it needs to function
optimally can aid immensely in preventing these same reactions from
occurring.

REFERENCES

Adams, R. *Megavitamin Therapy*. New York: Larchmont Books, 1973.
Airola, P. *Health Secrets from Europe*. New York: Arc Books, 1970.

8

Bricklin, M. "Linus Pauling: How to Live 15 Years Longer." *Prevention,* January 1975.

Davis, A. *Let's Eat Right to Keep Fit.* New York: Harcourt Brace Jovanovich, 1974.

Jennings, J. "Nutritional Therapy for Troubled Minds." *Prevention,* September 1975.

Lappe, F.M. *Diet for a Small Planet.* New York: Ballantine Books, 1971.

Pauling, L. and Hawkins, D. *Orthomolecular Psychiatry.* San Francisco: W.H. Freeman Co., 1973.

Watson, G. *Nutrition and Your Mind.* New York: Bantam Books, 1972.

Williams, R.J. *Nutrition Against Disease.* New York: Bantam Books, 1973.

Books

Body Pollution. *Null, Gary*
An examination of substances having varying degrees of toxicity, which we knowingly and unknowingly ingest, and an alternative program of natural nutrition are presented. New York: Arco Publishing Co., 1973. 216 pp.

Growth and Development of the Brain: Nutritional, Genetic, and Environmental Factors. *Brazier, Mary A.B.*
The nutritional, genetic, and environmental factors in the growth and development of the brain are surveyed, beginning at the cellular level with stress on the ontogenesis of key cellular components, and including data on human and lower animal forms. Even at this level it is possible to tie neuronal anomalies to psychological disturbances and mental retardation. The important neurochemical factors at work in the malnourished immature brain and the disorders caused by enzyme deficiencies, by inadequate protein energy metabolism, and by neural transmitter disturbances are discussed. Information is given on the effects of inborn errors of metabolism and on sensitive methods of detecting the extent of resulting brain damage. The aberrations resulting from such diverse environmental influences as oxygen deficiency and distorted visual conditions at critical periods of brain development are included. The scope and impact of human malnutrition is reviewed, and the extent of malnutrition in India and the United States is assessed. $28.50. New York: Raven Press, 1975. 390 pp.

Malnutrition and the Retarded Human Development.
Monacha, Sohan, L.
Malnutrition and its effects upon human development are discussed, especially with regard to deficiencies of calories and protein. The book begins with a survey of the nutritional background, including some general information concerning function and the effect of malnutrition on development. A short section is included on obesity and cardiovascular disease, after which the effect of malnutrition on mental development is considered in some detail. The following chapters discuss how and why maternal deprivation during pregnancy and lactation can be serious and the sometimes disastrous effects of bad food habits, social customs, and taboos. The last sections are devoted to a discus-

sion of the fight against malnutrition by organizations such as WHO and FAD, and the clinical treatment of calorie and protein deficiencies. $19.75. Springfield, IL: Charles C Thomas, 1972. 382 pp.

Nutrition and Mental Functions.   *Serban, George*
Volume 14 of the series Advances in Behavioral Biology is presented in which the relationship between nutrition and mental development is discussed by various authorities. The consequences of and some working solutions to the worldwide hunger problems are investigated. New findings on the interrelation of nutrition, environmental factors, timing, and mental development are presented. The effect of malnutrition during the infant's critical developmental period and the importance of the social environment in the possible reversal of malnutrition are explored, as well as the controversial use of vitamin megadoses in the treatment of schizophrenia. $22.50. New York: Plenum Press, 1975.

Nutrition and Your Mind.   *Watson, George*
The hypothesis that mental and emotional disorders are usually due to metabolic malfunction is supported by data that indicate the necessity to pay more attention to nutrition and the body's need for rest. The attitudes expressed are in extreme opposition to the theory that the only valid cures to emotional problems are releasing unconscious memories or opening relationship possibilities. $6.95. New York: Harper and Row, 1972.

Obesity: And Its Management.   *Craddock, Denis*
The predisposing factors of obesity and the important considerations in its treatment are summarized. The evidence that refined sugar is a major cause not only of obesity per se but also of general vascular degenerative disease is emphasized. Diet and psychology are the keys to successful treatment. Various diets and food tables are included. $9. 2nd Ed. London: Churchill Livingstone, 1973. 205 pp.

Psychodietetics.   *Cheraskin, E.*
Dieting and the promotion of good eating habits are related to individual psychology and to the environment. A few of the common dangers of reducing diets that are deficient in calories and essential nutrients are dealt with in some detail. The major importance of good nutrition is discussed, including reference to the literature. The therapeutic uses of optimum nutrition and megavitamins with al-

coholics, schizophrenics, and children with learning and behavior disorders are described. $1.95. New York: Bantam Books, 1976. 227 pp.

The Psychology of Obesity: Dynamics and Treatment.
Kiell, Norman
The psychology of obesity is discussed. The complexities of the problem and the people involved are discussed, from dynamics and etiology to body image and self-concept. Techniques and therapies are scrutinized, from hypnosis with children, adolescents, and adults, to dieting and psychometrics. $13.95. Springfield, IL: Charles C Thomas, 1973. 480 pp.

Why Your Child Is Hyperactive.   *Feingold, Ben F.*
Dietary management advice for use by parents of hyperactive children is offered. It is maintained that diet can adversely affect a hyperactive child with learning disabilities, and that particularly foods with synthetic coloring and additives should be avoided, along with natural salicylates. A list of permitted and undesirable food is included with menus and recipes. $7.95. New York: Random House, 1975. 211 pp.

Articles

Administration of Massive Doses of Vitamin E to Diabetic Schizophrenic Patients.   *Deliz, Antonio J.*
Treatment with massive doses of vitamin E of 20 diabetic schizophrenic patients exhibiting acute perceptual cognitive disorder and signs of incipient gangrene of the toes and feet is reported. Successful results are reported, including progressive disappearance of the patients' complaints of acute pains and numbness of the toes, fading of areas of ischemia on the legs, and disappearance of signs of secondary infected ulcers. *Journal of Orthomolecular Psychiatry* (Regina), 4(1):85–87, 1975.

Aging and Nutrition.   *Mayer, Jean*
Relationships between nutrition and aging are explored. It is noted that nutrition may play a role in preventing death from the degenerative diseases of old age, but it is by no means certain that it retards death from old age itself. The need for proper nutrition and diet in the

elderly is stressed. Although the need for quantity of food decreases in the elderly, the need for quality increases, since they are no longer as active. Poverty, lack of transportation, lack of mobility, and lack of companionship are factors that oppose a nutritionally adequate diet. Suggestions are offered for delaying the diseases of old age. Two references. *Geriatrics,* 29(5):57–59, 1974.

Depression Induced by Oral Contraception and the Role of Vitamin B₆ in Its Management.   *Leeton, John*
The appearance of pharmacological depression in women taking oral contraceptives is examined. The resulting depressive syndrome may be suppressed by Vitamin B₆ therapy in those women who have an absolute Vitamin B₆ deficiency. As laboratory confirmation of this deficiency is difficult, a safe daily dose of 50mg Vitamin B₆ can be given to all women complaining of depressive symptoms while taking oral contraceptives. 22 references. *Australian and New Zealand Journal of Psychiatry* (Carlton), 8(2):85–88, 1974.

Emotions and Attitudes Related to Being Overweight.
Plutchik, Robert
It was found that the tendency to have problems in the areas of depression, anxiety, and impulsivity increased with the degree of obesity. The number of overweight persons in one's immediate family also was related to the person's degree of obesity. It is suggested that therapy for obesity should involve a multidimensional approach to determine the psychosocial forces, familial role models, and metabolic factors which cause the problem. Nine references. *Journal of Clinical Psychology,* 32(1):21–24, 1976.

Etiologic Factors in Mental Retardation.   *Valente, Mario; and Tarjan, George*
The etiology of mental retardation is discussed. In describing causation, the new manual of the American Association on Mental Deficiency is followed. Diagnosis is analyzed. It is noted that in only 20 percent to 25 percent of all mentally retarded individuals does one find a definitive biomedical etiologic factor. It is suggested that the majority of mentally retarded individuals are in the mildly retarded range, and that among those, socioeconomic, nutritional and environmental factors appear to play a major role. 20 references. *Psychiatric Annals,* 4(2):22–37, 1974.

History of Orthomolecular Psychiatry. *Hoffer, A.*

The concern of orthomolecular psychiatry with the provision of the optimum molecular environment for the mind is discussed, treatments entailing orthomolecular psychiatry are described, and the history of this approach to mental illness is outlined. Theoretical and practical roots for orthomolecular psychiatry are discussed in terms of megavitamin therapy, mineral therapy, and changes in the development of current foodstuffs. The need for accurate diagnosis based on both clinical examination and accurate laboratory tests is noted, with treatment discussed in terms of supernutrition and needs of patients with allergies. 27 references. *Journal of Orthomolecular Psychiatry* (Regina), 3(4):223–30, 1974.

Hypoglycemia. *Ross, Harvey M.*

Etiology and treatment of hypoglycemia are discussed. Hypoglycemia is recognized as an important condition occurring with schizophrenia, and as having both physical and emotional symptoms. Important physical causes are noted; however, the greatest number of cases are termed of unknown origin and probably result from overconsumption of sugar. Mode of diagnosis is outlined, and treatment is discussed in terms of vitamin supplementation and dietary regulation. Four references. *Journal of Orthomolecular Psychiatry* (Regina), 3(4):240–45, 1974.

Malnutrition and Mental Deficiency. *Kaplan, Bonnie J.*

The effects of inadequate nutrition on both psychological and physiological developments in humans are discussed. The nine months of gestation and the first several years of life are the most critical in the growth of brain tissue and are also the periods of greatest vulnerability to malnutrition. Some variables that mediate the effect of nutrition on mental development include prematurity, birth weight, and the nutritional status of the mother during her childhood. A model for thorough research is suggested and is employed to evaluate the major studies in the literature of the relationship between malnutrition and mental deficiency. 70 references. *Psychological Bulletin*, 78(5):321–34, 1972.

Megavitamins. *Ross, Harvey M.*

Psychiatric disorders of children and adults which have been successfully treated with megavitamins are outlined, and indications for the use of supernutrition therapy are discussed. Consideration is given to determination of proper dosages and the need to combine megavitamin therapy with other modes of treatment. Seven references. *Journal of Orthomolecular Psychiatry* (Regina) 3(4):254–58, 1974.

Megavitamin and Orthomolecular Therapy of Schizophrenia.
Brown, W.T.
The literature on megavitamin and orthomolecular therapy of schizophrenia is reviewed, and the controversy between practitioners of conventional and orthomolecular psychiatry is outlined. *Canadian Psychiatric Association Journal* (Ottawa), 20(2):97–100, 1975.

On the Orthomolecular Environment of the Mind: Orthomolecular Theory. *Pauling, L.*
Orthomolecular psychiatry is discussed as the achievement and preservation of good mental health by the provision of the optimum molecular environment for the mind, especially the optimum concentrations of substances normally present in the human body, such as the vitamins. It is suggested that there is sound evidence for the theory that increased intake of such vitamins as ascorbic acid, niacin, pyridoxine, and cyanocobalamin is useful in treating schizophrenia. 35 references. *American Journal of Psychiatry*, 131(11):1251–57, 1974.

Orthomolecular Psychiatry, Vitamin Pills for Schizophrenics.
Ross, Harvey M.
Orthomolecular psychiatry, a school of psychiatry that believes thoughts, emotions, and actions are affected by the physical condition of the body, is discussed as it relates to individual cases of schizophrenia. The historical development of orthomolecular psychiatry from the 1950's onward is studied. Differences between the approaches of an orthomolecular psychiatrist and a traditional psychoanalyst are examined. The inclusion of the family as a necessary instrument in treating schizophrenics by orthomolecular psychiatry is analyzed. Both the patient's psychological and physical condition are evaluated to determine if there may be underlying biochemical reasons for illnesses such as schizophrenia. Results of actual cases using orthomolecular therapy are discussed. 5 references. *Psychology Today*, 7(11):82–85, 1974.

An Orthomolecular Study of Psychotic Children. *Rimland, Bernard*
An orthomolecular study of 191 psychotic children who were treated

with megavitamins is reported. Findings are based on questionnaires completed by parents which covered the child's medical and birth history, symptomatology and other information as well as detailed reports by both parents on the child's behavior while receiving vitamins and after treatment was discontinued. Reports confirm the value of megavitamin therapy and indicate that certain dysnutritional conditions produce highly predictable behavioral manifestations. 6 references. *Journal of Orthomolecular Psychiatry* (Regina), 3(4):371–77, 1974.

Orthomolecular Therapy Review of the Literature.   *Hall, Kay*
Research studies pointing to a biochemical etiology of mental illness in which transient factors such as history and experience play much the same role as in other physical disorders are reviewed. Vitamin and mineral deficiency diseases are covered. Schizophrenia (genetic transmission, biochemical defects, and orthomolecular treatment) and childhood schizophrenia and autism are reviewed. Also discussed are: learning disabilities; mental retardation; alcoholism; drug addiction; neuroses; allergies; and hypoglycemia. The role of psychotherapy in the treatment of biochemically induced illness is considered. 147 references. *Journal of Orthomolecular Psychiatry* (Regina), 4(4):297–313, 1975.

Progress in Research: Child Behavior Disorders.   *Rimland, Bernard*
Several concepts of treating children with behavior disorders are outlined. The use of high dosage vitamins is compared with the use of drugs to improve behavior; the former is more likely to help and less likely to cause harm. Some research on vitamin metabolism is cited. The difficulties of many autistic-type children and their families to cope with sugar and other carbohydrates in their diets is discussed. Allergies of the nervous system that may involve wheat, milk, grain cereals, citric acid, chocolate, and chicken are noted. Suggestions for coping with the problem are made. 1 reference. In: *Autism: 4th Annual Meeting of the National Society for Autistic Children.* pp. 21–32. Washington, DC: U.S. Government Printing Office, 1973. 161 pp.

Psychological Aspects of Obesity.   *Bruch, Hilde*
The psychological aspects of obesity are examined. Weight loss alone will not solve the underlying problems of living. The fat person must be made aware of the conflicts from which he has tried to escape by

excessive eating and that he needs help in growing beyond his basic sense of incompetence and helplessness. *Medical Insight,* 4(7):23, 26–28, 1973.

Pyridoxine and Trace Element Therapy in Selected Clinical Cases. *Cutler, Paul*
Pyridoxine and trace element therapy and their application to selected clinical cases are described. Vitamin-mineral disturbances are relatively common in schizophrenia, children with learning disabilities, obesity, alcoholism, and nonschizophrenic psychiatric disorders and many of these patients have been helped by orthomolecular therapy. 8 references. *Journal of Orthomolecular Psychiatry* (Regina), 3(2):89–95, 1974.

Relation between Orality and Weight. *Keith, Regina R.; and Vandenberg, Steven G.*
The psychoanalytic theory of obesity, which holds that overeating by obese individuals represents a regression to the oral stage of psychosexual development, was tested. The dynamic personality inventory of T. G. Grygier was administered to two groups of females (obese and normal weight). No significant differences between groups were found, and the tenability of the theory of obesity and suitability of the scales were questioned. 11 references. *Psychological Reports,* 35(3):1205–06, 1974.

Senility and Chronic Malnutrition. *Hoffer, A.*
The hypothesis that senility is a manifestation of chronic malnutrition is considered. Evidence drawn from previous studies and the successful treatment of senility with nicotinic acid support this hypothesis. The orthomolecular approach, including use of proper nutrition plus reinforcement with megadoses of vitamins is recommended to treat and prevent senility. 56 references. *Journal of Orthomolecular Psychiatry* (Regina), 3(1):2–19, 1974.

Starved Brains. *Lewin, Roger*
The effects of malnutrition and an impoverished environment on the development of the human brain are discussed. The stages and timing of human brain growth are described. It is noted that even moderate degrees of malnutrition produce side-effects and deficiencies that cannot be repaired by normal feeding once the brain growth spurt has passed. Studies are cited which show how nutrition and environment

are related to the physical, mental, and emotional development of children. It is concluded that the mental capacity of 300 million children is being eroded daily by a combination of malnutrition and deprived environments. Eight references. *Psychology Today,* 9(4):29–33, 1975.

Taking the Fun Out of Overeating
In an ongoing, long term study conducted in order to evaluate the role physiologic factors play in regulating food intake in both lean and obese subjects, food intake monitoring indicates obese subjects respond to external cues for feeding while normal subjects respond to internal hunger and satiety cues. Lean individuals tend to adjust consumption to caloric content and needs, maintaining weight, while obese subjects under conditions affording no external feeding cues take in fewer calories than needed, do not adjust for caloric variations in formula and lose weight. *Medical World News,* 13(29):56, 1972.

Audio Tapes

Effects of Nutrition on Behavior: Studies in Animal and Man
(Sessions I–II)
Data on the effects of different kinds of malnutrition, the effects on different species and the effects on human children in different countries. (Judy R. Rosenblith, Wheaton College; Harry F. Harlow, University of Wisconsin; etc.) $24. Each session about 3 hours long. Number 3-69. American Association for the Advancement of Science (AAAS).

Schizophrenia
Issues in the recognition and treatment of schizophrenia are examined by Dr. A. Hoffer. An explicit guide to the diagnosis and prognosis of psychotic and affective disorders, and a detailed outline of treatment by the orthomolecular paradigm are presented. The individual tape titles are: (1) The Development of a Theory of Schizophrenia; (2) Models of Schizophrenia; (3) The Diagnosis of Schizophrenia; (4) The Development of Orthomolecular Therapy; (5) Orthomolecular Therapy: Phase One; (6) Orthomolecular Therapy: Phases Two and Three; (7) The Treatment of Children; (8) Corroboration: Positive and Negative; (9) The Biochemistry of Schizophrenia; (10) The Quality of

Recovery; (11) The Genetics of Schizophrenia; and (12) The Importance of Good Nutrition in Treating Mental Illness. $7.95 each. At
1⅞ IPS. Cassette. 60 min each. 1974. Behavioral Sciences Tape Library.

Films

Drag
The childhood and teenage influences on a young man who becomes a
chain smoker. The psychology of the smoking habit. Animated.
Rental: $7.75. 9 min. 16mm. Color. 1965. Film Library–Oregon.

How We Adapt
Why is it that some live to a great age, retaining their mental and
physical health, while others seem unable to cope with the stress and
tensions of everyday living. Understanding the roles of exercise and
diet in achieving physical health, and the relationship of mind and
body in adapting to an increasingly demanding environment is a basic
concern of scientists—and all of us. Sale: $275. Rental: $20. 20 min.
Color. 1973. Films, Inc.

Human Body: Nutrition and Metabolism
Basal metabolism, active metabolism, energy requirements of
metabolism in units of calories. The five classes of chemical substances
in natural foods: carbohydrates, fats, protein, vitamins, and minerals.
Their function in body growth and repair. Rental: $10.50. 14 min.
16mm. Color. 1962. Film Library–Oregon.

Prenatal Development
The influences of heredity and prenatal environment on the development of the fetus are examined. Interviews with researchers and actual
footage of the developing fetus are combined to present up-to-date
information on this topic. Studies on the effects of malnutrition, drugs,
and maternal emotional state on the developing embryo are reported.
Sale: $295. Rental: $35. 23 min. 16mm. Optical color. 1974. Federal
Marketing Services Films, P.O. Box 7316, Alexandria, VA 22307.

Smoking and You
How smoking affects the lungs and general health of a person. Ani-

mated sequence on the throat and lungs. Rental: $7.75. 11 min. 16mm. Color. Film Library–Oregon.

You're Too Fat
Obesity is a disease of an abundant and comfortable society. Over 70 million Americans are overweight. In a culture that sets up an ideal of the slim body, overweight people feel isolated and rejected. They suffer not only psychological problems but physical ones as well. Ten to twenty pounds of excess weight increases the chances of early death by 15 percent. This study looks at some of the scientific explanations of obesity, ways of reducing from the sensible to the extreme, and possibilities of painless diets for the future. Sale: $550. Rental: $40. 52 min. Color. Films Inc.

Contacts

BOOKS

Back to Eden.   Jethro Kloss, Beneficial Books, Box 404, New York, NY 10016

Common & Uncommon Uses of Herbs for Healthful Living.   Richard Lucas, Arc Books

The Complete Book of Nutrition.   Gary Null & Staff, Dell, 1 Dag Hammarskjold Plaza, New York, NY 10017

Earth Medicine—Earth Foods.   Michael A. Weiner, Macmillan Co., 866 Third Ave., New York, NY 10022

Get Well Naturally.   Linda Clark, M.A., Arc Books, 219 Park Ave. So., New York, NY 10003

God-Given Herbs.   William K. McGrath, Historical Mennonite Faith Publications, Route 2, Seymour, Missouri 65746.

A Guide to Medicinal Plants of Appalachia.   Agric. Handbook 400, Supt. of Documents, Washington, DC 20402

Herbs for the Seventies.   Gary Null & Staff, Dell, 1 Dag Hammarskjold Plaza, New York, NY 10017

Herb Teas for Health.   Shirley A. Boie, Boie Enterprises, P.O. Box 66235, Los Agneles, CA 90066

Magic in Herbs.   Leonie de Sounin, Gramercy Publishing Co., 519 Park Ave. So., New York, NY 10016

Nature's Healing Grasses.   H.E. Kirschner, M.D., H.C. White Publications, P.O. Box 8014, Riverside, CA 92505

Nature's Medicines. Richard Lucas, Aware Books, P.O. Box 500, Farmingdale, NY 11735

Of Men and Plants. Maurice Messegue, The Macmillan Co., 866 Third Ave., New York, NY 10022

Proven Herbal Remedies. John H. Tobe, Pyramid Books, 9 Garden St., Moonachie, NJ 07074

Raw Vegetable Juices. N.W. Walker, D.Sci., Pyramid, 919 Third Ave., New York, NY 10022

MAGAZINES & NEWSLETTERS

Bestways Magazine. 466 Foothill Blvd., La Canada, CA 91011

Better Nutrition Magzine. 25 West 45 St., New York, NY 10036

Dr. Shelton's Hygienic Review. P.O. Box 1277, San Antonio, TX 78295

Eden Ranch. Betty Lee Morales, Topanga, CA 90290

The Healthway Advisor. 1920 Irving Park Rd., Chicago, IL 60613

Herald of Health. P.O. Box 552, Mount Ayr, IO 50854

Hygiene Magazine. 3519 Thom Blvd., Las Vegas, NV 98106

The Layman Speaks. 6231 Leesburg Pike, Falls Church, VA 22044

Let's Live Magazine. 444 No. Larchmont Blvd., Los Angeles, CA 90004

Natural Food News. P.O. Box 210, Atlanta, TX 75551

Natural Health Bulletin. P.O. Box 109, West Nyack, NY 10994

NHF Bulletin. P.O. Box 688, Monrovia, CA 91016

Organic Gardening. Rodale Press, 33 East Minor St., Emmaus, PA 18049

Pathways to Health. 693 Main St., Hackensack, NJ 07601

Prevention Magazine. Rodale Press, 33 E. Minor St., Emmaus, PA 18049

The Provoker. John Tobe, St. Catherines, Ontario, Canada

Report to the Consumer. Ida Honorof, P.O. Box 5449, Sherman Oaks, CA 91403

The Total You Magazine. Suite 518, 4605 Lankershim Blvd., No. Hollywood, CA 91602

Vegetarian Voice. 501 Old Harding Highway, Malaga, NJ 08328

ORGANIZATIONS & CLUBS

American Foundation for Homeopathy. 6231 Leesburg Pike, Suite 506, Falls Church, VA 22044

American Natural Hygiene Society. 1920 Irving Park Road, Chicago, IL 60613

American Physical Fitness Research Institute (APFRI). 641-A No. Sepulvega Blvd., Los Angeles, CA 90049

American Schizophrenia Association. 1114 First Ave., New York City, NY 10021

Cancer Control Society. 2043 No. Berendo St., Los Angeles, CA 90027

Center for the Study of Aging, Inc. 706 Madison Ave., Albany, NY 12208

Citizens for Health Information, Inc. 10120 Chapel Road, Potomac, MD 20854

Huxley Institute for Biosocial Research. c/o The Charlotte Moen Library, 1114 First Ave., New York, NY 10021

IACVF, International Association for Cancer Victims and Friends. 155-D So. Highway 101, Solana Beach, CA 92075

The International School of Living. Route 1, Freeland, MD 21053

Lee Foundation. 2023 W. Wisconsin Ave., Milwaukee, WI 53201

McNaughton Foundation. P.O. Box A, Sausalito, CA 94965

National Food News. P.O. Box 219, Atlanta, TX 75551

NHF, National Health Federation. P.O. Box 688, Monrovia, CA 91016

National Scleroderma Club. c/o Mrs. John Barlet, 704 Gardner Center Road, New Castle, PA 16101

Natural Health Bulletin. P.O. Box 109, West Nyack, NY 10994

North American Vegetarian Society. 501 Old Harding Highway, Malaga, NJ 08328

Price-Pottenger Nutrition Foundation. 2901 Wilshire Blvd., Suite 345, Santa Monica, CA 90403

Report to the Consumer. P.O. Box 5449, Sherman Oaks, CA 91403

Wholistic Health and Nutrition Institute. 150 Shoreline Highway, Mill Valley, CA

If you would like further information on smoking and health, write to:
The National Congress of Parents and Teachers
700 North Rush Street
Chicago, IL 60611

8

Sex

THE FIELD OF SEXOLOGY WAS dramatically brought before the public in 1948 with Alfred Kinsey's *Sexual Behavior in the Human Male*. Later, in 1953, Kinsey released his *Sexual Behavior in the Human Female*. Both of these books brought Kinsey great fame but also tremendous persecution. The public was divided; many were interested in their sexuality and were glad it was finally being studied—others were outraged and considered Kinsey to be dangerous and immoral. Some, like Senator Joseph McCarthy, even thought he was destroying the foundations on which America rested. The years 1954 to 1957 were a time of oppression and persecution to those involved in the field of human sexuality. There were no funds available for research, hate mail and public speeches condemned those involved in this research, and many suffered socially and financially because of this. In 1956 Kinsey died. He was considered by many to have been a victim of overwork and the onslaught of hate that followed the publication of his books. With McCarthy dead and discredited, 1957 initiated the period of funding and recognition of the importance of sexuality to a person's emotional well being. This same year the Society for the Scientific Study of Sex was formed, the first of its kind by professionals engaged in this field. Since then, many groups have formed, each with their own interests and publications, bringing an abundance of valuable research and knowledge. Almost all recent major studies agree with Kinsey's data; his study stands unreplicated as the most thorough study of sexuality ever conducted in the United States.

It should be stressed that almost all studies have excluded nonwhite and lower-class subjects; hopefully in the future this will be rectified. The field of sexology is relatively new, and although it has

144

had great accomplishments, it should be recognized as still being in its infancy.

Attitudes

Two-thirds of the adults polled rejected the idea that sex is primarily for pleasure—over 50 percent rated their attitudes toward sex as conservative. However, a majority of adults, 57 percent, feel that young people today have healthier attitudes toward sex than their parents. Although people are now openly discussing sex, and there is certainly a great deal more freedom in sexual matters, in reality there has been almost no change in sexual attitudes or behavior in the last thirty years. The conclusion must be that there has definitely not been a sexual revolution and society is not dominated by a permissive morality concerning sex.

Sensitivity

For women, the clitoris is the center of female sexuality, the most erogenous zone on a woman's body. In several research studies women ranked their erogenous zones as follows: clitoris, vestibule of vagina, labia minora, vagina, breasts, and labia majora. If they were given a choice, 64 percent preferred clitoral stimulation, 36 percent vaginal.

For men, the glans of the penis is the most sensitive area on the male body, the center of male sexuality.

Sexual Peak

The female reaches her sexual peak in her late twenties to early thirties; the male reaches his peak soon after adolescence.

Masturbation

Ninety-two percent of the men and sixty-two percent of the women engaged in masturbation. Educated people, regardless of gender, masturbate earlier and more frequently than less educated people.

Petting

Premarital noncoital activity has increased in the last few years but is no longer used as a compromise to intercourse. Instead it has become a brief period of education that soon transforms into coital foreplay.

Premarital Sex

Ninety-two percent of the men and fifty percent of the women had intercourse before marriage. Younger males and females reported an earlier age for first intercourse than their elders. Both genders have a later experience if they go to college. An average age for first intercourse by men is 18, women 20. More than 50 percent of the women had only one premarital coitus partner, the men had an average of six. Forty percent of the men and twenty percent of the women found their first coitus pleasurable; however, two-thirds of the women and one-third of the men had moral and emotional conflicts, and anxiety about venereal disease and unwanted pregnancy.

Foreplay

Precoital activity. The more education a male has, the more he will engage in foreplay. Foreplay is limited to ten minutes or less by 47 percent of American couples, with only 22 percent beyond twenty minutes.

Position

Kinsey found that an estimated 70 percent of the population of the United States had used only the missionary position (male superior) in intercourse. The missionary position is one of the least satisfying to both partners since it results in poor clitoral stimulation and does not allow full penetration of the penis. The female superior, lateral, and rear positions are much more satisfying to both partners.

Coitus

Married couples are engaging more frequently in intercourse than before. Coital frequency is highest among couples using modern contraceptive devices. Age and education (but not gender) are also associated with frequency; the younger and better educated have coitus more frequently. Seventy-five percent of the men had intercourse for only two minutes or less before ejaculating.

Orgasm

Vasocongestion is the process of blood moving into the pelvic area and being trapped. Muscle tension and vasocongestion are brought about by sexual stimulation; the release of these two results in orgasm. Men have a smaller area for vasocongestion than women (childbearing increases the area) and this explains why women have more intense and prolonged orgasm. It should be noted that there is no such thing as either a vaginal or clitoral orgasm. Orgasm for a woman is reached by release of vasocongestion and the muscle tension of the circumvaginal venous chambers. As soon as a woman has orgasm, the supply of blood and edema fluid is refilled, enabling multiple orgasms to result. The more orgasms a woman has the stronger they become, with women reporting the second and third to be the most pleasurable. Men who have multi-ejaculatory experiences normally report the first to be the most pleasurable. The longer the foreplay and the coitus, the more chance a woman has to reach orgasm. Only 38 percent of married women had orgasm consistently in coitus, while 95 percent reached orgasm consistently in masturbation. Methods for a woman to reach orgasm, ranked by Masters and Johnson according to intensity, are as follows: masturbation, partner manipulation, and intercourse.

Marriage

Ninety-two percent of the population were married or would eventually marry. There has been an increase in the percentage of people married in the last twenty years. The increasingly high divorce rate is usually viewed as a threat to the institution of marriage. It is not; most people remarry so it just means more partners than before. Along with the increasing marriage rate there has also been a tremendous increase in the number of people cohabiting. Between 1960 and 1970 it rose 841 percent.

Extramarital Intercourse

Kinsey found that by the age of forty over 50 percent of men and 26 percent of women have had extramarital intercourse. The highest incidence was among lower-class males, with their wives expecting it. The upper class was found to be most tolerant—the middle class the least tolerant. Many more men than women who were divorced, 51 percent to 27 percent, believed their partner's extramarital experience to be the primary factor in their divorce. Women are much more tolerant of extramarital intercourse than men, except when it is their own husband.

Swinging

Swingers are usually married, in their twenties to thirties, educated, white, and middle class. When compared to nonswingers they were found to be just as happy in their marriages, had more premarital sexual relations, made a separation between love and sex, and were less religious. In swinging, homosexuality is rare among men but common among women, usually with encouragement by the males. Oral sex, group sex, and intercourse are common, anal sex is very rare. The male is five times as often as the female the initiator of swinging. Terms: TV (transvestite), AC-DC (bisexual), B&D (bondage and discipline), S/M (sado-masochism), Roman (orgies), French (oral-genital), Greek (anal intercourse), Straight (genital sex), Gay (homosexual).

Children

Children are full sexual beings, able to reach orgasm from birth. Although a preadolescent boy is not developed enough to ejaculate he can still reach orgasm. A preadolescent girl can also reach orgasm. Modern society does not let children express their sexuality; it is denied, punished, and believed to be unnatural. The fact is, that it is totally natural, but is suppressed by uncomfortable, frightened adults. The psychological damage to children (soon to be adults) is incalculable.

Teenagers

Half the population between 15 and 19 are sexually active. More than one out of every ten teenage girls becomes pregnant each year. Six

hundred thousand babies are born each year to teenagers, 21 percent
out-of-wedlock, with less than a third of all teenage mothers wanting a
baby. The rule has been to deny contraceptives and sex education to
teenagers because it was felt this promoted sexual activity. This has
certainly not worked: the only result has been to burden many young
people with babies they neither want nor are able to cope with emotionally or financially.

Elderly

Elderly people, male and female, are capable of an active sex life well
into very old age. The most important variable is a person's attitude:
"if you want to, you can, and will." Society frowns on elderly sexuality; this strong disapproval and severe interference has hampered the
sex life of many elderly.

Sodomy

Recently the Supreme Court of the United States ruled that sodomy
statutes are constitutional. Most sodomy offenses are felonies and
prohibit anal intercourse, fellatio, or cunnilingus, no matter what the
sex of those engaged in the act. According to numerous sex surveys
over 80 percent of the adult population has engaged in at least one of
these, making the vast majority of Americans felons under the law.

Homosexuality

About 20 percent of adult females and 30 percent of adult males
have had some homosexual experience. It is estimated there are twenty
million people in the United States who are homosexual, approximately
one-tenth of the population. Great amounts of money and time have
been spent in trying to figure out the cause and cure of homosexuality. Many noted researchers feel this is totally absurd, pointing to
current information stating there is nothing psychologically wrong
with homosexuals, aside from the effects on them of a society that
is hostile to their lifestyle. In 1973, the American Psychiatric Association voted, with great debate, to take homosexuality off their list
of mental disorders. Although this is significant, homosexuality is

still regarded by many in the helping professions and by the public at large as "sick and unnatural."

Fantasy

The younger and better educated a person is the more likely he/she is to fantasize that the coital partner is someone else. Over 16 percent of the population have such fantasies, with no difference between men and women. More than 66 percent of the population have dreamed about sex, with young people more frequently than older ones, men more than women, and the better educated more than those less educated.

Incest

Kinsey felt incest was virtually nonexistent, but many researchers feel it is only hidden. At this time no one really knows the extent of incest; it is a new area of study that promises to be very difficult to examine because of severe taboos and strong reservations by participants about admitting involvements.

Male Impotence and Female Frigidity

Both are extremely common conditions in our culture. However, they should be looked at as overwhelmingly coital, since other forms of sex (manual, oral, etc.) frequently eliminate impotency or frigidity. Since our society is coitally fixated, sex is viewed from this narrow perspective, resulting in emotional problems and labeling of those who do not respond to coitus as well as they would to other forms of sex. Impotency, frigidity, and premature ejaculation occur in over half the United States population and account for almost all sex therapy cases.

Mental Health Field

The mental health field has not been a liberator of sexuality, in fact quite the opposite is true. They have labeled as sick or infantile any form of sex that is not heterosexual coitus. Women were diagnosed as frigid, infantile, or prone to hysteria if they did not move their sexuality at puberty from their clitoris to their vagina. Recently this has proved to be a cruel hoax, but many mental health professionals still believe it, as well as believing that any sexual behavior that is not coital is sick and unhealthy. Freud, the father of so much wrong information about human sexuality, is still highly regarded in this area by many therapists. The fact is that most therapists, including medical doctors, have had absolutely no training in human sexuality and are totally ignorant about it. In the entire world there is not one medical school or teaching hospital that has a department of sexology. Today the field of sex research/education is advancing the knowledge of human sexuality, but much of the mental health field is still back in the dark ages.

REFERENCES

Fong, Betty. "Swinging in Retrospect." *The Journal of Sex Research,* 1976, 8:220–37.

Kinsey, Alfred C. et al. *Sexual Behavior in the Human Male.* Philadelphia: W.B. Saunders Co., 1948.

Kinsey, Alfred C. et al. *Sexual Behavior in the Human Female.* New York: Pocket Books, 1970.

Masters, William H. and Johnson, Virginia E. *Human Sexual Response.* Boston: Little, Brown & Co., 1966.

Money, John. "The Development of Sexology as a Discipline." *The Journal of Sex Research,* 1976, 5:83–7.

Wagner, Sally. *The Institution of Marital Coitus.* Master's Thesis, California State University-Sacramento, 1974.

Wilson, Cody. "The Distribution of Selected Sexual Attitudes and Behaviors Among the Adult Population of the United States." *The Journal of Sex Research,* 1975, 2:46–64.

Books

Female Sexuality. *Chasseguet–Smirgel, Janine*
A collection of writings on female sexuality. In the introduction, different theoretical approaches to women's psychosexual development are explored to provide a background against which the reader might consider the ideas of the contributors of the book. $8.95. Ann Arbor, MI: University of Michigan Press, 1970. 220 pp.

Group Sex. *Bartell, Gilbert D.*
A middle-class, suburban group is the basis for a study of group sex. The study was in agreement with other findings indicating that: (1) swinging (mate swapping) is usually initiated by the husband; (2) swingers do not force any individual to do something against his/her wishes; (3) there is a high rate of female homosexual behavior but male homosexuality is rare; (4) there is no evidence that swingers have any more personal problems than nonswingers of similar backgrounds; (5) most swingers feel swinging has helped their marriages but do not feel it would help a marriage in trouble; (6) there is a belief by many swingers that they are honest and open about sex and that this is a desirable quality. Case material is included. $1.25. New York: New American Library, 1973. 294 pp.

Human Sexuality. *Goldstein, Bernard*
Providing the tools for distinguishing between research facts and opinions that create myths, this text offers the reader an accurate and in-depth explanation of the basics of human sexuality. The text distinguishes clearly between evidence derived from scholarly research performed on the general population and clinical observations of psychiatric patients. For each major topic, the author presents the current theories—summarizing supporting data, noting the criticisms of other researchers of the validity of particular experiments and observations, and providing references to the scholarly literature. $11.95. $8.95 (pb). New York: McGraw-Hill, 1977. 352 pp.

The Illustrated Manual of Sex Therapy. *Kaplan, Helen Singer*
In an illustrated manual of the erotic techniques most frequently employed in sex therapy, designed for professionals dealing with sexual dysfunctions among patients, the basics of sex therapy are summarized

and the nature of sexual responses of men and women, dynamics of sexual dysfunctions, and concepts of causality are discussed. A method of sexual evaluation is presented, consisting of a multidimensional formulation for treatment decisions. Typical emotional responses of patient and spouse to each of the prescribed tasks are described, and therapeutic strategies, which can be used to deal with psychological issues indicated by these emotional responses, are covered. Implications of these emotional reactions are discussed in terms of causality of sexual problems. Thirty-nine illustrations accompany the text, for didactic training and to aid in conveying to the patient the tasks assigned at each stage of treatment. $6.95. New York: A & W Publishers, 1976. 181 pp.

The New Sex Therapy: Active Treatment of Sexual Dysfunction.
Kaplan, Helen
The active treatment of sexual dysfunction is discussed. Sex therapy is seen as a task centered form of crisis intervention which presents an opportunity for rapid conflict resolution. The basic conceptual framework is multicausal and eclectic. There are numerous case studies illustrating the points discussed. It is suggested that where the sexual symptom appears to be enmeshed in more extensive psychopathology, the therapist should try to circumvent the neurotic problem and deal with the sexual difficulties. The results of sex therapy are evaluated. $17.50. New York: Brunner/Mazel, 1974.

SAR Guide for a Better Sex Life. *National Sex Forum*
A self help program for personal enrichment. A step-by-step process for people who want to explore the joy of sexuality. $5.95. Berkeley: Bookpeople, 1976. 128 pp.

Sex Change: The Achievement of Gender Identity by Feminized Transsexuals. *Kando, Thomas*
A study is presented in deviance management, describing the postoperative adjustment of 17 feminized transsexuals. It is a sociological study of the social relations of a group of transsexuals who have already undergone the sex change. Focus is on how these subjects get along postoperatively, what they do with their new lives as reborn women, and what methods they use to achieve their sexual identity. $7.50. Springfield, IL: Charles C Thomas, 1973.

Sexuality and Psychoanalysis.   *Adelson, Edward T.*
Research by scientists and psychoanalysts incorporating recent advances in the study of the physiology, anatomy, biochemistry and psychology of sexuality are discussed in relation to the original concepts of Freud and the effect the newer concepts have on psychoanalytic theory and practice. $13.95. New York: Brunner/Mazel, 1975.

Studies in Human Sexual Behavior: The American Scene.
Shiloh, Ailon (Ed.)
Basic information about the post-Kinsey American sexual scene is presented in a collection of 40 articles written from psychological, sociological, legal, and anthropological points of view. They are arranged into three divisions: (1) the study of human sexual behavior; (2) heterosexual behavior and biocultural factors; and (3) the wider range of human sexual behavior. $16.50. Springfield, IL: Charles C Thomas, 1970. 460 pp.

Articles

APA & Homosexuality.
On December 15, 1973, the Trustees of the American Psychiatric Association, by a unanimous vote (with two abstentions) stated that homosexuality shall no longer be listed as a 'mental disorder.' For a copy of this five page report, write to: APA, 1700 18th St., N.W., Washington, DC 20009.

Bisex Teamwork: Sex Therapy Today.   *Shearer, Marguerite; Shearer, Marshall; and Sproule, George*
The interview of Drs. Marguerite and Marshall Shearer, excerpted from a live radio show, is presented in a series of questions and answers regarding their approach and techniques in sex therapy. The Shearers treat primarily three types of problems: the individual who ejaculates very rapidly, not giving his female partner an opportunity to reach an orgasm; impotence; and women who have difficulty having an orgasm. The impact of publicizing sex therapy is discussed. This team emphasizes the need for sex to be understood and experienced as a natural function. If people take away value judgments on feelings, and self-expression, a feeling of acceptance will facilitate sexual ad-

justment. It is concluded that in verbal and nonverbal communication partners must be able to give, receive, take, and be taken from. *Impact,* 2(4–5), 16–19, 1973.

Counseling Parents with Sexually Active Young Teenagers.
Gadpaille, Warren J.
The parental role in intervention in adolescent sexual activities and the function of the therapist in guiding parents to a better comprehension of their position and the problems involved are discussed. Primary to the task is getting the parents to understand the real issue involved— the meaning of adolescent sexual activity. The importance of maturity over age is stressed as a determinant of when an adolescent is ready for sex. *Medical Aspects of Human Sexuality,* 8(7):127–28, 1974.

Helping Elderly Couples Become Sexually Liberated:
Psycho-social Issues. *Sviland, Mary Ann P.*
Some of society's negative social attitudes toward elderly sexuality are discussed, valuable information about the sexual capacities and activities of the elderly is provided, and a discussion on how counseling for the elderly must take into account cultural and physiological factors which affect sexuality among older persons is given. Specific treatment approaches and special considerations which are critical to effective sex therapy with the aged are discussed. 20 references. *Counseling Psychologist,* 5(1):67–72, 1975.

An Informal History of Sex Therapy. *Ellis, Albert*
A short account of the human endeavor to describe and convey sexual information over the centuries is presented. Starting with the ancients, sex therapy is traced through the Havelock Ellis generation, the "marriage manual" period, Kinsey's research, Masters and Johnson's work, to the latest developments from a variety of sources. The reasons why psychoanalysis fails to help individuals are examined, and it is predicted that cognitive behavior therapy will win out over other forms of sex therapy as additional clinical and research evidence accumulates. 43 references. *Counseling Psychologist,* 5(1):9–13, 1975.

Multivariate Approaches to Psychotherapy with Sexual
Dysfunctions. *Obler, M.*
The thesis is presented that many of the latest sex therapies, including the Masters and Johnson approach, were designed for middle-class,

married couples who are maintaining a relatively stable relationship. It is suggested that most people with sexual problems are single, have unstable relationships, and often cannot afford the expense of treatment. It is suggested that flexible treatment programs, which use the most effective techniques at each specific stage of therapy, must be designed. Further, carefully controlled research is essential to provide empirical data on the success of therapy. Findings are presented on research. Nine references. *Counseling Psychologist,* 5(1):55–60, 1975.

Sex Knowledge Test Instrument
An interview test instrument to determine the level of factual knowledge about sex possessed by mentally retarded adolescents has been initiated for future use in education programs and counseling young retarded persons. Available from: National Association for Retarded Children, 2709 Avenue E East, P.O. Box 6109, Arlington, TX 76011.

Sex in Psychotherapy: The Myth of Sandor Ferenczi.
Kaplan, Alexandra G.
The impact of sexual relations in terms of the theory or practice of psychotherapy is discussed, with focus on the psychoanalytic theory of Sandor Ferenczi, which has been used in justifying sexual relations in psychotherapy. It is felt that Ferenczi is invalid. Sex in psychotherapy is concluded to parallel and highlight the traditional and problematic status of women within a sexual relationship. 15 references. *Contemporary Psychoanalysis,* 11(2):175–87, 1975.

Sex Therapy in the 1970s.   *Renshaw, Domeena C.*
The types and treatment of sexual dysfunctions are surveyed, exploring the development of treatment methodologies to the present. The common sexual dysfunctions are listed, and the qualities of male and female orgasm are considered. The basic principles of the Masters-Johnson sex therapy are surveyed and discussed. Although the Masters-Johnson method has been termed simplistic, it has produced remarkable improvements in sexual functioning. Common factors which should be sought by the clinician when confronted with cases of sexual dysfunction are briefly examined, and the therapist is cautioned to observe the personal and cultural background of each patient before treatment is begun. 13 references. *Psychiatric Opinion,* 12(5):6–11, 1975.

Sex Therapy: Making It as a Science and an Industry.
Holden, Constance
The rapid spread of sex therapy programs is discussed, a few programs
are briefly described, and issues relating to research, training and
therapy in sexology are suggested. It is noted that most programs are
based on techniques developed by Masters and Johnson. The chief
controvery relating to training and clinical work on sex relates to
quality control in sex counseling. Training, accreditation and licensing
procedures are discussed in terms of public protection, integrity of the
field, and insurance reimbursement. *Science,* 186(4161):330–34,
1974.

Sexual Dysfunction: A Four-Approach Treatment Utilizing Peer
Pressure. *Codner, Rhoda Rand; and Gustafson, Donald Allen*
Four approaches to sex therapy are discussed: didactic information,
behavior modification, insight, and fantasy. Each approach is examined in reference to its values and limitations, and to its particular
advantages and disadvantages in a group setting. Several useful concepts which can be used in conjunction with these approaches, such as
sensate focus, aggressive physical exchanges, and the Gestalt "hot
seat," are examined. The superiority of an eclectic approach to
therapy is suggested. One reference. *Marriage and Family Counselors
Quarterly,* 10(1):1–10, 1975.

The Sexual Fantasies of Women. *Hariton, E. Barbara*
From a study of the sexual fantasies of women it was concluded that
erotic fantasies are common among women, that they are not escape
mechanisms, and that they often enhance sexual desire and pleasure.
Participants in the study were 141 women from upper-middle-class
New York suburbs who ranged in age from 25 to 50. The study was
carried out through both questionnaires and interviews. *Psychology
Today,* 6(10):39–44, 1973.

The Sexual World of the Adolescent. *Elias, James E.;
and Elias, Veronica D.*
Data gathered from adolescents concerning self-image and sexuality
and attitudes about masturbation, petting, and sexual intercourse are
presented. The strong influence of the family in determining the adolescent's values and behavior suggest that families might best serve to
guide and counsel, rather than to criticize young people as they learn

about sexuality, and thus prevent some of the psychological disturbances that develop later. *Counseling Psychologist,* 5(1):92–97, 1975.

Sexuality and the Severely Disabled Person.   *Smith, Jim; and
Bullough, Bonnie*
Specific questions are offered for nurses who are interested in either
primary or secondary sex counseling for disabled people. It is asserted
that a major cause of frustration and anxiety among the severely disabled is fear of sexual inadequacy. The importance of sex counseling
for the disabled is emphasized, and the primary need to find a mate
who is willing to work through the problems involved is noted.
Guidelines are offered for counseling the disabled. 14 references.
American Journal of Nursing, 75(12):2194–97, 1975.

Audio Tapes

Call Off Your Old and Tired Ethics
Addressing herself to the question of which one is the criminal, the one
who pays or the one who lays, Margo St. James, president of
COYOTE, the first civil rights organization for prostitutes, argues
against the arrest of prostitutes unless there is a complaining witness
and for the decriminalization of prostitution. $9. 60 min. 1974. Big
Sur Recordings.

Co-Marital Sex: Beyond Swinging, Swapping & Sexual Deviance
An exploration of some recent research findings concerning the
emergence of what are conveniently presumed to be deviant patterns
and styles of marriage. The speakers attempt to reorient this common
theoretical perspective by showing that research to date does not support the conception that these styles and patterns can be understood
primarily in terms of deviance vs. normalcy. Albert Ellis and Barbara
Taylor. $9. 90 min. 1972. Big Sur Recordings.

Dealing with Sexual Material
A symposium on the inner feelings of the therapist when dealing with
sexual material. Participants are Dr. Albert Ellis (on premarital sex),
Dr. Harold Greenwald (on sexual approaches from patients), Mrs.

Virginia Satir (sexual material in family therapy), and Dr. Arthur Sea-
gull (on risk-taking in psychotherapy). $10 including script. $1 extra
scripts. Cassette. 30, 30 min. AAP Tape Library.

Homosexual Marriage: Pro and Con
A debate over whether homosexuals should be allowed to marry. In
this program, it is argued that the legalization of homosexual marriage
would benefit society by providing means of stabilizing the personal
relationships of some 15 million Americans, while on the other hand it
is argued that such legalization would "mimic and debase the institution of the family." $16.95. 52 min. Center for Cassette Studies.

Incest: The Last Word in Taboos
A documentary, with Miriam Kennedy of McGill University's forensic
clinic, psychiatrist Dr. Julian Bigras of the Albert Prevost Institute in
Montreal, and an anonymous woman who lives with the memory of
an incestuous past. $12.95. 30 min. Center for Cassette Studies.

Lesbian-Feminist Dialogue
After two years of dispute during which lesbians accused various
women's groups of discriminating against them and attempting to
bury the lesbian question, a conference was called to make amends
with straight women. This exploration of the politics of the conflict is
also an exploration of the feelings that gay and straight women have
towards each other and towards life, with comments by Gloria
Steinem and Jill Johnston. $14. 65 min. Pacifica Tape Library.

New Attitudes on Homosexuality
Dr. Howard Brown discusses the ending of old stereotypes. Dr.
Brown, a professor of medicine at New York University, was one of
the first to break that silence and publicly admit his homosexuality.
Here he describes his life both before and after he "came out of the
closet." $16.95. 56 min. Center for Cassette Studies.

Report on Pornography
The Chairman of the National Committee on Obscenity and Pornography, Dr. William B. Lockhart, assesses the committee's findings;
namely, that people are not influenced in their behavior by hearing,
seeing or reading pornography. $12. 41 min. Pacifica Tape Library.

Films

About Sex
This film for adolescents deals with such common concerns as sexual fantasies, body growth, masturbation, homosexuality, birth control, abortion and the responsibilities of both sexes. It received the Blue Ribbon Award in 1973 for the best film on sex education at the American Film Festival sponsored by the Educational Film Library Association. Sale: $290. 24 min. 16mm. Color. 1973. Herman Engel, Texture Films, Inc., 1600 Broadway, New York, NY 10019.

Give to Get
The act of sexual intercourse is portrayed with special emphasis on the technique of genital massage and the use of body lotion. Genital massage is applied to the male, bringing him to a swift erection. This technique may be of great value in therapy with the impotent male. The latter portion of the film demonstrates intercourse on a water bed. Throughout the film the couple are at ease and not hurried. Sale: $175. Rental: $30. 11 min. 16mm. Optical color. 1970. Multi Media Resource Center, 340 Jones St., Box 439 E, San Francisco, CA 94102.

A Three Letter Word for Love
This film presents problems related to sex education with adolescents and stresses the difficulties which this group has in gaining clear information. Although not specifically related to group techniques, the film portrays discussion of sex information in a group. Sale: $330. 30 min. 16mm. Sound. Color. Herman Engel, Texture Films, Inc., 1600 Broadway, New York, NY 10019.

Unwed Mothers in Today's World
This film gets in touch with the feelings, fears, and loneliness of four young women who discuss informally with a counselor their experience as unwed mothers. The film emphasizes the need for sensitive counseling and sound prenatal care, and presents convincing evidence of the need for sex education. Sale: $225. Rental: $25. 28 min. 16mm. Optical. Color. 1972. Lawren Productions, Inc., P.O. Box 1542, Burlingame, CA 94010.

Contacts

CERTIFICATION

The American Association of Sex Educators and Counselors has recently established certification standards for sex therapists. For a copy of their standards and a list of AASEC-certified sex therapists in your area, write:
Sex Therapy Certification Committee
American Association of Sex Educators and Counselors
5010 Wisconsin Ave., N.W., Suite 304
Washington, DC 20016
They also have many publications of interest.

Another organization that has strict certification and membership requirements for sex therapists is:
Eastern Association of Sex Therapy (EAST)
10 East 88th St.
New York, NY 10028

Erickson Educational Foundation. 1627 Moreland Avenue, Baton Rouge, LA 70808. Information on all aspects of transsexualism.

Institute for Sex Research. 416 Morrison Hall, Indiana University, Bloomington, IN 47401
The research collections of the Institute for Sex Research (popular name: Kinsey Institute) are available to any qualified researcher with demonstrable research needs. The Information Service processes requests for information and provides the following types of services by mail: requests to visit the collections; bibliographic searches; copying of requested materials; referrals to individuals engaged in similar research; assistance in locating materials; gathering of specific information; and other related services. While the Information Service does not provide free pamphlets or packets of materials, it does have available a number of subject bibliographies, prepared in response to frequent requests at very low cost. Bibliographies on more specific topics can be obtained by contacting the Information Service and clearly outlining the scope of your research.
The Institute for Sex Research Library currently holds approximately 34,000 volumes, adding about 500 books and 1500 re-

prints of articles to its behavioral science collection each year. It also subscribes to about 60 journals primarily in the fields of psychiatry, psychology and sociology. Comprehensive coverage, including historical works and current research, has been attempted in topics related to sex behavior such as:

Disorders due to surgery, injury, etc.	Masturbation	Sex Ethics
	Orgasm	Sex Knowledge
Erotica Research	Pedophilia	Sex Laws
Exhibitionism	Prostitution	Sex Offenders
Fetishism	Sadism	Sex Response
Homosexuality	Sex Attitudes	Transsexualism
Incest	Sex Counseling	Transvestism
Masochism	Sex Dysfunctions	Voyeurism

Partial coverage is also available for the following topics:

Abortion	Family	Sex Differences
Anthropology	Gender Identity	Sex Education
Aphrodisiacs	Intersex	Sex in the Mass-Media
Biography	Marriage	Social History
Censorship	Nudism	Symbolism
Contraception	Psychosexual	Venereal Disease
Divorce	Development	Witchcraft
Drugs	Religion and Sex	Women
	Sex Customs	

In addition, the library has a collection of erotic literature and art, of records and tapes, and of ephemeral sex materials such as "girlie magazines," underground press publications, advertisements, and articles clipped from newspapers and magazines.

The Institute for Sex Research Archive Collections contain approximately 25,000 pieces of flat art, 10,800 slides of erotic art, 1,300 art objects, 1,500 films, and 50,000 photographs. In scope it covers both fine art representations of the erotic motif and the simplest dime-store novelty representation of the same theme. An attempt has been made to cover the full range of erotic production, and to gather examples from historical periods and cultures. The collections have been classified into a geographic and historical sequence. The Archives also include a collection of medical and pseudo-medical devices related to sex, collections of prison art, psychotic art, and children's art. The films and photographic collections include representative examples from the early development of the erotic theme in these media to the most recent representations and themes.

Continuing Education

The Institute for Sex Research has held an annual training program each summer since 1970. The Reproductive Biology Research Foundation (4910 Forest Park Blvd., St. Louis, MO 63108) offers several programs each year. Further listings of programs are published in various professional journals with an extensive listing appearing in *SIECUS Report*. (See Journals listing.)

SEX BEHAVIOR JOURNALS

Archives of Sexual Behavior. Subscription orders to: Plenum Publishing Corp. (see appendix). $19 (individual); $54 (institution). 6 issues per year.

Forum: The International Journal of Human Relations. Subscription orders to: Forum Subscription Dept., 155 Allen Blvd., Farmingdale, NY 11735. $10. 12 issues per year.

Gay Sunshine Press. Journal and books. Box 40397, San Francisco, CA 94140.

Homosexual Counseling Journal. Subscription orders to: HCCC, Inc., 30 East 60th St., New York, NY 10022. $10 (individual); $15 (institution). 4 issues per year.

Journal of Homosexuality. Subscription orders to: Haworth Press, Inc., 174 Fifth Ave., New York, NY 10010. $12 (individual); $25 (institution). 4 issues per year.

Journal of Sex Education and Therapy. Subscription orders to: American Association of Sex Educators and Counselors, Suite 304, 5010 Wisconsin Ave., N.W., Washington, DC 20016. Free (members); $6 (nonmembers).

Journal of Sex and Marital Therapy. Subscription orders to: Human Sciences Press, 72 Fifth Ave., New York, NY 10011. $15 (individual); $35 (institution). 4 issues per year.

Journal of Sex Research. Subscription orders to: Charles Ihlenfeld, M.D., Treasurer, Society for the Scientific Study of Sex, Inc., 12 West 72nd St., New York, NY 10023. $20/year. 4 issues per year.

Medical Aspects of Human Sexuality. Subscription orders to: Hospital Publications, Inc., 609 Fifth Ave., New York, NY 10017. $25. 12 issues per year.

SIECUS Report (The Sex Information and Education Council of the United States). Subscription orders to: Behavioral Publications, 72 Fifth Ave., New York, NY 10011. $9. 6 issues per year.

Sex News. P. K. Houdek, 7140 Oak, Kansas City, MO 64114. $4 per year, $4.50 if invoice is required. 12 issues per year.

Sexology. Subscription orders to: SXO Corporation, 200 Park Ave. South, New York, NY 10003. $10. 12 issues per year.

Sex Roles: A Journal of Research. Subscription orders to: Plenum Publishing Corp., 227 West 17th St., New York, NY 10011. $14 (individual); $35 (institution).

SEX THERAPISTS / SEX CLINICS

Center for Sex Education and Medicine, 4025 Chestnut St., Director, Harold Lief, M.D., Philadelphia, PA 19104

Human Sexuality Program, University of California Medical School, San Francisco, CA 94143

Loyola University Foster McGaw, Hospital Sexual Dysfunction Clinic, Domeena Renshaw, M.D., Director, 2160 S. First Ave., Maywood, IL 60153

Mount Sinai Medical School, Program in Human Sexuality, Paul Schiavi, M.D., Director, 11 East 110th St., New York, NY 10029

Payne Whitney Clinic of New York Hospital, Sex Therapy and Education Program, Helen Singer Kaplan, M.D., Ph.D., Director, 525 E. 68th St., New York, NY 10021

Reproductive Biology Research Foundation, William Masters, M.D., and Virginia Johnson, 4910 Forest Park Blvd., St. Louis, MO 63108

Philip E. Veenhuis, M.D., and Joanne Veenhuis, M.A., 1220 Dewey Ave., Wauwatosa, WI 53213

The Whitman-Radclyffe Foundation, 2131 Union St., San Francisco, CA 94123. Provides social service activities, legal/constitutional research, public information campaigns, and regular mailings of information on the area of homosexual men and women. Write for information on their services and activities.

Alcohol*

9

ANALYSIS OF SOCIAL CLASSES shows that rates of frequent, heavy drinking and rates of infrequent drinking are higher in lower socioeconomic groups. Alcoholism and drinking problem rates tend to be low among groups whose drinking habits are well integrated with the rest of their culture.

Farm owners have the lowest proportion of heavy drinkers. Professionals and businessmen have the highest proportion of drinkers. Semiprofessional men have the highest proportion of heavy drinkers. Among women who drink, service workers have the highest proportion of heavy drinkers.

There is a high proportion of heavy drinkers among Catholics. Jews had the lowest proportion of abstainers, a large proportion of light drinkers and the lowest proportion of heavy drinkers. Liberal Protestants were similar to Catholics, while conservative Protestants had the largest proportion of abstainers and the lowest proportion of heavy drinkers among the four groups.

As far as education and heavy drinking are concerned: 6 percent of heavy drinkers have grammar school educations; 13 percent have postgraduate training; and 15 percent have college education.

Enlisted men and officers in the Army drink more than civilians of the same age. In the Navy, enlisted men were more often heavy and problem drinkers than officers who drank. In both the Army and Navy populations, about 3 percent were nondrinkers, compared to 23 percent of civilian men.

Separated persons have higher rates of problem drinking than do single or divorced persons. Alcoholism is less frequent among elderly

*with Rose L. Reiwitch

persons than among the young, but some people become problem drinkers in later life and for reasons specifically connected with aging.

Men and Women

A breakdown of men and women in the United States shows the following: Men—31 percent abstainers or infrequent drinkers, 30 percent light drinkers, 24 percent moderate drinkers, 15 percent heavy drinkers; Women–51 percent abstainers or infrequent drinkers, 33 percent light drinkers, 12 percent moderate drinkers, 4 percent heavy drinkers.

In alcoholism, women and men differ in the following ways: the hospital referral is usually due to domestic stress for women, and employment difficulties for men; the duration of alcoholism prior to treatment is shorter for women; women usually drink in the home, whereas men drink more often in public establishments; females have more problems with sexual inadequacies than men; females had previously received more psychiatric treatment, had more suicide attempts, more marital disruption, and had experienced more traumatic childhoods, but the appearance of alcoholism came later in life for women than men; the presence of depression is more common for women; and while men prefer group therapy with informal contact with fellow patients (such as in Alcoholics Anonymous), women are more responsive to individual therapy, such as interviews with a psychotherapist. The most successful treatment for women alcoholics includes her family in the therapy.

The Family

It is estimated that one of 15 persons over age 18 in the United States is suffering from alcoholism. Each of these victims adversely affects the lives of at least four other persons—a wife or husband, children, other relatives, an employer, or friends. In a nationwide survey (NIAAA) one out of five people interviewed said that someone close to them drinks too much, and that this heavy drinking has gone on for at least ten years. In an outpatient clinic for alcoholism most of the patients still had a wife and children, but the family was in some stage of disorganization.

When the mother is alcoholic, the children describe both parents as unable to have a strong, satisfying relationship either with the spouse or their children. The nonalcoholic father is described as being too busy doing his own job and his wife's to pay attention to the children. These marriages seemed to be held together by extreme neurotic interaction, apathy, and fear. The children of these marriages felt more deeply affected by disharmony and rejection, than excessive drinking.

The backgrounds of the children of alcoholics and the backgrounds of alcoholics themselves are strongly similar, including alcoholism of a parent, financial difficulty, premature assumption of adult responsibilities, parental rejection, and parental incompatibility. At times the intensity of the tragedy and conflict is more severe with the spouse and the children than with the alcoholic.

Health

Alcoholics more frequently fall victim to all sorts of illness, directly and indirectly connected with alcohol. Their life span is reduced by as much as ten to twelve years. The risk of developing cancer of the mouth, throat, esophagus, and other sites having direct contact with, particularly, strong alcohol solutions, is increased by prolonged heavy drinking and is even increased further still when combined with heavy smoking. Primary liver cell cancer is also more frequent with alcoholic cirrhosis. Alcoholic cardiomyopathy, a disease of the heart muscle, can be caused by even moderate amounts of alcohol. In the long known association between heavy alcohol intake and liver disease, the first and most common effect is fatty liver. It is usually reversible with withdrawal of alcohol, but sometimes is suspected of causing sudden death. Alcoholic hepatitis, a more serious condition, causes severe pathological alterations in the structure and function of the liver. The most serious condition is cirrhosis, a degenerative, often fatal, liver disease which can occur if drinking is not stopped. Alcohol abuse is implicated as a primary or related causal factor in many pathological conditions including: brain disorders such as Wernicke's syndrome, Korsakoff's psychosis, niacin deficiency, and Marchiafava's disease; disorders of the digestive system, such as malabsorption of vital nutrients, gastritis, pancreatitis, fatty liver, hepatitis, and cirrhosis; generalized myopathy and cardiomyopathy, numerous nutritional diseases in addition to some of the encephalopathies, including polyneuropathy, beriberi heart, pellagra, scurvy, and anemia; atrophy of some endocrine glands; disturbances of metabolism that may aggravate or precipitate such conditions as gout and hypoglycemia; increased risk of accident, injury, and death from intake of other drugs that interact additively or potentiatively with alcohol.

Hazards

There is a strong association between problem drinking and driving problems. Alcoholic drivers had nearly twice as many crashes and traffic citations as nonalcoholic drivers. Alcoholic drivers involved in accidents more frequently had alcoholic parents, marital problems, were over 20 and under 69, and were mostly male, than nonalcoholics. Fatal and other crashes of teenagers and young adults also frequently involve hazardous amounts of alcohol.

There is a relationship between alcohol intake and a variety of crimes. Crimes of physical violence are associated with intoxicated persons: stabbings 11 to 1; carrying concealed weapons 8 to 1; and other assaults 10 to 1.

Social Cost

The epidemic health and social problem of alcohol misuse and alcoholism drains an estimated $25 billion from the American economy each year and the figure is probably conservative. This is about 68 times the amount spent by the federal government on prevention and control of all health problems. The specific cost areas are:

Loss of production	$9.35*
Health and medical	8.29
Motor vehicle accidents	6.44
Alcohol programs and research	.64
Criminal justice	.51
Social welfare	.14
	$25.37

* In billions of dollars per year.

These figures only hint at the personal cost suffered by alcoholics and their families.

The Issue

Fifty percent of mental hospital admissions of males 46 to 64 years old are for alcoholism. Some hospitals have found that as many as 50 percent of their inpatients in various service categories, orthopedic or general medicine, for example, were admitted because of an involvement with alcohol.

The causes of alcoholism are unknown. Most probably, the condition reflects a response to an interactive combination of psychological, environmental, and sociological factors in an individual. The alcoholic is a medically, socially ill person and has no place being introduced into the criminal justice system for punishment any more than any other sick individual. The alcoholic should be treated.

The most essential part of a treatment program is to pull together for the individual patient the potential healing forces that are available in any community. It seems clear that no single treatment approach or method has been demonstrated to be superior to all others for the treatment of alcoholism. This viewpoint is consonant with that of most investigators, i.e., alcoholism is not a unitary disease condition treatable by a single therapy. There is a tendency, because of this, for alcoholics to become involved in the "revolving door" system (jail, hospital, welfare, courts). Alcoholics have been treated as criminals by the legal system and as mentally disordered by the medical systems, but rarely as alcoholics, with any differentiated special attention being paid to the alcoholic syndrome itself. Except for the use of Antabuse and the method used by Alcoholics Anonymous, the treatment modalities employed were those available for other psychological disturbances including:

Individual therapy
Group therapy
Family therapy
Milieu therapy
Drug therapy
Aversion therapy
Transactional analysis
Behavior modification

Treatment for alcoholics is provided by many facilities in the community:

State alcoholism programs
Outpatient clinics

General hospitals
Private psychiatric hospitals
General practitioners
Psychiatrists in private practice

Emergency care services for the alcoholic should perform these three essential functions: sophisticated diagnosis; physical detoxification; effective referral to other medical, psychiatric and social needs. Successful alcoholism programs are those that have an aggressive outreach program. Current data show that alcoholism is treatable. A variety of treatment strategies should be available in each community, and they should be used discriminately by care-giving personnel. A community oriented program should be aware of the differences among the patients, as well as their interactions with society, and systematically seek to fit the appropriate treatment to each individual.

REFERENCES

"Alcohol Use on the Rise." *Sacramento Bee Newspaper,* January 7, 1976.

Cork, R. *The Forgotten Children.* Toronto: Paper Jacks, 1969.

Curlee, J. "Sex Differences in Patient Attitude Toward Alcoholism Treatment." *Quarterly Journal of Studies on Alcoholism,* 32(1), 1971.

Economic Costs of Alcohol Related Problems, Rockville, MD: National Clearinghouse on Alcohol Information, 1974.

Glasscote, R.M., et al. *The Treatment of Alcoholism: A Study of Programs and Problems.* Washington, DC: American Psychiatric Association, 1967.

O'Briant, R.G. and Lennard, H.L. *Recovery from Alcoholism: A Social Treatment Model.* Springfield, IL: Charles C Thomas, 1973.

Pavloff, G. (ed.). *Proceedings: On Alcoholism Emergency Care Services.* Washington, DC: DHEW, 1972.

Rathod, N.H. and Thomson, I.G. "Women Alcoholics: A Clinical Study." *Quarterly Journal of Studies on Alcoholism,* 32(1), 1971.

Scott, E.M. *Struggles in an Alcoholic Family.* Springfield, IL: Charles C. Thomas, 1970.

Siegal, H.H. *Alcoholic Detoxification Programs: Treatment Instead of Jail.* Springfield, IL: Charles C. Thomas, 1973.

Treating Alcoholism: The Illness, the Symptoms, the Treatment. Washington, DC: DHEW, 1974.

U.S. Dept. of Health, Education & Welfare. *First Special Report to the U.S. Congress on Alcohol and Health.* Rockville, MD: National Institute on Alcohol Abuse and Alcoholism, 1971.

U.S. Dept. of Health, Education & Welfare. *Proceedings of the National Conference of Vocational Rehabilitation & State Alcoholism Directors.* Washington, DC: Rehabilitation Services Administration, 1973.

U.S. Dept. of Health, Education & Welfare. *Second Special Report to the U.S. Congress on Alcohol and Health.* Rockville, MD: National Institute on Alcohol Abuse and Alcoholism, 1974.

"What Price Alcohol?" *Sacramento Bee Newspaper, Parade,* January 4, 1976, p. 6.

Who Cares About an Alcoholism Program in the General Hospital? Chicago: American Hospital Association, 1972.

Books

Alcohol: Drink or Drug? *Hyde, Margaret O.*
The author provides information about the positive and negative aspects of alcohol and discusses current research findings on the treatment and prevention of alcoholism. New York: McGraw-Hill, 1974. 157 pp.

Alcoholism in Industry. *Trice, Harrison M.*
Some basic outlines for a successful alcoholic employee rehabilitation program are discussed. The author presents conclusions derived from personal interviews with company executives, personnel managers, industrial nurses, union officials, and other key people from a variety of businesses and industries. New York: Christopher D. Smithers,1972. 77 pp.

Alcohol: Our Biggest Drug Problem ... And Our Biggest Drug Industry. *Fort, Joel*
Topics discussed include the effects of alcohol on the body, the history of alcohol, cultural drinking habits, causes of alcoholism, treatment, education, and prevention. $4.95. New York: McGraw-Hill, 1973. 185 pp.

Employee Assistance Program Training Manual and Supervisor's Guide. *Frey, Wayne; and Conboy, Carol Ann*
The authors present a guide designed to outline various aspects of a supervisor's role in an industrial alcoholism treatment program. Concord, NH: New Hampshire Division of Public Health, 1973. 88 pp.

The Person with Alcoholism. *Sexias, F.; Cadoret, R.; and Eggleston, S.*
Twenty-five papers on various aspects of alcoholism and its treatment are presented. Psychiatric, behavior and cognitive aspects of chronic alcohol abuse are examined. Various treatment modalities are described, including many innovative alternatives to contemporary therapeutic approaches, such as meditation and biofeedback. Other therapeutic procedures which are discussed include reality therapy, family therapy, videotaping, pastoral counseling, psychodrama, and group therapy. $25. New York: Annals of the New York Academy of Sciences, 1974. Vol. 223. 177 pp.

Second Special Report to the U.S. Congress on Alcohol and Health: New Knowledge. *U.S. Department of Health, Education and Welfare: National Institute on Alcohol Abuse and Alcoholism*
An appendix is devoted to prevention of alcoholism in the United States utilizing cultural and educational forces. The Secretary of HEW recommends that knowledge about alcohol and alcoholism be made more readily available for use by specialists and the public; that educational resources for professionals and schools be developed and expanded. 550 references. DHEW Pub. No. (ADM)75-212. Washington: Superintendent of Documents, U.S. Government Printing Office, 1975. 170 pp.

Skid Row: An Introduction to Disaffiliation. *Bahr, Howard M.*
This study draws together the extensive popular and research literature on the skid row alcoholic person, with special emphasis on the conditions which determine and perpetuate his disaffiliation from society. $6. New York: Oxford University Press, 1973. 335 pp.

What You Must Know About Drugs.
It is pointed out that alcohol is the most easily obtained, used and abused drug in the English-speaking world. A teaching guide is included. New York: Scholastic Book Services, 1971. 184 pp.

Articles

AA and the Alcoholic Employee.
Methods available to management for overcoming alcoholism among employees include utilizing an AA counselor and establishing their own AA group. Alcoholics Anonymous World Services, Inc., Box 459, Grand Central Station, New York, NY 10017. 1962. 24 pp.

Al-Anon Family Groups. *Ablon, J.*
This paper describes Al-Anon meeting format and group behavior in a west coast metropolitan area, and analyzes the operational principles which underlie the Al-Anon process. 19 references. *American Journal of Psychotherapy,* 29:30–45, 1974.

Alcoholism. *Chafetz, Morris E.*
A general discussion of alcoholism highlights such topics as history of alcohol, attitudes toward alcohol, a definition of alcoholism, preven-

tion and education efforts, early detection and diagnosis, organizing a community program, treatment, followup, and evaluation. 27 references. In: Bellak, L. (ed.). *A Handbook of Community Psychiatry and Community Mental Health*. $14.50. New York: Grune and Stratton, 1974. pp. 163–82.

Alcoholism and the Criminal Justice Population.   *Pavloff, George G.*
The author presents an overview of criminal justice systems, a detailed statistical analysis of crimes related to alcohol or alcoholism, and raises questions about the feasibility of improving treatment programs and facilities. 53 references. In: *NIAAA Seminar on Alcoholism Detection, Treatment, and Rehabilitation Within the Criminal Justice System*. Washington, DC: National Institute on Alcohol Abuse and Alcoholism, 1973. 18 pp.

Behavioral Assessment in Alcoholism Research and Treatment: Current Techniques.   *Miller, Peter M.*
The author reviews and discusses a variety of medical, social, psychodynamic, and behavioral approaches used in alcoholism therapy. 20 references. *International Journal of the Addictions*, 8(5):831–836, 1973.

Charismatic Leadership in Alcoholics Anonymous: A Case Study. *Groves, David H.*
The dynamics of an AA group and its leadership were studied for a 4-year period. *Quarterly Journal of Studies on Alcohol*, 33(3):684–691, 1972.

Clinical Application of Behavior Therapy in the Treatment of Alcoholism.   *Bhakta, Mohan*
In a discussion of behavior therapy as related to treatment of alcoholism, seven therapeutic techniques are listed. 24 references. *Journal of Alcoholism*, 6(3):75–83, 1971.

Elderly Alcoholic.   *Zimberg, S.*
A review of the literature concerning the extent of the problem of alcoholism among the elderly is presented. 11 references. *Gerontology*, 14(3):221–224, 1974.

Electrical Aversion Therapy with Alcoholics: An Analogue Study. *Miller, Peter M.; Hersen, Michael; and Eisler, Richard M.* The authors report that electrical aversion therapy did not produce any significant changes in reduced alcohol consumption or attitudes toward alcohol among chronic alcoholic patients. 15 references. *Behavior Research and Therapy*, 11(4):491–497, 1973.

Female Alcoholic. *Fraser, Judy* The influence of the women's liberation movement on the drinking habits of women and its contribution to elucidation of the problem of alcoholism among women are discussed. *Addictions*, 20(3):64–80, 1973.

The Key Role of Labor in Employee Alcoholism Programs. The significant contributions made by labor unions to successful company alcoholism programs are outlined and opinions of several labor leaders are included. New York: Christopher D. Smithers Foundation, 1970. 32 pp.

Management Guide on Alcoholism and Other Behavioral Problems. This company's program is described: supervisors are trained, not as experts in alcoholism, but as skilled observers with ability to correct performance problems; organizations and publications to provide assistance are listed. Public Relations Dept., Kemper Insurance Group, 4750 N. Sheridan Road, Chicago, IL 60640.

Social Modification of Drinking by Alcoholics. *Alterman, A.; Gottheil, E.; and Skoloda, T.* A 6-week experimental treatment program allowed alcoholic persons the option of abstinence or drink. 5 references. *Quarterly Journal of Studies on Alcohol*, 35(3):917–924, 1974.

Study of Alcoholism in Half Siblings. *Schuckit, Marc A.; Goodwin, Donald A.; and Winokur, George* For each comparison of genetic and environmental factors, the genetic factor seemed more closely associated with the development of alcoholism. 16 references. *American Journal of Psychiatry*. 128(9): 122–126, 1972.

Treatment of Alcoholism by Physicians in Private Practice.   *Jones, Robert W.; and Helrich, Alice R.*
Findings of a survey of 88,302 private physicians are presented. 2 references. *Quarterly Journal of Studies on Alcohol,* 33(1):117–131, 1972.

Audio Tapes

Alcohol through the Ages
William M. Usdane traces the history of intoxicating beverages. In this lecture Mr. Usdane tells the story of alcohol and its place in each of the world's great civilizations. $14.95. 28 min. Center for Cassette Studies.

Alcoholism and the Clinic
How alcoholics can be helped by medical institutions. In this discussion several specialists involved in the clinical rehabilitation of alcoholics consider ways in which the disease can be identified and arrested. $14.95. 27 min. Center for Cassette Studies.

Alcoholism and the Family
The surrogate families available to rehabilitated alcoholics. On this cassette a clergyman who has involved his church in this work and counselors at the Alpha Quarterway House discuss the ways they have created artificial families for alcoholics. $14.95. 27 min. Center for Cassette Studies.

Alcoholism and the Man
An executive explains his firm's innovative approach. In this program John Matheus, a vice-president of a progressive Milwaukee firm, describes the program his company has devised to detect and defeat alcoholism before it becomes a major problem. $14.95. 25 min. Center for Cassette Studies.

Alcoholism and the Teenager
Teenagers describe their problem and their rehabilitation. Here two teenagers tell how that situation has affected them, and two experts on the problem tell how it is affecting the country. $14.95. 26 min. Center for Cassette Studies.

Alcoholism and Therapy
Doctors discuss innovative treatments of alcoholism. Two of the most innovative and successful of these facilities, the Southwood Mental Health Center in California and the Tidewater Psychiatric Institute in Virginia, are examined in this program. $14.95. 27 min. Center for Cassette Studies.

Alcoholism and the Woman
Two women tell sad stories with happy endings. In these moving and cautionary tales of two near-disastrous experiences, the listener will learn how to recognize alcoholism's danger signals as well as the humiliating consequences of ignoring them. $14.95. 27 min. Center for Cassette Studies.

Films

Alcohol—Drug of Choice
This film examines the causes of alcoholism and reports on several detoxification and rehabilitation programs. Producer: NBC. Sale: $325. Rental: $23. 25 min. 16mm. Color. 1973. Films Incorporated.

Alcohol: Our Number One Drug
Dramatic sequences illustrate the life-shattering effects often produced by "hidden alcoholics." Complementing the dramatic portion of the film, documentary sequences complete a comprehensive view of the danger of misusing alcohol. Rental: $7.75. 11 min. 16mm. Color. 1973. Film Library–Oregon.

Problem Drinking: A Call to Action
A typical day in one community's fight against alcoholism—Reading, Pennsylvania's program. Providing speakers and experts for schools and community groups, assisting the police to handle alcoholics as sick people, and helping industry to handle the problems. The rehabilitation facet of referral for those who need it. Rental: $12.75. 25 min. 16mm. Color. 1970. Film Library–Oregon.

Contacts

NATIONAL ORGANIZATIONS

All of the following national organizations have extensive publications (many are free or at very low cost) as well as many other services. Write for information.

Alcohol and Drug Problems Association of North America (formerly the North American Association of Alcoholism Programs). 1130 Seventeenth St., N.W., Washington, DC 20036.

Local Alcoholics Anonymous chapters and Al-Anon Family Groups are also listed in virtually every telephone book. For further information you may wish to contact the national headquarters: Al-Anon Family Groups Headquarters, Inc., P.O. Box 182, Madison Square Station, New York, NY 10010. Alcoholics Anonymous, P.O. Box 459, Grand Central Station, New York, NY 10017.

National Council on Alcoholism, Inc. 2 Park Avenue, New York, NY 10016. This organization has a list of major nonprofit organizations in many cities that can refer clients to private physicians, as well as public and private agencies providing treatment for alcoholism. Some of these referral organizations not only provide generalized information services, but also have individualized counseling and treatment services.

The National Institute on Alcohol Abuse and Alcoholism maintains a state-by-state listing of most private and public treatment facilities currently available. For the appropriate list, write to: National Clearinghouse for Alcohol Information, P.O. Box 2345, Rockville, MD 20852.

The Salvation Army. 120 West 14 St., New York, NY 10011. Most facilities sponsored by this organization provide food, shelter, or rehabilitation and take the form of halfway houses. In some areas, the Salvation Army provides a broad range of other services.

Veterans Administration, Alcohol and Drug Dependent Service. 810 Vermont Ave., N.W., Washington, DC 20420. Any veteran who is eligible for VA medical benefits may receive alcoholism treatment at no charge. Treatment of acute intoxication for alcohol-related problems is available at any VA hospital in the country. A number of VA hospitals now also offer special comprehensive treatment programs for the disorder.

STATE ORGANIZATIONS

ALABAMA
Alcohol Program Contact, Alabama State Alcoholism Program, 145 Moulton St., Montgomery, AL 36104 (205) 265-2301

ALASKA
Alcohol Program Contact, Division of Mental Health, Office of Alcoholism, Pouch H, Juneau, AK 99801 (907) 465-3020

ARIZONA
Alcohol Program Contact, Division of Behavioral Health Services, Alcoholism Program, 2500 East Van Buren St., Phoenix, AZ 85008 (602) 271-4525

ARKANSAS
Office on Alcohol Abuse and Alcoholism, 1515 West 7th St., Suite 202, Little Rock, AR (501) 371-2003

CALIFORNIA
Alcohol Program Contact, Office of Alcohol Program Management, 825 15th St., Sacramento, CA 95814 (916) 445-1940

COLORADO
Alcohol and Drug Abuse Authority, 4210 East 11th Ave., Denver, CO 80220 (303) 388-6111

CONNECTICUT
Alcohol Program Contact, State Alcohol Advisory Council, 90 Washington St., Hartford, CT 06115 (203) 566-3424

DELAWARE
Alcoholism Services, 3000 Newport Gap Pike, Wilmington, DE 19808 (302) 998-0483

DISTRICT OF COLUMBIA
Alcohol Program Contact, Department of Human Resources, District Building, Washington, DC 20004 (202) 629-5443

FLORIDA
Division of Mental Health, Bureau of Alcoholic Rehabilitation, 1323 Winewood Blvd., Room 324, Tallahassee, FL 32301 (904) 499-8922

GEORGIA
Alcohol & Drug Services, 618 Ponce de Leon Ave., Atlanta, GA 30308 (404) 894-4785

GUAM
Alcohol Program Contact, Division of Mental Health, Guam Memorial Hospital, Agara, Guam 96910

HAWAII
Alcohol Program Contact, Advisory Commission on Drug Abuse and Controlled Substances, Governor's Office, State Capitol, Honolulu, HI 96813 (808) 531-1907

IDAHO
Alcohol Program Contact, Division of Field Operations, Statehouse, LBJ Building, Room 343, Boise, ID (208) 384-2336

ILLINOIS
Department of Mental Health, James F. Griffin, Jr., Program Policy Advisor for Alcoholism, 188 West Randolph St., Room 1900, Chicago, IL 60601 (312) 793-2907

INDIANA
Alcohol Program Contact, Division of Addictive Services, 3000 West Washington St., Indianapolis, IN 46222 (317) 633-4777

IOWA
Alcohol Program Contact, Division of Alcoholism, Lucas State Office Building, Des Moines, IA 50319 (515) 281-5604

KANSAS
Commission on Alcoholism, Ward A. Rogers, Executive Director, 535 Kansas Ave., Room 1106, Topeka, KS 66603 (913) 296-3991

KENTUCKY
Alcohol Program Contact, Bureau of Health Services, 275 East Main St., Frankfort, KY 40601 (502) 564-3970

LOUISIANA
Mental Health Division, William P. Addison, M.D., Director, 655 North Fifth St., Baton Rouge, LA 70804 (504) 389-5791

MAINE
Bureau of Rehabilitation, Office of Alcoholism and Drug Abuse Prevention, Marilyn L. McInnis, Director, 32 Winthrop St., Augusta, ME 04330 (207) 289-2141

MARYLAND
Division of Alcoholism Control, Maxwell N. Weisman, M.D., Director, 2305 No. Charles St., Baltimore, MD 21201 (301) 383-2784

MASSACHUSETTS
Division of Alcoholism, Edward Blacker, Ph.D., Director, 755 Boylston St., Boston, MA 02116 (617) 536-6983

MICHIGAN
Office of Substance Abuse Services, J. Irvin Nichols, Director, 1019 Trowbridge Rd., East Lansing, MI 48823 (517) 373-8600

MINNESOTA
Alcohol Program Contact, Metro Square Building, Room 402, Saint Paul, MN 55101 (612) 296-4610

MISSISSIPPI
Alcohol Program Contact, Division of Alcohol Abuse and Alcoholism, 125 Lelia Court, Jackson, MS 39216 (601) 982-6436

MISSOURI
Alcoholism Section, Joel W. Donovan, Acting Director, 722 Jefferson St., Jefferson City, MO 59601 (314) 751-4122

MONTANA
Alcohol Services Division, Robert L. Soloman, Administrator, Cogswell Building, Helena, MT 59601 (406) 449-3176

NEBRASKA
Alcohol Program Contact, Division of Alcoholism, Box 94728, Lincoln, NE 68509 (402) 471-2231

NEW HAMPSHIRE
Program on Alcohol and Drug Abuse, Jesse E. Trow, Exec. Director, 61 South Spring St., Concord, NH 03301 (603) 271-3531

NEW JERSEY
Alcoholism Control Program, William J. Chamberlain, Chief, P.O. Box 1540, John Fitch Plaza, Trenton, NJ 08625 (609) 292-8947

NEVADA
Alcohol Program Contact, Bureau of Alcohol & Drug Abuse, Capitol Complex, 1803 No. Carson St., Carson City, NV 89701 (702) 885-4790

NEW MEXICO
Alcohol Program Contact, New Mexico Commission on Alcoholism, PO Box 1731, Albuquerque, NM 87103 (505) 877-1000

NEW YORK
Division of Alcoholism, John R. Butler, Assistant Commissioner, 44
Holland Ave., Albany, NY 12208 (518) 474-5417

NORTH CAROLINA
Department of Mental Health, R.J. Blackley, M.D., Deputy Commissioner on Alcoholism, P.O. Box 26327, Raleigh, NC 27611 (919)
733-4670

NORTH DAKOTA
Division of Alcoholism and Drug Abuse, Richard D. Elefson, Director,
320 Avenue B, East, Bismark, ND 58501 (701) 224-2767

OHIO
Alcoholism Unit, Terrance J. Boyle, Chief, 450 East Town St., P.O.
Box 118, Columbus, OH 43215 (614) 466-3543

OKLAHOMA
Alcohol Program Contact, Division on Alcoholism, 408-A North
Walnut St., Oklahoma City, OK 73105 (405) 521-2811

OREGON
Alcohol Program Contact, Alcohol & Drug Section, Mental Health
Division, 2570 Center St., N.E., Salem, OR 97310 (503) 378-2163

PENNSYLVANIA
Alcohol Program Contact, Governor's Council on Drug & Alcohol
Abuse, Office of the Governor, Commonwealth of Pennsylvania, 2101
No. Front St., Harrisburg, PA 17110 (717) 787-9857

PUERTO RICO
State Alcoholism Program, Carlos A. Aviles Roig, M.D., Box 1276,
Hato Rey, PR 00919 (809) 764-6573

RHODE ISLAND
Alcoholism Coordinator, Myra Jones, Rhode Island Medical Center,
Box 8281, Cranston, RI 02920 (401) 464-3291

SAMOA, AMERICAN
Comprehensive Health Planning, Charles McCuddin, Director, Pago
Pago, American Samoa 96920

SOUTH CAROLINA
Alcohol Program Contact, South Carolina Commission on Alcohol &
Drug Abuse, P.O. Box 4616, Landmark East, 3700 Forest Dr., Suite
300, Columbia, SC 29240 (803) 758-2521

SOUTH DAKOTA
Division of Alcoholism, Richard Barta, Acting Director, Office Building No. 2, State Capitol, Pierre, SD 57501 (605) 224-3459

TENNESSEE
Section on Alcohol and Drugs, William Howse, Director, 300 Dordell Hull Building, Nashville, TN 37219 (615) 741-1921

TEXAS
Alcohol Program Contact, Texas Commission on Alcoholism, 809 Sam Houston State Office Building, Austin, TX 78701 (512) 475-2577

TRUST TERRITORY OF THE PACIFIC ISLANDS
Alcohol Program Contact, Division of Mental Health, Saysan, Marianas Islands

UTAH
Alcohol Program Contact, Division of Alcoholism & Drugs, 554 So. 300 East Street, Salt Lake City, UT 84111 (801) 328-6532

VERMONT
Alcohol Program Contact, Alcohol & Drug Abuse Division, 81 River St., Montpelier, VT 05602 (802) 828-2721

VIRGINIA
Bureau of Alcohol Studies and Rehabilitation, Thomas R. Dundon, Ph.D., M.P.H., Director, James Madison Building, 109 Governor St., Richmond, VA 23219 (804) 770-3082

VIRGIN ISLANDS
Mental Health Services, Eldra L.M. Shulterbrandt, Director, P.O. Box 1442, St. Thomas, VI 00801 (809) 774-0117

WASHINGTON
Alcohol Program Contact, Office of Mental Health, P.O. Box 1788, Olympia, WA 98504 (206) 753-5866

WEST VIRGINIA
Division of Alcoholism and Drug Abuse, Raymond E. Washington, Director, State Capitol, Charleston, WV 25302 (304) 348-3616

WISCONSIN
Bureau of Alcoholism and Other Drug Abuses, Frank N. Coogan, Director, 1 West Wilson St., Madison, WI 53702 (608) 266-3442

WYOMING

Mental Health and Mental Retardation Services, Cone J. Munsey, Ed.D., Director, State Office Building, Cheyenne, WY 02001 (307) 777-7351

Drugs* 10

History

THE USE OF DRUGS is as old as the history of man. In the United States special periods have had special drug abuse problems. During the Civil War opium was used medically, and since its addictive properties were not clearly understood, many wounded soldiers became addicted. Following the Civil War, the practice of opium smoking became popular on the West Coast and spread to many urban areas.

Throughout this century, there were periodic "drug scares" created by the use of cocaine at the turn of the century, heroin in the 1920s, marihuana in the 1930s, and heroin again in the 1950s. The 1960s saw a social explosion of drug use of all kinds from LSD to heroin and marihuana.

Treatment

Many programs exist for drug abuse treatment and related problems. They come from a variety of sources: federal (Veterans Administration), state (Department of Justice, State Office of Narcotics and Drug Abuse, State Department of Education), county mental health services, school programs, law enforcement, and a large number of private groups. These private groups include religion-oriented programs (Salvation Army, Youth for Christ, Teen Challenge), quasi-religious or-

*with Les Bowman and Kristina Martin. Acknowledgment to the United States Government for material we have used copiously in this report.

185

ganizations (Synanon, and Scientology), drop-in and residential homes, private hospitals, and other social services (YMCA, Lions).

The types of services they provide include: referral (hotline, switchboard, information services, legal assistance); emergency services (detoxification, withdrawal talk-down, shelter, free clinic, other medical/psychiatric); and rehabilitation which includes methadone maintenance, group counseling, individual and family counseling, medical/psychiatric treatment, vocational/employment rehabilitation, residential care, drop-in centers, and consultation and advice. Most of these services do not require payment.

It appears that drug treatment programs are biased in favor of the male patients. At the National Drug Abuse Conference in 1975, the following information was revealed. It appears that drug treatment center staff feel that the women patients' main problems stem from unsatisfactory interpersonal heterosexual relationships, so the female patients are encouraged to develop stable ties. The staff's theory on their male patients is that their main problems stem from unsatisfactory competence in achievement areas, so the male is given vocational training education, and aided in finding satisfying jobs. The reality is that the main problem voiced by both male and female patients is lack of money and a satisfying job. If both men and women were given equal opportunities and vocational training, women in the drug programs would be more satisfied, and helped toward developing more independence and self-assurance.

The mental health profession is one of the greatest of drug abusers. The most common therapy treatment today is chemotherapy (drugs). Unfortunately, drugs do not alleviate the underlying problems, they only temporarily relieve the symptoms, and they produce various negative side effects. Antidepressant drugs are used to relieve mild to moderate cases of depression. Stimulants are used to relieve depression, fatigue, and especially for treatment of obesity. A growing problem among housewives is the use of amphetamines to maintain a positive mood level, reduce the appetite, and maintain their energy level. Adverse side effects are tolerance build-up (regular use of the drug necessitates increased doses to get the same results), increased irritability, restlessness, jitteriness, and eventually the long-term effect is the development of hostility and suspiciousness or paranoia. Tranquilizers are prescribed for the relief of tension and anxiety. Barbituates are sometimes used to relieve anxiety and tension, but more often for insomnia and to produce a state of relaxation.

It seems logical that alternatives to drugs should relate to the motives which drive persons toward experimentation with or continued use of drugs. Therefore it seems essential to attempt an understanding of the motives for drug preference. The reasons for drug dependency vary among individuals, which in turn leads to different choices of drugs and patterns of usage.

Summary of Drug Use

The following information has been taken from material prepared by Abelson and Fishburne (1976):

Marihuana: Of all the psychoactive drugs studied, marihuana is the substance which the public is most likely to have experienced. Among youth (age 12–17), about one in five (22.4 percent) report having used marihuana and about half of these (12.3 percent) report current use. For adults (age 18 and over) the prevalence rate (21.3 percent ever used) is similar to that of youth but the adult current rate (8 percent) is substantially lower.

The proportion of 12–17-year-olds who have ever used marihuana (22.4 percent) did not increase over the twelve months following the 1974 study. Beginning with the first national study in 1971, lifetime prevalence estimates for youth are: 1971–14 percent; 1972–14 percent; 1974–23 percent; 1975/6–22.4 percent.

The prevalence figure among all adults of 21.3 percent represents an increase of 2.3 percent over the 1974 study. This slight increase continues the gradual upward trend in lifetime prevalence among adults (1971–15 percent; 1972–16 percent; 1974–19 percent; 1975/6–21.3 percent).

In the current study, overall levels of youth and adult experience are quite similar. However, this masks the fact that marihuana use is strongly related to age. Among the adult public, young adults between ages 18 through 25 have more experience with marihuana than older adults, those age 26 and over. In fact, more than half the young adults have used marihuana while about one in eight older adults have experienced it. Those age 18 through 25 also have higher current use rates. Fully one in four in this age group are current users compared to one in twenty-five older adults.

The fact that 18–25-year-olds report the highest level of marihuana experience coincides with other age-related findings. In every psychoactive drug studied, young adults form the highest experience cohort.

Hashish: One in ten 12–17-year-olds, and a similar proportion of all adults, have ever used hashish. Among young adults, the proportion rises to three in ten, whereas only one in twenty-five older adults report hashish experience. Current use: youth, 2.8 percent; all adults, 1.4 percent; young adults, 5.6 percent; older adults, less than .5 percent.

Inhalants: 8.1 percent of the 12–17 age group report having had experience with inhalants, with .9 percent current use. Among all adults, 3.4 percent ever used with less than .5 percent current use. Comparable figures for those age 18–25 are 9.0 percent and .5 percent. Among those 26 years and over, the figures are 1.9 percent and less than .5 percent.

Hallucinogens: Among youth and all adults, one in twenty have experienced hallucinogens. However, adult experience differs dramatically by age; one in six young adults has ever used hallucinogens compared to one in fifty older adults. Current use: youth, .9 percent; all adults, less than .5 percent; young adults, 1.1 percent; older adults, less than .5 percent.

Cocaine: 3.4 percent of 12–17-year-olds have had cocaine experience and 1.0 percent report current use. Of all adults, 4.1 percent have ever used, and .7 percent are current users. Among 18–25-year-olds, 13.4 percent have cocaine experience and 2.0 percent are current users. Comparable figures for those 26 years and over are 1.6 percent and less than .5 percent.

Heroin: Half of one percent (.5) of youth and 1.2 percent of all adults have experienced this substance. Among young adults and older adults, the prevalence figures are 3.9 and .5 percent, respectively. Current use is less than .5 percent for any age group studied (12–17, 18–25, 26–34, 35+).

Methadone: Of the 12–17 age group, .6 percent, and .8 percent of all adults had ever used methadone. Among young adults and older adults, the prevalence figures are 2.3 percent and less than .5 percent, respectively. Current use is less than .5 percent for each of the four age groups.

Other Opiates: In the 12–17-year-old group, 6.3 percent had ever used other opiates and 2.3 percent were current users. Of all the adults, 5.3 percent have had experience with other opiates, and .5 percent were current users. Prevalence among 18–25-year-olds rises to 14.0 percent and 1.3 percent current users. Comparable figures for those age 26 and over are 2.9 percent and less than .5 percent.

Nonmedical Use of Psychotherapeutic Drugs

In terms of experience, nonmedical use of psychotherapeutic drugs ranks second to marihuana among youth and all adults. One in ten young people and one in seven adults report having some nonmedical experience with an over-the-counter or prescription sedative, tranquilizer, or stimulant. Among 18–25-year-olds, fully one-fourth report such experience, whereas one in eight of those age 26 and over have used a psychotherapeutic drug for nonmedical purposes. Current use rates are: youth, 2.0 percent; all adults, 3.2 percent; young adults, 8.2 percent; older adults, 1.8 percent.

The public tends to have more experience with nonmedical use of *prescription* drugs than with nonmedical use of *OTC* (over the counter) drugs. Among youth, 7.5 percent have used a prescription drug nonmedically, while 5.5 percent have used an OTC drug nonmedically. Comparable proportions for all adults are 11.4 percent and 6.4 percent, respectively. Among 18–25-year-olds, the proportions rise to 22.0 percent and 11.5 percent, whereas for those age 26 and over, the proportions drop to 8.6 percent and 5.0 percent.

Social Cost

An estimate of the cost of drug abuse indicates a current cost of $10 billion annually. This is a conservative figure subject to change as better methodologies for measuring the extent of the problem are developed.

Simply stated, social cost is a function of the number of people currently abusing drugs and the effect of their drug abuse. To help us understand the extent to which drug abuse exists in our society, we must look at supportive evidence which indicates the magnitude of the problem. Examples of phenomena suggestive of dramatic changes in the number of abusers can be found on both national and local levels. For example, there has been a ten-fold increase in hepatitis related to intravenous drug use; a fact which demonstrates the rapidity with which profound changes in drug abuse can occur. In addition, there are several other illustrations of the extent of the susceptibility of America's population to heroin addiction. The finding that 20 percent of the enlisted men in the Army released from Vietnam in September 1971 reported themselves addicted to heroin, and Washington, DC's report that 20 percent of the young men born in 1952 were treated for heroin addiction between 1970 and 1973, both indicate a high potential vulnerability.

In the past, estimates were limited by the lack of information in important areas that affect the total costs of drug abuse. Most estimates focused exclusively on the relationship of heroin addiction to property crime. Out of context, the crime factor has fostered negative stereotypes and unnecessary generalizations about heroin users, further complicating the data.

The current cost of $10 billion annually does not include the indirect costs of individual, family, and community impairment or welfare, insurance, and public health costs associated with drug abuse. The estimates of drug abuse costs are just beginning; obviously these other categories must be measured. With that in mind, the estimate of $10 billion annual cost in the United States is broken down as follows:

Health Costs: Within this category, the number of primarily drug-related emergency room visits, inpatient general care, and mental hospital days devoted to the treatment of drug disorders accounted for almost $200 million.

Productivity Losses: For those drug abusers who are employed or looking for work, productivity losses of approximately $1.5 billion can be assumed, based on the number of drug-related deaths and consequent foregone earnings; number of drug-related inpatient hospital days resulting in foregone productivity costs; and estimated number of unemployed individuals whose unemployment is associated with drug use.

Criminal Justice System Costs: The proportion of state and local police salaries, estimated share of state and local legal, court and correction costs, and Federal correction costs devoted to drug-related crime and offenders total $620 million.

Property Loss: The drug-related social cost of income-producing crime committed to support heroin habits is estimated at $6.3 billion. This figure is derived by multiplying the number of addicts times the days per year of heroin use times the average cost per day of habit times a fencing factor for stolen goods.

Direct Program Costs: Government and private efforts devoted to drug abuse education, treatment, rehabilitation, and drug prevention cost an estimated $1.1 billion annually.

A second important area for consideration is that of improved assessment of the size of the drug abuse population. With the exception of the cost component for "Property Losses Attributable to Drug Abuse" which pertains to heroin addiction only, both opiate and nonopiate social costs, as available, were estimated. However, the combined drug abuse costs may not reflect the situation accurately in every instance. Until recently, the federal government focused on the prevention of heroin addiction as its top priority. Consequently, far more information is available on the heroin addict than on the nonopiate abuser. This is reflected in the heavy representation of heroin-related data in this estimate. Now, however, we can begin to understand and calculate the size of the population who are primarily nonopiate abusers, exclusive of alcoholics. Exploratory studies suggest that this group of "polydrug" abusers may include between 2 and 2.5 million citizens. As these numbers are scrutinized and refined, an account of the "polydrug" factor can be made in future social cost estimates.

Understanding any social phenomenon involves a recognition that it is a process rather than an event which occurs at a given point in time. A few years ago, the field of drug abuse was in its infancy, largely devoid of information about the nature, course, or effects of drug abuse. Since then, viable systems have been developed to expand and quantify knowledge of drug abuse. This process will lead to improvement in social cost estimates. Despite these limitations, though, the current figure is significant for several reasons. It helps to view the drug abuser in a social context and to understand how his behavior affects our institutions, expenditures of government funds and the quality of life in our communities. Likewise, the social cost estimate serves as a barometer of United States attempts to grapple with the drug abuse situation and provides a measure against which evaluation of prevention efforts can be made.

An estimate of the problem is a necessary first step. It shows the effects on individuals and society, and the necessity for applied research to continue.

Types of Drugs

The following is a list by Pawlak (1974) of the most commonly used drugs:

Barbiturates:
Classification: Depressant
Overdose potential: High when taken in large numbers or mixed with alcohol.
Physical addiction: Yes, high.
Method of consumption: Ingestion, in capsule or tablet form, occasionally injected.

Amphetamines:
Classification: Stimulant
Overdose potential: Possible, but generally not fatal. Long term damage to body and mind can result through prolonged use. Overdose and death possibility increase when injected, due to impurities in drug.
Physical addiction: No, but there are serious effects when the chronic user stops the drug use. Tolerance does occur.
Method of consumption: Ingested or injected, capsules, powder, or tablets.

Cocaine:
Classification: Stimulant
Overdose potential: Improbable, unless used intravenously.
Physical addiction: Debatable, speed-like, no withdrawal.
Method of use: Snorting (sniffing), also intravenous.

Marijuana and Hashish:
Classification: Mild hallucinogen is possible, but classification also referred to in some respects as relaxant, appetite enhancer, etc. Actually, this drug may defy rigid classification completely.

Overdose potential: None
Physical addiction: None
Method of use: Smoked, occasionally ingested.
Common forms: Green leafy plant substance (marijuana). Solid brown substance (hashish) which may vary from very hard to crumbly. Strengths vary primarily due to climatic influences on growth, as well as general variations of plant types.

PCT and Angel Dust:
Classification: Tranquilizer anesthetic with hallucinogenic properties.
Overdose potential: Yes, alone or in combination with alcohol or "downers."
Physical addiction: Possible with extended use.
Common forms: Caps, tabs, powder, usually sold as "THC," occasionally "Mescaline."

LSD:
Classification: Hallucinogen
Overdose potential: Clinically, none.
Physical addiction: None
Method of use: Ingestion
Common forms: Tablets, capsules, paper squares, gelatin squares.

Morning Glory Seeds:
Classification: Hallucinogen
Overdose potential: Clinically, none. Chemical coating on certain types will produce adverse effects.
Physical addiction: None
Method of use: Ingestion

Mescaline/Peyote:
Classification: Hallucinogen
Overdose potential: None
Physical addiction: None
Method of use: Organically (peyote), by chewing peyote buttons or grinding up into capsules. Synthetically, available only as white needlepoint crystals, two to three doses per gram.

Psilocybin:
Classification: Hallucinogen

Overdose potential: None
Physical addiction: None
Method of use: Mushrooms, fresh or dried. (Note: frozen chopped up
mushrooms are really LSD, but are peddled as psilocybin.)

Belladonna:
Classification: Poison in large doses, analgesic in minute doses (cold
tablets, etc.).
Overdose potential: Yes
Physical addiction: Unlikely
Common forms: Contact capsules, etc. (low dosage), asthmador
(strong), and Jimson weed (very strong).

Heroin:
Classification: Opiate
Overdose potential: Yes, due to unknown dosage levels, occasionally
due to impurities in the cutting agents.
Physical addiction: Yes, high.
Method of use: Injection, also snorting (sniffing).

REFERENCES

Abelson, Herbert and Fishburne, Patricia. *Non-medical Use of Psychoactive
Substances.* Rockville, MD: National Institute on Drug Abuse, September,
1976.
Cohen, A. *Alternatives to Drug Abuse: Steps Toward Prevention.* Rockville,
MD: National Clearinghouse for Drug Abuse Information, 1973.
"Drug Use Shows No Signs of Decreasing." *Sacramento Bee Newspaper,*
February 27, 1976, p. A13.
DuPont, R. *Federal Strategy for Drug Abuse and Drug Traffic Prevention
1975.* Washington, DC: U.S. Gov't. Printing Office, 1975.
Levy, S.J. and Broudy, M. "Sex Role Differences in the Therapeutic Commu-
nity." *Second Annual National Drug Abuse Conference—Workshop on
Women in Treatment.* New Orleans, 1975.
Levy, S.J. and Doyle, K.M. "Attitudes Toward Women in Drug Abuse Treat-
ment." *Journal of Drug Issues,* Fall, 1974.
The National Drug Abuse Treatment Utilization Survey. Rockville, MD: National Institute on Drug Abuse, September, 1975.
Pawlak, Vic. *Conscientious Guide to Drug Abuse.* Phoenix: Do It Now Foun-
dation, 1974.

Social Cost of Drug Abuse. Rockville, MD: National Institute on Drug Abuse, December, 1974.

"Young People Turn to Drugs at an Earlier Age." *Sacramento Bee Newspaper,* October 1, 1975, p. A20.

Books

Connections: Notes from the Heroin World.   *Gould, L.C.;
Crane, L.E.; Walker, A.L.; and Lidz, C.W.*
Using quotations from their field notes, a lawyer and three sociologists
describe how people involved in the use and control of heroin perceive
themselves and each other. $12.50. New Haven: Yale University Press,
1974. 268 pp.

Drug Abuse Control: Administration and Politics.   *Rachin, R.L.;
and Czajkoski, E.H.*
A collection of seven essays dealing with drug abuse, drug abuse
causes, methods of drug abuse prevention and control, drug treatment,
and the effects of drug control legislation. $14.50. Heath Lexington
Books, 125 Spring St., Lexington, MA 02173, 1975. 194 pp.

Drug Abuse: Psychology, Sociology, Pharmacology.
Hafen, Brent Q. (Ed.)
A collection of readings from the literature on drug abuse and related
problems is presented. Provo, UT: Brigham Young University Press,
1973. 610 pp.

Drug Abuse in Industry.   *Carone, Pasquale, A.; and Krinsky,
Leonard W. (Eds.)*
The many disciplines of medicine, psychiatry, psychology, and
neuropathology, plus the expertise of labor, management, and state
enforcement agencies are brought together in this major overview on
drug abuse and alcoholism in industry. 69 references. $11.50.
Springfield, IL: Charles C Thomas, 1973. 190 pp.

**Drug Experience, Attitudes, and Related Behavior Among Adolescents
and Adults, Part I: Main Findings**
Multi-drug study which ranges over commonly used and approved
substances such as cigarettes and alcoholic beverages, to selected
pharmaceuticals to more esoteric and illicit substances of current concern. Response Analysis, Research Park, Route 206, Princeton, NJ
08540, 1973. 200 pp.

Drug Use, the Labor Market and Class Conflict.   *Helmer, John; and Vietorisz, Thomas*
Narcotics use is analyzed in relation to labor market conditions, and it is argued that narcotics use is one of several interrelated social responses to labor market failure. A historical survey shows that the socioeconomic pattern of narcotics use is the same as it was a century ago, and that the problem of widespread addiction is a recurrent and cyclical one. 46 references. $1.25. Washington, DC: Drug Abuse Council, 1974. 44 pp.

Drugs and the Criminal Justice System.   *Inciardi, J.A.; and Chambers, C.D.*
A collection of 10 papers which provide a multidisciplinary investigation of the effect of drug law enforcement, treatment of the drug abuser, and the relationship of crime and drug abuse. $7.50. Beverly Hills: Sage Publications, Inc., 1974. 249 pp.

Drugs and Youth: Medical, Psychiatric and Legal Facts.
Coles, Robert; Brenner, Joseph; and Meagher, Dermot
Medical, legal, and psychiatric aspects of drugs and drug use are discussed. Descriptions of various drugs, including the nature and effects of the substances, are presented. Advice on how to protect oneself if confronted with the enforcement of drug use laws is included. Social and cultural factors contributing to drug use among adolescents are explored. This book is especially oriented toward parents and young people. $2.95. New York: Liveright, 1971. 258 pp.

Guide to Films (16MM) About the Use of Dangerous Drugs, Narcotics, Alcohol and Tobacco
Synopsis of 230 films and 60 filmstrips dealing with drugs, narcotics, alcohol and tobacco. Alexandria, VA: Serina Press, 1971. 61 pp.

Psychiatric Complications of Medical Drugs.   *Shader, Richard I.*
Data on the psychic effects of drugs often prescribed by physicians are presented. Literature on the psychic effects of digitalis, resperine, belladonna alkaloids and synthetic anticholinergics, antituberculosis agents, levodopa, various hormones, oral contraceptives, amphetamines, vitamins, and placebos is reviewed. Drugs alone are not sufficient cause for mental and behavioral symptoms. Management of toxic effects and therapeutic benefits of some drugs for the emotion-

ally disturbed are discussed. $14.50. New York: Raven Press, 1972.
394 pp.

Research Advances in Alcohol and Drug Problems, Vols. 1–3.
Gibbins, R.; Israel, Y.; and Kalant, H. (Eds.)
Comprehensive information about the causes and consequences of
drug and alcohol use is presented. Vol. 1, $25.50; Vol. 2, $25.; Vol. 3,
$31. Toronto, Canada: John Wiley and Sons, 1974. 427 pp.

Stoned Age: A History of Drugs in America.   *Rublowsky, John*
The author offers a historical perspective on the use of drugs in the
United States as the first step in alleviating what he believes to be the
most intractable social problem of our age. $2.95. New York: G.P.
Putnam's Sons, 1975. 218 pp.

**Therapeutic Effectiveness of Methadone Maintenance Programs in the
Management of Drug Dependence of Morphine Type in the USA.**
Wilmarth, S.S.; and Goldstein, A.
This document provides an overview of the history and pharmacological effects of methadone, discusses the rationale of methadone maintenance, and describes the features and outcomes of three methadone
programs. $6.80. Geneva, Switzerland: World Health Organization,
1974. 53 pp.

Articles

**Alcohol and Drug Abuse Among Native American Youth on
Reservations: A Growing Crisis.**   *Pinto, Leonard J.*
The author examines the complex problems of alcohol and drug abuse
among American Indian youth and reviews relevant research in this
area. 50 references. *Drug Use in America: Problem in Perspective,*
Appendix, Vol. 1. Washington: Superintendent of Documents, U.S.
Government Printing Office, 1973. pp. 1151–1178.

Alcohol and Drug Abuse: Causes of Sudden Death.
Keeley, Kim A.; Kahn, Peter; and Keeler, Martin H.
Mortality associated with substance abuse was investigated in a review
of DOA and emergency room sudden deaths in a metropolitan area
over a two-year period. It was found that three of four sudden death

and DOA patients with substance abuse histories had visited the emergency room at least once within six months of their deaths; this figure was higher than that for death involving patients with other psychiatric symptoms, and significantly higher than that for death from medical and other causes. *Scientific Proceedings: 126th Annual Meeting of the APA,* Washington, DC: American Psychiatric Association, 1973.

But It's Against the Law.   *Fort, Joel*
The history and efficiency of federal and state laws to control drug use are discussed. The Harrison Act of 1914, the Volstead Act, the Marihuana Tax Act of 1937, the Narcotic Drug Control Act of 1956. The effects of two presidential commissions and legal tests of existing law, as well as federal bureaucratic reorganization and legislation are discussed. The author claims that severe penalties have not proven efficient as a deterrent. In: *The Pleasure Seekers,* Fort, J. pp. 67–96. $6.50. Indianapolis: Bobbs-Merrill, 1969. 255 pp.

Poly-Drug Abuse: Drug Companies and Doctors.   *Kunnes, Richard*
The author asserts that, in recent years, a new form of polydrug abuse has emerged as a direct consequence of efforts by pharmaceutical companies to bolster their profits. *American Journal of Orthopsychiatry,* 43(4):530–532, 1973.

Parent-Child Drug Abuse: Generation Continuity or Adolescent Deviancy?   *Tech, Nechama*
Based on a review of the literature as well as a survey of adolescents, the authors examine the relationship between parent and child drug usage. *Adolescence,* 9(35):351–364, 1974.

Patrolmen and Addicts: A Study of Police Perception and Police-Citizen Interaction.   *Coates, R.B.; and Miller, A.D.*
It was observed that officers considered 50 to 75 percent of the total crime in the community to be related to heroin addiction. Negative opinions were expressed with respect to addicts, methadone maintenance, and the "permissiveness" of the courts in their treatment of addicts. *Journal of Police Science and Administration,* 2(3):308–321, 1974. International Association of Chiefs of Police, 11 Firstfield Road, Gaithersburg, MD 20760.

Personality Dynamics of Heroin Use.   *Kurtines, William; Hogan, Robert; and Weiss, Daniel*
Fifty-nine white male heroin addicts were compared with 26 psychiat-

ric patients, 142 incarcerated delinquents, 37 undergraduate marihuana users, and 108 police officers, using the California Psychological Inventory. The results suggested that the heroin users were relatively normal in terms of social poise and self-esteem; however, they were significantly more hostile, rebellious, and irresponsible than any of the comparison groups. The addicts seemed relatively well adjusted, suggesting that their drug use is symptomatic not of neurosis but of a generalized antisocial disposition. 12 references. *Journal of Abnormal Psychology*, 84(1):87–89, 1975.

Report on Research Visit to Synanon Foundation, Inc.   *Maillet, E.L.* This report describes the Synanon Foundation. Synanon is an alternative lifestyle which has been successful in the rehabilitation of drug addicts, alcoholics, and other character-disordered people. Synanon Foundation, Inc., Box 786, Marshall, CA 94940, 1972. 48 pp.

The Sick Physician: Impairment by Psychiatric Disorders, Including Alcoholism and Drug Dependence
The effect of alcoholism and drug dependence on physicians is discussed. The incidence of narcotic addiction in physicians varies from 30 to 100 times that found in the general population. *Journal of the American Medical Association*, 223(6):684–687, 1973.

Youthful Drug Use.   *Brotman, Richard; and Suffet, Frederick* An overview of the dimensions of the drug problem includes discussion of types of drug use and drug users, theories of causes of drug abuse, consequences of drug use, and forms of control. 30¢. Washington, DC: Superintendent of Documents, Government Printing Office, 20402, 1970. 39 pp.

Audio Tapes

Community Drug Abuse Guidance Program
Intended for use both by guidance persons and by individuals using or considering using drugs. The four-part program is entitled as follows: "Facing Reality through Responsibility;" "Prevention Education;" "Permanent Rehabilitation;" "Vocational Rehabilitation." The narration focuses on the individual's relation to society and on his develop-

ment of goals rendering drug use unnecessary. Communications Through Cassettes, Inc.

Drugs and Society
Margaret Mead talks about the religious and moral stigma surrounding drug use in America. Recorded in 1970 in New York City. $13. 37 min. Pacifica Tape Library.

Films

Dead Is Dead
Produced and narrated by comedian and actor Godfrey Cambridge as one concerned citizen's contribution to the fight against drugs. *Dead Is Dead* seeks to fight drug addiction with shocking truth. Traces the step-by-step destruction of humans addicted to pills and needles. Also offers concrete and timely suggestions for action that can be taken by all concerned. Rental: $10.50. 21 min. 16mm. Color. 1973. Film Library–Oregon.

Drug Age: What Can We Do?
Guideline Series. How to prevent people from becoming dependent on chemicals or drugs. Responsibility of parents, schools, community members to help solve the drug problem. The generation gap. Panel of adults and students. Rental: $8.75. 29 min. 16mm. 1969. Film Library–Oregon.

Marathon: The Story of the Young Drug Users
Highlights from a 30-hour encounter session among young drug addicts undergoing voluntary treatment at New York's Daytop Village. Rental: $14.75. 51 min. 16mm. 1967. Film Library–Oregon.

Or Die
A very short film on the work of Synanon and the particular kind of group which is used. The film gives a brief picture of the group and a short introduction to the work of Synanon. Rental: $8. 18 min. 16mm. b/w. 1968. Restricted. Penn State University, Psychology Cinema.

Release

True story of one woman's experiences after release from jail to Horizon House, a Milwaukee County (WI) halfway house for female drug offenders. This film covers the Horizon House program and the difficulties of re-entry into the community, reestablishing relationships with children and other family members, and resisting the temptation to go back to using drugs. Sale: $350. Rental: $35 per day. 30 min. 16mm. Color. 1974. Odeon Films, Inc., P.O. Box 315, Franklin Lakes, NJ 07417.

You Can't Grow a Green Plant in a Closet

This film records portions of the National Marijuana Symposium held March, 1968, at the University of California Medical Center in San Francisco. The Symposium was designed to answer questions about marijuana such as whether or not it is a narcotic, whether it leads to heroin addiction, what laws control it, and what barriers exist to further research on marijuana. Most of the speakers agree on some basic issues: marijuana is legally misclassified; this misclassification results in overly harsh penalties for abusers and "manufactures criminals" out of otherwise innocent people; factual information about marijuana is suppressed from the public; and overreaction to marijuana use is frequent on the part of legislators and parents. The participants, made up of psychologists, medical doctors, sociologists, criminologists, and writers, include Joel Fort, M.D.; David E. Smith, M.D.; Price Cobbs, M.D.; and James Carey, Ph.D. Purchase: $375 b/w; $425 color. Rental: $25 b/w; $30 color. 52 min. 16mm. Sound. 1969. Zip Film Distributing Co., 2220 B Bridgeway, Sausalito, CA 94965.

Contacts

SOURCES OF INFORMATION ON DRUG ABUSE

Extensive publications (many free) and services; write for information.

Drug Enforcement Administration
U.S. Department of Justice
Washington, DC 20530
(202-382-4315)

National Clearinghouse for Alcohol
 Information
P.O. Box 2345
Rockville, MD 20852
(301-948-4455)

National Clearinghouse for Drug
  Abuse Information
11400 Rockville Pike
Room 110, Rockwall Building
Rockville, MD 20852
(301-443-6500)

National Library of Medicine
8600 Rockville Pike
Bethesda, MD 20014
(301-496-4441)

National Organization for the
  Reform of Marijuana Laws
2317 M St., N.W.
Washington, DC 20037
(202-223-3170)

Drug Information Sources: A Survey of Selected Drug-Related Repositories and Information Sources. *Mangad, Fong*
Lists over 100 services providing information on drug abuse. Washington: Bureau of Narcotics and Dangerous Drugs, 1972.

Special Action Office for Drug Abuse Prevention (SAODAP) has been terminated. Requests and inquiries should be sent to the National Clearinghouse for Drug Abuse Information at the above address.

11

Crisis*

CRISIS COUNSELING IS A recent innovation in clinical practice. Probably the first agency that came close to this type of counseling, as it is thought of today, was the Salvation Army. In its conception, the Salvation Army was concerned with spiritual salvation. It soon became apparent that other problems were perhaps better dealt with first, poverty, for example. When it became obvious that suicide was an increasing social problem, the Salvation Army established the Anti-Suicide Bureau. This bureau was established in 1905 in London, England, supported by voluntary contributions. The treatment consisted of advice, or assistance as needed, with the offer of evangelical teachings.

Probably the first record of a crisis center in the United States occurred in New York City with the National Save A Life League, established in 1906 by Rev. Warren after a traumatic episode during which a woman who had overdosed told him she might not have attempted suicide had she someone to talk to. Still in existence today, this center is sponsored by voluntary contributions. Staffed by both professional employees and volunteers, the center offers 24-hour service and personal counseling.

In 1958, a project involving suicide prevention was sponsored by the federal government. Dr. Shneidman and Dr. Farberow established the Suicide Prevention Center and the Institute for Studies of Self-Destructive Behaviors in Los Angeles, California. More information about suicide prevention has come from this pilot research project than from any other single source. No other crisis center has even come close to conducting the amount of research done by this agency.

*with David Fox

This center provides both 24-hour telephone service and psychotherapy. A large percentage of the staff are paid professionals.

Another crisis center was established in Boston in 1959 by Rev. Kenneth Murphy. In direct contrast to the Los Angeles Center, Rescue Incorporated, as it is called, has no paid staff. It has a 24-hour telephone service, but no personal counseling. It works in conjunction with the Boston City Hospital Psychiatric Department, which offers counseling and group therapy. Rescue Incorporated is supported by the Catholic Church.

In 1958, three crisis centers existed in the United States; by 1966 only 37 such centers were functioning. In 1966, in an attempt to study further the problem of suicide, the federal government created the Center for Studies of Suicide Prevention of the National Institute of Mental Health. Most crisis centers have been created since the founding of this federal agency.

Programs and Services

All crisis centers assume responsibility for getting people in crisis to appropriate help. The telephone is a necessity in crisis counseling because of immediate access. Crisis centers differ in the services they offer. From studies done by Fisher (1972), suicide prevention and crisis intervention are two areas of responsibility taken by most centers. Of the 192 centers 84 percent had suicide prevention services, 94 percent offered intervention services, 52 percent offered community education, 83 percent offered referral services, 32 percent conducted research, and 3 percent had a religious message to offer. Over 80 percent of crisis centers are using 24-hour telephone coverage. Probably less than 5 percent have no phone coverage; 56 percent in Fisher's study said they offered both telephone and direct contact.

There are hundreds of different services offered by crisis centers from rape clinics to psychiatric counseling.

Characteristics of Clients Using Crisis Services

Suicide prevention personnel adhere to the belief that anonymity is an important therapeutic technique in the highly personal area of self-destructive behavior. For this reason, the personal information gathered by crisis workers is only from those clients who volunteer this information. Keeping that in mind, it appears that the 21–40-year age group is the most popular caller to crisis centers, with 61 percent of the callers between the ages of 21–30. When the services are directed toward youth the overwhelming majority of calls are received from the 10–20 age group.

The implications of these findings are that crisis centers are attracting a younger age group than is indicated by current statistics on suicide. Many suicidal people over 40 are not using suicide prevention services. The male, as he ages, commits suicide three times more often than the female, yet his calls comprise only one-third of the total calls received. In all age groups, females outnumber males in the number of calls they make to crisis centers. A younger male is more likely to call a crisis center than an older male.

Disorders Involved in Crisis Counseling

Crisis counseling by definition involves any disorder thought by the client to be a crisis. As a general rule, crisis centers accept most calls regardless of the problem stated. There is such a large array of problems and concerns expressed by callers that referral services are a necessary part of all crisis centers.

The problem most often encountered in primary contact with crisis centers is marital conflict. Following closely are multiple problems, alcohol, drugs, and sex problems. Suicidal thoughts are not the most frequently encountered problems, although many centers are oriented in that area.

Budget

In a study of 60 crisis programs, yearly budgets ran from under $500 to $50,000, with the majority operating at between $8,000 and $15,000 a year. There are certain basic costs, of which the telephone is, in most cases, the largest item. Another large item for many programs is the salary of a full or part-time coordinator-director. Almost all of the programs rely heavily on volunteers in one capacity or another. It is clear that expenses for operating crisis centers would be much higher if community resources were not used. Volunteers, free building space, and supplies greatly cut down on expenses of crisis centers.

REFERENCES

Aguilera, Donna C. and Messick, Janice M. *Crisis Intervention: Theory and Methodology.* St. Louis: C.V. Mosby, 1974.

Crow, Gary A. *Crisis Intervention.* New York: Associated Press, 1977.

Edwards, Romaine V. *Crisis Intervention and How It Works.* Springfield, IL: Charles C Thomas, 1976.

Ewing, Charles P. *Crisis Intervention as Psychotherapy.* New York: Oxford University Press, 1978.

Fisher, Sheila. *The Voice of Hope to People in Crisis.* Canton, OH: Case Western Reserve Bibliography, 1972.

Frederick, Calvin J. and Lague, Louise. *Dealing with the Crisis of Suicide.* Public Affairs Pamphlet No. 406A. Rockville, MD: National Institute of Mental Health, 1972.

Haughton, Anson. "Suicide Prevention Programs in the United States." *Bulletion of Suicidology,* No. 6. Rockville, MD: National Institute of Mental Health, 1970.

Hyde, Margaret O. *Hotline,* 2nd ed. New York: McGraw-Hill Book Co., 1975.

Jaffe, D.T. "The Organization of Treatment on a Short-Term Psychiatric Ward." *Psychiatry,* 38(1), February 1975.

Levine, Murray and Kay, Peter. "The Salvation Army's Anti-Suicide Bureau." *Bulletin of Suicidology,* No. 8. Rockville, MD: National Institute of Mental Health, 1971.

Pattee, C. "Population Characteristics and Sex Role Patterns in a Youth Run Crisis Center." *Journal of Youth and Adolescence,* 3(3), 1974.

Resnick, H.L.P. and Ruben, H. *Emergency Psychiatric Care: The Management of Mental Health Crises.* Bowie, MD: Charles Press Pub. Inc., 1975.

Robinson, S. *What It's All About, A Training Guide for a Youth Operated Hotline.* Rockville, MD: National Institute of Mental Health, 1976.

Books

Crisis Intervention: Theory and Methodology. *Aguilera, Donna C.; and Messick, Janice M.*
An historical overview of the development of crisis theory and a paradigm for understanding crisis and crisis intervention are presented. A differentiation is made between crisis intervention and long-term and short-term therapies, and discussions of situational and maturational types of crises are included. Case discussions of crisis intervention illustrate the theory and methods involved in this form of therapy. 2nd Ed. $6.00. St. Louis: C.V. Mosby, 1974. 153 pp.

Crisis Intervention Theory and Practice: A Review of the Literature and a Synthesis of a General Theory. *Smith, Larry Lorenzo*
The literature on crisis intervention up to and including December of 1972 was reviewed in a four part study to develop a general conceptual framework for crisis intervention that could be put into practice across a variety of problem areas. Various concepts of crisis intervention are reviewed and compared, and a description is given of how these conceptual frameworks have been put into practice and used with such selected problems of living as marital and family conflicts, emergency hospitalization, and suicide. The similarities and differences between these various concepts and practices of crisis intervention and planned short-term treatment procedures are analyzed, and a general concept is developed. HC $12.50. MF $4. (D.S.W. Dissertation, University of Utah.) Dissertation Abstracts International. Ann Arbor, MI, University Microfilms, No. 74-17519. 265 pp.

The Minister as Crisis Counselor. *Switzer, David*
Theories and experiences in the treatment of individual and family crises are presented, including new resources for counseling people in crisis in a community. Implications for the minister as a professional with a special perspective are emphasized. Distinction is made between the pastoral counselor and the secular psychotherapist, noting that the counselor represents a community of faith. Procedures, problems, and possibilities involved in developing community crisis services are outlined. Family systems theory is applied to crisis intervention counseling. Three kinds of systems are described with the counseling approaches appropriate to each. Divorce is also discussed in relation

to the minister's role as counselor. $6.95. Nashville, TN: Abingdon Press, 1974. 288 pp.

Suicide.   *Choron, Jacques*
Suicide is discussed in a framework encompassing the insights and contributions of anthropology, psychology, psychiatry, and sociology. Historically, suicide is shown to be a problem for the ethical and religious structures of most societies. Anecdotes and accounts of suicides and attempts at suicide are used to illustrate the history of the phenomenon. Suicide is seen as man's privilege to reject an unwanted existence and to possess mastery over life and death. Self-annihilation is seen as a legitimate human function. $7.95. New York: Charles Scribner's Sons, 1972.

Suicide: Preventable Death.   *Seiden, Richard*
Single copies of this outstanding report are free. Write to: Editor, Institute of Governmental Studies, 109 Bernard Moses Hall, University of California, Berkeley, CA 94720, 1976.

Articles

An Approach to Helping Individuals Who Have Entered Unfamiliar Life Situations.   *Weiss, Robert S.*
At the 52nd annual meeting of the American Orthopsychiatric Association, a program whose aim is enhancement of coping capacity through the provision of information regarding the unexpected situation was discussed. The approach has been used with individuals in three types of situations: marital separation, the loss of a spouse through death, and long-term single parenthood. Evaluations for the problem of marital separation indicate that the approach is very helpful. Program format was outlined, and areas where the program should be modified were identified. *American Journal of Orthopsychiatry*, 45(2):309–310, 1975.

Attempted Suicide by Males and Females.   *Beck, Aaron T.;*
Lester, David; and Kovacs, Maria
A study of 240 attempted suicides indicated different patterns for males and females. The attempts for females seemed motivated more by severe interpersonal friction whereas the attempts by males tended

to be preceded more by job loss, difficulties with the law and alcoholism. The female attempters were more depressed than the males but the males were more likely to be loners. The sexes did not differ in the lethality of their attempts and neither did they differ in age. Two references. *Psychological Reports,* 3(3):965–966, 1973.

Bibliography on Suicide and Suicide Prevention.   *Farberow, N.L.*
Good list available, free. NIMH, Office of Health, Education and Welfare Publication No. 72,9080, 1972.

Crisis Intervention: Implications for the Nurse.   *Shields, Leona*
The use of crisis intervention principles by nurse practitioners is illustrated and discussed. It is felt that when an emotional hazard or external event causes a crisis, the individual often responds to the hazardous situation with an inadequate habitual range of problem-solving methods; aid provided at this critical point can make the difference between an adaptive and a maladaptive reaction to change. Four levels of crisis intervention (environmental manipulation, general support, generic support, and individual intervention) are discussed with case histories illustrating the interventive use of nurse practitioners at each level. 6 references. *Journal of Psychiatric Nursing and Mental Health Services,* 13(5):37–42, 1975.

Crisis Intervention and Short-Term Therapy: An Approach in a Child Psychiatric Clinic.   *Berlin, Irving N.*
This paper outlines efforts in understanding and teaching crisis intervention and brief therapy with families. Case examples illustrate learning experiences that have led to the development of a model. Emphasis is placed on the requirement of training in dynamic psychiatry as a basis for understanding and applying lessons from ego psychology developed by Anna Freud, Erikson, Lindemann, and Caplan. 18 references. *Journal of the American Academy of Child Psychiatry,* 9(4):595–606, 1970.

Crisis Telephone Services.   *Hoey, Henry P.*
Problems in proper training of the growing number of volunteer staff members on local crisis telephone services are briefly discussed. All nonprofessionals should be carefully screened, demonstrate emotional maturity, and receive a minimum of 40 hours of training. Many crisis services have diversified into drug abuse programs, abortion informa-

tion centers, draft counseling, etc. Three references. *American Psychologist*, 27(8):776–777, 1972.

**A Selective Bibliography on Disaster and Human
Ecology.** *Harshbarger, Dwight; and Moran, Garrett*
A total of 101 publications concerning various aspects of disaster and human ecology are listed. International journal articles are included. Subjects deal with organizational aspects of crisis intervention, social processes in disaster, psychological and emotional reactions of survivors, and delivery of human services in the aftermath of a crisis. 101 references. *Omega,* 5(1):89–95, 1974.

The Use of Paraprofessionals in Crisis Intervention.
Getz, William L.; Fujita, Byron N.; and Allen, David
Single session crisis intervention services by paraprofessionals (graduate students and community volunteers) in the emergency room of a community hospital were offered to 293 clients. The clients were followed up 6 to 12 months after their last contact and asked about: (1) the effectiveness of the service; (2) their use of referrals; (3) the major source of change in their crisis situation; and (4) their rating of improvement for their presenting problem. Results support the interpretation that timely intervention by paraprofessionals has long-lasting results in specific problem areas, including client evaluation, referral usage, major source of change, and improvement rating. Seven references. *American Journal of Community Psychology*, 3(2):135–144, 1975.

Uncovering the Precipitant in Crisis Intervention.
Hoffman, David L.; and Remmel, Mary L.
A treatment method called crisis psychotherapy is described and its value to clients is examined. Crisis psychotherapy represents an attempt to integrate psychoanalytic personality theory and crisis theory. The method was developed by a family agency in recognition of the fact that most clients seek help during a crisis that has a natural life of 4 to 6 weeks and that they want quick, economical help. It has been found that the presenting complaint is rarely what stimulates the client's call for help. The therapist must discover the true precipitant—the client's unverbalized anxiety or pain. If the client feels he is understood, he will return to the agency for additional counseling. Crisis psychotherapy is an orderly, structured process

which takes place in three distinct phases: the initial, middle, and termination phases. Case histories which illustrate these phases are presented. Six references. *Social Casework,* 56(5):259–267, 1975.

Audio Tapes

Hotline Professional Cassettes
This series was recorded during the second International Hotline Conference at Asilomar, California, in 1971. The discussions, primarily of interest to participants in the Conference but also useful to other professionals, include the following: opening session with four professional participants; round table discussion on the handling of crisis calls; rap session with nine psychologists and hotline representatives; and a discussion on how to handle a bad trip. $5 for each cassette. 1971. Elaine Lynn & Associates.

The Suicidal Patient
Dr. Irwin Rothman discusses the suicidal client and offers systematic mnemonics and specific suggestions for the evaluation and treatment of high-risk patients. There is also a discussion of suicide risk in the healing professions. Excellent audio. $10 including script. Extra scripts $1. Cassette. 31, 28 min. AAP Tape Library.

Films

Point of Return
Introducing this film, Dr. Karl Menninger points out that suicide can be reduced only through understanding of the problem and appreciation of its seriousness. The story recounts the events of a day culminating with a suicide attempt. Using flashbacks, Dr. Howard P. Rome, Dr. Edwin S. Shneidman, Dr. Floyd S. Cornelison, and Mrs. Mary Hall comment on the important incidents of suicide, its effects on the survivors, and the need for preventive programs. The tendency of suicide-minded persons to cry out for help while planning self-destruction and the usual behavioral changes are discussed. Pointing out that there must be more thinking and discussion about suicide, the panel denies that one has no right to interfere in another's life, but

insists it is an obligation. Produced by the University of Oklahoma for the Oklahoma State Department of Health. Sale: $150. Rental: $9. 24 min. 16mm. b/w. 1965. International Film Bureau, Inc.

Psychiatric Emergencies

Different clinical situations which might well either be defined as emergencies or require close scrutiny and analysis are depicted for use in the training of health and mental health personnel. The vignettes cover: severe retarded depression; angry, hostile depressed man; suicidal man; bitchy lady who says she is depressed but doesn't give that appearance; potentially murderous woman furious after a family argument; delusional paranoid woman; agitated postpartum depression; confused, elderly woman with memory loss; agitated depression in elderly woman; woman who becomes confused and delusional at night; flamboyant, possibly manic woman; parents and adolescent girl in violent family fight; and couple fighting in a counselor's office. Rental: $25. Sale: $100. ½ inch videotape (Sony) b/w. 1974. Mental Health Media (GI–80). University of Washington, Department of Psychiatry and Behavioral Sciences, Seattle, Washington 98105.

Suicide

Perched on a rooftop threatening to jump, a young woman is talked out of becoming one more grim statistic. The common denominator of suicides is aloneness, a sense of being worthless and unloved, a feeling that "there is no other way out." The search must continue for a way to answer the needs of these people and prevent their self-destruction. Purchase: $325. Rental: $23. 25 min. Color. 1975. Films, Incorporated.

Contacts

American Association of Suicidology.   AAS has extensive publications, training programs, conferences, etc. Of special interest is their *New Directory of Suicide and Crisis Intervention Agencies* available for $6.35. AAS will be glad to respond to all interested individuals. Write to: Betsy S. Comstock, M.D., Secretary, AAS, Department of Psychiatry, Baylor College of Medicine, 1200 Moursund Ave., Houston, TX 77025.

National Institute of Mental Health.   Reports, publications, will send information to all who inquire. National Institute of Mental Health, Emergency Mental Health Section, 5600 Fishers Lane, Rockville, MD 20852. Attn: Dr. Calvin Frederick.

Rape* 12

FORCIBLE RAPE IS A CONSIDERABLE THREAT to the mental well being of many women in America. In this country, the incidence of rape is 35 per 100,000 population. The rates for other countries (per 100,000 population) are: Luxemburg 2.7; France 1.9; Holland 1.2; and Belgium 0.8.

Rape by its very nature is humiliating to the victim. This is especially true, since it is usually accompanied by violence and various sexual acts.

There seem to be three emotional response phases common among rape victims. The first is the initial reaction of distress and emotional disturbance. This is followed by a period of outward pseudo-adjustment characterized by denial of the impact of the assault, and a return to normal activities. In the third phase, the woman feels depressed and has a need to talk about the rape experience and her feelings. This last phase is important for the integration and resolution of her experience.

Although women statistically see therapists more often than men, few rape victims are seen in mental health agencies or private practices. These women may be adjusting or perhaps shame and guilt prevent them from seeking help. Fortunately, the feminist movement has formed rape crisis centers providing victims with someone to talk to and practical advice on coping with unsympathetic laws, policemen, and hospitals. Centers can provide information on how to obtain free medical and legal care, self-defense lessons, and rape prevention courses.

The feminist movement has made the following recommendations

*with Kristina Martin

215

on future treatment for rape victims: 1. To have a supportive nurse or social worker accompany the police officer on his investigation; 2. To have hospitals accept and treat rape victims with qualified and supportive personnel. These seem like reasonable recommendations; it is unfortunate that many times laws, policemen, and hospitals are not supportive in their treatment of rape victims. In the future, possibly the mental health field can also take a more active part in aiding rape victims.

REFERENCES

Barnes, Dorothy L. *Rape: A Bibliography 1965–1975.* Troy, NY: Whitestone Publishing Co., 1977.

Chappell, Duncan, et al. *Forcible Rape: The Crime, the Victim and the Criminal.* New York: Columbia University Press, 1977.

Cimons, Marlene. "Rape Concern Reaches the Federal Level." *Los Angeles Times,* May 9, 1974.

Gager, Nancy and Schurr, Cathleen. *Sexual Assault, Confronting Rape in America.* New York: Grosset & Dunlap Inc., 1976.

Goldberg, Jacob A. and Goldberg, Rosamond W. *Girls on the City Streets: A Study of 1400 Cases of Rape.* New York: Arno Press, 1974.

Hilberman, Elaine. *The Rape Victim.* New York: Basic Books, 1976.

Hursch, Carolyn J. *The Trouble With Rape: A Psychologist's Report on the Legal, Medical, Social and Psychological Problems.* Chicago: Nelson-Hall Inc., 1977.

Kemmer, Elizabeth J. *Rape and Related Issues: An Annotated Bibliography.* New York: Garland Publishing Inc., 1977.

Russell, Diana E. *Politics of Rape.* New York: Stein and Day, 1975.

Schultz, LeRoy G. *Rape Victimology.* Springfield, IL: Charles C Thomas, 1975.

Wilson, Cassandra and Connell, Noreen. *Rape: The First Sourcebook for Women.* New York: New American Library, 1974.

Books

Against Our Will: Men, Women and Rape. *Brownmiller, Susan*
Historical, legal, criminological, and psychological aspects of rape are discussed. Rape is described as a conscious process of intimidation by which all men keep all women in a state of fear. Legal sanctions against rape are outlined, beginning with ancient Babylonian law and continuing through the world wars and Vietnam. Attitudes and actions of the police in rape cases are considered, and the question of race is discussed. Specific types of sexual assault are included in the discussion: homosexual rape in prisons, police rape, and sexual abuse of children. The importance of the victim's personality, attitudes, and reactions, and influences of the crime on the victim are emphasized. Action taken by women to prevent rapes is also described. 402 references. $2.75. New York: Bantam Books, 1976. 472 pp.

How to Say No to a Rapist and Survive. *Storaska, F.*
Handbook that presents a detailed program on how women can protect themselves from rape and other violent attacks and emphasizes both what should and what should not be done when dealing with an attacker. $1.95. New York: Random House, 1976. 252 pp.

Patterns in Forcible Rape. *Amir, Menachem*
A study of patterns in forcible rape emphasizes the social characteristics and social relationships of the offender and victim, the offensive act itself and the situations in which rape is likely to occur. Certain aspects of the offense, such as group rape, victim-precipitated rape, felony rape, and the relationship between alcohol and rape, are studied intensively. Many of the myths and misconceptions surrounding the crime are refuted. $17.50. Chicago: University of Chicago Press, 1971. 394 pp.

Rape and Its Victims: A Report for Citizens, Health Facilities, and Criminal Justice Agencies—Prescriptive Package.
Gates, M.J.; Chapman, J.R.; and Barnett, E.
Results of national surveys of citizen action groups, medical facilities, and criminal justice agencies to determine their approach to and handling of rape cases, with suggestions for innovative changes. Law Enforcement Assistance Administration, Washington, DC 20531, NCJRS Document Loan Program, 1975. 373 pp.

Rape: How to Avoid It and What To Do If You Can't.
Csida, June-Bundy; Csida, Joseph
Written for the general reader, this book is heavily laced with anecdotal material and covers the major problems of victims as well as discussion of rape crisis centers and other efforts to assist victims. Chicago & London: University of Chicago Press, 1971.

Rape in Prison.   *Scacco, A.M., Jr.*
This book discusses the different acts of sexual aggression that occur in all correctional institutions and develops various theories relative to the extent that race, ethnic background, and institutional conditions affect what takes place. Emphasis is placed on juvenile and young adult institutions. A bibliography of books, articles, law reviews, task force reports, newspaper articles, unpublished papers, and booklets and pamphlets is provided. $10.50. Springfield, IL: Charles C Thomas, 1975. 138 pp.

Rape: The First Sourcebook for Women.   *Connell, Noreen;*
and Wilson, Cassandra (Eds.)
This book is based on the premise that "the act of rape is a logical expression of the essential relationship now existing between men and women." Using summaries of consciousness raising sessions, papers delivered at the New York Radical Feminists Rape Conference, reprints, and interviews, the book covers a number of issues from the feminist perspective. It includes a model rape law, medical issues, political action, self defense, and a critical bibliography. $3.95. New York: New American Library, 1974.

Rape: Offenders and Their Victims.   *MacDonald, John M.*
The nature of the crime of rape is examined from the viewpoint of the offender, his victim, the physician, psychiatrist, police officer, and attorney. Authoritative information is presented from actual case material on the scope of rape, forcible rape, characteristics of victims, and characteristics of offenders. Special attention is given to cases of child rape, the psychology of the rapist, the nature of group acts of rape, and the incidence of homicide which often follows. Incest is also considered, along with the situation of false accusation of rape. Finally, the specifications of the law regarding crimes of rape are examined, taking into account injustice in the courts, judicial review of rape convictions, criminal investigation, punishment, treatment, and prevention. $14.50. Springfield, IL: Charles C Thomas, 1971. 342 pp.

Rape: Victims of Crisis. *Burgess, Ann Wolbert; and Holmstrom, Lynda Lytle*
The authors' experiences in the Victim Counseling Program they established at Boston City Hospital underlie the rape victim counseling approach presented in the book. The book is intended particularly for those involved in the immediate crisis situation. $6.95. Bowie, MD: Robert J. Brady Co., 1974.

Articles

Alcoholism and Forcible Rape. *Rada, R.T.*
Data collected in this study of the autobiographies of 77 convicted rapists revealed that 50 percent of them were drinking at the time of the rape and that 35 percent were alcoholics. The author reviews several theories which have been suggested to explain the relationship between alcohol and the commission of sexual and/or violent crimes. It is stated that the strong association between alcohol and rape indicated by these results highlights the importance of followup treatment programs for the ex-offender. Such programs, the author maintains, should focus on adequate control of the offender's drinking behavior as well as on his sexual adjustment. *American Journal of Psychiatry,* 132(4):444–446, 1975.

Crisis Intervention and Investigation of Forcible Rape.
Bard, Morton; and Ellison, Katherine
The idea that crisis intervention theory has particular relevance to the police in their interactions with the victims of forcible rape is discussed. Guidelines for investigation of rape cases are presented in detail. Two references. *Police Chief,* 41(5):68–74, 1974.

Crisis Intervention with Victims of Rape. *Fox, Sandra Sutherland; and Scherl, Donald J.*
Three predictable and sequential phases that represent a normal cycle of emotional responses by victims of sexual assault are described: (1) acute reaction; (2) outward adjustment; and (3) integration and resolution of the experience. A series of interventions was developed to help patients work through each phase as smoothly as possible. The response patterns described provide only a general context in which to help such patients. *Social Work,* 17(1):37–42, 1972.

Counseling Rape Victims.   *Crum, Roger S.*
A crisis intervention program for rape victims at the University of
Chicago's emergency rooms and the associated responsibilities of
chaplains are described. A case verbatim is presented and analyzed.
Journal of Pastoral Care, 28(2):112–121, 1974.

Rape Trauma Syndrome.   *Burgess, Ann Wolbert;*
and Holmstrom, Lynda Lytle
One hundred and forty-six patients admitted during a 1 year period
to the emergency ward of a city hospital with a presenting complaint
of having been raped were studied. Based upon the analysis of the 92
adult women rape victims, the existence of a rape trauma syndrome is
documented, and its symptomatology delineated. Two variations,
compounded reaction and silent reaction, are also discussed. Specific
therapeutic techniques are required for each of the three reactions. It is
suggested that crisis intervention counseling is effective with typical
rape trauma syndrome; additional professional help is needed in the
case of compounded reaction and the silent rape reaction means that
the clinician must be alert to indications of the possibility of rape
having occurred even when the patient never mentions such an attack.
17 references. *American Journal of Psychiatry,* 131(9):981–986, 1974.

Films

Question of Consent—Rape
The film dramatizes a portion of the events that precipitate a rape
charge against a casual acquaintance of a resident of a singles' apart-
ment. The major portion of the film consists of the courtroom
questioning and cross-examination of the woman as the prosecutor
attempts to establish the use of force and the defense attorney seeks to
indicate consent. The detailed verbal descriptions pressed on the
woman by both prosecutor and defense attorney as necessitated by legal
definitions of rape are frankly presented. The narrator interjects
interpretive comments to define the content of the rape laws underlying
what is happening in the trial. The film concludes with a redirect by the
prosecution that is considered to preclude a directed verdict of not
guilty, and the film closes with the verdict left to the judgment of the
jury. Rental fee: $50. 20 min. 16mm. Color. 1974. Motorola Tele-
programs, Inc., 4825 No. Scott St., Suite 26, Schiller Park, IL 60176.

Rape Alert
A film which outlines steps for rape prevention, demonstrates self-defense techniques and indicates several potentially dangerous situations which should be avoided by the aware woman. Rental $30. 17 min. 16mm. Color. 1975. Aims Instructional Media, Inc.

Rape: A Preventive Inquiry
Practical advice on how women can decrease their chances of being raped, together with survival alternatives in case an attack occurs. "Be informed, be aware" is the central theme of this film which was produced in cooperation with the sex crimes detail of the San Francisco Police Department. Police Department inspectors, rape victims, and convicted rapists from California's Vacaville Medical Facility all give advice on how a woman should deal with a rape-assault situation. Emphasized is the need for the victim to remain cool and use her wits to avoid severe physical injury, talk her way out of the situation, or find a way to escape. Rental fee: $50. 18 min. 16mm. Color. 1974. Motorola Teleprograms, Inc., 4825 N. Scott St., Suite 26, Schiller Park, IL 60176.

Contacts

MISCELLANEOUS PUBLICATIONS: HANDBOOKS, PAMPHLETS, BROCHURES, NEWSLETTERS

Counselor's Manual. Rape Crisis Center. P.O. Box 1312, Madison, WI 53701. November 1973.
Feminist Alliance Against Rape Newsletter. P.O. Box 21033, Washington, DC 20009.
Freedom From Rape. Women's Crisis Center. 306 N. Division St., Ann Arbor, MI 48108. 1974.
How to Organize a Woman's Crisis Service Center. Women's Crisis Center. 306 N. Division St., Ann Arbor, MI 48108. 1974.
How to Start a Rape Crisis Center. Rape Center Women. P.O. Box 21005, Kalorama Street Station, Washington, DC 20009. August, 1972.
Lay Advocate Training Manual: A Guide to Assist Rape Victims. Chicago Legal Action for Women, 5609 N. Broadway, Chicago, IL 60660.

Orientation Guide for Counselors. New York Women Against Rape. P.O. Box 487, New York, NY 10011. November, 1973.

Rape: A Problem for All Women. Los Angeles Commission on Assaults Against Women. P.O. Box 74786, Los Angeles, CA 90004.

Rape: A Reference for Women in D.C. (Prepared for distribution in public schools) Rape Crisis Center. P.O. Box 21005, Washington, D.C. 20009.

Rape: A Survey of the Care and Treatment of Rape Victims in Dallas. Dallas County National Organization for Women. Dallas Women Against Rape, P.O. Box 12701, Dallas, TX 75225.

Rape Kit. NOW Task Force on Rape. 5 So. Wabash, Suite 1516, Chicago, IL 60603.

Rape: Medical and Legal Information. Rape Crisis Center. 46 Pleasant St., Cambridge, MA 02139.

Rape Prevention Tactics. Rape Crisis Center. P.O. Box 21005, Washington, DC 20009.

Report of the Public Safety Committee Task Force on Rape. District of Columbia City Council, City Hall, 14th and E Streets, N.W., Room 507, Washington, DC, July 9, 1973.

Stop Rape. Women Against Rape. 2445 W. 8 Mile, Detroit, MI 48203.

Training Manual. Women Against Rape. P.O. Box 4442, Tri Village Station, Columbus, OH 43212.

Volunteers Handbook. Rape Crisis Service. Planned Parenthood of Rochester and Monroe County, Inc., 24 Windsor St., Rochester, NY 14605. May, 1974.

We Are Women: How to Defend Ourselves Against Rape. SERMDTA Project. 4332 Maple Ave., Dallas, TX 75219.

NATIONAL ANTI-RAPE CONTACTS

NIMH. National Institute of Mental Health. National Center for the Prevention and Control of Rape. Room 8C-23, Parklawn Building, 5600 Fishers Lane, Rockville, MD 20852. Extensive information, contacts, and publications. Will be glad to try to help anyone who writes.

NOW. The National Organization for Women (NOW) has rape task forces in almost 200 chapters around the country. The National Rape Task Force coordinator for NOW is Mary Ann Largen, who can be reached through the NOW Legislative Office, 1107 National Press Building, Washington, DC 20004. (202) 347-2279.

COMMUNITY ANTI-RAPE PROJECTS

The following is a list of citizen action and community projects designed to help rape victims. For reasons of privacy and security, names and addresses of individuals are not included.

ALASKA

Fairbanks Crisis Line
P.O. Box Fairbanks, Alaska
Fairbanks, AK 99701
(907) 452-4403

ARIZONA

Assault Crisis & Prevention Center
P.O. Box 26851
Tempe, AZ 85282
(602) 257-8095

ARKANSAS

Rape Crisis, Inc.
P.O. Box 5181
Hillcrest Station
Little Rock, AR 72205
(501) 375-5181

CALIFORNIA

Bay Area Women Against Rape
P.O. Box 240
Berkeley, CA 94701
(415) 845-RAPE

Feminist Task Force
Rape Crisis Service
P.O. Box 368
Fairfield, CA 94533
(707) HER-AIDE

Harbor Free Clinic
615 S. Mesa
San Pedro, CA 90731
(231) 547-0202

L.A. Commission on Assaults
Against Women
P.O. Box 74786
Los Angeles, CA 90002
(213) 653-6333

Marin County Rape Crisis Center
P.O. Box 823
Kentfield, CA 94904
(415) 924-2100

Peninsula WAR
c/o YWCA
4161 Alma St.
Palo Alto, CA 94306
(415) 493-7273

Rape Crisis House
127 W. Main St.
El Cajon, CA 92020
(714) 444-1194

Rape Crisis Service
c/o Family Service Agency
1669 N. "E" St.
San Bernardino, CA 92405
(714) 886-4889

Rape Information & Prevention
Center
San Fernando Valley Free Clinic, Inc.
P.O. Box 368
Canoga Park, CA 91303
(213) 888-6515

Sacramento Women Against Rape
Sacramento Women's Center
1221 20th St.
Sacramento, CA 95814
(916) 447-RAPE

San Diego Rape Crisis Center
P.O. Box 16205
San Diego, CA
(714) 239-RAPE

San Jose Rape Crisis Center
YWCA, 375 S. 3rd St.
San Jose, CA 95112
(408) 287-3000

Santa Barbara Rape Crisis Center
1220 Santa Barbara St.
Santa Barbara, CA 93101
(805) 963-1696

South County Women's Center
Rape Crisis Center
c/o 25036 Hillary
Hayward, CA 94544
(415) 537-2112

Stop Rape, Inc.
P.O. Box 651
Placentia, CA 92670
(714) 525-HELP

Women Against Rape
c/o River Queen Women's Center
P.O. Box 726
Monte Rio, CA 95462
  (mailing address)
17140 River Road
Guerneville, CA 95446
  (street address)
(707) 869-0333

Women Against Sexual Abuse
12818 Morningside Ave.
Downey, CA 90242
(213) 653-6333

COLORADO

Community Crisis & Information
  Center
202 Edwards St.
Fort Collins, CO 80521
(303) 493-3888

Denver Anti-Crime Council
1313 Tremont Place, Suite 5
Denver, CO 80204
(303) 893-8551

Denver Coalition on Sexual Assault
227 Clayton St.
Denver, CO 80206
(303) 355-5510

Denver Victim Crisis Line
c/o Southeastern Denver
  Neighborhood Services Bureau
227 Clayton St.
Denver, CO 80206
(303) 321-8191 (crisis)
(303) 321-1793 (office)

Pueblo Rape Crisis Center
509 Colorado Ave.
Pueblo, CO 81004
(303) 545-RAPE (crisis, 24-hr)
(303) 545-8271 (business)

Rape Counseling Service
P.O. Box 2518
Colorado Springs, CO 80901
(303) 471-HELP

Rape Prevention Program
Department of Psychiatry
Denver General Hospital
8th & Cherokee
Denver, CO 80204
(303) 623-8252

CONNECTICUT

People Against Rape (P.A.R.)
448 Birch Road
Fairfield, CT 06430
(203) 366-0664

Prudence Crandall Center for
  Women
P.O. Box 895
New Britain, CT 06050
(203) 229-6939

DELAWARE

Rape Crisis Center of Wilmington
901 Washington St.
Wilmington, DE
(302) 658-5011

DISTRICT OF COLUMBIA

D.C. Rape Crisis Center
P.O. Box 21005
Washington, DC 20009
(202) 333-RAPE

Feminist Alliance Against Rape
P.O. Box 21033
Washington, DC 20009

FLORIDA

Community Relations Commission
330 E. Bay St.
Room 406
Jacksonville, FL 32202
(904) 633-2010

Hillsborough County Stop Rape, Inc.
P.O. Box 1495
Tampa, FL 33601
(813) 228-RAPE

Rape Information & Counseling
  Service
P.O. Box 12888
Gainesville, FL 32604
(904) 377-RAPE

Rape Treatment Center
Emergency Department
c/o Jackson Memorial Hospital
1611 N.W. 12 Ave.
Miami, FL 33136
(305) 325-RAPE (hotline)
(305) 325-6901

Women's Rape Crisis Center
P.O. Box 10572
Jacksonville, FL 32207
(904) 384-2234

GEORGIA

Carroll Crisis Intervention Center
201 Presbyterian Ave.
Carrollton, GA 30117
(805) 963-1696

Mayor's Commission on the Status of
  Women
501 Running Ave.
Fort Benning, GA 31905
(404) 658-6100

Rape Crisis Center
Grady Memorial Hospital
Atlanta, GA 30303
(404) 659-1212 x4460

ILLINOIS

Chicago Coalition Against Rape
c/o ACLU
5 South Wabash, Room 1516
Chicago, IL 60603
(312) 236-5564

Chicago Legal Action for Women
Northside Rape Crisis Line
5609 N. Broadway
Chicago, IL 60660
(312) 728-1920

Chicago Women Against Rape
37 S. Wabash
Loop Center, YWCA
Chicago, IL 60603
(312) 372-6600

DuPage Women Against Rape
Box 242
Clarendon Hills, IL 60514
(312) 629-0170

Emma Goldman Women's Health
  Center
1317 W. Loyola
Chicago, IL 60626
(312) 262-8870

Feminist Action Coalition
Southern Illinois University
Washington Square "a"
Carbondale, IL 62901
(618) 536-2103

NOW Rape Task Force
833 N. Cooper (upstairs)
Peoria, IL 61606
(309) 685-2346

Women Against Rape
1001 S. Wright
Champaign, IL 61801
(217) 344-0721 (business)
(217) 384-4444 (hotline)

Women's Development Council
1751 Felten, Apt. 3
Aurora, IL 60505
(312) 851-3675 or 897-4241

INDIANA

Indiana University Police
  Department
428 N. Lansing
Indianapolis, IN 46205
(317) 264-7971

Women's Committee on Sex Offense
P.O. Box 931
South Bend, IN 46624
(219) 282-2323

Women United Against Rape
(WUAR)
Indianapolis Anti-Crime Crusade
5343 N. Arlington Ave.
Indianapolis, IN 46226

IOWA

Ames Hotline
Box 1150
Iowa State University
Ames, IA 50010
(515) 292-7000

Iowa City Rape Crisis Line
c/o Women's Center
3 East Market St.
Iowa City, IA 52240
(319) 338-4800

Iowa Women's Political Caucus
P.O. Box 1941
Des Moines, IA 50306
(515) 282-8191

Polk County Rape/Sexual Assault
  Care Center
700 E. University
Des Moines, IA 50316
(515) 262-4357 (24-hr)
(515) 283-5666

Women's Counseling Service
310 W. 3rd St.
Davenport, IA 52802
(319) 322-1719

KANSAS

Lawrence Community/University of
  Kansas
Rape Victim Support Service
220 Strong Hall
University of Kansas
Lawrence, KS 66045
(913) 864-3686

Manhattan Rape Crisis Center
Kansas State University
Center for Student Development
Holtz Hall
Manhattan, KS 66506
(913) 532-6432

KENTUCKY

Rape Relief Center
c/o YWCA
604 S. 3rd St.
Louisville, KY 40202
(502) 585-2331

LOUISIANA

Rape Crisis Center of Baton Rouge,
  Inc.
P.O. Box 65037
Baton Rouge, LA 70806
(504) 383-7273
(504) 383-RAPE

YWCA Rape Crisis Service
3433 Tulane Ave.
New Orleans, LA 70119
(504) 488-2693

MARYLAND

Montgomery County Sexual
  Offences Committee
  Commission for Women
64 Courthouse Square
Room 5
Rockville, MD 20850
(301) 279-8346

Passage Crisis Center
Montgomery County Health
  Department
8500 Colesville Road
Silver Spring, MD 20910
(301) 589-8610

Rape Action Center, Baltimore
  County
Sheppard Pratt Hospital
6501 North Charles St.
Windy Brae, Room 103
Baltimore, MD 21204
(301) 823-8200

University Women's Crisis Hotline
Health Center
University of Maryland
College Park, MD 20742
(301) 454-4616 or 4617

MASSACHUSETTS

Boston Area Rape Crisis Center
c/o Women's Center
46 Pleasant St.
Cambridge, MA 02139
(617) 492-RAPE

Rape Crisis Intervention Team
Beth Israel Hospital
330 Brookline Ave.
Boston, MA 02215
(617) 734-4400 x2179

Springfield Rape Crisis Center, Inc.
292 Worthington St., Room 215
Springfield, MA 01103
(413) 737-RAPE

MICHIGAN

Copper County NOW
Rape Task Force
943 Summit St.
Hancock, MI 49930

Detroit Rape Crisis Line
P.O. Box 35271
7 Oaks Station
Detroit, MI 48235
(313) 872-RAPE

Rape Crisis Team
Box 6161, Station C
Grand Rapids, MI 49506

Women Against Rape
2445 W. 8 Mile
Detroit, MI 48203
(313) 892-7161

Women's Alternatives Crisis Center
203 15th St.
Bay City, MI 48706
(517) 892-1551

Women's Crisis Center
306 N. Division St.
Ann Arbor, MI 48108
(313) 994-9100

MINNESOTA

Center for Rational Living
2130 Fairways Lane
Roseville, MN 55113
(612) 631-2046

Family Tree
1599 Selby Ave.
St. Paul, MN 55104
(612) 645-0478

NOW Task Force on Rape
2851 E. Lake of the Isles Blvd.
Minneapolis, MN 55408
(612) 825-6080

Rape Counseling Center
Neighborhood Involvement Program
2617 Hennepin Ave.
Minneapolis, MN 55408
(612) 374-4357

Sex Offense Services Committee
c/o Department of Social Work
St. Paul-Ramsey Hospital
St. Paul, MN 55101
(612) 222-4260 x402

MISSISSIPPI

Rape Counseling Service
P.O. Box 4902
Jackson, MS 39216
(601) 354-1113

Rape Crisis Center
P.O. Box 2971
University City, MS 63160
(314) 773-1313

MISSOURI

Metropolitan Organization to
    Counter Sexual Assault
P.O. Box 15492
Kansas City, MO 64106

MONTANA

Rape Relief Program
Woman's Place
1130 W. Broadway
Missoula, MT 59801
(406) 543-7606

NEBRASKA

Lincoln Coalition Against Rape
c/o Women's Resource Center
Room 116 Nebraska Union
University of Nebraska
Lincoln, NB 68508
(402) 472-2597

NEVADA

Community Action Against Rape
1212 Casino Blvd.
Las Vegas, NV 89104
(702) 735-1111 (crisis)
(702) 385-0158 (office)

Rape Crisis Center
325 Flint St.
Reno, NV 89501
(702) 329-RAPE

NEW MEXICO

Rape Crisis Center
1824 Las Lomas N.E.
Albuquerque, NM 87131
(505) 277-3393

Rape

229

NEW YORK

Citizens Advisory
  Committee—Chairperson
Anti-Rape & Sexual Assault Program
YWCA
190 Franklin St.
Buffalo, NY 14202
(716) 852-6120

Crime Victims Service Center
Center for the Study of Social
  Intervention
Albert Einstein College of Medicine
Ginsburg Building, Room 3-14
Bronx, NY 10461
(212) 829-5522

Crisis Intervention Center
C.W. Post Center
Long Island University
Greenvale, NY 11548
(516) 299-2575 (all-purpose crisis
  hotline)
(516) 299-2578 (office)

Crisis Service
3258 Main St.
Buffalo, NY 14214
(716) 838-5980

Director of Education
Planned Parenthood
210 Franklin St.
Buffalo, NY 14202
(716) 853-1771

Erie County Anti-Rape & Sexual
  Assault Program
95 Franklin St., Room 1376
Buffalo, NY 14202
(716) 846-6462

Mayor's Task Force on Rape
52 Chambers St., Room 112
New York, NY 10017
(212) 566-0382

National Association of Junior
  Leagues
825 Third Ave.
New York, NY 10022
(212) 355-4380

NOW Rape Task Force
119 Strong Ave.
Syracuse, NY 13210
(315) 472-4200

Rape Crisis Service
Planned Parenthood of Rochester &
  Monroe County, Inc.
24 Windsor St.
Rochester, NY 14605
(716) 546-2595

NORTH CAROLINA

Chapel Hill-Carrboro Rape Crisis
  Center
P.O. Box 871
Chapel Hill, NC 27514
(919) 967-RAPE

North Carolina Memorial Hospital
Emergency Room Rape Crisis
  Program
c/o Department of Psychiatry
School of Medicine
University of North Carolina
Chapel Hill, NC 27514
(919) 966-4551

OHIO

Akron Women Against Rape
c/o Humanity House
475 W. Market St.
Akron, OH 44313
(216) 434-7273

Project Woman Rape Crisis Center
22 East Grand Ave.
Springfield, OH 45506
(513) 325-3707

Rape Crisis Center
Women Helping Women
2699 Clifton Ave.
Cincinnati, OH 45220
(513) 861-2959
(513) 861-8616

Rape Crisis Center
3201 Euclid Ave.
Cleveland, OH 44115
(216) 391-3912

Toledo United Against Rape
1831 W. Bancroft St.
Toledo, OH 43606
(419) 475-0494

Victim/Witness Division of the
  Montgomery County Prosecutor's
  Office
41 N. Perry St.
Dayton, OH 45402
(513) 223-8085

OKLAHOMA

Oklahoma County YWCA Rape
  Crisis Center
YWCA Women's Resource Center
722 N.W. 30th
Oklahoma City, OK 73118
(405) 528-5440 (YWCA/Resource
  Center)
(405) 528-5508 (hotline)

OREGON

Rape Prevention Center
P.O. Box 625
370½ W. 6th St.
Eugene, OR 97401
(503) 485-0234

Rape Relief Hotline
P.O. Box 1363
Portland, OR 97201
(503) 235-5333

Rape Victim Advocate Project
Multnomah County D.A.'s Office
600 County Court House
Portland, OR 97201
(503) 248-5059

Women's Crisis Service
Box 851
Salem, OR 97308
(503) 399-7722

PENNSYLVANIA

Center for Rape Concern
Philadelphia General Hospital
Mills Building C-16
700 Civic Center Blvd.
Philadelphia, PA 19104
(215) 823-7966

Chester County Rape Crisis Council
P.O. Box 738
West Chester, PA 19380
(215) 692-RAPE

Mon Yough-Allegheny County Rape
  Crisis Center
810 Walnut St.
McKeesport, PA 15132
(412) 664-0788

Pennsylvania State University
Department of University Safety
Police Services
University Park, PA 16802
(814) 863-1111

Pittsburgh Action Against Rape
  (PAAR)
932 Baldwin St. (rear)
Pittsburgh, PA 15234
(412) 678-8895 (McKeesport)
(412) 765-2731 (Pittsburgh)

Women Organized Against Rape
P.O. Box 17374
Philadelphia, PA 19105
(215) 823-7997

SOUTH CAROLINA

Greenville General Hospital
Greenville Hospital Systems
Mallard St.
Greenville, SC 29602
(803) 242-8377

RHODE ISLAND

Committee on Criminal Sex Offenses
c/o Women's Liberation Union of
Rhode Island
P.O. Box 2302
Eastside Station
Providence, RI 02906

TENNESSEE

Knoxville Rape Crisis Center
1831 Melrose Ave., S.W.
Knoxville, TN 37916
(615) 522-RAPE
(615) 522-7273

TEXAS

Austin Rape Crisis Center
P.O. Box 2247
Austin, TX 78701
(512) 472-RAPE

Dallas Women Against Rape
P.O. Box 12701
Dallas, TX 75225
(214) 341-9400

Fort Worth/Tarrant County Task
Force on Rape
512 W. 4th St.
Fort Worth, TX 76102
(817) 338-4211

Rape Treatment, Detection,
Prevention Program
City Health Department
1115 N. MacGregory, Rm. 206
Houston, TX 77025
(713) 222-4261

San Antonio Rape Crisis Line
P.O. Box 28061
San Antonio, TX 78228
(512) 433-1251
(512) 433-8282

Women Against Rape
Box 3334
El Paso, TX 79923
(915) 545-1500

VIRGINIA

Northern Virginia Hotline
P.O. Box 187
Arlington, VA 22210
(703) 527-4077

Roanoke Rape Crisis Center
3515 Williamson Road
Roanoke, VA 24012
(703) 366-6030

WASHINGTON

Feminist Coordinating Council
5649 11th N.E.
Seattle, WA 98105
(206) 325-8258

Rape Relief
4224 University Way, N.E.
Seattle, WA 98105
(206) 632-RAPE

Renton Rape Line
1525 North 4th St.
Renton, WA 98055
(206) 235-2315

Sexual Assault Center
Harborview Medical Center
325 Ninth Ave.
Seattle, WA 98104
(206) 223-3010 (nights & weekends;
  ask for social worker)
(206) 233-3047 (days)

WISCONSIN

Dane County Project on Rape
120 W. Mifflin St.
Madison, WI 53703
(608) 251-5440

Rape Crisis Center
P.O. Box 1312
Madison, WI 53701
(608) 251-RAPE

Wisconsin Task Force on Rape
2770 N. 44th
Milwaukee, WI 53210

Witness Support/Anti-Rape Unit
Office of the District Attorney
Room 206, Safety Building
East Milwaukee, WI 53208
(414) 278-4646

CANADA

Rape Relief
1027 West Broadway
Vancouver, British Columbia
Canada V6H1E2
(604) 732-1613

Toronto Rape Crisis Centre
Box 6597
Postal Station A
Toronto, Ontario
Canada M5W1X4
(416) 368-5695

Death

13

UNTIL RECENTLY, DISCUSSING DEATH has been taboo; however, now there is a significant increase in clinical, experimental, and popular literature on death and dying. Death and dying classes are becoming more prevalent in universities, high schools, and community mental health programs.

American society has been permeated by a socially repressive outlook which refuses to acknowledge death as natural or as inevitable. A leading authority in the field, Elisabeth Kubler-Ross, has said that death is seen as: "pathological, avoidable, preventable, postponable, and never welcome, celebrated, or acceptable." The media helps to perpetuate this attitude by portraying death as unnatural, unexpected, and violent.

Society emphasizes the preservation of youth and the denial of aging; death is made remote by the removal of the elderly from the family into nursing homes. With the advent of the industrial age, fewer people are exposed to farm life and the experience of the natural life and death cycle livestock provides. People have lost contact with nature and the life and death struggles that are part of it.

The combination of isolating the elderly, the media's portrayal of death as unreal and remote, and the lack of contact with death as a natural and predictable event—as with agrarian lifestyles—have made death mysterious and frightening.

Elisabeth Kubler-Ross has been in the forefront of the research on death and dying. She has defined several stages a dying person goes through when aware of impending death. (1) First, a dying person experiences denial and isolation, which may range from a refusal of medical assistance to a denial of the terminal illness itself. (2) The next stage is a confrontation with anger, a feeling that what has happened is

233

not fair. The dying person may lash out at doctors, nurses, and family, even blaming them for his suffering. (3) In the bargaining stage, the dying person makes promises to doctors, family, or God; in return, he expects a postponement of death. (4) The fourth stage is a deep depression, a preparatory grief over the eventual loss of important relationships and the self. (5) The last stage is acceptance. If the patient has had enough time to work through the previous stages, he will reach this last stage in which he is no longer depressed or angry, but accepts his fate.

Information on how to cope with the loss of a loved one or to face one's own death is an area that the mental health profession is just beginning to explore. The awareness of death as part of the natural life cycle can only enhance living.

Recent Studies

Bereavement studies have shown that there is a high risk of mortality for the young widowed person. The poorest risk is the survivor between ages 25 and 34, whose chances of dying are 4.31 times greater than his/her married counterpart. Most people who died within six months after losing their spouse, died from the same causes.

If death occurs at a location other than a hospital or at home, and if the death occurs suddenly (for example, in a car accident), the shock for relatives is much greater. In this instance, the risk of a close relative dying during the first year of bereavement is five times greater than that of a close relative of someone who died at home or in a hospital.

Married people have a lower death rate in every age group than those who are widowed, single, or divorced. For example, for widows between 25 and 34, the coronary death rate is more than five times that for married women.

The bachelors' death rate is 75 percent higher than for married men. The death rate for divorced men is more than double.

Divorced people have a higher incidence of medical problems; for example, lung cancer, strokes, and heart disease are double that of married people; while cirrhosis of the liver is seven times that of married people. Also, widowed, separated, and divorced people are four to five times more likely to take their own lives.

REFERENCES

Armstrong, Harry G. *The American Way of Dying.* Hicksville, NY: Exposition, 1977.

Brim, Orville G. Jr. et al. (ed.). *Dying Patient.* New York: Russell Sage Foundation, 1970.

Calvert, Sharon J. *Death Education: An Analysis of Changes in Cognitive, Affective, and Behavioral Reactions to Death.* Master's Thesis. California State University–Sacramento, 1976.

Carse, James P. and Dallery, Arlene B. (eds.). *Death and Society: A Book of Readings and Sources.* New York: Harcourt, Brace & Jovanovich, 1977.

Kastenbaum, Robert (ed.). *Death and Dying,* 40 vols. New York: Arno Press, 1977.

Kubler-Ross, Elisabeth. *Questions and Answers on Death and Dying.* New York: Macmillan Publishing Co., 1974.

Parkes, Colin M. *Bereavement: Studies of Grief in Adult Life.* New York: International Universities Press, 1972.

Prindiville, C.M. *The First Year after the Death of the Spouse: A Study of Widowers.* Master's Thesis. California State University–Sacramento, 1974.

Books

Bereavement: Studies of Grief in Adult Life. *Parkes, Colin Murray*
Human reaction to grief is studied, including the body's reaction to the loss of a love object, the devices by which grief is postponed or avoided, the ways in which anger and guilt complicate sorrow, and the gradual reconstruction of a person's world. Most studies refer to young and middle aged men and women, but basic information on the human grief process provides a framework for bereavement services for the aging. Care of the bereaved is a communal responsibility, involving family, friends, physicians, psychologists, psychiatrists, clergymen, and social workers. $10. New York: International Universities Press, 1972. 223 pp.

The Child in His Family, Vol. 2: The Impact of Disease and Death. *Anthony, E. James; and Koupernick, Cyrille*
Disease and death as they relate to the child in his family are discussed. Original contributions from international sources present an overview of the effects of serious illness, dying, death, suicide, and survival in relation to the child and his family. $15.95. New York: Wiley-Interscience, 1973. 544 pp.

Children's Experience with Death. *Zeligs, Rose*
Children's experience with death is discussed. Topics covered include the child's developmental concepts of death, his fear of death, his response to the loss of a parent, the part suicide plays in his life, the influence of his religion on his attitudes toward death, and the dying child himself. $10.75. Springfield, IL: Charles C Thomas, 1974.

Death as a Fact of Life. *Hendin, David*
A survey of (1) impersonal medical, legal, and historical facts; (2) interpersonal attitudes toward the dying and the dead; and (3) intrapersonal conflicts of the patient and those caring for the patient toward the patient's dying is presented. The medical criteria of death, transplants, euthanasia, the psychogy of the dying patient and that of his doctor, children's notions of death, grief, and the cryonics society are discussed. $7.50. New York: W.W. Norton, 1973. 255 pp.

Deaths of Man. *Shneidman, Edwin S.*
The place of death in life, as seen through the experiences of the

psychologist in dealing with dying persons and their survivors, is analyzed, stressing the need to accept the effects of the concept of death on human behavior. Preoccupation of some persons with death is analyzed via scientific assessment of Herman Melville's writings. The stages through which the dying person passes in arriving at final acceptance are described, based on Kübler-Ross' work. New terms are also conceptualized, including postvention, the work to be done with and for the survivors; subintention, the unconscious state of mind that precipitates or hastens death; megadeath, the massive death possible in a nuclear war, its threat, and its alienating, dehumanizing effects on the younger generation; partial death, or the loss of aspects of the self, such as a limb or a spouse through divorce; postself, the fantasy of survival through reputation or children, as well as other efforts to achieve immortality. Other topics include the psychological autopsy, medico-legal aspects of death, and a national survey of the attitudes on death. $8.95. New York: Quadrangle/New York Times Book Co., 1973. 232 pp.

Death's Single Privacy: Grieving and Personal Growth.
Phipps, Joyce
A first-person account, written in the style of an autobiographic novelette, depicts a young widow's and her two children's thoughts and reactions to the father's sudden death. Clumsy attempts by friends, neighbors, and some professionals to console the bereaved family point up the ineffective, unwelcome behavior toward the bereaved on the part of well meaning sympathizers. Dialogues of the children (aged two and a half, and five and a half) are excellent depictions of the differences in problems, attitudes, and thoughts of children between those ages on the subject of death. $5.95. New York: Seaburg, 1974. 143 pp.

The Discovery of Death in Childhood and After.   *Anthony, Sylvia*
The progressive understanding by children of the concept of death is described, and attitudes of children of different ages in China, England, France, Sweden, Switzerland, and the United States are studied and compared. The relationship between a child's idea of death and his feelings about separation, aggressiveness, and guilt are analyzed. An extensive bibliography is included. $6.95. New York: Basic Books, Inc., 1972.

Effects of Early Parent Death, Vol. 1:   *Birtchnell, J. et al.*
The relationship of early parent death to adult mental illness is ex-

plored. Topics covered include: diagnostic groups particularly vulnerable to pathology resulting from early bereavement; the interrelationship between social class, early parent death, and subsequent mental illness; early parent death in relation to size and constitution of sibship; parental deprivation in childhood and type of future mental disease; parental loss and its consequence on marriage relationships; and children's response to bereavement. $17. New York: MSS Information Corp., 1973. 176 pp.

Normal and Pathological Responses to Bereavement, Vol. 2:
Ellard, J. et al.
Management of grief, conjugal bereavement, parental response to child death, and loss and grief are considered. Articles discuss emotional reactions to the death of loved ones, recognition and prevention of pathological grief, factors affecting the outcome of conjugal bereavement, the mourning of parents confronting infant death, response to a dying child, linking objects of pathological mourners, "seeking" and "finding" a lost object, and the impact of object loss in childhood. $19.50. New York: MSS Information Corp., 1973. 235 pp.

On Death and Dying.   *Kübler-Ross, E.*
This book focuses in on the patient and the need to treat him as a human being and the need to talk openly with him. The information in this book is based on the author's experiences with dying patients. An essential book to read on the subject. $1.95. New York: Macmillan, 1970.

The Psychology of Death.   *Kastenbaum, R.; and Aisenberg, R.*
Clinical experimental and empirical findings in the field of the psychology of death are reviewed. Functions of today's physicians, funeral directors, nurses, clergymen, and the mental health specialists are examined and psychological responses to dying and the role of death systems in past and present societies are traced. The logical and methodological issues involved in defining death, suspended animation, and sham death are discussed. The development of our notions and confrontation of death in childhood and adolescence and the psychological factors linked to death and longevity are considered with   emphasis   on   suicide,   murder,   accidents,   and   illness.

Thanatomimesis, contemporary personifications of death, and the future association between man's control over death are also included. $9.95. New York: Springer Publishing, 1976. 498 pp.

Articles

Aging is Dying: Now to Make the Most of It.   *Loeb, Martin B.*
At the Foundation of Thanatology Symposium, the family and death—social work, the need for providing better social conditions for the aging was discussed. It was noted that the elderly must accept and cope with the fact that aging implies death. Young people were said to project their terrors about death onto the old, leaving no place for genuine interaction and leading to the generation gap. Specific interventions were recommended to help the aged to grow old in a dignified manner and to make the most out of life. These interventions involve reducing both physical and psychosocial pain and providing appropriate housing, food, sociability, work, love, and sex. *Archives of the Foundation of Thanatology,* 5(1):77, 1975.

Attitudes Toward Living and Death in 100 Elderly Heart Subjects.
Results of a survey of attitudes of elderly patients with heart disease toward living and death are presented, along with an assessment of their goals, values, perceptions, significance of and adaptation to illness, and their views on the meaning of death. *Gerontologist,* 13(3, Part II):51, 1973.

Children and Dying: An Exploration and a Selective Bibliography.   *Cook, Sarah Sheets; Renshaw, Domenna C.; and Jackson, Edgar N.*
The problem of children and dying is explored through four papers on the following subjects: children's perceptions of death, the dying child, helping children cope with death, and understanding the teenager's response to death. An extensive bibliography is provided after each chapter. Discussions of research on the perceptions, understanding, and reactions to death of children of various ages suggests ways in which care providers can help individuals adjust to the process of fatal illness and death. Thought provoking questions are asked and suggested solutions given. Emphasis is placed on the cooperation needed by all who are involved in evaluating and adapting to the

shock, anger, guilt, or despair of terminal illness and death in children. $1.95. New York: Health Sciences Publishing Corp., 1973. 37 pp.

Family Communication in the Crisis of a Child's Fatal Illness: A Literature Review and Analysis. *Share, Lynda*
An examination of family communication during the crisis of a dying child is presented. When faced with the tragedy of losing a child to a terminal illness, communication is a crucial factor in alleviating stresses and anxieties experienced by the child and his family. Two opposing modes of communication have been advocated: (1) the protective approach in which the ill child is shielded from knowledge of the disease diagnosis and prognosis; and (2) the open approach, which encourages provision of an environment in which the child feels free to express concerns and ask questions about his condition. The rationale for the protective and open approaches is discussed in terms of the sources of the child's anxiety, his conception of death, and his observed behavioral response to the illness. 44 references. *Omega*, 3(3):187–201, 1972.

On Widowhood: Discussion. *Blau, David*
A mutual help program for elderly widows which utilized widow helpers who had adapted well to their own bereavement is critically discussed. It is agreed that widow helpers' visits served an important humanitarian and public health function. However, there is a danger that unresolved or unrecognized grief may adversely influence the aide in trying to assist the newly bereaved widow. The widowed aide who volunteers must still be dealing with the remnants of her own bereavement, and the very act of volunteering to help other widows may be motivated by her own needs. Untrained people may have a heavy investment in their own methods of coping with problems and ignore the ones employed by other people. 15 references. *Journal of Geriatric Psychiatry*, 8(1):29–40, 1975.

Primary Crisis Intervention. *Kliman, Ann S.*
At a symposium on Death, the Press, and the Public, held in New York City, February 1976, primary crisis intervention as practiced by the Center for Preventive Psychiatry was discussed. Intervention is focused on children who are going through potentially damaging situations. The death of a parent or other family member accounts for many of the Center's crisis cases. In these situations, the bereaved child (or adult) is helped to deal with the loss and to mourn in a

healthy, constructive way. The Center's approach to bereavement counseling is basically that of helping the patients to remember so that they can forget. *Archives of the Foundation of Thanatology,* 5(4):462, 1976.

The Relationship Between Death Anxiety and Religion in Psychiatric Patients. *Templer, Donald I.; and Ruff, Carol F.*
In light of previous and conflicting findings on the link between death anxiety and religious attitudes and behaviors of undergraduates, the relationship between death anxiety and religion was investigated in a state hospital. Results reveal a significant relationship only between belief in an afterlife and fear of death: those patients who had the most death anxiety also had the strongest belief in a life after death. Patients who had changed religious affiliation since childhood also tended to experience more death anxiety than others. *Journal of Thanatology,* 3(3):165–68, 1975.

Symposium on Death and Attitudes Toward Death
Changing attitudes toward death and dying are examined in a panel discussion presented by Bell Museum of Pathology and the University of Minnesota Medical School. The discussion focuses on attitudes of society, the dying patient, and the physician. Panelists agreed that discussions of death are currently in vogue in society, although individual discussions between dying patients and physicians are often avoided or strained. While not personally agreeing with the principle of euthanasia, they foresee voluntary statutory euthanasia as a cure for the social problems caused by old age. The importance of thinking about dying as preparation for death is stressed. The work of groups such as Equinox which hold group therapy sessions with dying patients is discussed as one means of preparation; another is through personal meditation before illness or accidents occur. *Geriatrics,* 27(8):52–55, 58–60, 1972.

Audio Tapes

Crib Death: A Sudden Infant Death Syndrome . . . A Documentary
Parents who have experienced the loss of a child through sudden infant death syndrome discuss the guilt and self-criticism that exacerbates their normal grief reaction. Dr. John I. Coe presents recent research findings and nurse Carolyn Szybist offers suggestions on how

to help parents recover from their loss. $15. Cassette. 59 min. 1972.
Charles Press Publishers, Inc., Bowie, MD 20715.

Death and the Child
A psychologist/clergyman directs his remarks to parents and to those
in the care-giving professions who will ultimately shape children's
attitudes toward death. Direct, honest answers to questions on death
provide a basis for a healthy philosophy that can sustain an individual
throughout life. $15. Cassette. 45 min. 1972. Charles Press Publishers,
Inc., Bowie, MD 20715.

Death and the Family: From the Caring Professions' Point of View
Children's attitudes toward death are discussed by Delphie Fredlund,
emphasizing the need for children to be made aware of death and for
them to learn to accept loss in a realistic and healthy manner. $15. 3¾
IPS 5 inch reel. 30 min. 1971. Center for Death Education and Research, 1167 Social Sciences Building, University of Minnesota, Minneapolis, MN 55455.

Death and Life
A documentary, illustrating what people from all walks of life think
about death, what it means to them, how they visualize it, their fear of
it. These same people are then asked what they think about life, and
their answers reflect their experience of it. $15.95. 60 min. Center for
Cassette Studies.

Death and the Self
Dr. John Brantner observes that even in the absence of anything that
can be called education for death, people manage, from early childhood on, to learn certain attitudes toward death. It is his premise that
individuals rarely examine or question these attitudes which today
present serious difficulties for many. He discusses the changes necessary in such attitudes that could make possible more fully developed
lives. $15. 3¾ IPS 5 inch reel. 28 min. 1970. Center for Death Educa-
tion and Research, University of Minnesota, Minneapolis, MN 55455.

Parents and the Dying Child
Ms. Eugenia Waechter works with children who suffer from terminal
diseases (most commonly, leukemia) and extends her concern to include the children's families. She discusses her attitude and approach,
which are directed toward helping the dying and their families to cope

with the reality of death. Her interest in this subject was formalized in her doctoral thesis, published in 1968. $9. 90 min. 1974. Big Sur Recordings.

Problems in the Meaning of Death (Sessions I–II)
Different ideas about life and death and how these ideas affect and are affected by medical and scientific practice (Leon R. Kass, National Research Council; William F. May, Indiana University) $24. Each session about 3 hours long. Number 57-70. American Association for the Advancement of Science.

Talking to Children About Death
Dr. George G. Williams discusses ways to open the channels of communication between parent and child on the sensitive issue of death. It is cautioned that thwarting a child's efforts at a greater understanding of death can result in serious emotional problems in later life. Concrete suggestions of how to approach the topic of death with children are offered. $15. Cassette. 57 min. 1972. Charles Press Publishers, Inc., Bowie, MD 20715.

Films

All the Way Home
The impact of the sudden death of a husband on his wife and child is considered. Attitudes toward aging, religion, illness, child rearing, and family relationships are interwoven. 103 min. 16mm. Optical b/w. 1963. Films, Inc., 35-01 Queens Blvd., Long Island City, NY 11101.

Confrontations of Death
Documentary of the Confrontations of Death Seminar, one of the courses in the gerontology curriculum. How the seminar is taught, experiences of the students, and how students feel about these experiences. Rental: $26.50. 36 min. 16mm. Color. 1971. Film Library–Oregon.

Death
A set of five full color filmstrips (average 60 frames each), with an accompanying 12-inch long playing record or three cassettes, 5 audio script booklets, and discussion guide, is designed to advise the care-

giver or parent on explaining death to children. It is felt that death is
not a reality of life for most children. Thus, the death of a family
member, much loved pet, or friend can be a traumatic experience. It is
suggested that adults help a youngster learn about and understand
death gradually. Aspects of death covered include: death as a reality;
expressing grief; ages of understanding; explaining death to children;
and the importance of funerals. Photographed sequences illustrate,
among other things, how children express grief, and the three phases it
involves. The need for honesty and openness on the part of the care-
giver is emphasized. $49 with record; $58 with cassettes. Filmstrip.
Color. 1975. Parents' Magazine Films, Inc., 52 Vanderbilt Ave., New
York, NY 10017.

What Man Shall Live and Not See Death?
There is a "conspiracy of silence" surrounding the subject of death.
Through conversations with doctors, clergymen, terminally ill patients
and bereaved people, the silence is lifted to provide insight into a
profound and universal experience. Sale: $575. Rental: $42. 57 min.
Color. 1971. Films, Incorporated.

Contacts

Ethel Percy Andrus Gerontology Center.   University of Southern
California, Los Angeles, CA 90007. Major research, teaching and
study center.
Hospice, Inc.   765 Prospect St., New Haven, CT 06511. An organization that believes dying is a normal part of life and should be
treated as such, patterned after the London St. Christopher Hospice. Hospice provides dying persons and their families with counseling, medical services, aid, and coordinated home/hospital service.

Potpourri

14

Books

Barriers and Bridges: An Overview of Vocational Services Available for Handicapped Californians, January 1977
This is a publication of the California Advisory Council on Vocational Education authored by Linda Phillips. Thomas Bogetich, Executive Director of CACUE, has done an outstanding job in the management and goals of this agency. *Barriers and Bridges* describes the current state-of-the-art in vocational services for handicapped persons in California. The monograph describes the resources available in the state and the barriers that prevent handicapped persons from reaching their career and vocational goals. Practical recommendations are made to facilitate change and to bridge those barriers. The recommendations are directed to government agencies, elected officials, employers, program implementors, handicapped persons themselves and their families, preservice and inservice educators and Californians at large. Definitely has implications fot the United States as a whole. $3. State Department of General Services, Office of Procurement, Publications Section, P.O. Box 1015, North Highlands, CA 95660.

Counseling the Severely Disabled
Special issue of Rehabilitation Counseling Bulletin. Civil rights and the disabled, industry projects, sex and the spinal cord patient. $3. Washington, DC: American Personnel and Guidance Association. 1975. 96 pp.

Directory of Counseling Services
Published by the International Association of Counseling Services, an

APGA affiliate. Lists over 350 counseling services and agencies in the United States and Canada. $4. Washington, DC: American Personnel and Guidance Association. 1975. 302 pp.

Dream Issue.   *Grossinger, Richard; and Hough, Lindy (Eds.)*
The *Dream Issue* contains extensive dream material from different cultures, plus articles on telepathic dreams, precognitive dreams, symbolism in dreams, dream interpretation and physiology. $5. Illustrated. Berkeley: Bookpeople, 1973. 276 pp.

The Encyclopedia of Careers and Vocational Guidance.
Hopke, William E. (Ed.)
1972 revision, two volumes. Published by J.G. Ferguson Co. A guide for the career planning of students. Vol. 1 contains 71 articles by leaders of industry; Vol. 2 discusses the specifics of 650 occupations. $26.95 to APGA members. $39.50 nonmembers. Washington, DC: American Personnel and Guidance Association.

An Introduction to Environmental Psychology.
Ittleson, W.H.; Proshansky, H.M.; Rivlin, L.G.; and Winkel, G.H.
Man's changing conceptualization of his environment is examined in a historical perspective, methodological aspects of environmental psychology are discussed, and theoretical speculations are presented. Emphasis is on a dynamic interchange between man and the environment which leads to a preference for holistic, naturalistic methods of observation and to a multidisciplinary approach to research problems. Consideration is also given to the interdependence of physical environment and social systems and environmental decision-making processes. $9.95. New York: Holt, Rinehart & Winston, 1974. 406 pp.

A Guide to Psychologists and Their Concepts.   *Nordby, Vernon J.; and Hall, Calvin S.*
Brief biographies of 42 persons whose thinking has been important in psychological theory are presented. A summary of the principal concepts of each individual is given along with the biography. $8. San Francisco: W.H. Freeman, 1974. 187 pp.

Guidelines for Family Care Home Operators.   *Schrader, Paul J.; and Elms, Roslyn R.*
Guidelines for persons providing family living services to selected mentally ill persons are presented. Family care is a placement program

of persons in supervised private homes as an intermediate step during treatment. It focuses on resocialization, return to employment, and personal dependence. Topics covered include health care for residents, first aid, nutrition, practical solutions for behavior problems, caring for the mentally retarded, motivation and remotivation techniques, and some legal implications for family care home operators. $4.25. New York: Springer Publishing, 1972. 158 pp.

The Handbook of Animal Welfare: Biomedical, Psychological and Ecological Aspects. *Allen, Robert D.; and Westbrook, William (Eds.)*
$22.50. New York: Garland STPM Press, 1978. 300 pp.
This handbook, the first of its kind, comprehensively reviews the various aspects of animal welfare concerning the problems that pets present, and their control. It also offers information on training, and resources necessary for individuals or groups to understand, conduct research, and provide solutions for pet problems in their communities. Topics include: the problems of animal control; the ecology of urban dogs; pet owner psychology; biomedical aspects; animal welfare; personality profiles and information surveys; and techniques for solving animal-related problems.

Of interest to veterinarians, animal behaviorists, humane society members, and anyone else working in the field of animal welfare. $22.50. New York: Garland STPM Press, 1978. 300 pp.

Hypnosis in the Relief of Pain. *Hilgard, Ernest R.; and Hilgard, Josephine R.*
Technical and very complete. $10. Berkeley: Bookpeople, 1975. 264 pp.

International Collaboration in Mental Health. *Brown, Bertram S.; and Torrey, E. Fuller*
A report of international cooperation in the field of mental health and summaries of research supported by NIMH are presented. The following research projects are described: studies of schizophrenia in the USSR; an international reference centers network for psychotropic drugs; an international pilot study of schizophrenia; a six country study of the effects of modernization; multi-ethnic studies of psychopathology and normality in Hawaii; psychotherapeutic drug trials in England, megavitamin treatment, culture and tranquilizers and drugs for the aged in Canada; the discharge of schizophrenic patients in Turkey and the U.S.; an 8-year followup study of autistic

children in England; Danish studies of heredity and schizophrenic disorders; Danish factors which influence criminality; psychiatric case registers in Yugoslavia; suicides; Swedish laboratory methods, child-rearing; and perspectives on thinking. Other studies concern mental health services, training for researchers, drug abuse, alcohol abuse, and the future for international collaboration. 129 references. $2.10. Rockville, MD: NIMH, 1973. 291 pp.

Law, Psychiatry and the Mental Health System.
Brooks, Alexander D.
The junctures between the fields of law and psychiatry, particularly in the areas of due process and equal protection, are addressed. These points of contacts are covered in a topical fashion, in three distinct categories: (1) How the law deals with the mentally disabled offender; (2) Civil commitment; and (3) The general area of competence. The book is a collection of articles and cases intended as a casebook. $22.50. Toronto: Little, Brown & Co., 1974. 1150 pp.

Mental Health and Law: A System in Transition.   *Stone, A.A.*
This monograph, written by a professor of law and psychiatry, provides a review and discussion of the interactions of the legal and mental health systems. Among the issues covered in this text are civil vs. criminal confinement, treatment and prediction of dangerous behavior, the legal criteria and goals of civil commitment, and inpatient care. Legal issues involved in the treatment of such groups as the mentally retarded, juveniles, the aging, sexual psychopaths, and defective delinquents are also discussed. The role of law and mental health treatment is then examined with respect to the right to treatment, the right to refuse treatment, competency to stand trial, and the insanity defense. An appendix which updates the major legal issues in light of recent judicial decisions is also provided. Washington, DC: U.S. Gov't. Superintendent of Documents, 1975. 280 pp.

NVGA Bibliography of Current Career Information
Lists and evaluates 2,300 books and pamphlets, describes and evaluates occupational films, and has a special section on career-related information. 6th ed. $2. Washington, DC: American Personnel and Guidance Association, 1973. 129 pp.

**Prisoners of Psychiatry: Mental Patients, Psychiatrists,
and the Law.**   *Ennis, B.J.*
The author's opinion is that the legal rights of mentally disturbed

persons are abrogated by present mental hygiene laws. The author
served as legal defender for most of the cases in this book. The narra-
tives exemplify the ambiguity in usage of the term "mental illness" and
the variety of legal and psychiatric attitudes towards mental illness.
Ennis suggests tightening of commitment criteria, the imposition of
absolute or presumptive limits on length of involuntary hospitalization
and the creation of community-based outpatient treatment facilities as
steps toward the abolition of involuntary commitment. $1.65. New
York: Avon Books, 1974. 232 pp.

**A Social History of Helping Services: Clinic, Court, Schools, and
Community.**   *Levine, M.; and Levine, A.*
The history of American psychology in the areas of the clinic, courts,
schools, and community is reviewed. Each of these chapters helps to
bring insights into how American society perceived educational and
psychological problems at a particular time in our history. A variety of
helping services are described and the thesis that social and political
conditions exert profound influences upon mental health problems
and the particular forms of help that develop is explored. $10.95. New
York: Appleton-Century-Crofts, 1970. 315 pp.

Source Book on the Teaching of Psychology.   *Woods, Paul J. (Ed.)*
An organized but flexible reference source for teachers of psychology
containing course outlines and teaching bibliographies in traditional
and recently developed areas of psychology. The materials are contained in a loose-leaf format so that revision and new materials can be
periodically incorporated. The intention is to maintain a "living" and
"evolving" source of ideas and stimulation for teachers of psychology.
This publication developed from the course outlines project of the
Division on the Teaching of Psychology of the American Psychological
Association which the editor coordinated for over ten years. $22.50.
The Scholars' Press Ltd., P.O. Box 7231, Roanoke, VA 24019. 1973.

Stranger and Traveler: The Story of Dorothea Dix.
Wilson, Dorothy Clarke
Almost single-handedly, Dorothea Dix reformed American views of
the "insane" and improved their care. Before she died in 1887, she
helped found or enlarge 32 state institutions, two overseas hospitals, and 15 training schools for patients. She started her crusade
in 1841, when after hearing screams in a jail she investigated and saw
the plight of "mad folks." $8.95. Boston: Little, Brown & Co., 1975.

Theories of Psychology: A Handbook.   *Neel, Ann*
An account of many of the theories of the major writers and thinkers
in psychology is presented. Each theory presented is examined in terms
of a common framework to make comparisons between concepts clear
and systematic. $9.95. New York: Halsted Press, 1977. 482 pp.

Understanding Understanding.   *Osmond, Humphrey;*
Osmundsen, John A.; and Agel, Jerome
The need for the understanding of individuals' differeing viewpoints is
explored personally and psychologically. A typology of personality,
which delineates 16 types is presented. Several internal and external
environmental factors that affect people's behavior and their understanding of each other are discussed. The megavitamin therapy for
schizophrenics as a rigorous and viable method is discussed. Diagnostic and evaluative methods in the treatment of mental illness are summarized. A theory of group-member relations termed "typo-
methetics" is described, and its application to management practices in
the business world and to the structuring of various types of organizations is discussed. $7.95. New York: Harper and Row, 1974. 216 pp.

Victimology.   *Drapkin, I.*
The initial stages of victimology are discussed along with the controversy surrounding them, and the international spread of the idea.
Examples are cited for several nations. Psychiatric and psychoanalytical aspects of the problem are noted. It is concluded that biological,
sociological, psychological, and legal aspects of the victim have been
neglected, and that victimology should be a separate and autonomous
science with its own institutions. $15. Lexington, MA: Lexington
Books, 1974. 263 pp.

Articles

Directory of Institutions for Mentally Disordered Offenders.
Eckerman, W.C.
Listing by states of institutions, including federal, state, and municipal
facilities, and providing addresses, a brief description, number and
type of inmates, and the name of the program director. Washington,
DC: Superintendent of Documents, 1972. 28 pp. (HSM) 72-9055.

New Directions for Social Work in Mental Health. *Wittman, Milton*
Implications for social work practice in recent changes and anticipated
modifications in the system of mental health services in the United
States are discussed. A history of the changes in structure and function
of the mental health services is sketched, and trends in direct and
indirect practice of social work attributable to those changes are described. Modes for service delivery which can be expected in the near
future are suggested, with emphasis on the expected enactment of a
national health insurance system. Explication of these trends is accompanied by commentary on the current state of professional development and the impact of mental health knowledge on social work
education and practice. 25 references. Unpublished paper. Rockville,
MD: NIMH, 1976. 26 pp.

Oneiromancy: An Historic Review of Dream Interpretation.
Kurland, Morton L.
A review of early writings confirming current views concerning the use
of dreams to understand the dreamer and reaffirming many specific
methods in current use is presented. Such things as symbolic representation, proverbial expression, puns, forgetting portions of dreams,
were described two millenia ago in much the same fashion as they are
today. Repeated mention of the use of dreams as a tool for divination
of the future and for diagnosis of physical ills is made in the ancient
writings. It is suggested that these areas may be as fruitful for further
exploration as were those pursued by Freud into the realm of wish
fulfillment. 13 references. *American Journal of Psychotherapy,*
26(3):408–16, 1972.

Overview: Current Trends in Mental Health Law.
McGarry, A. Louis; and Kaplan, Honora A.
Trends in mental health law beginning with early law and proceeding
to the present time are delineated. Recent mental health related judicial decisions and statutory changes such as class actions, the right to
treatment, admission statuses, classification of mentally ill and mentally retarded patients, involuntary commitment, and patient rights are
discussed. 65 references. *American Journal of Psychiatry.*
130(6):621–30, 1973.

**Program Development Theme for the 70s: The Development of
Alternative Mental Health Services.** *Shore, Milton F.*
Specific themes in various historical periods are discussed which form

a basis for the development of programs in mental health. They include: (1) the evolution of hospitals for the mentally ill in place of the
inhumane, punitive settings of jails; (2) the child guidance movement,
with stress on outpatient work, interdisciplinary team functioning,
and prevention; and (3) the development in 1963 of community mental health centers arising from the major commitment by the federal
government to mental health as a national problem. Consideration is
given to alternative ways of delivering mental health care and services,
especially the alternative service movement and alternative schooling.
Alternatives to incarceration, to hospitalization, and services for youth
are also mentioned. 4 references. (Unpublished paper.) Rockville, MD:
NIMH, 1975. 5 pp.

The Voluntary Agency and Community Mental Health Services
National voluntary agencies and a cross-section of community services
involved in mental health are listed, with their services detailed. Services offered by these agencies are in the areas of alcoholism, children
and youth. Services for patients, services for unwed mothers, rehabilitation, home care, referral, education and counseling, and cooperative
financing. Collaborative services and planning for changing needs are
also detailed. 50¢. Rockville, MD: NIMH, 1973. 33 pp.

Audio Tapes

Alan Watts Interviewed by Michael Murphy
The interview takes place on Alan Watts' ferry boat in Sausalito.
Watts discusses concentration, technology, nature, materialism, and
many other topics. $9. 75 min. 1964. Big Sur Recordings.

Authority vs. Authoritarianism: The Willingness to Submit
Is there a difference between genuine authority and authoritarianism?
Panel members Peter Marin, Thomas Szasz and Claudio Naranjo discuss the pros and cons of this question, but generally come to one
point of agreement: authority is bestowed upon an individual by the
respect of other people for his outstanding expertise in one field. The
authoritarian is one who tries to make other people regard him as an
authority, whether or not he merits their respect. $9. 90 min. 1973.
Big Sur Recordings.

The Black Experience
In a confrontation which explodes in rage and indignation, Blacks and Whites engage in an exploration unique to the meeting rooms of psychologists. $18. 3 hours, 2 tapes. 1969. Big Sur Recordings.

Divine Madness. *Alan Watts*
"Sanity" is nothing more than a name given to a statistical norm by a frightened majority, and the consequences to us all, he says, are criminal. $9. 90 min. 1968. Big Sur Recordings.

Fear
Psychologist Maria Piers compares those fears which come from outside causes—pain, death, destruction, and indignity—with those which emanate from inner impulses of hate, greed and aggression. $10.95. 28 min. Center for Cassette Studies.

Freud, Jung and Kundalini Yoga
A voyage up through each of the seven chakras according to the Hindu tradition is lucidly described in this talk, which shifts to the Tibetan system for its return journey. Dr. Joseph Campbell then relates these traditions to the development of Western psychology and religion. $9. 60 min. 1967. Big Sur Recordings.

Future Shock
An interview with Alvin Toffler, author of *Future Shock,* about the social pathologies caused by ever increasing rates of change. $15. 88 min. Pacifica Tape Library.

Guilt: The Psychic Censor
The most personal of emotions is considered from different standpoints. In this program doctors from different disciplines—including theologian Harvey Cox and anthropologist Margaret Mead—discuss the problem of guilt from the viewpoints of their various specialties. $16.95. 50 min. Center for Cassette Studies.

Human Potentialities. *Aldous Huxley*
The field of choice is originally infinite; untapped and undeveloped potentialities; the ultimate positive nature of man. $9. 45 min. Big Sur Recordings.

Is I.Q. Inherited?

According to Dr. R.J. Hernstein, I.Q. tests have shown that intelligence is primarily inherited. According to Dr. Thomas Berber, they only show the extent to which a child reflects society's values. Both psychologists agree, however, that the tests are designed to be predictive. In this program they debate the value of the predictions obtained and offer contrasting views of what it is that the tests predict. $16.95. 29 min. Center for Cassette Studies.

Madness and Civilization

Citing a history of neglect, custodial brutality and a tidal wave of new patients, Dr. Rappaport here outlines some greatly needed mental health alternatives. He stresses the preventive service of community psychiatry and new, active approaches for professionals who must stem the flood of emotional ills proliferating in our overcrowded society. $15.95. 58 min. Center for Cassette Studies.

Overview of Transpersonal Psychology

Ira Progoff, Thomas Weide, Sonja Margulies, and Elmer Green speak of the basic concerns and intentions that have inspired the establishment of Transpersonal Psychology as an association, and as a journal and as a means for continuing research. $9. 90 min. 1971. Big Sur Recordings.

Physiological Feedback Research

In a concise and informative lecture on understanding alpha feedback, Joe Kamiya and Robert Ornstein discuss how to detect the alpha wave, how to make the alpha state occur more frequently, and the relationship of the state to traditional religious practices. $9. 90 min. 1971. Big Sur Recordings.

Safety of the Cyclone's Center

During this two-hour recording, Dr. Lilly shares the contents of several chapters from a book then in manuscript, titled *The Center of the Cyclone*. This part of the book contains advice for navigators in unknown spaces, reports Dr. Lilly's own experience with inner space travel, and tells some of the things he learned. $18. 2 hours. 2 tapes. 1970. Big Sur Recordings.

Violence (Series of 2 programs)

Encounter therapy sessions recorded in Oak Ridge, the maximum security section of the Ontario psychiatric hospital at Penetanguishene, whose patients include killers, child molesters, rapists, and arsonists. A discussion of the taped material follows: In Part II of the program two psychiatrists, a patient, and a sociologist deal with the question, "Is it possible to define violence so that people can recognize it before it takes over their lives?" Also, "Are there any roots from which overt violence grows?" $29.95. 60 min. each. Center for Cassette Studies.

Violence in Sport
A documentary on the psychology of hitting to hurt. On this cassette men who have excelled in two of the most violent contact sports—football and hockey—attempt to answer this question and try to explain the weird exhilaration they experience from incapacitating an opponent. $15.95. 54 min. Center for Cassette Studies.

Visionary Experience.   *Aldous Huxley*
Exploring that "other world of the mind" familiar to mystics and artists, to children and poets, where intellect gives way to luminous vision. $9. 45 min. Big Sur Recordings.

What Is Love?
Anthropologist and author Ashley Montague discusses the nature of love, its physical and psychological aspects. He offers a definition of what we mean by love, drawing on his knowledge of scientific research on the subject. $14.95. 30 min. Center for Cassette Studies.

Wilhelm Reich and the Bioenergetics of Feeling
Personally acquainted with Wilhelm Reich, Dr. Charles Kelley gives a concise, informative history of the man's life and work, followed by a description of some current applications of Reichian methods. $9. 90 min. 1970. Big Sur Recordings.

Wilhelm Reich: His Life and Work
Reich's oldest daughter reminisces about her father in his role of philosopher, teacher and researcher. $9. 90 min. 1974. Big Sur Recordings.

World of Psychic Phenomena I
In this program, Dr. Thelma Moss of UCLA, one of the nation's foremost authorities in the world of parapsychology, discusses in detail the evidence relating to these and other phenomena, and also

reveals some of the astonishing results produced by her own laboratory experiments. $15.95. 45 min. Center for Cassette Studies.

The World of Sleep
Dr. Margaret Mead talks about the results of some investigations and reveals the surprising extent to which our sleep patterns—and even our dreams—can be controlled by society. $14.95. 38 min. Center for Cassette Studies.

Films

Ages of Man

Part I: Selections from Shakespeare's dramatic and poetic works presenting lyrical pieces of love and longing. Readings by Sir John Gielgud. Youth. 23 min.

Part II: Sir John Gielgud presents selections from Shakespeare's dramatic and poetic works portraying problems of ambition and authority. Adulthood. 29 min.

Part III: Sir John Gielgud presents selections from Shakespeare's dramatic and poetic works concerned with questions of decision and doubt. Maturity. 25 min.

Part IV: Sir John Gielgud presents selections from Shakespeare's dramatic and poetic works concerned with moments of remorse and reflection and the breaking and mending of the spirit. Death. Rental: $8.75 each. 27 min. 16mm. 1966. Film Library–Oregon.

Be An Effective Teacher

This film was developed by Dr. Thomas Gordon as a companion approach to parent effectiveness training (PET). The teacher effectiveness training (TET) approach provides a basis for promoting a powerful learning environment in the classroom. Sale: $300. Rental fee: $30/day. 55 min. (2 reels). 16mm. Color and sound. American Personnel and Guidance Association.

Should Man Play God?

Controversy surrounding psychosurgery and fetal research. Sale: $215. Rental: $20. 15 min. Color. 1973. Films Incorporated.

Special Education—Training Deaf & Blind
Demonstrations by a blind and deaf girl and her teacher on sensitivity
of other senses. Use of fingertips on teacher's lips for communication.
Rental: $4.25. 45 min. 16mm. Film Library—Oregon.

Touching
This film is a conversation with Dr. Ashley Montagu, famous
sociologist and anthropologist on the key concepts of his recent volume, *Touching*. Utilizing psychological research and medical opinion,
Dr. Montagu develops the case that touching is necessary for human
life. He utilizes much experimental research (including the work of
Harry Harlow) and clinical work in various settings to develop his
thesis. Sale: $350. Rental: $30. 35 min. 16mm or Videocassette.
Color. Psychological Films, Inc.

Two Faces of Group Leadership
This film gives a clear view of the two basic functions which leaders
use in all groups: mobilizing and managing. This film makes it clear
that groups are only as good as their leaders and leaders are only as
good as their leadership skills. It is especially appropriate for group
encounter and counselor training programs. Sale: $325. Rental: $30.
30 min. 16mm or Videocassette. Color. Psychological Films, Inc.

Understanding Aggression
This film is intended for use by psychology, sociology and education
departments. Noted Psychologist Roger Ulrich presents significant re-
search findings in this discussion of man's own aggressive behavior.
Sale: $420. Rental: $48. 29 min. 16 mm. Color/sound. 1972.
Prentice-Hall Film Library.

Contacts

SOME ORGANIZATIONS INTERESTED IN RECREATION FOR HANDICAPPED PEOPLE

American Alliance for Health, Physical Education and Recreation,
    Programs for the Handicapped, 1201 16th St., N.W., Washington,
    DC 20036
American Blind Bowling Assn., 3701 Connecticut Ave., N.W.,
    Washington, DC 20008

American Wheelchair Bowling Assn., 2635 N.E. 19th St., Pompano Beach, FL 33062

Boy Scouts of America, Scouting for the Handicapped, North Brunswick, NJ 08902

The 52 Assn., Inc. (Veterans), 147 E. 50th St., New York, NY 10022

Girl Scouts of the USA, Scouting for the Handicapped, 830 Third Ave., New York, NY 10022

Joseph P. Kennedy, Jr. Foundation, 1701 K St., N.W., Washington, DC 20006

Indoor Sports Club, 3445 Trumbull St., San Diego, CA 92106

National Association of the Physically Handicapped, Inc., 6473 Granville Ave., Detroit, MI 48228

National Association for Retarded Citizens, 2709 Avenue E East, P.O. Box 6109, Arlington, TX 76011

National Council for Therapy Through Horticulture, 5606 Dower House Rd., Upper Marlboro, MD 20870

National Easter Seal Society for Crippled Children and Adults, 2023 W. Ogden Ave., Chicago, IL 60612

National Inconvenienced Sportsmen's Assn., 3728 Walnut Ave., Carmichael, CA 95608

National Therapeutic Recreation Society, 1601 N Kent St., Arlington, VA 22209

National Wheelchair Athletic Assn., 40–23 62nd St., Woodside, L.I., NY 11377

National Wheelchair Basketball Assn., Box 100, Rehabilitation & Education Center, Oak St. and Stadium Dr., Champaign, IL 61820

CONTACTS FOR INFORMATION ON MENTAL RETARDATION

American Association on Mental Deficiency, 5201 Connecticut Ave., N.W., Washington, DC 20015 (Publishes *Mental Retardation*)

Bureau of Education for the Handicapped, Office of Education, U.S. Dept. of Health, Education and Welfare, 7th and D Sts., S.W., Washington, DC 20203

Children's Bureau, Office of Child Development, U.S. Dept. of Health, Education and Welfare, Washington, DC 20201

Council for Exceptional Children, 1920 Association Drive Highway, Reston, VA 22091 (Publishes *Exceptional Children*)

Division of Mental Retardation, Rehabilitation Services Administration, 330 C St., S.W., Room 3068, Washington, DC 20201

National Association for Retarded Citizens, 2709 Avenue E, East, Arlington, TX 76010

National Clearinghouse for Mental Health Information, National Institute of Mental Health, U.S. Dept. of Health, Education and Welfare, 5600 Fishers Lane, Rockville, MD 20852

Office of Mental Retardation Coordination, U.S. Dept. of Health, Education and Welfare, Washington, DC 20201 (Publishes *Programs for the Handicapped*)

The President's Committee on Mental Retardation, 7th and D Sts., S.W., Washington, DC 20201 (Publishes *PCMR Message*)

PSYCHOLOGY INDEPENDENT STUDY PROGRAM

Psychology Today magazine offers an independent study program in psychology. The sixteen-week course is offered in cooperation with the University of California Extension, eight college credits are granted upon completion. A selection of materials is mailed, there are no classes to attend. The cost is $105. Write for free information: *Psychology Today* Independent Study Program, Room 715, One Park Ave., New York, NY 10016.

Rehabilitation Services Administration. Division of Monitoring and Program Analysis, Statistical Analysis and Systems Branch, Washington, DC 20201. Reports, publications and detailed information on rehabilitation may be obtained by writing.

Stanford's Sleep Disorders Clinic. Stanford University, Medical Center, Stanford, CA 94305. Exploring the mysteries of sleep. Write for information.

ANTIPSYCHIATRY & MENTAL PATIENTS' RIGHTS ORGANIZATIONS

Advocates for Freedom in Mental Health, 928 No. 62nd St., Kansas City, KS 66102

Alliance for the Liberation of Mental Patients, 112 S. 16th St., Room 1305, Philadelphia, PA 19103

American Association for the Abolition of Involuntary Mental Hospitalization, c/o Post Office, University of Santa Clara, Santa Clara, CA 95053

Cahiers pour la Folie, c/o Mme. Hubert, 68 Rue d'Assas 75006, Paris, France

Campaign Against Psychiatric Atrocities, c/o R. Povall, Box 6899, Auckland, New Zealand

Center for the Study of Legal Authority and Mental Patient Status (LAMP), Box 277, Hartford, CT 06101

Center for the Study of Psychiatry, 4628 Chestnut St., Bethesda, MD 20014

Citizens Against Shock, c/o Adamski, 8417 S.W. Beaverton Hillsdale Hwy., Portland, OR 97225

Elizabeth Stone House, 128 Minden St., Jamaica Plain, MA 02130

de Gekkenkrant, P.O. Box 3286, Amsterdam, The Netherlands

Heavy Daze, 111 Tavistock Crescent, London W11, England

Madness Network News, Box 684, San Francisco, CA 94101

Mental Health Law Project, 84 Fifth Ave., New York, NY 10011

Mental Health Law Project, 1220 19th St., N.W., Suite 300, Washington, DC 20036

Mental Patients Association, 2146 Yew St., Vancouver, B.C., Canada

Mental Patients Liberation Front, Box 156, West Somerville, MA 02144

Mental Patients Liberation Project, Box 1745, Philadelphia, PA 19105

Mental Patients Liberation Project, Box 158, Syracuse, NY 13201

Mississippi Mental Health Project, P.O. Box 22571, Jackson, MS 39206

Network Against Psychiatric Assault, 2150 Market St., San Francisco, CA 94114

Network Against Psychiatric Assault, c/o Beattie, H-16 Koshland, UCSC, Santa Cruz, CA 95064

Network Against Psychiatric Oppression, P.O. Box 667F, New York, NY 10010

Patients Rights Organization, 2108 Film Bldg., Room 707, Cleveland, OH 44114

Project Release, 4 West 76th St., New York, NY 10023

Scarlet Letter Group, Box 12106, Richmond, VA 23241

State and Mind, Box 89, West Somerville, MA 02144

Vermont Health Rights Committee, c/o Helvarg, 76 N. Union St. #6, Burlington, VT 05401

Welcome Back, 3206 Prospect Ave., Cleveland, OH 44115

Women Against Psychiatric Assault, 2150 Market St., San Francisco, CA 94114

PART III

The
Profession

Graduate Programs

15

GRADUATE EDUCATION IS RAPIDLY CHANGING; distinctions between programs are vanishing, and there is an increasing diversity in objectives. The best source of information about a program is the department itself. It will send its brochures on admission requirements, degree objectives, and study programs, upon request. It is wise to remember that uninformed preconceptions about a certain program can be misleading and also wasteful of time and money.

The field in which a person is thinking of making a career should be thoroughly reviewed before entering a graduate program. Many people find themselves in a graduate program with no idea of the actual career work involved, employment opportunities, or licensing requirements for that particular discipline. Many students would not have entered a certain graduate program, or would have switched programs, if they had acquired this knowledge. For example, a person really needs a doctorate in psychology to establish credibility in the field. A Master's degree in psychology is very limiting, while a Master's in counseling offers a wide range of opportunities. A poor position for a person to be in is to find out, after receiving a Master's in psychology, that in order for career objectives to be met, he/she must go on for the doctorate, when a Master's in counseling might have fulfilled the objectives. There are literally hundreds of examples like this; it all depends on what a person wants to do. After that has been decided and the area evaluated, then a program and field that meets those objectives is chosen.

In the field of psychology there are ten applications for every graduate opening, thirty to one in the clinical area. The other mental health professions are very similar, although not quite so bad. This should not discourage anyone who is serious. If a person really wants to enter a graduate program, acceptance will come. A high GPA (grade point average) and GRE (Graduate Record Examination score) are important in most cases, but it is much more important to "stand out" from other applicants. Graduate school is not a circus (some would disagree), yet it is still the best policy to be noticed, and to be unique and unusual. The selection committee reads hundreds of applications; all of them similar. If one is unusual it will command their attention. By commanding their attention (as long as it is not offensive) a person has an edge over all the look-alikes. There are many ways to do this: letters of recommendation; research; publications; projects; personal statements and objectives; a different format for the application or resume; and personal contacts.

Several questions should be asked before entering a graduate program. (1) Do I really need or want to go to graduate school? (2) What are my career objectives? Have I thoroughly checked out the field I want to enter? (3) What type of program is best for me personally? Professionally? (4) What are my financial resources? Does the program offer any stipends, fellowships, or scholarships? Can I obtain any student loans? (5) Do I need an accredited program? If the answer is yes, then the program should be thoroughly checked. There is a great difference between a program that is accredited or is a candidate for accreditation, and one that has applied for accreditation (any program can apply). Many programs apply, just to say they have, knowing that there is no chance they will be accepted. So be careful.

Programs

In this chapter there are lists of External Degree Programs and Innovative Degree Programs. Traditional programs are not listed because there are three sources readily available listing them. One source is this chapter itself. Another is the public or university library where there is a plentiful supply of catalogs and source books. A third source is the chapters in this book on Professional Associations and Service Organizations. By writing the associations and organizations that cover an interest area, one cannot only obtain lists of traditional graduate programs but also many other types of educational and training programs not readily available in standard reference works on the subject.

External Degree Program: Abolition of residency requirements, plus a willingness to give the student a great deal of study areas freedom.

Innovative Degree Program: Residency required, student involvement in program design, credit for past work experience, independent individualized study, increased use of internships and practicums, and a stronger emphasis on career oriented public service programs are the chief characteristics.

Classification: Most programs are not totally external degree or innovative degree, but a combination of both, so we have made no distinction in the classification of them.

Adelphi University, Waldorf Institute for Liberal Education, Garden City, NY 11530. Degree: MA in elementary education.
Alfred University, Psychology Department, Alfred, NY 14802. Degree: BA, MA.
American University College of Continuing Education, Massachusetts & Nebraska Avenues, Washington, DC 20016. Degrees: wide variety of programs and degrees.
Antioch College, Master of Arts in Community Education Program, 5829 Banneker Road, Columbia, MD 21044. Degree in community education.
Antioch: New England, Antioch Graduate School, One Elm Street, Keene, NH 03431. Degree: Master of Education degree in counseling and guidance; M.A. degree in counseling psychology.

Antioch College: West, 3663 Sacramento St., San Francisco, CA 94118. Degree: MA degree in psychology.

Appalachian State University, Boone, NC 28607. Degrees: MA and Ed.S. in Education.

Associates for Human Resources, Box 727, Concord, MA 01742. Degree: M.Ed. in conjunction with Antioch College.

Auburn University, Auburn, AL 36830. Degrees: Ed.D. in Educational Administration and Supervision and Counselor Education.

Baltimore Center for Social Research and Action (Antioch College), 525 St. Paul Street, Baltimore, MD 21202. Degree: MA in media studies.

Boston University, School of Education, 264 Bay State Road, Boston, MA 02215. Degrees: BA, MA, Ph.D., Ed.D., MED, BS in Education.

California Graduate Institute, 1321 Westwood Blvd., Los Angeles, CA 90024. Degrees: MA, Ph.D. in variety of areas.

California School of Professional Psychology, 2450 Seventeenth St., San Francisco, CA 94122. Degrees: MA and Ph.D. in psychology. The school has other branches at the following locations: 3755 Beverley Blvd., Los Angeles, CA 90004; 3974 Sorrento Valley Blvd., San Diego, CA 92120; 1350 M St., Fresno, CA 93721.

California State University, Fullerton, 800 North State–College Blvd., Fullerton, CA 92631. Degree: A terminal MS degree in psychology with concentration in Clinical and Community Psychology.

California State University, Long Beach, School of Applied Arts and Sciences, 6101 E. 7th St., Long Beach, CA 90801. Degree: MA in Vocational Education.

California State University, Sonoma, Rohnert Park, CA 94928. Degree: MA in Psychology.

Campus Free College, 466 Commonwealth Avenue, Boston, MA 02212. Degrees: AA, BA, MA in a variety of areas.

Case Western Reserve University, School of Management, Wilberforce, OH 45384. Degrees: MS, Ph.D.

College for Human Services, 201 Varick St., New York, NY 10014. Degree: Master of Human Services degree which is supposed to be equivalent to an MSW.

Consortium of the California State University and Colleges, 400 Golden Shore, Long Beach, CA 90802. Degrees: MA in Early Childhood Education and Vocational Education.

D-Q University, Box 409, Davis, CA 95616. Degrees: AA, MA in Humanities.

E.W. Cook Institute, Master's Program in Counseling and Psychotherapy (Antioch College), P.O. Box 917, Fairbault, MN 55021. Degree: MA in counseling and psychotherapy.

The Extended University, Systemwide Administration, 570 University Hall, University of California, Berkeley, CA 94720. Degrees: BA, MA, Ph.D. in various fields of study.

Farleigh Dickinson University, Center for Human Development, Rutherford, NJ 07070. Degree: MA.

The Fielding Institute, 225 Butterfly Lane, Santa Barbara, CA 93108. Degrees: Ph.D., BA, in Education. Ph.D., Psy.D. in Clinical and Counseling Psychology.

Friends World College, Plover Lane, Lloyd Harbor, Huntington, NY 11743. Degree: BA.

George Williams College, Counseling Psychology, 555 31st St., Downers Grove, IL 60515. Degree: MA.

Goddard College, Plainfield, VT 05658. Contact: Robert Belenky. Degree: MA in many areas.

Grand Valley State College, Thomas Jefferson College, Allendale, MI 49401. Degree: Ph.B.

Humanistic Psychology Institute, 325 Ninth St., San Francisco, CA 94103. Part of the Association for Humanistic Psychology. Degree: Ph.D. in many areas.

Institute for Child Study—University of Maryland, College Park, MD 20742. Degrees: MA, MED, Ph.D., Ed.D.

International (Community) College, 1019 Gayley Ave., Westwood Village, Los Angeles, CA 90024. Degrees: BA, MA and Ph.D. in education and psychology.

International Graduate School of Behavioral Science. Contact: Director of Admissions, The International Graduate School of Behavioral Science, Executive Office: Suite P, 205 West End Ave., New York, NY 10023. Degrees: Doctoral in psychology, behavioral science and mental health sciences.

Iowa State University of Science and Technology, Ames, IO 50010. Degree: MA in education and psychology.

Juarez-Lincoln Bilingual University, (Antioch Graduate School of Education) 715 E. 1st Street, Austin, TX 78701. Degrees: M.Ed. in counseling and guidance. They also offer a nonresidential BA degree in cluster areas in Texas and Colorado. For more information write: *Austin:* 715 E. 1st St., Austin, TX 78764. *Denver:* 825 Delaware Street, Denver, CO 80204.

Lehigh University, Psychology Department, Bethlehem, PA 18015. Degrees: BA, BS, DA, Ph.D.

Logos West, Brook Dewing Medical Bldg., 914 Dewing Avenue, Lafayette, CA 94549. Offers: Certificate of training in marriage/family/child counseling.

Lone Mountain College, 1005 Valencia St., San Francisco, CA 94110. Degree: Masters in psychology.

Montclair State College, Human Organizational Processes, Upper Montclair, NJ 07043. Degree: MA in education and personnel.

New York University, Department of Human Relations, 239 Greene Street, New York, NY 10003. Degrees: MA, Ph.D.

North Dakota State University of Agriculture and Applied Science, Fargo, ND 58102. Degree: MS in Educational Counseling and Guidance.

Nova University, 3301 College Avenue, Fort Lauderdale, FL 33314. Degree: Ph.D. in the behavioral sciences is offered in an off-campus format. Ed.D. in community college teaching. Masters degree in counseling and guidance.

Pacific States University, Graduate Programs, 1516 South Western Avenue, Los Angeles, CA 90006. Degrees: MA, Ed.D., Ph.D. Areas: psychology, counseling, administration, and general education.

Peter Sammartino College of Education, Farleigh Dickinson University, Office of Doctoral Studies, Teaneck, NJ 07666. Degree: Ed.D.

Philadelphia Center (Antioch Graduate School of Education), 5538 Wayne Avenue, Philadelphia, PA 19144. Degree: MA in Education.

The Rand Graduate Institute, Santa Monica, CA 90406. Degree: Ph.D. in policy analysis.

The Teachers, Inc. (Antioch College), 2248 Broadway, New York, NY 10024. Degree: M.Ed.

Union Graduate School: Antioch College, Yellow Springs, OH 45387. Degree: Ph.D. in many areas.

United States International University, School of Human Behavior, 10455 Pomerado Road, San Diego, CA 92131. Degree: MA, Ph.D. in variety of areas.

University of Alabama, New College, Box 6211, University, AL 35486. Degrees: BA, BS interdisciplinary studies.

University of Connecticut, Inner College, Storrs, CT 06268. Degrees: MA, Ph.D. in combined philosophy and psychology.

University of Denver, Denver, CO 80210. Degree: Ph.D. in Higher Education.

University of Iowa, Iowa City, Iowa 52242. Degree: Master of Social Work.

University of Massachusetts, Higher Education Center, Graduate School of Education, Amherst, MA 01002. Degree: MA and Ed.D. in Education.

University of Mississippi, University, MS 38677. Degrees: Masters in Education and an Ed.D. and Ph.D. in Education.

University of Northern Colorado, Center for Special and Advanced Programs, Greeley, CO 80639. Degree: Graduate programs in psychology (counseling and guidance) and education at various military and civilian areas across the nation.

University of Redlands, Johnston College, Redlands, CA 92373. Contact: Hugh Redmond. Degree: BA in humanities or psychology.

University of Sarasota, 2080 Ringling Blvd., Sarasota, FL 33577. Degree: Doctorate in Education.

University of Toledo Graduate School, Community Information Specialist Program, Department of Library and Information Services, University Hall, Room 309, 2801 W. Bancroft Street, Toledo, OH 43606. Degree: MA as a community information specialist.

University of Washington, Seattle, WA 98195. Degree: Ph.D. The program offers a specialized individual Ph.D. in fields not already being given at the University of Washington.

University of Wisconsin: Madison, Institute for Environmental Studies, 1225 West Dayton Street, Madison, WI 53706. Degrees: MA and Ph.D. interdisciplinary.

Wake Forest University, Box 7266, Reynolds Station, Winston-Salem, NC 27109. Degrees: MA in education, MA in counseling.

Walden University, Institute of Advanced Studies in Education, 1191 8th Street South, Naples, FL 33940. Degree: Ph.D. in a variety of areas.

Webster College, 470 East Lockwood, Webster Groves, MO 63119. Degree: BS.

The Wright Institute, Graduate School, 2728 Durant Avenue, Berkeley, CA 94708. Degree: Ph.D. in psychology.,

References

Accredited Institutions of Postsecondary Education and Programs 1976-77
Published for the Council on Postsecondary Accreditation. A national directory of junior and senior colleges, universities, professional, and specialized schools shows, alphabetically by state, all the institutions accredited by the recognized agencies at the beginning of the academic year. It also reports the latest accrediting actions of 35 professional agencies for the accreditation of 41 programs; it is the latest accurate list of institutional names and addresses, names of presidents, and enrollment data. There is also a list of major changes in institutions: name changes, mergers, and closings. Each institutional entry includes: name of president; academic calendar; branch campuses, or affiliated institutions; enrollment; student body; date of first regional accreditation and latest renewal; professional accreditation; level of degrees offered; type of institution; control–public or private; religious relationship, if any. Candidates for accreditation as well as institutions belonging to the 10 member accrediting associations are separately listed. $9.50. Washington, DC: American Council on Education, 331 pp.

A Directory of College Programs for Paraprofessionals in Human Services. *Gartner, Alan.*
$9.95. Behavioral Publications, 72 Fifth Ave., New York, NY 10011. 1975.

Graduate Study in Psychology 1977-1978.
American Psychological Association
An excellent source book on 476 programs in the United States and Canada. This book lists mostly traditional universities and 4-year colleges. Information is given on the degrees offered, application and admission requirements, degree requirements, financial assistance, tuition fees, and a description and orientation of the programs. $6. Washington, DC: American Psychological Association.

A Guide to Graduate Study. *Quick, Robert (Ed.)*
A comprehensive guide to, and directory of, programs leading to the Doctor of Philosophy in United States universities. Entries on each graduate school and its programs give information on admission and

residence requirements, requirements for admission to candidacy for the Ph.D. degree, fees, first-year financial aid, housing, and special facilities for study and research. Fields of study leading to the degree and areas of specialization within them are detailed. For large institutions, fields are grouped for easy reference. An extensive index of the fields of study enables the reader to identify the institutions offering various programs. A brief introductory section, intended for the college undergraduate contemplating graduate study and his adviser, considers such topics as selecting and gaining admission to graduate school and financing graduate study. $19. Washington, DC: American Council on Education, 1969. 637 pp.

Innovative Graduate Programs Directory.
This book lists innovative graduate programs, along with who to contact, degrees offered, accreditation of the institution, and a brief description of the program. Over 100 programs are listed in the directory. $4. Learning Resources Center, Empire State College, S.U.N.Y., Saratoga Springs, NY 12866, 1976.

International Handbook of Universities.   *Keyes, H.M.R.; and Aitken, D.J. (Eds.)*
A companion volume to American Universities and Colleges, the volume describes, in English, universities and other institutions of higher education in 108 countries outside of the United States and the Commonwealth. Entires give the title, address, and principal officers of the institution and information concerning faculties, institutes and schools, history, structure and status, academic year, admission requirements, fees, language(s) of instruction, degrees and duration of studies, libraries, publications, and the size of academic staff and student enrollment. The index lists each institution under its official title and under the English translation. $32. Washington, DC: American Council on Education, 1975.

Women in Higher Education.   *Furniss, W. Todd; and Graham, Patricia Albjerg (Eds.)*
Discrimination against women in higher education exists and must be eliminated, according to 38 leaders in education, feminism, law, and government who reflect the consensus of participants in the 55th Annual Meeting of the American Council on Education. Their analyses, opinions, and suggestions are collected in a source book to establish a sound basis for endeavors to remove prejudice and to extend oppor-

tunities for women in academe. Threaded throughout the discussions
are the issues of academic ability and double standards for judging
credentials and performance for men and women; social barriers to
women in colleges and universities; the role of women's colleges;
women's studies; feminism; black feminism; affirmative action
policies, especially those with legal and academic implications for university autonomy. $12. Washington, DC: American Council on Edu-
cation, 1974. 336 pp.

World List 1974–75.   *Keyes, H.M.R.; and Aitken, D.J. (Eds.)*
A world directory covering more than 6,000 universities and other
institutions of higher education in 146 countries, this work lists the
principal national and international organizations concerned with
higher education. It is informative about bodies responsible for inter-
university cooperation and for facilitating exchanges of academic staff
and students. $9. Washington, DC: American Council on Education,
1974. 500 pp.

The college reference guides listed below are available at most public
libraries and contain facts about each college or university—costs,
course offerings, size, areas of specialization, scholarship possibilities,
and professional accreditation.

Barron's Profiles of American Colleges. $4.95. Woodbury, NY:
Baron's Educational Series, Inc., 1972.
**Comparative Guide to American Colleges: Professional and Guidance
Edition.**   Cass, James; and Birnbaum, Max. $7.95. New York:
Harper & Row, 1977.
Financial Information National Directory: Health Careers.   Chicago:
American Medical Association. $2.95. FIND, 535 No. Dearborn,
Chicago, IL 60610.
Lovejoy's College Guide.   Lovejoy, Clarence E. $5.95. New York:
Simon & Schuster. 1976.

Licensing

16

Introduction

If a state does not require individuals from a particular field to be licensed, then there are no minimum standards. In this instance, clients must "beware" and check the qualifications of professionals with whom he deals. Licensing insures minimum standards of competency and protects the public. If a person is not required to be licensed then what professional associations does she/he belong to? Professional associations have set standards for membership, and one is scrutinized by one's peers, both of these help to keep professional competency high. Write to professional associations concerned for information or for a referral to a member in good standing in your area, they are always more than pleased to help. Also check the chapter on professional associations in this book for information.

Counselor

For the general term "counselor" there are no license requirements in any of the states in the United States. Depending on a person's expertise and experience, many of the professional associations give registration or certification in a particular phase of counseling.

Marriage & Family Counselor

At present only six states in America require licensing for marriage and family counselors: California, New Jersey, Georgia, Nevada, Utah, and Michigan. As Georgia only recently passed its licensing law, no State Board has yet been established.

CALIFORNIA
Board of Behavioral Science Examiners
1020 N. St.
Sacramento CA 95814

NEW JERSEY
Board of Marriage Counselor Examiners
1100 Raymond Blvd.
Newark, NJ 07102

NEVADA
Board of Marriage and Family Counselor's Examiners
1101 N. Virginia St.
Reno, NV 89503

MICHIGAN
Dept. of Licensing and Regulation
1033 S. Washington Ave.
Lansing, MI 48926

UTAH
Bureau of Business Regulations
330 E. 4th South
Salt Lake City, UT 84111

The American Association of Marriage and Family Counselors (AAMFC) stands firmly for the highest standards in marriage counseling. A member of AAMFC must be fully qualified to practice, meeting training, experience and ethical standards. If you wish information about marriage counseling, write AAMFC, 225 Yale Ave., Claremont, CA 91711.

Occupational Therapist

There are license requirements for OTR's in only four states: New York, Florida, Ohio and Georgia. For further information write the American Occupational Therapy Association, Inc. (AOTA), 6000 Executive Blvd., Rockville, MD 20852. All members of AOTA have had to meet the highest requirements.

Psychiatric Social Workers

These professionals are trained in a wide range of mental health roles. Individual therapy, diagnosis, referral, consultation, and group therapy are some of the tasks they are trained to perform. Psychiatric social workers have master's degrees in social work and have completed field-placement programs designed to train them in basic techniques in several areas, including therapy, community organization, administration and consultation. They will usually, but not necessarily, be members of the Academy of Certified Social Workers and the National Association of Social Workers.

Nineteen states have laws regulating social workers. In order: name of state, title, degree, examination required, experience required, and current employment *if* required.

Arkansas: Registered Social Worker—BSW. Exam—NO. Experience—NO. Registered Master Social Worker—MSW or ACSW. Exam—NO. Experience—NO.

California: Registered Social Worker—BA-MSW. Exam—YES. Experience—1–5 years. Licensed Clinical Social Worker—MSW. Exam—YES. Experience—1 year.

Colorado: Licensed Social Worker II—MSW. Exam—YES. Experience—5 years. Licensed Social Worker I—MSW. Exam—YES. Experience—2 years. Registered Social Worker—BA or MSW. Exam—YES. Experience—2 years.

Idaho: Independent Practice—MSW. Exam—NO. Experience—2 years. Certified Social Worker—MSW. Exam—YES. Experience—NO. Social Worker—BSW. Exam—YES. Experience—NO.

Illinois: Certified Social Worker—MSW. Exam—YES. Experience—NO. Social Worker—BA. Exam—YES. Experience—2 years. Employment—YES.

Kansas: Independent Practice—MSW. Exam—YES. Experience—2 years. Master Social Work—MSW. Exam—YES. Experience—NO. Bacc. Social Worker—BSW. Exam—YES. Experience—NO. Social Work Associate—AA. Exam—YES. Experience—NO.

Kentucky: Independent Practice—MSW. Exam—YES. Experience—2 years. Certified Social Worker—MSW. Exam—YES. Experience—NO. Social Worker—BSW. Exam—YES. Experience—NO.

Louisiana: Board Certified Social Worker—MSW. Exam—YES. Experience—2 years.

Maine: Registered Social Worker—MSW. Exam—YES. Experience—NO. Associate Social Worker—BA. Exam—YES. Experience—2 years.

Maryland: Certified Social Worker—MSW. Exam—YES. Experience—2 years. Graduate Social Worker—MSW. Exam—YES. Experience—NO. Social Work Associate—BSW. Exam—YES. Experience—NO.

Michigan: Certified Social Worker—MSW. Exam—NO. Experience—2 years. Social Worker—MSW or BA. Exam—NO. Experience—2 years. Employment—YES. Social Worker Technician—BA. Exam—NO. Experience—NO. Employment—YES.

New York: Certified Social Worker—MSW. Exam—YES. Experience—NO.

Oklahoma: Registered Social Worker—MSW. Exam—NO. Experience—2 years. Employment—YES. Social Work Associate—BA. Exam—NO. Experience—2 years. Employment—YES.

Puerto Rico: Social Worker—BA to MSW. Exam—NO. Experience—2 years.

Rhode Island: Registered Social Worker—MSW. Exam—NO. Experience—NO.

South Carolina: Registered Social Worker—MSW. Experience—NO.

South Dakota: Independent Practice—MSW. Exam—YES. Experience—2 years. Certified Social Worker—MSW. Exam—YES. Experience—NO. Social Worker—BSW. Exam—YES. Experience—NO. Social Work Assistant—AA to BA. Exam—YES. Experience—NO.

Utah: Independent Practice—MSW. Exam—YES. Experience—2 years. Certified Social Worker—MSW. Exam—YES. Experience—

NO. Social Service Worker—BSW. Exam—YES. Experience—NO.
Social Service Aide. Exam—YES. Experience—NO.

Virginia: Registered Social Worker in Private Practice—MSW.
Exam—YES. Experience—2 years. Registered Social Worker—
MSW. Exam—YES. Experience—NO. Employment—YES. As-
sociate Social Worker—BA. Exam—YES. Experience—2 years.

Academy of Certified Social Workers (ACSW): The Certification of
Competence Program administered by the National Association of
Social Workers, Inc. (NASW). A professional recognition program
designed to assure high standards of social science delivery. Also
has developed Manpower Classification Standards for Differential
use of six personnel groups in social work. For more information
write: NASW, 1425 H St., N.W., Suite 600, Washington, DC
20005.

Psychiatrists

A psychiatrist is a medical doctor who specializes in mental disorders.
He/She must be licensed to practice medicine. A board certified psychiatrist has, in addition, practiced for two years and passed the written and oral examinations of the American Board of Psychiatry and
Neurology. Of the mental health professionals, only psychiatrists can
prescribe drugs and medical therapies. Further information can be
obtained from the American Psychiatric Association, 1700 Eighteenth
St., N.W., Washington, DC 20009, or from the American Board of
Psychiatry and Neurology, 1603 Orrington Ave., Evanston, IL 60201.

Psychologists*

Clinical psychologists are trained to provide therapy to individuals
and groups. In addition, they are skilled in the use of diagnostic techniques to measure personality and intellectual traits. Other psychologists specialize in child development, counseling and guidance, work-

* Information supplied by the American Psychological Association (APA). For further
information write APA, 1200 Seventeenth St., N.W., Washington, DC 20036, (202)
833-7600.

ing with schools and schoolchildren, or in research areas. A clinical
psychologist should have a Ph.D. from a university and have had at
least two years experience in a mental health facility. In addition,
he/she may have a diploma from the American Board of Examiners in
Professional Psychology and may be licensed by the state in which
he/she practices. In order: name of state, title, degree, examination
required, experience required, and definition.

DEFINITIONS

1. Licensing Law: Anyone practicing psychology by any title
   without a license will be penalized.
2. Specific definition of title.
3. Psychotherapy is included in definition of title.
4. Circular definition of title: a person who does psychological
   work and calls himself a psychologist is one.
5. Examination may be waived if the standards are no lower in a
   state or province where the candidate is licensed or certified.
6. Examination may be waived for Diplomates of the American
   Board of Professional Psychology.

Alabama: Practice of Psychologists—Doctorate. Exam—not mandatory. Experience—NO. 1, 2, 3, 5, 6.

Alaska: Practice of Psychology—Doctorate. Exam—YES. Experience—1 year. 1, 2, 3, 5, 6.

Alberta: Psychologist—MA. Exam—not mandatory. Experience—
NO. 4.

Arizona: Psychologist—Doctorate. Exam—evaluation of candidate's
credentials. Experience—NO. 4.

Arkansas: Psychologist—Doctorate. Exam—YES. Experience—1
year. 1, 2, 3, 5. Psychological Examiner—MA. Exam—YES.
Experience—NO.

California: Psychologist—Doctorate. Exam—YES. Experience—2
years, of which 1 must be postdoctoral. 1, 2, 3, 5, 6.

Colorado: Psychology—Doctorate. Exam—YES. Experience—2
years postdoctoral. 1, 2, 5, 6.

Connecticut: Psychologist—Doctorate. Exam—YES. Experience—1
year postdoctoral. 2, 5, 6.

Delaware: Psychologist—Doctorate. Exam—YES. Experience—1
year, 2 years if clinical. 2, 3, 5, 6.

Washington, DC: Practice of Psychology—Doctorate. Exam—YES. Experience—2 years. 1, 2, 3, 5, 6.
Florida: Practice of Psychology—Doctorate. Exam—YES. Experience—2 years, 1 must be postdoctoral. 1, 2, 5, 6.
Georgia: Practice of Applied Psychology—Doctorate. Exam—not mandatory. Experience—1 year. 1, 2, 5.
Hawaii: Practice of Psychology—Doctorate. Exam—YES. Experience—NO. 1, 2, 3, 5, 6.
Idaho: Practice of Psychology—Doctorate. Exam—not mandatory. Experience—2 years postdoctoral. 1, 2, 3, 5.
Illinois: Psychologist—Doctorate. Exam—YES. Experience—2 years. 2, 5.
Indiana: Psychologist in Private Practice—Doctorate. Exam—YES. Experience—3 years postdoctoral. 2, 5, 6. Basic Psychologist— Doctorate. Exam—YES. Experience—NO.
Iowa: Practice of Psychology—Doctorate. Exam—YES. Experience—1 year postdoctoral; Master's—5 years experience. 2, 5, 6. Practice of Associate Psychology—Master's. Exam—YES. Experience—NO.
Kansas: Psychologist—Doctorate. Exam—either regular or evaluation of candidate's credentials. Experience—2 years. 2, 5.
Kentucky: Practice of Psychology—Doctorate. Exam—YES. Experience—1 year. 1, 2, 5.
Louisiana: Psychologist—Doctorate. Exam—YES. Experience—2 years postdoctoral. 2, 3, 5, 6.
Maine: Psychologist—Doctorate. Exam—YES. Experience—2 years. 1, 2, 3, 5. Psychological Examiner—Master's. Exam—YES. Experience—1 year.
Manitoba: Psychologist—Doctorate. Exam—YES. Experience—NO. 5.
Maryland: Psychologist—Doctorate. Exam—YES. Experience—2 years, 1 must be postdoctoral. 2, 5.
Massachusetts: Practice of Psychology—Doctorate. Exam—YES. Experience—2 years, 1 must be postdoctoral. 1, 2, 3, 5, 6.
Michigan: Consulting Psychologist—Doctorate. Exam—YES. Experience—5 years. 2, 5, 6. Psychologist—Doctorate. Exam—not mandatory. Experience—1 year. Psychological Examiner or Technician—Master's. Exam—not mandatory. Experience—1 year.
Minnesota: Consulting Psychologist—Doctorate. Exam—YES. Ex-

perience—2 years postdoctoral. 1, 2, 5, 6. Psychologist—Master's.
Exam—YES. Experience—2 years post-Master's.

Mississippi: Psychologist—Doctorate. Exam—not mandatory. Experience—1 year. 2, 5, 6.

Montana: Practice of Psychology—Doctorate. Exam—YES. Experience—2 years postdoctoral. 1, 2, 3, 5, 6.

Nebraska: Practice of Psychology—Doctorate. Exam—YES. Experience—NO. 1, 2, 3, 5.

Nevada: Psychologist—Doctorate. Exam—YES. Experience—1 year postdoctoral. 2, 3, 5.

New Brunswick: Psychologist—Doctorate. Exam—YES. Experience—1 year. 4, 5, 6.

New Hampshire: Psychologist—Doctorate. Exam—YES. Experience—2 years. 4, 5, 6.

New Jersey: Practice of Psychology—Doctorate. Exam—YES. Experience—2 years, 1 must be postdoctoral. 1, 2, 3, 5, 6.

New Mexico: Psychologist—Doctorate. Exam—YES. Experience—2 years postdoctoral. 2, 5, 6.

New York: Psychologist—Doctorate. Exam YES. Experience—2 years. 2, 3, 5, 6.

North Carolina: Psychologist—Doctorate. Exam—YES. Experience—2 years postdoctoral. 1, 2, 3, 5, 6. Psychological Examiner—Master's. Exam—YES. Experience—NO.

North Dakota: Psychologist—Doctorate. Exam—YES. Experience—NO. 2, 5, 6.

Ohio: Practice of Psychology—Doctorate. Exam—YES. Experience—2 years, 1 postdoctoral. 1, 2, 3, 5, 6. Practice of School Psychology—Master's. Exam—YES. Experience—1 year.

Oklahoma: Practice of Psychology—Doctorate. Exam—YES. Experience—2 years. 1, 2, 5.

Ontario: Psychologist—Doctorate. Exam—YES. Experience—1 year. 4, 5, 6.

Oregon: Practice of Psychology—Doctorate. Exam—YES. Experience—2 years. 1, 2, 3, 5, 6. Psychologist Associate—Master's. Exam—YES. Experience—3 years.

Pennsylvania: Practice of Psychology—Doctorate. Exam—YES. Experience—2 years postdoctoral. 1, 2, 5, 6. Master's. Exam—YES. Experience—4 years post-Master's.

Quebec: Psychologist—Doctorate or Master's. Exam—not mandatory. Experience—NO. 2, 5, 6.

Rhode Island: Psychologist—Doctorate. Exam—YES. Experience—

2 years, 1 must be postdoctoral. 2, 5, 6.

Saskatchewan: Registered Psychologist—Doctorate. Exam—not mandatory. Experience—NO. 4, 5.

South Carolina: Practice of Psychology—Doctorate. Exam—not mandatory. Experience—NO. 1, 2, 3, 5, 6.

Tennessee: Psychologist—Doctorate. Exam—YES. Experience— NO, except if clinical, then 1 year. 1, 2, 3, 5, 6. Psychological Examiner—Master's. Exam—YES. Experience—NO.

Texas: Psychologist—Doctorate. Exam—YES. Experience—2 years, 1 must be postdoctoral. 1, 4, 5, 6.

Utah: Psychologist—Doctorate. Exam—YES. Experience—2 years. 2.

Virginia: Practice of Psychology—Doctorate. Exam—YES. Experience—2 years with clinical psychologists having completed a practicum internship of at least 1 year. 1, 2, 3, 5, 6.

Washington: Psychologist—Doctorate. Exam—YES. Experience—1 year postdoctoral. 2, 3, 5, 6.

West Virginia: Practice of Psychology—Doctorate. Exam—YES. Experience—2 years postdoctoral. 1, 2, 3, 5, 6. Master's. Exam—YES. Experience—8 years post-Master's.

Wisconsin: Practice of Psychology—Doctorate. Exam—not mandatory. Experience—1 year. 1, 2, 3, 5, 6.

Wyoming: Psychologist—Doctorate. Exam—YES. Experience— NO. 2, 3, 5, 6.

Psychotherapists

There are no licensing requirements in any of the states in the United States. The term psychotherapy describes what all mental health professionals do who work with clients; however, some people who call themselves psychotherapists are not professionals and do not have adequate training. If there is doubt concerning the credentials of a "therapist," check with his/her professional association.

Rehabilitation Counselor

There are no licensing requirements in any of the states in the United States. However, there is certification by the Commission on Rehabilitation Counselor Certification formed a few years ago by the American Rehabilitation Counseling Association and the National Rehabilitation Counseling Association. The primary purpose of certification is to establish professional standards whereby disabled individuals, related professionals, agency administrators, and the general public can evaluate the qualifications of persons practicing rehabilitation counseling. Certification has as its primary impetus the provision of assurances that professionals engaged in rehabilitation will meet acceptable standards of quality in practice. Such standards are considered to be in the clients' best interests.

The Commission consists of five appointees from NRCA, five appointees from ARCA, and one each from the Council on Rehabilitation Education, Council of State Administrators of Vocational Rehabilitation, Association of Rehabilitation Facilities, National Association of Non-White Rehabilitation Workers, Council of Rehabilitation Counselor Educators, and a national consumer representative.

To be eligible for the Certification Examination, a candidate must meet one of the following requirements of education combined with experience:

—A Master's degree in Rehabilitation Counseling from a rehabilitation counselor training program, plus a supervised internship, plus one year of acceptable experience as defined below; or

—A Master's degree in Rehabilitation Counseling without a supervised internship, plus two years of acceptable experience as defined below; or

—A Master's degree in a related area (such relatedness to be determined by CRCC on the basis of the candidate's transcript), plus two years of acceptable experience as defined below; or

—A Master's degree in an unrelated area plus five years of acceptable experience as defined below; or

—A Bachelor's degree in rehabilitation plus four years of acceptable experience as defined below; or

—A Bachelor's degree in any other area plus five years of acceptable experience as defined below.

Acceptable experience in rehabilitation counseling is defined as full-time employment acceptable to the Commission in the use of rehabilitative counseling techniques; vocational evaluation; psychological assessment; social, medical, vocational psychiatric information; and rehabilitative methods in an agency (public or private), hospital or clinic, in which the applicant is under professional supervision and has employed such methods and measures. Effective January 1, 1977, experience submitted as meeting certification requirements must include at least one year under the supervision of a Certified Rehabilitation Counselor. Questions concerning the acceptability of an individual's experience are considered on a case-by-case basis by the Commission's Credentials Committee. Commission on Rehabilitation Counselor Certification, 520 North Michigan Ave., Chicago, IL 60616, (312) 644-4329.

School Psychologist

The National School Psychology Certification/Licensure Project has completed data collection and analysis leading to the publication of *The Handbook of Certification/Licensure Requirements for School Psychologists*. The *Handbook* is an authoritative, accurate and comprehensive reference source which incorporates certification requirements in all fifty states. It is designed to serve as a ready reference for trainers, state department personnel and students in school psychology. It includes a glossary of descriptive terms frequently used by state agencies. Since the National School Psychology Certification/Licensure Project is an ongoing research effort, revisions of state requirements, if any, will be available approximately every six months. The project was established to provide a service to professionals interested in the field of school psychology. Proceeds from the handbook are used to cover the cost of research, publication and distribution and insure continued up-dating of all information relevant to the certification/licensure of school psychologists.

The *Handbook of Certification/Licensure Requirements for School Psychologists* is published in two editions. The student edition is a soft cover volume and costs $5.95. The faculty and library edition is ring bound and costs $8.95. Both prices include the cost of postage and handling. NASP Certification Handbook, 1511 K St., N.W., Suite

927, Washington, DC 20005. Or write to: The National Association for School Psychologists (NASP) for information on one state or for other areas of interest, (202) 347-3956. Local libraries and university libraries should have a copy of this book, if not request that it be ordered.

Sex Therapist

There are no laws, in any of the states in the United States to enforce minimum standards of education and experience for sex therapists. Recently two organizations have established certification standards for sex therapists. For a copy of these requirements and a list of certified sex therapists in your area write:

American Association of Sex Educators and Counselors, 5010 Wisconsin Ave., N.W., Suite 304, Washington, DC 20016, (202) 686-2523.
Eastern Association of Sex Therapy, 10 East 88th St., New York, NY 10028.
Of the 4,000 to 5,000 sex clinic/treatment centers in the United States, William Masters and Virginia Johnson (highly respected experts in the field) estimate that only 50 to 100 are *legitimate*. In fact, William Masters went a little further when he appeared at the 128th Annual Convention of the American Psychiatric Association, and said that seduction of clients by therapists is tragic; the therapist should be charged with rape, not malpractice.

Vocational Guidance Counselors

No licensing requirements in any of the American states. However, members of the National Vocational Guidance Association (NVGA) have had to meet the highest standards. NVGA, 1607 New Hampshire Ave., N.W., Washington, DC 20009, (202) 483-4633.

Employment*   17

ALTHOUGH IT WAS NOT POSSIBLE to obtain facts and figures on specific jobs within the mental health field, much of the information supplied by Janet M. Cuca of the American Psychological Association regarding the psychologist is relevant (not only because many of those in the mental health field come from a psychology background, but because the material reflects general trends within the current job market).

Ms. Cuca in her 1975 paper, "Ph.D.s in Psychology: Supply and Demand," compared the 1974 doctorate (psychology) labor force of 30,049 to a projected 1980 labor force of 42,658. This growing supply of doctorates would necessitate the creation of 11,780 new positions by the year 1980 in order to see full employment (in 1974 there were 30,950 full-time positions, enough for that year's labor supply). This trend would seem to reflect a quickly tightening job market.

However, the job market is making some attempts to adjust to the large numbers of Ph.D.s. Positions which have more traditionally been held by those with a Master's degree are being filled by Ph.D.s. Also, the salary once paid the more scarce Ph.D. is declining. There has also been a shift in the traditional employer. Due partially to revenue sharing, federal and local governments have begun to employ a greater percentage of psychologists, becoming almost as significant a factor in employment as the academic institutions.

Among general trends in 1973 and 1974, the ratio of applicants to positions was better at the Master's level than at the Ph.D. level; the numbers were more disproportionate in the academic area than

*with Marilyn Bader

285

elsewhere; they were less disproportionate in the clinical-counseling area; and most in balance in the industrial-applied area.

One aspect of psychology which has suffered high unemployment is the scientific subfield. While 36 percent of the 1974 unemployment in psychology was in clinical psychology, 42 percent was in scientific psychology (experimental, comparative-physiological). It is important to realize that 42 percent of psychology degrees are in clinical while only 23 percent are in scientific psychology!

Ms. Cuca's article, "Survey Shows Deteriorating Job Market for New Doctoral Psychologists," indicates that the percentage of 1975 Ph.D.s with no positions has increased over that of 1974. She suggests that the number of those whose status remains undecided for a considerable length of time, is increasing. She attributes this to decreasing academic job opportunities, the "crunch" on scientific jobs, the popularity of the "social" psychology field among doctoral students (and hence the oversupply), and the fact that newer fields do not contain many job opportunities.

Fortunately, a somewhat brighter picture of the job market is offered by the U.S. Labor Department in their 1974–1975 *Occupational Outlook Handbook,* which projects job opportunities through 1985.

The outlook for sociologists at the Ph.D. level is favorable. However, there will be considerably more competition at the Master's level. The widest job choice will exist for those with research training.

The projection for employment counselors (Master's) is favorable in public and community agencies. The market for employment counselors should increase with government funding and recognition of the need to train unskilled, unemployed people.

The outlook for rehabilitation counselors is favorable. The best prospects are for those with graduate work in rehabilitation counseling. This job also depends largely upon government funding.

The prospects for college career planning and placement counselors are favorable for the well qualified. Opportunities should increase as college enrollments are expected to increase through the early 1980s.

The *Handbook* states that the outlook for psychologists is good. The prospects for the Ph.D. are seen as very good and for the Master's degree, good in the areas of clinical and counseling. Settings which have an increasing need for psychologists include: mental hospitals; correctional institutions; mental hygiene clinics; and community mental health centers. There are also expected federal openings in the

Veterans Administration and the Department of Defense. A great deal of competition will continue for preferred academic settings.

The projection for social workers with Master's degrees is very good, and favorable for those with Bachelor's degrees (through the 1970s).

The conflicting projections for psychologists may be explained by at least two factors. First, Ms. Cuca is dealing with all aspects of psychology which include several subfields particularly hard hit by unemployment. (By contrast, the U.S. Labor Department's projection is based on openings in one of the least affected subfields, clinical-counseling.) Second, Ms. Cuca is also dealing with areas of psychology (scientific, and new fields) which have depended to a great extent on the academic institutions which are now hiring fewer psychologists. However, the clinical counseling opportunities (projected by the U.S. Labor Dept.) are rapidly increasing, thanks to government aid.

In summary the U.S. Labor Department predicts that professional occupations in all fields will be the fastest growing and the most in demand, with a very significant demand occurring in the field of mental health for all professions.

REFERENCES

Cuca, Janet M. "Graduate Enrollments Leveling Off." *APA Monitor,* November, 1974.

_____. "Job Crunch Hits Scientists Harder than Professionals." *APA Monitor,* July, 1975.

_____. "Ph.D.'s in Psychology: Supply and Demand." Paper presented at The American Psychological Association convention, Chicago, 1975.

_____. "Placement Report." *American Psychologist,* November, 1975.

_____. "Survey Shows Deteriorating Job Market For New Doctoral Psychologists." *APA Monitor,* November, 1975.

Lathrop, Richard. *Who's Hiring Who,* 3rd ed. Berkeley: Ten Speed Press, 1977.

Lecht, Leonard A. *Occupational Choices and Training Needs.* New York: Praeger Publishers, 1977.

National and International Marketing and Employment Directory, 7th ed. New York: World Trade Academy Press, 1976.

Occupational Outlook Handbook, 1974–1975. Washington, DC: U.S. Dept. of Labor.

U.S. Dept. of Labor. *Jobs, Jobs, Jobs for the College Graduate.* Woodbury, NY: Barron's Educational Series Inc., 1977.

Sources of Information

APA Employment Bulletin

The *Employment Bulletin* is a monthly publication, providing listings of full-time employment opportunities for psychologists and self-descriptions of psychologists seeking employment. In addition to specific vacancies, the *Employment Bulletin* can serve as a resource to identify trends in the supply and demand situation for psychologists in the United States as well as an indication of starting salary ranges. Listings are solicited and accepted from employers of psychologists for positions which require a minimum of either a Master's degree plus one year of experience in psychology to two years of full-time graduate study in psychology. Each month the *Bulletin* lists 125–150 position openings grouped by geographical areas (East, Midwest, South, West, and outside the United States), and employment field (Clinical and Counseling, Academic, Industrial, and Research). A General Openings Section is used for employers having a continuing, widespread need for psychologists who may be recruited through a central office, or for positions of a very general nature.

Applicant Availability Notices are also listed by employment field (Clinical and Counseling, Academic, Industrial and Research). Only members of the APA may submit their availability notices for publication. Notices include applicants' qualification, geographic preference, as well as date and conditions of availability. Confidentiality is assured through the use of coded applicant identification numbers.

APA Member Rates:

One Year Subscription (mailed 3rd class)	$ 7.
One Year Subscription (mailed 1st class)	11.
One Year Subscription (mailed Air Mail)	12.

APA Nonmember Rates:

One Year Subscription (mailed 3rd class)	$14.
One Year Subscription (mailed 1st class)	18.
One Year Subscription (mailed Air Mail)	19.

Subscription must be prepaid to: Subscription Department, American Psychological Association, 1200 Seventeenth St., N.W., Washington, DC 20036 (202) 833-7600. Also APA has a 30-page booklet titled *Careers in Psychology* which is free for a single copy. For a very detailed report APA has a 307-page publication, *Career Opportunities for Psychologists;* write for price and ordering information.

APGA Career Placement Service   (for Counseling and Related Professions)
This service is designed to facilitate and improve job searches by APGA members and employers. It provides a central location for the collection of APGA members' resumes. APGA promotes by advertisement job seeking members who participate in this service. This serves not only students who are looking for initial employment but also those interested in moving on to other jobs advancing their careers or service. Participating employers are able to systematically screen candidates and receive resumes from one source. There is a one-time fee of $15 for subscribing candidates which includes a minimum size advertisement. The advertisement is then broadly exposed in APGA's *Guidepost.*

   When members join the service, they submit copies of resumes and an ad which will appear in the next issue of *Guidepost.* When employers join the service and place ads, they receive copies of all previous advertisement listings of registered candidates and continue to receive issues of *Guidepost.* From this list, employers may request from the APGA Placement Office selected resumes of candidates. As subscribers, candidates and employers have the opportunity to use the Convention Placement Service. This provides the opportunity for candidates and employers to meet and interview there.

American Personnel and Guidance Association, 1607 New Hampshire Ave., N.W., Washington, DC 20009, (202) 483-4633.

American Students and Teachers Abroad
A 66-page publication, costing 90¢, that is loaded with information on services of organizations concerned with employment, travel, and study abroad. Order by stock number: 1780-01377, from: Superintendent of Documents, U.S. Government Printing Office, Washington, DC 20402.

Chronicle of Higher Education.   1717 Massachusetts Ave., N.W., Washington, DC 20036, (202) 667-3344
Weekly newspaper for the academic community, read nationwide with a circulation of over 20,000. They have a regular space in their paper,

"Bulletin Board," in which one can advertise: 35¢ per word for regular classified ads, for larger print the price goes up. The "Bulletin Board" is also full of ads from institutions seeking persons to fill jobs.

College Placement Council, Inc. P.O. Box 2263, Bethlehem, PA 18001, (215) 868-1421
CPC has one publication that deserves special interest (write for free catalog of publicatbns):

College Placement Annual is an occupational directory with career information on approximately 1,300 employers. Circulation: approximately 400,000 copies to more than 1,200 college placement offices and 600 Armed Services installations. 448 pages. Individual copies available directly from CPC at $3 each for members, $5 for nonmembers (payment must accompany order).

The Cooperative College Register. P.O. Box 298, Alexandria, VA 22314
Persons interested in being considered for teaching or administrative positions at colleges and universities complete a registration form and submit it to the Register with an enrollment fee of $20 for a full year's service. This confidential file is maintained at the Alexandria, VA office and lounge reserved for Register visitors. Once each year, in February, a personnel catalog is sent to deans and department heads at each of the 1,200 colleges and universities listed in the American Council on Education (ACE) Directory. This list reflects condensed information on all registered applicants under a coded identification to preserve confidentiality. Institutions indicate preliminary interest by requesting files by code number which are promptly furnished. Also, institutions list position vacancies or request searches for specific profiles or specialties. The Register office reproduces and forwards registration files from the talent bank. Any or all further contact is directly between the institution and the applicant. Each spring, a summary tabulation of all "positions available" listed by the colleges and universities is sent to each registered applicant. This is the only communication between applicant and the Register after confirmation of registration.

Cosmopolitan Professional Placement, Inc. 1st Floor, Howard Johnson's Motor Lodge, Monroeville, PA 15146, (412) 372-3451 or 243-7264
For teachers, school administrators, and college personnel. No charge

unless they actually find you a job, then a percentage of your first year's salary.

Directory of Nonprofit Organizations.   200 Park Ave. South, New York, NY 10003, (212) 777-8210
The *Directory* is available from the American Council of Voluntary Agencies of Foreign Service, Inc. for $6. At over 1,000 pages, it lists information for more than 400 nonprofit organizations with programs abroad. An excellent service book for those interested in working with organizations doing this type of work.

Educational Career Service/Health Career Service.   12 Nassau St., Princeton, NJ 08540, (609) 924-4660
ECS/HCS memberships are open to anyone seeking instructional or administrative positions in universities, colleges, independent schools, hospitals, allied health and social service agencies, foundations, state and federal governments, museums and other cultural organizations. As notices of position openings are filed by institutions, ECS/HCS mail confidential notices to individual members whose training, experience, and career objectives match the position specifications. Each notice contains a summary description of the position, an indication of compensation, benefits, responsibilities and desired qualifications.

ECS/HCS never disclose a member's identity to an institution without written authorization from that member. Thus, the individual member can examine all position vacancy notices without prejudice to current employment. The number of position vacancy notices which an individual may receive during the annual membership varies widely depending upon the fields of interest. ECS/HCS members who receive no notices during their membership year may request a 50 percent refund or continue their membership for an additional twelve months without payment of the renewal fee.

The annual fee for ECS/HCS individual membership is $36. A special introductory membership fee of $18 for six months is available to members of certain national and regional associations. Annual renewal of a membership is $24. There are no additional costs for ECS/HCS services in the United States. ECS/HCS never charge contingent placement fees.

Federal Jobs Overseas.   Superintendent of Documents, U.S. Government Printing Office, Washington, DC 20402
A 20-page pamphlet listing Federal agencies employing overseas per-

sonnel, positions, and conditions. The cost is 30¢. Use pamphlets code when ordering: CS 1.48 BRE 18/5.

Friends of World Teaching. P.O. Box 1049, San Diego, CA 92112 Friends of World Teaching is an independent teachers' information agency, dedicated entirely to assisting American and Canadian educators in locating teaching/administrative positions in foreign countries. Files contain updated listings for American Community Schools, International Schools, Church-related, and industry-supported schools and colleges in more than 120 foreign countries. During the past six years Friends of World Teaching has assisted thousands of teachers throughout the United States and Canada in finding jobs with English-language oriented schools and colleges abroad. The application fee is $5 for three countries (your choice), $1 per country after that. Write for further information.

Higher Education Administration Referral Service (HEARS). Suite 510, One Dupont Circle, Washington, DC 20036, (202) 296-2344 HEARS guarantees its registrants complete confidentiality. All correspondence is sent to the individual's home address. Only the HEARS staff knows the names of those professionals who have registered. By registering with the Service, you can be apprised of professional vacancies in all areas of the country—at public, private, land-grant, church-related, private secondary, medical, and research institutions. Once you have registered, you will be informed of all positions listed for which your background meets the institution's specifications. Positions are prescreened for you by the HEARS staff, to be certain they meet the criteria of salary/location/position level you wish to consider. Credentials are released to a prospective employer only on your signature. To date, more than 1,000 institutions have used HEARS as part of their professional staff recruitment programs. A number of major colleges and universities lists all top-level management openings with the Service.
Fees for the professional:
Individual registration (first year) $30.
Individual Re-registration (subsequent year) $25.

International Director of Youth Internships. c/o U.S. Committee for UNICEF, 331 East 38th St., New York, NY 10016. Attn: Connie Crosson. (212) 686-5522
Annual directory that lists more than 400 intern/volunteer positions.

This is work involving the United Nations as well as other international programs. There is no charge for a copy of the directory, but a donation would be appreciated.

VA Hospitals

VA Hospitals at locations shown below range in capacity from approximately 100 to over 2,000 beds. Average bed capacity is about 800. Most have general medical and surgical, pulmonary disease, and psychiatric units. Others are predominantly psychiatric. Many have research programs, outpatient clinics, or domiciliaries. Write directly to the Personnel Officer of the VA Hospital(s) you are interested in.

Alabama, Birmingham 35233, Montgomery 36109, Tuscaloosa 35401, Tuskegee 36083

Alaska, *Juneau 99802

Arizona, Phoenix 85012, Prescott 86301, Tucson 85723

Arkansas, Fayetteville 72701, Little Rock 72206

California, Fresno 93703, Livermore 94550, Loma Linda 92354, Long Beach 90801, Los Angeles (Brentwood) 90073, Los Angeles (Wadsworth) 90073, *Los Angeles 90013, Martinez 94553, Palo Alto 94304, San Diego 92161, San Francisco 94121, Sepulveda 91343

Colorado, Denver 90220, Fort Lyon 81038, Grand Junction 81501

Connecticut, Newington 06111, West Haven 06516

Delaware, Wilmington 19805

District of Columbia, Washington 20422

Florida, Bay Pines 33504, Gainesville 32602, Lake City 32055, Miami 33125, Tampa 33612

Georgia, Augusta 30904, Decatur (Atlanta) 30033, Dublin 31021

Hawaii, *Honolulu 96801

Idaho, Boise 83702

Illinois, Chicago (Lakeside) 60611, Chicago (West Side) 60680, Danville 61832, Downey 60064, Hines (Maywood) 60141, Marion 62959

Indiana, Fort Wayne 46805, Indianapolis 46202, Marion 46952

Iowa, Des Moines 50310, Iowa City 52240, Knoxville 50138

Kansas, Leavenworth 66048, Topeka 66622, Wichita 67218

Kentucky, Lexington 40507, Louisville 40202

Louisiana, Alexandria 71301, New Orleans 70146, Shreveport 71130

Maine, Togus 04330

Maryland, Baltimore 21218, Fort Howard 21052, Perry Point 21902

Massachusetts, Bedford 01730, Boston 02130, *Boston 02108, Brockton 02401, Northampton 01060, West Roxbury 02132

Michigan, Allen Park 48101, Ann Arbor 48105, Battle Creek 49016, Iron Mountain 49801, Saginaw 48602

Minnesota, Minneapolis 55417, St. Cloud 56301

Mississippi, Biloxi 39531, Jackson 39216

Missouri, Columbia 65201, Kansas City 64128, Poplar Bluff 63901, St. Louis 63125

Montana, Fort Harrison 59636, Miles City 59301

Nebraska, Grand Island 68801, Lincoln 68501, Omaha 68105

Nevada, Reno 89502

New Hampshire, Manchester 03104

New Jersey, East Orange 07019, Lyons 07939

New Mexico, Albuquerque 87108

New York, Albany 12208, Batavia 14020, Bath 14810, Bronx 10468, Brooklyn 11209, *Brooklyn 11205, Buffalo 14215, Canadaigua 14424, Castle Point 12511, Montrose 10548, New York 10010, Northport (Long Island) 11768, Syracuse 13210

North Carolina, Asheville 28805, Durham 27705, Fayetteville 28301, Salisbury 28144

North Dakota, Fargo 58102

Ohio, Chilicothe 45601, Cincinnati 45220, *Columbus 43210, Dayton 45428

Oklahoma, Muskogee 74401, Oklahoma City 73104

Oregon, Portland 97207, Roseburg 97470, **White City 97501

Pennsylvania, Altoona 16603, Butler 16001, Coatesville 19320, Erie 16501, Lebanon 17042, Philadelphia 19104, Pittsburgh (Highland Drive) 15206, Pittsburgh (University Drive C) 15240, Wilkes-Barre 18711

Philippines, *Manila (APO San Francisco) 96528

Puerto Rico, San Juan 00921

Rhode Island, Providence 02908

South Carolina, Charleston 29403, Columbia 29201

South Dakota, Fort Meade 57741, Hot Springs 57747, Sioux Falls 57101

Tennessee, Memphis 38104, Mountain Home (Johnson City) 37684, Murfreesboro 37130, Nashville 37203

Texas, Amarillo 79106, Big Spring 79720, Bonham 75418, Dallas 75218, *El Paso 79905, Houston 77031, Kerrville 78028, *Lubbock 79401, Marlin 76661, *San Antonio 78285, San Antonio 78284, Temple 76501, Waco 76703

Utah, Salt Lake City 84113
Vermont, White River Jct. 05001
Virginia, Hampton 23667, Richmond 23249, Salem 24153
Washington, American Lake (Tacoma) 98493, Seattle 98108, Spokane 99208, Vancouver 98661, Walla Walla 99362
West Virginia, Beckley 25801, Clarksburg 26301, Huntington 25701, Martinsburg 25401
Wisconsin, Madison 53705, Tomah 54660, Wood (Milwaukee) 53193
Wyoming, Cheyenne 82001, Sheridan 82801
   *Outpatient clinic only
   **Domiciliary only

Additional Contacts

There are over 200 occupations in the health field. Educational requirements range from a few months of on-the-job training following high school graduation through a college degree plus additional specialized training. Almost all of the Professional Associations and many of the Service Organizations (refer to these chapters in the *Almanac* for additional sources) have career placement services, plus publications with job listings. For additional information on careers in the health field, refer to the *Health Careers Guidebook* or the *Occupational Outlook Handbook*, published by the U.S. Department of Labor, copies of which are generally available from a school guidance counselor or public or school library. Of course, one of the best ways of getting information about health careers is by talking to the people involved in this field. Visit your local hospital. Arrange to speak with as many people in the health professions as possible. Whatever your interests, this first-hand knowledge can be valuable.

The following is a list of sources, not only for mental health, but for the health field as a whole since many overlap.

American Academy of Family Physicians, Volker Blvd. at Brookside, Kansas City, MO 64112
American Academy of Pediatrics, 1801 Hinman Ave., Evanston, IL 60204
American Academy of Physical Medicine and Rehabilitation, 30 No. Michigan Ave., Chicago, IL 60602

American Art Therapy Association, 6010 Broad Branch Rd., N.W., Washington, DC 20015

American Association for Health, Physical Education, and Recreation, 1201 Sixteenth St., N.W., Washington, DC 20036

American Association for Rehabilitation Therapy, Box 93, North Little Rock, AR 72116

American Association of Industrial Nurses, Inc., 79 Madison Ave., New York, NY 10016

American Association of Medical Assistants, One East Wacker Dr., Chicago, IL 60601

American Association of University Professors, Suite 500, One Dupont Circle, N.W., Washington, DC 20036

American Cancer Society, 219 East 42nd St., New York, NY 10017

American College of Nurse-Midwives, 50 East 92nd St., New York, NY 10028

American Congress of Rehabilitation Medicine, 30 No. Michigan Ave., Chicago IL 60201

American Corrective Therapy Association, Public Relations Officer, 1781 Begen Ave., Mountain View, CA 94040

American Dance Therapy Association, c/o Diana Cook, 865 West End Ave., New York, NY 10010

American Dietetic Association, 620 No. Michigan Ave., Chicago, IL 60611

American Heart Association, 44 East 23rd St., New York, NY 10010

American Home Economic Association, 2010 Massachusetts Ave., N.W., Washington, DC 20036

American Hospital Association, 840 No. Lake Shore Dr., Chicago, IL 60611

American Industrial Hygiene Association, 25711 Southfield Rd., Southfield, MI 48075

American Journal of Art Therapy, Box 4918, Washington, DC 20008

American Library Association, 50 East Huron St., Chicago, IL 60611

American Medical Association, 535 No. Dearborn St., Chicago, IL 60610

American Medical Women's Association, Inc., 1740 Broadway, New York, NY 10019

American National Red Cross, 17th and D Streets, N.W., Washington, DC 20006

American Nurses' Association, 10 Columbus Circle, New York, NY 10019

American Nursing Home Association, 1025 Connecticut Ave., N.W., Washington, DC 20036

American Occupational Therapy Association, 251 Park Ave. So., New York, NY 10010

American Physical Therapy Association, 1156 15th St., N.W., Washington, DC 20005

American Physiological Society, 9650 Rockville Pike, Bethesda, MD 20014

American Psychiatric Association, 1700 18th St., N.W., Washington, DC 20009

American Psychoanalytic Association, One E. 57th St., New York, NY 10022

American Psychological Association, 1200 17th St., N.W., Washington, DC 20036

American Public Health Association, 1015 18th St., N.W., Washington, DC 20036

American Rehabilitation Counseling Association, 1605 New Hampshire Ave., Washington, DC 20036

American Speech and Hearing Association, 9030 Old Georgetown Rd., Washington, DC 20014

American Social Health Association, 1740 Broadway, New York, NY 10019

American Society of Electroencephalographic Technologists, University of Iowa, Division of EEG & Neurophysiology, 500 Newton Rd., Iowa City, IA 52240

American Society of Biological Chemists, 9650 Rockville Pike, Bethesda, MD 20014

American Society of Safety Engineers, 850 Busse Highway, Park Ridge, IL 60068

ANA-NLN Committee on Nursing Careers, 10 Columbus Circle, New York, NY 10019

Arthritis Foundation, 1212 Ave. of the Americas, New York, NY 10036

Association for School, College, & University Staffing, Mr. James Akin, Assoc. Director, Educational Placement, Kansas State University, 8 Anderson Hall, Manhattan, KS 66506

Association of American Medical Colleges, One Dupont Circle, N.W., Washington, DC 20036

Association of Medical Rehabilitation Directors and Coordinators, Franklin Delano Roosevelt VA Hospital, Montrose, NY 10548

Association of Paraprofessional Therapists, 419 Boylston St., Room 403, Boston, MA 02116

Blue Cross Association, 840 No. Lake Shore Dr., Chicago, IL 60611

Goodwill Industries of America, Inc., 9200 Wisconsin Ave., Washington, DC 20014

Institute of Food Technologists, 211 No. La Salle St., Suite 2120, Chicago, IL 60601

International Association of Milk, Food, and Environmental Sanitarians, Inc., P.O. Box 437, Shelbyville, IN 46176

Maternity Center Association, 48 East 92nd St., New York, NY 10028

National Association for Mental Health, 1800 No. Kent St., Rosslyn, VA 22209

National Association for Music Therapy, Inc., P.O. Box 610, Lawrence, KS 66044

National Association for Practical Nurse Education & Services, 1465 Broadway, New York, NY 10036

National Association for Retarded Children, 2709 Ave. E East, Arlington, TX 76011

National Association of Hearing and Speech Agencies, 919 18th St., N.W., Washington, DC 20006

National Association of Human Services Technologies, 1127 11th St., Sacramento, CA 95814

National Association of Social Workers, Two Park Ave., New York, NY 10016

National Commission for Social Work Careers, Two Park Ave., New York, NY 10016

National Council for Homemakers-Home Health Aide Services, Inc., 1740 Broadway, New York, NY 10019

National Council on the Aging, 1828 L St., N.W., Washington, DC 20036

National Easter Seal Society for Crippled Children and Adults, 2023 West Ogen Ave., Chicago, IL 60612

National Environmental Health Association, 1600 Pennsylvania Ave., Denver CO 80203

National Federation of Licensed Practical Nurses, Inc., 250 West 57th St., New York, NY 10019

National Health Council, Inc., 1740 Broadway, New York, NY 10019

National Medical Association, 1717 Massachusetts Ave., N.W., #602, Washington, DC 20036

National Recreation and Park Association, 1700 Pennsylvania Ave., N.W., Washington, DC 20006

National Rehabilitation Counseling Association, 1522 K St., N.W., Washington, DC 20005

National Society for the Prevention of Blindness, Inc., 79 Madison Ave., New York, NY 10016

National Therapeutic Recreation Society, 1601 No. Kent St., Arlington, VA 22209

Planned Parenthood-World Population, 810 Seventh Ave., New York, NY 10019

Society for Public Health Education, 655 Sutter St., San Francisco, CA 94102

United Cerebral Palsy Association, 66 East 34th St., New York, NY 10016

Additional Resources

Food and Drug Administration, Parklawn Personnel Office, Parklawn Building, 5600 Fishers Lane, Rockville, MD 20852

MEDIHC Program, National Institutes of Health Manpower Education, 9000 Rockville Pike, Bethesda, MD 20014

National Institutes of Health Bureau of Health Manpower Education Information Office, 9000 Rockville Pike, Bethesda, MD 20014

Public Inquiries, Health Services and Mental Health Administration, Public Health Service, Room 5-B-29, 5600 Fishers Lane, Rockville, MD 20852

Public Health Service, Office of Public Inquiries, Bethesda, MD 20034

U.S. Employment Service, Department of Labor, Washington, DC 20202.

U.S. Office of Education, Division of Vocational and Technical Education, Health Occupations, Washington, DC 20202

Veterans Administration (054), 810 Vermont Ave., N.W., Washington, DC 20420

Additional Publications

Careers in Counseling and Guidance, Shelley Stone and Bruce Shertzer. Houghton Mifflin Co., 1972, 168 pp. $5.95.

Counseling Occupations, U.S. Dept. of Labor, Bureau of Labor Statistics, Reprint Bulletin No. 1785-102, 1974, 25¢. Available from the U.S. Superintendent of Documents.

The Counseling Psychologist, Teachers College Press, 1968, 18 pp. 25¢.

Personnel Workers, U.S. Department of Labor, Bureau of Labor Statistics, Reprint Bulletin No. 1785-23, 1974, 25¢. Available from U.S. Superintendent of Documents.

Psychologist, Clinical, Careers, 1975, 2 pp. 20¢.

Psychology, Career Opportunities Series C19, Catalyst, 1973, 24 pp. 95¢.

Psychology, Education Opportunities Series E19, Catalyist, 1973, 16 pp. 70¢.

Rehabilitation Counselor, Science Research Associates, 1975, 4 pp. 49¢.

School Counselors, Science Research Associates, 1971, 4 pp. 49¢.

School Psychologist, Careers, 1973, 2 pp. 20¢.

ADDRESSES:

Careers, Largo, FL 33540

Catalyst, 6 East 82nd St., New York, NY 10028

Houghton Mifflin Co., One Beacon St., Boston, MA 02108

Science Research Associates, Inc., 259 E. Erie St., Chicago, IL 60611

Superintendent of Documents, U.S. Government Printing Office, Washington, DC 20402

Teachers College Press, Columbia University, 525 West 120th St., New York, NY 10027

Funding

18

LEARNING HOW TO PREPARE a grant proposal is a valuable educational experience. It makes you put together a proposition that is clear and concise, filters out irrelevant parts, leaving you with a solid statement that is valuable to any research or study, whether it is funded or not. Once you learn this system it will be easy for you in the future to prepare other proposals. Don't be put off by the whole operation, it really isn't overwhelming, it just needs a little time and study. Money is the name of the game, and is available for those who try.

There are literally thousands of grants for thousands of different reasons and circumstances. Whether you are an individual looking for a grant to complete your studies or part of an organization that needs funding to carry on its work, there is money available if you know how to go about it. To this end, you should be aware of the following:

(1) Use this chapter for resources and contacts on funding before beginning or submitting your proposal. If you are unsure of how to write a grant proposal, consult one of the many pamphlets and books available, they are easy to understand and should not be a problem to any serious person.

(2) Find out about agencies and foundations, what they are interested in, what they want, and what they expect. It is surprising how many people do not check this out and submit proposals to organizations that have no interest in that area. It is obvious what happens to these proposals.

(3) Keep your proposal clear and short, no one likes reading rambling, wordy papers. At the beginning state what is to be accomplished, who is going to do it, the cost, and the length of time. Next show what benefits there will be, who will benefit, and how they will benefit.

After giving this some thought, test your ideas on others for critical reviews. Then consult a source on how to write a proposal. Put your ideas into the correct format and the result will be a well conceived, and well documented proposal. Now your proposal is ready to be submitted.

Types of Grants

Conference: A grant awarded to support the costs of meetings.

Consortium: A grant made to one institution in support of a project in which the program is being carried out through a cooperative arrangement between or among the grantee institution and one or more participating institutions (profit or nonprofit).

Construction: A grant made to provide support for building, expanding, or modernizing health facilities.

Continuing Education: A grant, usually short term, made to provide support for additional or updated training to individuals practicing or wishing to practice in a given health field.

Demonstration: A grant, generally of limited duration, made to establish or demonstrate the feasibility of a theory or approach.

Discretionary or Project: A grant made in support of an individual project in accordance with legislation which permits the grantor agency to exercise judgment in selecting the project, the grantee and the amount of the award.

Fellowship: A grant made to an individual to support specific training which will enhance that individual's level of competence in that particular health area of concern.

Formula: A grant in which funds are provided to specified grantees on the basis of a specific formula, prescribed in legislation or regulation, rather than on the basis of an individual project review. The formula is usually based on such factors as population, per capita income, enrollment, mortality, and morbidity. These grants are generally mandatory.

Planning: A grant made to support planning, developing, designing, and establishing the means for performing research, delivering health services, or accomplishing other approved objectives.

Research: A grant made in support of investigation or experimentation aimed at the discovery and interpretation of facts, revision of accepted theories in the light of new facts, or the application of such new or revised theories.

Service: A grant made to support costs for the purpose or organizing, establishing, providing, or expanding the delivery of health or mental health services to a specified community or area.

Staffing: A grant made to an institution to provide support for salaries of professional and technical personnel and their inservice training.

Study and Development: A grant awarded to study and develop innovative and experimental programs leading to an established health care component.

Training: A grant awarded to an organization to support costs of training students, personnel, or prospective employees in research, or in the techniques or practices pertinent to the delivery of health services in the particular area of concern.

National Institute of Mental Health Research Grants (1975)

I. *By Division,* amount in millions, $62.7. Behavioral Sciences 25 percent, Clinical 17 percent, Psychopharmacology 19 percent, Small Grants 1 percent, Epidemiology 3 percent, Service Development 13 percent, Metropolitan 3 percent, Minority Groups 5 percent, Crime and Delinquency 6 percent, Applied 8 percent.

II. *By Discipline* of Principal Investigator, N = 1,064. Medical and Biological Sciences 14 percent, Social Sciences 15 percent, Psychiatry 15 percent, Other 6 percent, Psychology 50 percent. Psychology is broken down as follows: Experimental 13 percent, Clinical 10 percent, Physiological 11 percent, Social 6 percent, Developmental 5 percent, Other 5 percent.

III. *By Type of Institution,* N = 1,064. Hospitals and Clinics 8 percent, Independent Organizations 9 percent, Other Institutions 2 percent, Colleges and Universities 81 percent. Colleges and Universities are broken down as follows: Medical Schools 25 percent, Arts and Sciences 38 percent, Other Schools 18 percent.

Sources of Information

Alcohol, Drug Abuse, and Mental Health Administration (ADAMHA)
National Research Service Awards
ADAMHA provides National Research Service Awards to individuals for research training experiences in specified areas of biomedical and behavioral research (a detailed description of these areas is available from the Government Information Service). Individual applicants receive the awards for specified training proposals. A limited number of awards are available for predoctoral training; ADAMHA will give priority to applicants for postdoctoral training. Applicants must be citizens, noncitizen nationals, or permanent residents of the United States. A predoctoral applicant must have completed two or more years of graduate work as of the proposed activation date of the award and have a doctoral prospectus. A postdoctoral candidate must have received the doctorate as of the activation date of the proposed fellowship. The award provides a maximum of 3 years of support. ADAMHA, 5600 Fishers, Rockville, MD 20852

Alcohol, Drug Abuse, and Mental Health Administration (ADAMHA)
Research Project Grants
Research Project Grants provide funds to institutions on behalf of principal investigators who have designed and will direct a specific project or set of projects. This support mechanism is common to all three of ADAMHA's Institutes:

National Institute of Mental Health (NIMH): Studies of the processes—biological, psychological, and social—underlying normal development and functioning form the core of NIMH's research program. NIMH also supports research into the etiology, treatment, and prevention of mental and emotional illnesses and research on a great number of public health problems related to mental health. Research on schizophrenia, the affective disorders, psychoneuroses and personality disorders, psychosomatic illnesses, organic brain disorders, and childhood mental illness accounts for a significant portion of NIMH research support.

National Institute on Drug Abuse (NIDA): NIDA provides support for studies concerned with the epidemiology, etiology, treatment and prevention of narcotic addiction and drug abuse and with the adverse effects of abused drugs. It also supports clinical and preclinical research and basic research on the sites and mechanisms of action of abused drugs. Areas of interest include all life science disciplines relevant to drug abuse.

National Institute on Alcohol Abuse and Alcoholism (NIAAA): NIAAA supports biomedical research in the areas of the central nervous system, neuroendocrine, pathologic conditions related to alcohol and fetal alcohol syndrome; and psychosocial research into areas of the moderate use of alcohol as a stabilizing factor, drinking among the elderly, history of alcoholism, and diagnosis and treatment. ADAMHA, 5600 Fishers Lane, Rockville, MD 20852

American Association of University Women (AAUW)

The AAUW's Educational Foundation awards fellowships to women of the United States who have achieved distinction or show promise of distinction in their fields of scholarly work. There are no restrictions as to age of applicant or academic field or place of study. AAUW attaches great importance to the project on which the applicant wishes to work, its probable significance as a contribution to knowledge, and the applicant's qualifications to pursue it. The awards will support 12 months of full-time research. AAUW, Educational Foundation, 2401 Virginia Ave., N.W., Washington, DC 20037

American Council of Learned Societies (ACLS)
Grants-in-Aid

Grants-in-Aid support specific programs of humanistic research in progress by contributing to the scholar's essential personal expenses. These expanses may include personal travel and maintenance away from home necessary to gain access to materials, research or clerical assistance, and reproduction or purchase of materials. The grants will be available to the recipient immediately following acceptance of the award (within three months after the deadline) and should be expended within one year after acceptance. Applicants must have a doctorate or its equivalent and must be citizens or permanent residents of the United States or Canada. ACLS, 345 E. 46th St., New York, NY 10017

The Aquinas Fund

Interested in research in psychology, mental health and social sciences. Will give research grants, scholarships and fellowships. Grants from a high of $20,500 to a low of $400. 345 Park Ave., 27th Floor, New York, NY 10022

Basic Educational Opportunity Grants

Grants range from a minimum of $50 a year to a maximum of $1,000. Only students starting their first, second, or third years of college may apply. In 1975 over $135 million was left over because people did not apply. P.O. Box 84, Washington, DC 20044

Cattell Fund

Interested in aiding psychologists in universities by supplementing their sabbatical allowances. Grants from a high of $25,000 to a low of $3,000. Cattell Fund, c/o Robert Thorndike, 525 West 120th St., New York, NY 10027

Center for Research for Mothers and Children (CRMC)
Major Research Program Grants

The Center for Research for Mothers and Children, part of the National Institute of Child Health and Human Development, is soliciting program grant applications to develop new knowledge about diseases and disorders during pregnancy, infancy, and childhood. CRMC will award Major Research Program grants to promote and support multidisciplinary research efforts, particularly those involving the behavioral and natural sciences in clinical and laboratory settings. Areas of concern include, but are not necessarily limited to: infants at risk for mortality and morbidity; birth defects; disorders of growth and development; and accidents and poisonings. Center for Research for Mothers and Children, DHEW, 330 Independence Ave., S.W., Washington, DC 20201

Davis Foundation

Interested in mental health, education and medical research. Grants from a high of $25,000 to a low of $300. Davis Foundation, W-2191 First National Bank Building, St. Paul, MN 55101

Department of Health, Education and Welfare
HEW Fellows Program

HEW invites applications for appointments to its Fellows program, which offers 200 men and women the opportunity to work for 12 months with major officials in the department. HEW promises that the individuals selected "will find here a unique experience in governmental policymaking and management." To be considered for the program, candidates must:

—be citizens of the United States
—have a record of demonstrated interest in community service and the
  nation's social problems
—provide a combination of education and specialized managerial or
  community experience with evidence of progressive responsibility
—qualify in the GS range 11-15, as determined by the U.S. Civil
  Service Commission

Fellows will receive the regular salaries for their assigned Civil Service
grade level. HEW Fellows Program, 330 Independence Ave., S.W.,
Washington, DC 20201

Falk Medical Fund
Interested in the mental health field in general, with particular interest
in mental health and racism and public policy. Grants from a high of
$375,000 to a low of $300. Falk Medical Fund, 3317 Grant Building,
Pittsburgh, PA 15219

Foundations' Fund for Research in Psychiatry
Interested in supporting postdoctoral scientists engaged in research in
mental health. Foundations' Fund for Research in Psychiatry, 100
York St., New Haven, CT 06511

The Grant Foundation
Interested in mental health, the nature and development of the human
mind with emphasis on psychology, biology and social bases. Preference given to young, unknown investigators. Grants from a high of
$300,000 to a low of $1,000. The Grant Foundation, 130 East 59th
St., New York, NY 10022

Green Foundation
Interested in mental health and medical research. Grants from a high
of $40,000 to a low of $5,000. Green Foundation, P.O. Box 452,
Mexico, MO 65265

The Harris Foundation
Interested in aid to teachers, graduate fellowships, educational television, and research in psychiatry. Grants from a high of $25,000 to a
low of $25. The Harris Foundation, First National Bank Building,
17th Floor, St. Paul, MN 60670

Ittleson Family Foundation
Interested in mental health and psychiatric research. Grants from a high of $40,000 to a low of $100. Ittleson Family Foundation, 660 Madison Ave., New York, NY 10021

Kennedy Foundation
Interested in research and studies into the problems of mental retardation. Grants from a high of $300,000 to a low of $500. Kennedy Foundation, 1701 K St., N.W., Suite 205, Washington, DC 20006

Leslie Fund, Inc.
Interested in the handicapped, hospitals, mental health, education, and child welfare. Grants from a high of $15,000 to a low of $50. Leslie Fund, Inc., 3600 West Lake Ave., Glenview, IL 60025

McCall Life Pattern Fund
The McCall Life Pattern Fund will award several $2,500 grants each year to mature women who want to go to school to improve their skills or complete their educations. Grants cover tuition, child care, bus fare and books. Applications from: The McCall Life Pattern Fund, Soroptomist Foundation, 1616 Walnut St., Philadelphia, PA 19103

Merck Family Fund
Interested in mental health, education, and conservation. Grants from a high of $9,500 to a low of $500. Merck Family Fund, c/o Mrs. Francis W. Hatch, Secretary, Preston Place, Beverly Farms, NJ 01915

National Center for Prevention and Control of Rape
The National Center for the Prevention and Control of Rape, part of the National Institute of Mental Health, supports research studies into the causes of rape, laws dealing with rape, the treatment of victims, and the effectiveness of existing programs to prevent and control rape. It is also authorized to fund research and demonstration projects to plan, develop, implement, and evaluate methods in treatment and counseling programs for victims of rape and their families, and efforts to rehabilitate offenders. The Center will promote the dissemination of educational, training, and other materials and facilitate the use of such information through conferences, technical assistance, and a clearinghouse. Efforts which address serious criminal sexual assaults committed against women and youth will receive special priority. The Center considers applications for research projects in the following

categories: Basic and Applied Research Studies; Research-Demonstration Projects; Research-Demonstration Projects on Consultation and Education. National Center for Prevention and Control of Rape, 5600 Fishers Lane, Rockville, MD 20852

National Endowment for the Arts (NEA)
Work Experience Internships
The 13-week program acquaints participants with the policies, procedures, and operations of the Endowment and gives them an overview of arts activities in this country. NEA plans the internship activities to provide a detailed knowledge of its programs, including policy development, grant-making procedures, and administration. In addition to working as members of the NEA staff in one program division throughout the session, interns attend a series of seminars and meetings with arts administrators, artists, and Endowment panelists. The grants include a stipend and travel allowance. Applicants must be sponsored by a college or university, state arts agency, or other nonprofit arts organization. National Endowment for the Arts, Washington, DC 20506

National Endowment for the Humanities (NEH)
General Research Program
Through the Genral Research Program the National Endowment for the Humanities offers support to a wide range of research needs. Inasmuch as it is not oriented to a specific area, this program provides the Endowment with the flexibility to respond constructively to a wide variety of requests which serve the general purpose of support for humanities scholarship. The program usually funds projects designed to explore specific research questions rather than to develop resources for research. The Endowment is particularly interested in promoting collaborative research projects in which scholars with different strengths pool their talents. NEH welcomes as models of research projects which address matters of common concern to scholarship. Grants tend to be one to three years in length, and to involve the efforts of more than one individual at the professional, assistant, or clerical level. The program accepts applications from all scholars engaged in humanities research. National Endowment for the Humanities, Washington, DC 20506

National Endowment for the Humanities (NEH)
Youthgrants in the Humanities
The program supports humanities projects developed and conducted

by students. To be considered for a Youthgrant award, a proposed project must meet three basic conditions: (a) it must relate in a clear way to the humanities; (b) it must have a specific purpose, a carefully designed scope, an identifiable end product, and a high promise of helping individuals to develop their critical faculties; (c) although instructors may be involved (and are encouraged to serve) as advisors and consultants, students must carry the major responsibility for its initiation, development, and execution. Proposed projects may concern: (a) designing or conducting an education program (of either a formal, institutional or informal, public nature); (b) study or research of a particular problem; (c) activities aimed at disseminating humanistic knowledge and materials or applying them to the understanding of ethical and social problems or basic issues of human and national life. National Endowment for the Humanities, Washington, DC 20506

National Institutes of Health (NIH)
National Research Service Awards
NIH will provide up to three years of support to individual, postdoctoral applicants for training experiences in biomedical and behavioral research. Applicants must be citizens, or noncitizen nationals, or permanent residents of the United States. As of the beginning date of the fellowship, an applicant must have received a Ph.D., M.D., D.D.S., etc., or an equivalent foreign or domestic degree. Applicants must apply in one of the research discipline areas specified by NIH and must arrange for appointment to an appropriate institution and acceptance by a sponsor who will supervise the research experience. National Research Service Awards are not made for study leading to the M.D., D.O., D.D.S. or similar professional degrees, nor will they support nonresearch clinical training. NIH, 9000 Rockville Pike, Bethesda, MD 20014

National Institute of Mental Health (NIMH)
Division of Extramural Research Programs
This program plans and supports research conducted throughout the country into the causes, prevention, diagnosis, and treatment of mental illnesses. Among the many types of research conducted with NIMH support are projects designed to improve understanding of the neural, psychological, and social factors underpinning human behavior. Clinical studies aim to sharpen understanding of the biological and biochemical bases of mental illness in order to develop effective treatments for mental illnesses; special emphasis is given such prob-

lems as schizophrenia, autism, and depression. Safe and effective drugs for the mentally ill are developed and tested through psychopharmacological research, while other innovative approaches to treatment and prevention are supported under applied research grants. The Division also conducts and supports epidemiological studies essential to mental health planning. The Division of Extramural Research Programs is composed of the Office of the Director and the following units: Clinical Research Branch, Psychopharmacology Research Branch, Applied Research Branch, and Behavioral Sciences Research Branch. The Office of the Director plans, directs, and coordinates all Division activities. Two research support units, the Small Grants Section and the Research Scientist Development Section, are located in the Office of the Director, as well as two staff units, the Administrative Office and the Program Analysis and Evaluation Section. Write or call for further information. NIMH, 5600 Fishers Lane, Rockville, MD 20852, (301) 443-4513

National Institute of Mental Health (NIMH)
Mental Health Small Grant Program
The small grant program of NIMH provides financial support in a relatively rapid and flexible manner for studies in behavioral, biological, and medical sciences relevant to mental health. These grants are intended primarily for younger, less experienced investigators who do not have regular research grant support or resources available from their universities. Small grants may be used to develop and test a new technique or method; to exploit an unexpected research opportunity; to analyze data previously collected; or to carry out exploratory or pilot studies. Applications for small grants may be submitted at any time, although NIMH must receive applications with June, July or August starting dates no later than February 1 in order to review them in time for the award of summer support. NIMH, 5600 Fishers Lane, Rockville, MD 20852

Rockefeller Foundation Humanities Fellowships
Fellowships are available to support the production of works of humanistic scholarship intended to illuminate and assess the values of contemporary civilization. Support will be given to applicants in the traditional areas of humanities, but proposals in fields not generally considered as humanities will also be encouraged as long as their humanistic implications and methodology are made clear. Awards cannot be made for the completion of graduate or professional studies;

nor can proposals for the writing of poetry or fiction be entertained. The ordinary grant will be of the magnitude of $10,000 to $15,000; generally no award will exceed $20,000. Rockefeller Foundation Humanities Fellowships, 1133 Avenue of the Americas, New York, NY 10036

Rosenthal Foundation, Inc.

Interested in demonstration projects, especially in the areas of mental health, child guidance and care of the sick. Grants from a high of $100,000 to a low of $500. Rosenthal Foundation, Inc., 680 Fifth Ave., Suite 1207, New York, NY 10019

Sandoz Foundation

Interested in medical research and all aspects of mental health. Grants from a high of $15,000 to a low of $500. Sandoz Foundation, 608 Fifth Ave., New York, NY 10020

Smithsonian Institution
Smithsonian Fellowship Programs

The Smithsonian Institution awards fellowships to support independent research in residence at the Smithsonian, in association with its staff and using its collections, laboratories, and other facilities. The fellowships are awarded for not less than 6 months or more than 12 months. The program offers two types of appointment: predoctoral fellowships to graduate students who have completed preliminary course work and examinations and are researching the dissertation; and postdoctoral fellowships to investigators who have recently completed the doctoral degree. Applicants must propose to conduct research in some field in which the Smithsonian has particular research strength, and must offer a specific research proposal, indicating clearly why the Smithsonian is the best place to conduct the studies proposed. The Smithsonian awards the fellowships in the following fields of research: history of science and technology; American history, American material, and folk culture; history of music and musical instruments; history of American and Oriental art; anthropology; geological sciences; radiation biology; evolutionary and systematic biology; ecological and behavioral studies in temperate and tropical zones; and astrophysics. Smithsonian Institute, 1000 Jefferson Dr., S.W., Washington, DC 20506

Stone Foundation
Looking for "positive mental attitude" to put into action in areas of mental health, religion, education, and youth. Grants from a high of $1,475,000 to a low of $216. Stone Foundation, 111 East Wacker Dr., Suite 510, Chicago, IL 60601

The Surdna Foundation, Inc.
Interested in mental health, higher education, child welfare, handicapped, aged, and medical research. Grants from a high of $800,000 to a low of $2,000. The Surdna Foundation, Inc., 200 Park Ave., South, Suite 1619, New York, NY 10017

Taubman Foundation
Interested in mental health and higher education. Grants from a high of $70,000 to a low of $50. Taubman Foundation, 1615 First National Bldg., Tulsa, OK 74103

U.S. Department of Labor, Employment and Training Administration
Program's Purpose—to develop greater capability in behavioral sciences related to the manpower field and to increase the availability of experts as manpower program administrators, specialists, consultants, and researchers. To direct the attention of doctoral candidates to the Nation's manpower problems. To guide social science research toward manpower problems.

Who is Eligible—Doctoral candidates who have completed all requirements for the degree except the dissertation, or those who will have completed them when the grant starts. Applications must be made through the university or college in the name of a specific candidate with the approval of the advisor. Candidates who have partially completed their dissertations may also apply. Institutions awarded grants must be accredited.

How to Apply—Guidelines for submission of doctoral dissertation grants are included in the publication, *Manpower Research and Development Projects*, and may be obtained free from: Director, Office of Research and Development, Employment and Training Administration, U.S. Department of Labor, 601 D St., N.W., Room 9100, Washington, DC 20213 (202) 376-7243. Closing dates for receiving applications are December 1, March 1, June 1, and September 1. All proposals are acknowledged when submitted and final determination made within 3 months.

Selection Procedure—Grants are made on the basis of evaluation and recommendation of the Small Grants Review Panel. The five-member panel of interdisciplinary experts from outside the government considers each proposal separately. Primary consideration is given to the proposal's originality and creativity within the manpower research area.

Grant Awards—Awards are made to the school for the use of the candidate. Funds are available for stipend (for candidate), allowance (for dependents), secretarial and clerical assistance, travel, materials and supplies, communication services, and computer usage. These costs may total up to $10,000 for a period not to exceed 1 year. The university or college may also receive indirect costs and an allowance for tuition and fees up to $3,000.

Study Areas—Topic of a candidate's dissertation must relate to the research objectives described in Title III, Part B of the Comprehensive Employment and Training Act (CETA) of 1973 (Public Law 93-203). Study areas include:

Apprenticeship System; Career Development; Discrimination in Employment; *Employment Service Operations;* Geographic and Occupational Mobility; Groups with Special Needs: Ex-Offenders, Females in the Labor Force, Migrant Workers, Minority Workers, Native Americans, Older Workers, Persons with Limited English-speaking Ability, Veterans, Youth; Implementation of CETA; Job Opportunities and Manpower Shortages; Labor Market Processes: Manpower Development, Training, and Utilization; Measurement of Labor Demand and Supply; Productivity; Quality of Work; Transition from School to Work; Unemployment and Underemployment; Unemployment Insurance Issues; Work and Welfare; Worker Motivation and Job Satisfaction.

U.S. Department of Labor Employment and Training Administration, Washington, DC 20213

U.S. Office of Education
Handicapped Research and Demonstration: Field Initiated Studies
The Field Initiated Studies program supports a broad range of activities focusing on the education of handicapped children. The basic objectives of this support are to: (a) identify, research, and demonstrate solutions to problems related to the education of handicapped children; (b) develop, demonstrate, and disseminate innovative support systems and techniques to improve the performance of handi-

capped children or teachers and others serving the handicapped; and (c) create means to produce the broadest possible dissemination and use of research and development products. The program's definition of handicapped children includes mentally retarded, physically handicapped, and emotionally disturbed children, as well as children with specific learning disabilities. U.S. Office of Education, Department of Health, Education and Welfare, Washington, DC 20202

U.S. Office of Education
Handicapped Research and Demonstration: Student Research
Under the Student Research program the Office of Education is interested in a broad range of student initiated and directed research and research-related projects focusing on the education of handicapped children. There are few restrictions on the types of activities eligible for support. However, proposals must represent activities concerned with the education, physical education, or recreation of handicapped children, and should relate directly to one or more of the objectives of OE's Bureau of Education for the Handicapped. Research must be applied in nature and must show promise of producing valid and relevant information. Within these broad constraints the program will support dissertations, theses, and other student directed projects. OE expects the award period for each project to be no more than 18 months. U.S. Office of Education, Department of Health, Education and Welfare, Washington, DC 20202

Van Ameringen Foundation, Inc.
Interested in promoting mental health through preventive measures, treatment, rehabilitation and research. Grants from a high of $50,000 to a low of $1,000. Van Ameringen Foundation, Inc., 509 Madison Ave., New York, NY 10022

White House Fellows
The program is open to men and women of all occupations who are not less than 23 and not more than 35 years of age. Fellows serve with senior members of the Administration and participate in seminars and other activities during a one-year period. Commission on White House Fellowship, Washington, DC 20415

Further Contacts

American Council on Education, One Dupont Circle, Washington, DC 20036

Andrew Mellon Foundation, 140 E. 62nd St., New York, NY 10021

Carnegie Foundation, 437 Madison Ave., New York, NY 10022

Charles Stewart Mott Foundatin, 510 Mott Foundation Bldg., Flint, MI 48502

Council for International Exchange of Scholars, 11 Dupont Circle, Suite 300, Washington, DC 20036

Danforth Foundation, 222 S. Central Ave., St. Louis, MO 63105

Duke Endowment, 200 S. Tryon St., Suite 1500, Charlotte, NC 28202

Exxon Education Foundation, 111 W. 49th St., New York, NY 10020

Ford Foundation, 320 E. 43rd St., New York, NY 10017

Lilly Endowment, 2801 N. Meridan St., Indianapolis, IN 46208

Resources for Proposal Writers

*Annual Register of Grant Support, Academic Media, Inc., 32 Lincoln Ave., Orange, NJ 07050

A Basic Guide for the Preparation and Submission of Proposals for Research Support, Western's Campus Bookstore, Western Michigan University, Kalamazoo, MI 49001

The Bread Game: The Realities of Foundation Fund-Raising, Glide Publications, 330 Ellis St., San Francisco, CA 94102

The Budget of the United States Government, Superintendent of Documents, U.S. Government Printing Office, Washington, DC 20402

Catalog of Federal Domestic Assistance, Superintendent of Documents, U.S. Government Printing Office, Washington, DC 20402

Division of Research Grants Newsletter, National Institute of Mental Health, NIH Building, Rockville Pike, Bethesda, MD 20014

The Foundation Center, 888 Seventh Ave., New York, NY 10019. Also has a library at 1001 Connecticut Ave., N.W., Washington, DC 20036. The Center compiles and disseminates information and publications about nongovernment foundations.

*Foundation Directory, Columbia University Press, 136 So. Broadway, Irvington-on-Hudson, NY 10533

*Foundation Grants Index, Columbia University Press, 136 So. Broadway, Irvington-on-Hudson, NY 10533

Foundation News, Council on Foundations, Box 783, Old Chelsea Station, New York, NY 10011. Published bi-monthly.

The Grantsmanship Center, 1015 West Olympic Blvd., Los Angeles, CA 90015. Educational organization that conducts training programs throughout the country on improving fund-raising skills. Also publishes the *Grantsmanship Center News* which gives information on how to obtain grants.

*Grantsmanship News, University Resources, Inc., 160 Central Park So., New York, NY 10019

*Grantsman Quarterly Journal, 950 6th St., Pine City, MN 55063

*Guide to European Foundations, Columbia University Press, 136 So. Broadway, Irvington-on-Hudson, NY 10533

Guide for Nonprofit Institutions, Superintendent of Documents, U.S. Government Printing Office, Washington, DC 20402

How to Prepare a Research Proposal: Suggestions for Those Seeking Funds for Behavioral Science Research by David R. Krathwohl, Syracuse University Bookstore, 303 University Press, Syracuse, NY 13210

How to Write Successful Foundation Presentations by Joseph Dermer, Public Service Materials Center, 104 East 40th St., New York, NY 10016

Library Information Service, University of Illinois, Room 212 Armory Bldg., Champaign, IL 61820. For $15. per hour will index manuscripts, compile a bibliography, locate pictures, persons, or any other type of information.

A Manual for Obtaining Foundation Grants, Robert J. Corcoron Co., Fund Raising Council, 40 Court St., Boston, MA 02108

*New York Times Guide to Federal Aid for Cities and Towns, Quadrangle Books, Inc., 300 Madison Ave., New York, NY 10017

*Private Foundations Reporter, Commerce Clearinghouse, Inc., 4025 Peterson Ave., Chicago, IL 60646

Where to Get Help: The Dollars and Sense of Fund Raising.   Virginia Kerr, June 1973, *MS. Magazine,* 370 Lexington Ave., New York, NY 10017

*These items are quite expensive. They may be available at a local public or university library.

19

Professional Associations

Index to Professional Associations

American Academy of Psychotherapists (AAP)
American Anthropological Association (AAA)
American Art Therapy Association, Inc. (AATA)
American Association of Marriage and Family Counselors (AAMFC)
American Association of Sex Educators, Counselors and Therapists (AASECT)
American Association of Suicidology (AAS)
American Association of University Professors (AAUP)
American Dance Therapy Association (ADTA)
American Group Psychotherapy Association, Inc. (AGPA)
The American Occupational Therapy Association (AOTA)
The American Orthopsychiatric Association, Inc. (AOA)
American Personnel and Guidance Association (APGA)
American Psychiatric Association (APA)
American Psychological Association (APA)
American Society of Group Psychotherapy and Psychodrama (ASGPP)
American Sociological Association (ASA)
Association for Advancement of Behavior Therapy (AABT)
Association for Humanistic Psychology (AHP)
Association for Psychotheatrics (AP)
Association for Transpersonal Psychology (ATP)
Association for Women in Psychology (AWP)
Association of Asian-American Psychologists (AAP)
The Association of Black Psychologists (ABP)

Behavior Therapy and Research Society (BTRS)
Eastern Association for Sex Therapy (EAST)
International Primal Association, Inc. (IPA)
National Association for Music Therapy, Inc. (NAMT)
National Association of School Psychologists (NASP)
National Association of Social Workers (NASW)
National Rehabilitation Counseling Association (NRCA)
PSI CHI
Western Association of Christians for Psychological Studies (WACPS)

List of Associations

American Academy of Psychotherapists (AAP)
Administrative Secretary: Thomas Robinson
Central Office: 1040 Woodcock Road, Orlando, FL 32803, (305)
894-0921
Membership:
1. A graduate degree in a field of study relevant to the practice of
   psychotherapy.
2. Specific training in psychotherapy, with acceptable supervision.
3. At least four years of full-time clinical experience (or the equivalent in part-time experience) for doctoral-level applicants, at
   least six years for others. In neither case may more than two of
   these years be in trainee status.
4. At least 100 hours of personal therapy. (This requirement may
   be waived in exceptional circumstances.)

Publications:
Quarterly journal *Voices, Newsletter,* and an extensive tape library
that members receive a discount on.

American Anthropological Association (AAA)
1703 New Hampshire Ave., N.W., Washington, DC 20009, (202)
232-8800
Extensive list of publications in all areas of anthropology, write for
free catalog.

Membership Benefits:
Members receive the *American Anthropologist Journal, Anthropology*

Newsletter, Annual Report, plus access to conferences and publications.

Dues and Qualifications:
Fellow: a Master's degree or doctorate in anthropology or an allied field with a demonstrated interest in anthropology. May vote and hold office. $40. Voting Member: professional interest in anthropology plus nomination by a Fellow in good standing. May vote but not hold office. $35. Student, $25. Corresponding Member: anyone who has a scholarly interest in anthropology. May not vote or hold office. $30. Student, $20.

American Art Therapy Association, Inc. (AATA)
Officers:
Public Information: Mickie Rosen, 70 Boucher Dr., Huntingdon Valley, PA 19006
Membership: Shellie David, 56 E. 11th St., New York, NY 10003
Professional Standards: Robert Ault, The Menninger Foundation, Topeka, KS 66601
Education: Gladys Agell, 37 Pike Hill Road, West Topskam, VT 05086

Founded: 1969
Art therapy provides the opportunity for nonverbal expression and communication. Within the field there are two major approaches. The use of art as therapy implies that the creative process can be a means both of reconciling emotional conflicts and of fostering self awareness and personal growth. When using art as a vehicle for psychotherapy, both the product and the associative references may be used in an effort to help the individual find a more compatible relationship between his inner and outer worlds.

Entrance into the field of art therapy on the professional level requires a Master's degree or its equivalent in institutional training. The AATA endorses and encourages the development of Master's degree programs, or their graduate level equivalent as the educational medium for the training of professional art therapists. It also approves of undergraduate programs that prepare students in the basic areas of the fine arts and the behavioral and social sciences. Preparation in these two areas is the basis for specialized art therapy training which includes knowledge of the history, theory, and practice of art therapy itself.

Guidelines for art therapy training have been prepared by the

AATA Education Committee and are offered to help educators plan effectively the development of programs of study and to help students choose intelligently among educational opportunities. The Guidelines are available upon request to the Education Committee Chairperson.

A list of centers and universities offering Art Therapy programs can be obtained also by writing the Education Committee Chairperson.

Membership:

Active Membership is open to all persons who are, or who have been engaged in the therapeutic use of art, including art specialists, psychiatrists, psychologists, administrators, and educators. Only active members have the right to vote and hold office. Annual dues: $65.

Associate Membership is open to volunteers or individuals who may or may not be professionally engaged in the therapeutic use of art. Annual dues: $55.

Student Membership is open to students officially enrolled in art therapy training courses. Annual dues: $30.

All classes of membership receive the following: The Constitution and By-Laws, the Code of Ethics, a Membership Directory, the *Newsletter, The American Journal of Art Therapy,* discounts on publications and discount on admission to the annual conference.

Applications for Active membership must be accompanied by letters of recommendation from two persons familiar with their work. A membership card and a Directory will be sent as verification that membership has been approved. Applications made between October 1 and April 30 must be accompanied by full payment of dues. These members will receive four issues of the *Newsletter* and four issues of *The American Journal of Art Therapy.* Applications made in the second half of the fiscal year, ending September 30, require one-half of the assessed dues. These members will receive two issues of the *Newsletter* and *The American Journal of Art Therapy.*

Registration:

The Association has established specific professional standards. Art therapists who have met those standards are awarded a certificate of registration by the AATA, are so listed in the AATA Registry, and may use the initials "ATR." There is an additional fee for registration, which is a separate procedure from membership. Only Active Members in the AATA are eligible to apply. Further information about qualifications for registration can be obtained from the Chairperson of the Professional Standards Committee.

American Association of Marriage and Family Counselors (AAMFC)
Executive Director: Ray Fowler, Ph.D.
National Office: 225 Yale Ave., Claremont, CA 91711, (714) 621-4749

The American Association of Marriage and Family Counselors is an organization dedicated to professional marriage counseling and to the field of marriage and family relations. Nearly 4,000 members throughout the United States and Canada include psychologists, psychiatrists, social workers, ministers, physicians, sociologists, attorneys, and educators—all of whom are highly-trained, professional marriage counselors working to help couples solve their marriage and family problems. Founded in 1942, AAMFC has national headquarters in Claremont, California, and regional divisions throughout the continent.

The American Association of Marriage and Family Counselors is concerned not just with the profession of marriage and family counseling but also with people and the needs and problems they face in relation to marriage—whether they are now married, will be married, have been married, or may somehow be affected by marriage in our society. AAMFC is also concerned with the institution of marriage itself—its strengths and weaknesses, its changing patterns, its role in the lives of all people. AAMFC firmly believes that this most important and intimate of human relationships demands increased understanding, research, and education at all levels, and that the professional marriage and family counselor must take the lead to insure that these needs are met.

For the public, AAMFC provides a nationwide referral service by supplying the names of qualified marriage counselors and general guidelines for seeking their help.

For interested professionals, AAMFC furnishes consultation about membership standards, application procedures, training, conferences, seminars, and related programs.

Publications:
Membership in AAMFC includes the quarterly *Journal* and the quarterly *Newsletter*. Nonmember subscription rates for the *Journal* are: $15 per year for individuals and $25 for institutions. AAMFC also has a wide variety of other publications.

Clinical Member:

1. Recognized graduate professional education with the minimum of an earned Master's degree from an accredited educational institution in an appropriate behavioral science field, mental health discipline, or recognized helping profession.

2. 200 hours of approved supervision of the practice of marriage and family counseling, ordinarily to be completed in a 2–3 year period, of which at least 100 hours must be in individual supervision. This supervision will occur preferably with more than one supervisor, and should include a continuous process of supervision with at least several cases. And 1,000 hours of clinical experience in the practice of marriage and family counseling under approved supervision, involving at least 50 different cases.

   or

   150 hours of approved supervision of the practice of psychotherapy, ordinarily to be completed in a 2–3 year period, of which at least 50 hours must be individual supervision. Plus: At least 50 hours of approved individual supervision of the practice of marriage and family counseling, ordinarily to be completed within a period of not less than one nor more than two years. And 750 hours of clinical experience in the practice of psychotherapy under approved supervision involving at least 30 cases. Plus: At least 250 hours of clinical practice of marriage and family counseling under approved supervision, involving at least 20 cases.

3. Applicants may be requested to have a screening interview with the national Membership Committee or a regional membership committee, or designated representative(s).

4. Demonstrated readiness for the independent practice of marriage and family counseling.

5. Upon completion of the graduate professional degree plus the required supervised clinical experience, the candidate will be expected to have mastered the important theory in the field of marriage and family counseling as defined in the document on supervision: "The Approved Supervisor is responsible for the supervisee's familiarity with the important and relevant literature in developmental psychology, personality theory, human sexuality, behavior pathology, marriage and family studies and marriage and family therapy."

Associate:

The designation "Associate" may be given to a person who has already completed graduate studies and achieved professional competence in an appropriate behavioral science or mental health field and who is now receiving supervision by arrangement with the Membership Committee in order to become qualified as a member. The Associate category shall ordinarily be for a maximum of five (5) years or until satisfactory completion of requirements for Member, whichever shall come first.

Student:
The designation "Student" may be given to a person who is currently enrolled in the graduate program of an accredited college or university in an appropriate discipline, or one who has completed such a program and is now serving on an internship basis in a training program approved by the Association or is under supervision by arrangement with the Membership Committee. The Student category shall ordinarily be for a maximum of five years, or until satisfactory completion of requirements for Member, whichever shall come first.

Dues Structure: (Annual)
Clinical Member: $65.
Associate: $35.
Student: $15.

American Association of Sex Educators, Counselors, and Therapists (AASECT)
Executive Director: Patricia Schiller, M.A., J.D.
Address: 5010 Wisconsin Ave., N.W., Suite 304, Washington, DC
    20016, (202) 686-2523

Membership:
Full Membership: is open to sex educators, therapists/counselors, researchers, administrators, and graduate program trainees.
Student Membership: is open to full-time, undergraduate students whose academic program is related to the field of sex education, counseling, and therapy. Statement of undergraduate year to accompany application.
Institution Membership: where staff or heads of an institution for any of the membership categories, membership may be taken in the name of the institution. Under institution dues, a maximum of three people are eligible for membership. They would be entitled to all of the services available to members.

Annual Dues:
Full Membership: $25.
Full-time Undergraduate Student Membership: $10.
Institutional Membership: $60.
Life Membership: $250.

AASEC has a general membership of over 2,600 members, about 350 certified sex educators, and 110 certified sex therapists. In cooperation with American University, AASEC offers degree and certificate programs. All AASEC members receive a quarterly *Newsletter* which consists of news about conferences, books, audio-visual aids, activities of members, professional news items and materials, and resources of interest to AASEC members and other professionals. A semi-annual publication, *Journal of Sex Education and Therapy,* is sent to all members. This sixty-four page *Journal* contains leading clinical and research articles dealing with sex education and therapy. All members are entitled to reduced registration fees at all AASEC sponsored workshops, courses, and institutes. AASEC has a publication list which offers, at reduced rates, leading papers and articles of interest to persons working in the field. The fee for a full day of professional services for workshops and curriculum development is $200. Where the contractor is interested in an entire course or a publication or a workshop involving several days and more than one person, including materials and audio-visual aids, then the fee is negotiable.

American Association of Suicidology (AAS)
Central Office: Sandra A. Lopez, Executive Secretary, P.O. Box 3264, Houston, TX 77001, (713) 644-7911

The American Association of Suicidology is a multidisciplinary organization of both professionals and concerned lay people who share a conviction that contributions to knowledge about suicide will help reduce human self-destruction. Participating in AAS activities are approximately 600 individual members and 200 Suicide Prevention and Crisis Intervention Centers throughout the country.

The AAS is a member of the International Association of Suicide Prevention. The American Association of Suicidology was founded by Edwin S. Schneidman, Ph.D. then chief of the Center for the Studies of Suicide Prevention, NIMH, in 1968 following the First Annual National Conference on Suicidology held at the University of Chicago.

The AAS provides a forum for mutual discussion of suicidology.

It holds annual meetings which attempt to draw upon different regions of the country and upon different disciplines and activities within the field. The AAS sponsors a journal, *Suicide,* which encourages workers to present their findings and to share their interests. The organization also sponsors a periodical, *Newslink,* which publishes center news, correspondence from association offices, and items of membership interest. The AAS is not limited to any single viewpoint, but hopes to enlist the contribution of everyone who believes that suicide and other life-threatening behavior are important problems that afflict the community of man.

Journal:
The official journal of the American Association of Suicidology, *Suicide,* is a quarterly publication. Manuscripts and inquiries regarding the journal should be addressed to Dr. Edwin S. Schneidman, Neuropsychiatric Institute, UCLA, 760 Westwood Plaza, Los Angeles, CA 90024. Subscription to this journal is included in the annual dues for regular members.

Membership:
Qualifications: Membership in the AAS is open to individuals from various disciplines and training and practice relating to suicide prevention and life-threatening behavior. There are three classes of active AAS members:

1. *Honorary Members:* Honary Members are nominated and designated by the Board of Directors.
2. *Members:* Members are individuals, who, in the judgment of the Board of Directors (or the Membership Committee to whom this function is delegated) manifest a substantial and responsible interest in suicide prevention or life-threatening behaviors. The dues for members are $35 per year.
3. *Student Associates:* Student associates are bonafide graduate students in M.D., Ph.D., D.D., LL.B., Master's or R.N. programs. Dues for student associates are $10 per year. Subscription to AAS journal is optional; annual subscription rate is $9.

Annual Meetings:
April 6–8, 1978   Monteleone Hotel, New Orleans, LA
1979   Pending
The membership roster is available for $2 to nonmembers and $1 for members.

American Association of University Professors (AAUP)

General Secretary: Joseph Duffey
Central Office: One Dupont Circle, Suite 500, Washington, DC
   20036, (202) 466-8050
Founded: 1915

The American Association of University Professors has members at more than 2,200 institutions with local chapters at 1,365 campuses, and 45 conferences, uniting chapter organizations on a statewide basis. Active membership is open to part-time and full-time teachers, research scholars, professional librarians, and counselors with faculty status. Membership is also open to professional appointees included in a collective representation unit with the faculty. Also graduate students and interested individuals are welcome to join.

Dues are based on the member's annual salary: $12 (under $8,000); $18 ($8,000–$9,999); $24 ($10,000–$11,999); $30 ($12,000–$14,999); $36 ($15,000 and up); $5 (graduate students); $15 (public members).

The AAUP sponsors conferences, provides advice and assistance to individuals and groups on educational matters, publishes important policy statements and reports accepted as the standards of the academic profession, and offers a group life insurance program and a reduced-rate, group travel program. Also, an AAUP member receives a subscription to the AAUP *Bulletin* and to *Academe,* the AAUP newsmagazine.

American Dance Therapy Association (ADTA)

President: Judith Bunney
Corresponding Secretary: Ivy Lee Cole
National Office: Suite 210, 1000 Century Plaza, Columbia, MD
   21044, (301) 997-4040
Founded: 1966

Dance therapy is the psychotherapeutic use of movement as a process which furthers the emotional and physical integration of the individual. There are many ways to become a dance therapist, but common to all is an intensive and extensive background in dance. Movement is a primary tool of the dance therapist and he or she must have deeply experienced a wide range of dance movement, so that it's spontaneously available to him or her. In addition to having creative awareness of the body, the dance therapist must acquire a physiological understanding of it. An undergraduate degree in dance will usually provide this. However, undergraduate degrees can be in many other related disciplines, such as special education or psychology, as long as the student has also experienced the necessary years of dance and movement studies.

A dance therapist works with patients or clients using a form of nonverbal psychotherapy within the framework of a therapeutic contract. The dance therapist may work with individuals or with groups. In addition to work as a clinician, the dance therapist may work as an educator, teaching dance therapy skills and/or in research. The dance therapist may also work as an administrator in any of these areas.

Regular Membership:
Open to any person or organization professionally involved in the field of dance therapy. Annual fee, $40.

Associate Membership:
Open to individuals, organizations, institutions and libraries. Annual fee, $30.

Student Membership:
Students must have proof of full-time school registration to qualify. Annual fee, $15.

Registry:
The Association has established specific professional standards. Registration is a separate procedure and all regular members may apply. Only those who have received the Registry Certificate may use the title "D.T.R." An additional fee is charged for the process of registration.

All members receive copies of the By-Laws, Code of Ethics, membership Directory, *Newsletter,* list of educational opportunities, and discounts on publications and the annual conference.

ADTA also has a wide range of special publications available.

American Group Psychotherapy Association, Inc. (AGPA)
Administrative Secretary: Marsha Block
National Office: 1995 Broadway, 14th Floor, New York, NY 10023, (212) 787-2618
Founded: 1943
Members: 3,000

Purposes for which AGPA has been formed are:
1. To provide a forum for the exchange of ideas among qualified professional persons interested in group psychotherapy and to publish and to make publications available on all subjects relating to group psychotherapy.
2. To encourage the training of group psychotherapists and to establish and maintain high standards in their qualifications and practice.
3. To encourage and promote research in group psychotherapy.

Membership Qualifications:

Full Members:
Clinical professionals who have had the equivalent of three years' full-time clinical practice supervised by qualified clinicians in mental health agencies, clinics and hospitals, this experience to include: at least 1800 hours of direct treatment of patients, in individual group or family treatment of which 600 must have been individual psychotherapy and 600 group psychotherapy; each of these must have been accompanied by 75 hours of qualified supervision. Applicants must have conducted, as responsible therapist or co-therapist, at least three psychotherapy groups, no one of which has extended for fewer than 60 hours.

Clinical Professionals means psychiatrists, psychologists, and social workers who meet the membership requirements of their respective national associations, or other mental health professionals who hold a Master's degree or its equivalent and who meet the above training requirements. In such cases where membership in a national organization is irrelevant, or where an organization does not exist, this criterion will not apply.

Exceptional professionals who meet the above training and professional standards in spirit, may be accepted on their individual merits by the membership committee and the Board of Directors.

Associate Members:
Clinical professionals who, after graduation from a recognized school or training facility, have had the equivalent of two years' full-time clinical experience, supervised by qualified clinicians in mental health agencies, clinics and hospitals. This experience is to include: at least 1200 hours in the direct treatment of patients—in individual, group or family treatment—of which 400 must have been in individual psychotherapy, with a minimum of 50 hours' qualified supervision.

Applicants must have conducted, as responsible therapist or co-therapist, at least one psychotherapy group, extending for no fewer than 60 hours, accompanied by at least 25 hours of qualified group psychotherapy supervision. Clinical professionals means properly licensed psychiatrists, psychologists, social workers, or other mental health professionals who hold a Master's degree or its equivalent, and who meet the above training requirements.

Member Benefits:
Participation in AGPA's Annual Institute and Conference at reduced fees. Full participation in the affairs of the Association including for full members, voting and holding office.

Free subscription to the *International Journal of Group Psychotherapy,* and a discount on all publications of the International Universities Press. Membership in local and regional affiliate societies.

Participation in the affiliate society's training institutes, seminars, workshops and conferences at reduced fees.

Conferences:
1978   February   21–25   New Orleans
1979   February   15–19   New York City

Annual Dues:
Members, $45. Associates, $35. Fellows, $60. Foreign (Full and Associate Members), $7.

Publications::AGPA has a variety of publications available. Write for free list.

The American Occupational Therapy Association (AOTA)
Information: Delores Hill
National Office: 6000 Executive Blvd., Rockville, MD 20852, (301) 770-2200

Official Rolls:
A. Registry of Certified Occupational Therapists. A member who has passed the Certification Examination for Occupational Therapists and has met other criteria set by the Representative Assembly shall be entitled to use the initials "OTR" following his/her name, which shall be maintained on the official registry.
B. Listing of Certified Occupational Therapy Assistants. A member who has met the criteria set by the Representative Assembly for

certified occupational therapy assistants shall be entitled to use the initials "COTA" after his/her name, which shall be maintained on the official list.

C. Roster of Fellows. An occupational therapist, registered (OTR) who maintains membership and meets the criteria established by the Representative Assembly may be nominated to the Roster of Fellows.

D. Roster of Honor. A certified occupational therapy assistant (COTA) who maintains membership and meets the criteria established by the Representative Assembly may be nominated to the Roster of Honor.

Annual conference: Always in the spring.

Member Benefits:
Newsletter, Bulletin on Practice, American Journal of Occupational Therapy and Registry
Establishment of standards
Wide variety of publications
Low-cost insurance
Workshops and conferences

The American Orthopsychiatric Association, Inc. (AOA)
Executive Director: Marion Langer, Ph.D.
National Office: 1775 Broadway, New York, NY 10019, (212) 586-5690

Founded in 1924, the American Orthopsychiatric Association brings together psychiatrists, psychologists, social workers, educators, nurses, sociologists, anthropologists, pediatricians, and behavioral science professionals in a collaborative approach to the promotion of mental health and the study of human behavior. Karl Menninger, David Levy, and George Stevenson were among the nine founding fathers who organized the first meeting in which psychiatrists, psychologists, social workers, and educators gathered to pool their knowledge and resources. Perhaps because the collaborative approach was first used in child guidance clinics, and because of AOA's continued concern with prevention of emotional disturbances, it is sometimes assumed that Ortho is concerned only with children and predominantly with psychiatric issues. Rather, the Association is equally concerned—and its Annual Meetings are devoted to—adolescents, adults, families, school and community mental health programs, services for the aging, and a broad range of related clinical and social concerns.

Membership Qualifications:
People working in the mental health field are eligible for membership under any of the following categories:

1. Those who meet the requirements set for membership in the professional organization appropriate to their discipline.
2. Those who have completed at least their Master's degree or its equivalent in their professional field.
3. Those who have extensive professional experience or community work in the mental health field.
4. Those who have at least two years experience in a mental health setting under professional supervision followed by three years of experience in a similar setting.
5. Those who are full-time students in a graduate university program in one of the mental health disciplines.

Benefits of Membership:
Benefits include voting rights; opportunity to serve on committees and Association task forces; subscription to *American Journal of Orthopsychiatry,* Association *Newsletter,* and AOA Membership Directory; listing in Directory, free 3-day registration for Annual Meeting and priority in advance reservations for Institutes, Workshops and Panels at annual meetings. (Members pay for Workshops and Panels and a lower fee for Institutes.)

Dues:
Members: $35/year
Student Members: $16/year

Dues are payable on receipt of notification of acceptance and dues bill.

American Personnel and Guidance Association (APGA)
Executive Vice President: Charles Lewis
National Office: 1607 New Hampshire Ave., N.W., Washington, DC 20009, (202) 483-4633

The American Personnel and Guidance Association is a scientific, educational organization serving members and the public through programs that advance guidance and counseling in all settings. APGA now represents more than 41,000 members and embraces 12 national divisions and 52 state branches. The Association's activities span counseling and guidance work at all educational levels, from kindergarten through higher education, and in community agencies, government, business/industry and corrections.

Services and Activities:
1. Workshops and conferences
2. Films
3. *Guidepost* newspaper
4. Insurance program
5. Career information center
6. *APGA Journal*
7. Placement service
8. Information and reference service
9. Publications: with more than 150 titles

Membership Definitions and Qualifications:
1. Individual: Open to any person whose responsibilities or interests are in the area of human development (guidance, counseling, personnel work, mental health workers, etc.). Eligible to vote and hold office.
2. Student: Open to graduate students engaged in counseling, guidance or personnel work more than ½ time.
3. Provisional: Member in APGA but no divisional affiliation. After one year must join a division.

National Divisions:
APGA has 12 special interest divisions that members may join. Each division publishes a journal and many publish a newsletter. They are: (1) American College Personnel Association; (2) Association for Counselor Education and Supervision; (3) National Vocational Guidance Association; (4) Association for Humanistic Education and Development; (5) American School Counselor Association; (6) American Rehabilitation Counseling Association; (7) Association for Measurement and Evaluation in Guidance; (8) National Employment Counselors Association; (9) Association for Nonwhite Concerns in Personnel and Guidance; (10) National Catholic Guidance Conference; (11) Association for Specialists in Group Work; (12) Public Defender Counselor Association.

Dues:
Regular: $31.
Student: $20.
Husband-Wife: $51.

Divisional Membership: Dues range from $7 to $16 depending on Division. Students pay one-half dues.

Annual Convention:
1978:   March 19–23   Washington, DC
1979:   April 2–5   Las Vegas, Nevada

American Psychiatric Association (APA)
Director: Melvin Sabshin, M.D.
Director Public Affairs: Robert Robinson, M.A.
National Office: 1700 Eighteenth St., N.W., Washington, DC 20009, (202) 232-7878

The American Psychiatric Association is the oldest national medical society in the United States. Founded in Philadelphia in 1844 by thirteen physicians who administered the mental hospitals of their day, it was then called the Association of Medical Superintendents of American Institutions for the Insane. In 1921 the present name of the organization, The American Psychiatric Association, was adopted. The membership of the Association has grown from 900 in 1918 to 21,000.

Categories of Membership:
All members, other than honorary, must be physicians with some specialized training and experience in psychiatry.

Fellowship: is the highest status the Association offers. It is conferred on general members who, over a period of at least five years, have proved a constructive influence in the Association and in the community they serve. A candidate's ability in clinical work, administration, teaching and research, and certification by the American Board of Psychiatry and Neurology are among the criteria carefully considered.

Members in Training: is a category to encourage residents in training to become members of the Association early in their professional careers. Residents are eligible to apply at the end of their first year of training. They may not retain the status for longer than five years. They are transferred on certification of their district branch to general membership status at the completion of their training; or, if they do not complete their training, they are then made Associate Members.

General Members: shall be physicians who have had at least three years of acceptable training and who have either a valid license to practice medicine or hold an academic, research, or governmental position that does not require licensure.

Associate Members: are physicians who have completed at least one year of acceptable training or experience in psychiatry but who are not eligible for General Membership or Member-in-Training status. It offers opportunity for physicians in other specialties who are interested in and have had some training and experience in psychiatry to share in furthering the Association's objectives.

Distinguished Fellows and Honorary Fellows: are elected from time to time. Distinguished fellows are physicians who have made outstanding contributions to psychiatry, and honorary fellows are nonphysicians who have rendered signal, outstanding, and unique service to the promotion of mental health and psychiatry.

Benefits of Membership:
1. Membership signifies that one has been accepted as a qualified psychiatrist by one's colleagues.
2. A certificate of membership is documentary evidence of one's qualification to be a psychiatrist.
3. A member receives tangible benefits such as *The American Journal of Psychiatry, Psychiatric News,* sharing and communication with other members, discounts on conferences and publications.

Dues:
For Members-in-Training: $30.
Associate and General Members and Fellows (less than 10 years' total membership): $125.
Associate and General Members and Fellows (more than 10 years' total membership): $165.

Conference:
The American Psychiatric Association holds an Annual Meeting each year. In 1978 the Annual Meeting will be in Atlanta, May 8–12; and in 1979 it will be in Philadelphia, May 7–11.

Publications:
Besides the monthly *Journal of Psychiatry* and the twice-monthly *Psychiatric News,* many other publications are available. Write for list and information.

American Psychological Association (APA)
Executive Officer: Dr. Charles Kiesler

National Office: 1200 Seventeenth St., N.W., Washington, DC 20036, (202) 833-7600

The American Psychological Association, founded in 1892 and incorporated in 1925, is a major psychological organization in the United States. With more than 40,000 members, it includes many of the qualified psychologists in the country.

Membership:
There are three classes of membership in APA: Associate, Member, and Fellow.

Associates:
To qualify as an Associate, an applicant must meet one of two sets of requirements:

1. He or she must have completed two years of graduate work in psychology at a recognized graduate school and be engaged in work or graduate study that is primarily psychological in character; or
2. He or she must have received the Master's degree in psychology from a recognized graduate school, have completed, in addition, one full year of professional work in psychology, and be engaged in work or graduate study that is primarily psychological in character.

Associates initially may not vote or hold office in the Association. After five consecutive years of membership, Associates may vote. Annual dues are $39.

Members:
The minimum standard for election to Member status is the receipt of the doctoral degree based in part upon a psychological dissertation, or granted from a program primarily psychological in nature, and conferred by a graduate school of recognized standing.

Members may vote and hold office.

Annual dues are $54, with a reduction to $42 for the first two years. (Applicants for Associate or Member status have their applications completed by August 1. New members are elected in the fall; their membership is dated as of the next year.)

Fellows:
Properly qualified Members may, upon nomination by one of the Divisions and election by the Council of Representatives, become Fel-

lows of the APA. Fellows must previously have been Members for at least one full year, have a doctoral degree in psychology and at least five years of acceptable experience beyond that degree, hold membership in the nominating Division, and present evidence of unusual and outstanding contribution or performance in the field of psychology. Fellows may vote and hold office.

Annual dues are $54.

All Associates, Members, and Fellows receive the *American Psychologist* and the *APA Monitor* automatically. They may also subscribe to all APA journals and to the Employment Bulletin and the Directory or Register at reduced rates. The services of the Placement Office are available to all members.

Foreign Affiliates:
Psychologists who are foreign nationals in countries other than the United States or Canada, and who desire affiliation with the APA may become Foreign Affiliates. They must either be members of regularly established psychological associations in other countries, or, if no such association exists, they must present evidence of appropriate qualifications and must be endorsed by two psychologists known to the Association.

The annual fee for Foreign Affiliates is $2.50. Subscription to any of the journals published by the Association are available at the special rates charged to members.

High School Teacher Affiliates:
Teachers of psychology classes in high schools who are not eligible for APA membership may become High School Teacher Affiliates. They must be endorsed by the principal of the high school in which the course is taught. The word "psychology" need not be a part of the course title.

The annual fee is $2.50. Subscriptions to any of the Association's journals are available at the special rates charged to members.

Students in Psychology:
Undergraduate or graduate students taking courses in psychology are eligible for participation as Student in Psychology subscribers. They must be endorsed by a member of the Association, preferably by a faculty member of the university or college where the student is registered.

The annual fee is $2.50. Subscriptions to any of the Association's journals are available at the special rates charged to members.

Foreign Affiliates, High School Teacher Affiliates, and Students in Psychology are not members of the Association and should not represent themselves as such.

Divisions:

To provide recognition to the specialized interests of different psychologists, the APA includes 34 Divisions. (There is no Division 4 or 11.) Any person, after becoming a member of the APA may apply for membership in as many Divisions as desired. The Divisions are:

1. General Psychology
2. Teaching of Psychology
3. Experimental Psychology
5. Evaluation and Measurement
6. Physiological and Comparative Psychology
7. Developmental Psychology
8. Personality and Social Psychology
9. The Society for the Psychological Study of Social Issues
10. Psychology and the Arts
12. Clinical Psychology
13. Consulting Psychology
14. Industrial Organizational Psychology
15. Educational Psychology
16. School Psychology
17. Counseling Psychology
18. Psychologists in Public Service
19. Military Psychology
20. Adult Development and Aging
21. The Society of Engineering Psychologists
22. Rehabilitation Psychology
23. Consumer Psychology
24. Philosophical psychology
25. Experimental Analysis of Behavior
26. History of Psychology
27. Community Psychology
28. Psychopharmacology
29. Psychotherapy
30. Hypnosis
31. State Psychological Association Affairs
32. Humanistic Psychology
33. Mental Retardation

34. Population Psychology
35. Psychology of Women
36. Psychologists Interested in Religious Issues

Each Division has its own officers. Each meets annually at the APA Convention. Each has its own membership requirements, which in some cases are higher or more specialized than the requirements for election to the APA.

Annual Convention:
The Annual Convention of the APA is held in late summer. Meeting sites are chosen so that attendance will be convenient for members in different sections of the country at different times.

Publications:
The APA publishes 18 psychological journals, a monthly newspaper, as well as other publications. Member rates for all publications are lower than for nonmembers. Write for information.

American Society of Group Psychotherapy and Psychodrama (ASGPP)
Secretary-Treasurer: Zerka T. Moreno
National Office: P.O. Box 311, Beacon, NY 12508. New York City
    telephone, (212) 260-3860.
Founded: 1942 by J.L. Moreno

The Society is dedicated to the development of the fields of group psychotherapy, psychodrama, sociodrama and sociometry, their spread and fruitful application.

Aims: To establish standards for specialists in group psychotherapy, psychodrama and allied methods, to increase knowledge about them and to aid and support the exploration of new areas of endeavor in research, practice, teaching and training.
    Through the newly established J.L. Moreno Fund it offers awards to such workers in the field whose prowess have opened new frontiers.

Membership Categories:
Student: $6 annually. Nonvoting membership, open to undergraduates.
Regular: $12 annually. Professionals in mental health may vote and hold office.
Fellowship: $20 annually. Regular members who have made special contributions. May vote and hold office.

Member Benefits:
Subscription to the *Journal Group Psychotherapy and Psychodrama.*
Attend annual meeting at reduced rate.

American Sociological Association (ASA)
Executive Officer: Hans Mauksch
National Office: 1722 N. St., N.W., Washington, DC 20036, (202)
   833-3410
Membership: 12,000

The American Sociological Association, founded in 1905, is an organization of persons interested in the research, teaching, and application of sociology. It seeks to stimulate and improve research, instruction, and discussion, and to encourage cooperative relations among
persons engaged in the scientific study of society.

Membership:
There are two classes of membership in the Association: *Nonvoting
   Associate and Voting Member.*
Both have subcategories as designated below. Members and Associates
have the right to attend and participate in the Annual Meeting. They
are entitled to a subscription to *Footnotes* and to a choice of other
publications.

Member: Persons with a Ph.D. in sociology or in closely related
fields or who have completed at least three years of graduate study in
such fields in good standing in accredited institutions; or persons lack-
ing these qualifications if they can present written evidence of comparable professional competence and commitment to the field. $30 to
$50 depending on income.
International Member: Persons fully qualified for Member classification but who are citizens of any country except the United States.
$30 to $50 depending on income.

Student Member: Persons who have completed at least three years of
graduate study in sociology or closely related fields and are continuing
as full-time students may be Student Members until completion of
their studies, but not for more than four years. $15.

Associate: Any person interested in the field of sociology who does
not qualify or does not wish Member status. $20.

International Associate: Any person interested in the field of sociology who is a citizen of any country outside the United States. Permanent residents of the United States are not eligible. $12.

Student Associate:　Undergraduate majors or graduate students currently enrolled in sociology in accredited institutions for as long as their status as full-time students is in effect. $10.

For each category of membership, reduced "No Journal" dues rates are available for those persons who do not want to receive the publications.

Publications:
Six journals and a *Newsletter*. Also many special publications: annual *Guide to Graduate Departments of Sociology,* Directory of Members, etc. Write for free list.

Annual Meeting:
Always at the end of summer for five days. Abstracts and copies of papers presented are available to those interested.

Sections:
Members and Associates with interest in special fields of sociology may join Sections of ASA. There are 14 sections, each with small annual dues, that range from Undergraduate Education to World Conflict.

Association for Advancement of Behavior Therapy (AABT)
Executive Director: Elizabeth Ann Kovacs
National Office: 420 Lexington Ave., New York, NY 10017, (212) 682-0065
Founded: 1966
Membership: 2,300

Membership:
Full Member:　Full membership in the AABT is open to all persons who agree with the purposes and objective of the organization and who meet the following requirements: Persons who are responsible professionals and members in good standing of either the American Psychological Association, or the American Psychiatric Association, or, in lieu, possess other acceptable qualifications and experience, and who are: (1) practicing behavioral clinicians; or (2) engaged in research or other activities pertinent to the development and advancement of behavior therapy; or (3) interested in acquiring professional

knowledge and competence in some aspect of the behavioral therapies, with a view toward eventual participation.

Associate Member: Associate membership is available to those who do not meet all of the professional requirements for full membership but whose credentials otherwise are acceptable to the membership committee.

Student Member: Student membership is available to graduate and undergraduate students, interns, and residents who currently are enrolled in a program of study.

Members receive the *Newsletter* free and reduced rates on all other publications and conferences.

Membership dues currently are $20 per year for full and associate members, plus an initiation fee of $10 for new members at those levels. Student membership dues are $10 per year, and there is no initiation fee. Annual dues cover the calendar year, January 1 to December 31. For application forms write to: Marsha Linehan, Ph.D., Membership Chairperson, Psychology Department, Catholic University of America, Washington, DC 20064.

Convention:
Held in early winter of each year in a major urban center for three days.

Publications:
Journal, Newsletter, Directory of Training Programs in Behavior Modification, plus other publications.

Association for Humanistic Psychology (AHP)
Executive Officer: Elizabeth Campbell
National Office: 325 Ninth St., San Francisco, CA 94103, (415) 626-
    2375

The Association for Humanistic Psychology is a world-wide network formed in 1962 for the development of the human sciences in ways which recognize distinctively human qualities and which work toward fulfilling the innate capacities of people—individually and in society. Humanistic psychology transcends the usual academic boundaries to include a broad spectrum of disciplines and approaches to human experience and behavior. It is devoted to exploring the ranges of human capacities and potentialities so as to enhance both the individual and the society.

AHP currently has some 4,500 members around the world, and welcomes into membership people from all backgrounds and vocations who wish to participate in and support these efforts. AHP is not a closed professional organization, but seeks dialogue with and membership of all who are interested in furthering the humanistic view of humankind.

AHP Offers:
A monthly *Newsletter*.
A quarterly *Journal of Humanistic Psychology*.
An annual meeting featuring both the theory and the practice of humanistic psychology.
Regional meetings throughout the United States.
International meetings in Latin America and Europe.
Local chapters and groups around the world.
Networks for members who wish to be in communication with others who share their special interest.
Current lists of colleges with humanistically oriented programs, and of growth centers.
An extensive bibliography of books in the field.
Reprints of selected materials at low cost.
Yearly Roster of AHP members plus updates.

The Journal of Humanistic Psychology began publication in 1961 and is the journal of the Association for Humanistic Psychology. It publishes experiential reports, theoretical papers, personal essays, research studies, applications of humanistic psychology, humanistic analyses of contemporary culture, and occasional poems. Topics of special interest are authenticity, encounter, self-actualization, self-transcendence, search for meaning, creativity, personal growth, psychological health, being-motivation, values, identity, and love. *The Journal* is a forum for diverse statements about humanistic psychology, including criticisms. Each writer speaks for himself or herself. The editor makes no effort to achieve an official AHP consensus.

The Humanistic Psychology Institute was founded by AHP in 1970 to offer an educational program at the doctoral level and to further the development of research in humanistic psychology. HPI grants the Ph.D. degree to Research Fellows (students) who successfully demonstrate scholarship and mastery in humanistic psychology, and who display the ability to accomplish and effectively communicate original research in the field. HPI is an external degree program designed for independent and self-directed study. The Home Faculty help

Research Fellows define their learning goals, identify resources and evaluate attainment of goals. Research Fellows assume responsibility for developing their own learning resources.

Dues:
$35 *regular membership*
$23 *student (full-time)*
$23 *retired (over 65 and no longer employed)*
$55 *couple*
$60 *two year regular (new members only)*
$50–$100 *Contributing; $100 or more, Supporting*

The membership fee entitles one to the quarterly *Journal of Humanistic Psychology,* the monthly AHP *Newsletter,* reduced registration fees for conferences and workshops, reduced prices on publications.

Association for Psychotheatrics (AP)
Executive Director: Robert D. Allen
National Office: P.O. Box 160371, Sacramento, CA 95816
Founded: 1976

Psychotheatrics (PT) is a process based on theories and techniques from theatre and the practice of psychotherapy. PT is action oriented, focuses on individual responsibility, enhances the discovery of options, and helps the individual create a design for behavior change. PT is adaptable for many purposes in a wide variety of settings with people of different levels of sophistication, it may be used as a therapy modality, educational process, theatre process or awareness process.

Member Benefits:
All members receive the AP *Newsletter,* reduced rates on publications (books, pamphlets, cassette tapes) and conferences. Registered members are recognized as qualified experts in PT. Special publications like *Yearly Events* (free to members and nonmembers who request it) will list Registered members, conferences, training workshops and information.

Dues and Qualifications:
Associate: $5. Open to all who are interested in PT, psychology, and theatre and performance. May not vote or hold office but receive all other member benefits.

Registered Facilitator (RF): $10. Recognizes one is qualified in the use of PT in one's specialty area(s). Must pass an exam in PT, theoretical and experiential. May vote and hold office, all member benefits.

Registered Teacher (RT): $15. Recognizes one is qualified in the use of PT in one's specialty area(s) and is also qualified to teach PT leading to RF status. Must have been an RF in good standing, then complete a training contract, resulting in RT status. May vote and hold office, all member benefits.

Association for Transpersonal Psychology (ATP)
Director: James Fadiman
Central Office: P.O. Box 3049, Stanford, CA 94305, (415) 327-2066
Founded: 1969
Membership: 1,500
Membership is open to all interested individuals.

ATP is a group of people drawn from a variety of fields of interest, many of whom are working in the transpersonal area. Some members are doing research in spiritual disciplines, biofeedback, personality theory, transpersonal and related therapies, to name a few. Other members are practitioners in professional areas, teachers, philosophers, or friends who have a common interest in Transpersonal Psychology.

Annual dues for the Association are $25 per calendar year. Members receive a one-year subscription to the *Journal of Transpersonal Psychology* (two issues), the ATP *Newsletter,* and a copy of the ATP mailing list for a specific related area. Mailing lists for other areas are available on request. Transpersonal organizations as well as individuals are eligible for membership and for mailing lists. Labels can be ordered at a nominal fee.

Since 1973, the Association has held an annual summer conference covering such topics as applications of transpersonal psychology to psychotherapy, counseling, research, education and everyday life. Association membership includes an invitation to the Annual Conference.

Association for Women in Psychology (AWP)
Information: Irene Frieze, University of Pittsburgh, Psychology Dept.,
    Pittsburgh, PA 15260, (412) 624-4141
Membership: Betsy Poland, Ball State University, Psychology Dept.,
    Muncie, IN 47306

The Association for Women in Psychology (AWP) is an independent group which began as a formal organization at the 1969 convention of the American Psychological Association.

Although AWP is composed largely of female psychologists, membership is open to all persons agreeing with AWP's objectives:

—ending the role which psychology has had in perpetuating unscientific and unquestioned assumptions about the "natures" of women and men;

—encouraging feminist psychological research on sex and gender;

—encouraging research and theory directed towards alternatives to sex roles, child-raising practices, nonsexist lifestyles and new vocabularies;

—expanding opportunities for women to achieve equality within psychology;

—educating and sensitizing the psychology profession and the public to the psychological, social, political and economic problems of women;

—ending the use of "mental health" professions and psychotherapy as a means of enforcing institutionalized sexism;

—helping women create individual sexual identities through which they may freely and responsibly express themselves (provided such expression does not oppress other individuals).

AWP holds two business meetings and one research conference each year.

AWP keeps its members informed of research, publications, conferences, and special events relevant to women in psychology through a bi-monthly *Newsletter,* and through activities at regional and national psychological conventions.

Membership Dues:
Regular membership: $10.
Institutional (libraries, organizations, etc.): $15.
Students and those of limited means: $3.

Association of Asian-American Psychologists (AAP)

Membership:
Marion Tinloy, California State University, Department of Educational Psychology, Hayward, CA 94542, (415) 881-3000

Early in 1972, several Asian-American social scientists organized an

Association of Asian-American Psychologists (AAP) aimed at encouraging inquiry and research on Chinese, Filipino, Japanese, Korean, etc., in order to promote the welfare of these groups. AAP was concerned that Asian-Americans constituted a neglected minority with pervasive stereotypes shared by the American public.

Since its original formation, membership has grown to nearly 150 members from a diversity of backgrounds (academicians, researchers, practitioners, etc.).

The goals of AAP are listed below:

1. To enlighten the public concerning the experiences, hopes, aspirations, and concerns of Asians in America.
2. To encourage research on Asian-Americans in order to assist in the development of special programs and services to fit the needs of Asians in America. The emphasis of these programs will be directed towards, (a) educational changes, (b) special psychological services, (c) community intervention programs, (d) problems in discrimination in housing, employment, etc.
3. Attempt to gain national representation on various agencies and committees that may have policy implications for Asian-Americans.
4. Seek private and public funds to support AAP's activities and goals. In order to implement some of these goals, it was decided that a working relationship be established between two major professsional organizations that had maximal impact not only upon fellow professionals, but the American public as well. These two organizations were the American Psychological Association (APA) and the American Personnel and Guidance Association (APGA).

Dues: Voluntary (would like at least $1)

The Association publishes a *Newsletter* which is devoted to the discussion of issues in psychology and Asian-American affairs, of research and applied programs in various communities, of employment opportunities, and the professional affairs of the Association. The Association sponsors conferences and has a placement service.

The Association of Black Psychologists (ABP)
Address: P.O. Box 2929, Washington, DC 20002, (202) 722-0779

The Association of Black Psychologists was founded at the 1968 San Francisco meeting of the American Psychological Association. Spearheaded by several individuals, the group charged that APA had not responded to the needs of the larger Black community. The basic unifying theme and focus of the initial group was at least twofold. The first was the desire and commitment to assess and develop mechanisms for addressing the needs of the Black community, particularly those of a psychological nature. The second aspect was to provide a vehicle for increasing the numbers and effectiveness of Blacks engaged in psychological services. Since 1968, the membership has shown a steady increase to over 500 Black psychologists. Members work individually and collectively in many ways. As priority areas for action have been identified, standing committees have been formed and strategies for change developed.

Publications of the National Association of Black Psychologists:
1. Quarterly *Newsletter*, $4 per year (free to paid members)
2. *1975 Biographical Directory*, $3 (free to paid members)
3. *Journal of Black Psychology*, subscription rates: $15—institutions; $10—regular.
4. *Proceedings of the 1975 Convention, San Francisco*, $4.
5. *Proceedings of the Drug Symposium*, $2.
   For further information, write: Nsenga Coppock, APB Headquarters, Washington, DC.

Behavior Therapy and Research Society (BTRS)

Address: c/o *Journal of Behavior Therapy and Experimental Psychiatry*
Joseph Wolpe, M.D., Editor, Temple University Medical School, c/o Eastern Pennsylvania Psychiatric Institute, Henry Ave., Philadelphia, PA 19129, (215) 842-4000
Members: 200

Membership:
The usual academic requirement for membership is an M.D. or Ph.D. An applicant shall provide evidence that he/she has been engaged in active postdoctoral practice of behavior therapy for at least two (2) years. Nondoctoral applicants will be acceptable in certain cases where there are very strong credentials. However, in keeping with the practices in other professional fields, membership will now be available to applicants actively engaged in graduate study for the doctorate. An applicant with a Master's degree should have engaged in the active practice of behavior therapy for at least three (3) years. An applicant with a Bachelor's degree should have engaged in the active practice of behavior therapy for at least four (4) years. Conferences: Annual sym-

posium held in conjunction with annual meeting of American Psychiatric Association.

Advises professionals and agencies seeking behavioral therapy service.

Eastern Association for Sex Therapy (EAST)
President: Donald Sloan, M.D., 10 East 88th St., New York, NY 10028, (212) 369-1777
Secretary: Oliver Bjorksten, M.D., Medical College of South Carolina, 80 Barre St., Charleston, SC

The Eastern Association for Sex Therapy was formed in January, 1974, by representatives from twenty-nine medical schools in the northeastern United States for the purposes of: (1) increasing communication between professionals involved in the treatment of patients with sexual dysfunctions; (2) promoting collaborative research between institutions; (3) establishing standards for accreditation of professionals engaged in sex therapy; and (4) educating the public on issues relevant to the therapy of sexual dysfunctions, including not only the competence of practitioners, but also their ethics and responsibilities as well. The impetus for the establishment of this organization came from a number of medical school faculty members who felt a void in communication existed between people engaged in sex therapy.

International Primal Association, Inc. (IPA)
President: Armand DiMele
Secretary-Treasurer: Thomas Rose
National Office: 186 West 4th St., #603, New York, NY 10014, (212) 989-2302
Founded: 1973
Members: Over 200

Since 1970, when Arthur Janov published his book, "The Primal Scream," thousands of individuals have become involved in Primal Therapy. In 1973, a group of over a hundred professionals came together in Montreal to form this Association. Their first decision was to break with the history of professional organizations and open their ranks to their clients and to all "feeling" people interested in the primal experience.

Member Benefits: *Newsletter,* magazine, membership directory. Workshops and conferences.

Dues: From $20 to $60 annually, depending on income.

National Association for Music Therapy, Inc. (NAMT)
Executive Director: Margaret Sears, RMT
Address: P.O. Box 610, Lawrence, KS 66044, (913) 842-1909

Types of Membership:
Active—All persons engaged in the use of music in therapy: music therapists, physicians, psychologists, administrators, and educators. Includes the right to vote and hold office. Sliding scale based on income: $30 to $50 per year.

Associate—Music volunteers or others not professionally engaged in the use of music in therapy but who wish to support the program. Does not include right to vote or hold office. $15 per year.

Student—Those enrolled in universities, colleges, or high schools. Students who do not qualify at this level are eligible for Associate membership. Does not include right to vote or hold office. $8 per year.

All memberships in NAMT include subscription to the *Journal of Music Therapy*.

Certification:
Active members who have completed a four-year degree course in music therapy, or its equivalent, from a university or college fully approved by the Association, and who have verification of a successfully completed six-month internship in a setting approved by the Association shall qualify for certification eligibility for registration as an R.M.T.

Placement Service:
The National Association for Music Therapy, Inc., provides a professional placement service for its members and employers in the field. Lists of position vacancies are available to all members in good standing upon request to the NAMT central office.

Publications:
The Journal of Music Therapy is published quarterly (March, June, September, and December). It contains reports of original investigations and theoretical papers pertaining to music therapy and sections devoted to Association business and activities. Single issue rate is $2, annual subscription rate is $7 for United States possessions, Canada

and Mexico. Foreign rate is $2.25 for single issue, $8.50 for annual subscription.

A *Career in Music Therapy* is a descriptive, information brochure, published by NAMT, listing minimum educational requirements and career information. A limited supply is available without cost through the NAMT Central Office.

Conferences:
Annual Conferences of the National Association for Music Therapy, Inc., are held each year during either October or November.

Information:
A list of universities offering Music Therapy programs may be obtained by writing NAMT.

National Association of School Psychologists (NASP)
National Office: Lois Leyda, 1511 K St., N.W., Suite 927, Washington, DC 20005, (202) 347-3956
Founded: 1969

Purposes:
1. Actively promote the interests of school psychology
2. Advance the standards of the profession
3. Secure the conditions necessary for the greatest effectiveness of its practice
4. Serve the mental health and educational interests of all children and youth

Membership Qualifications: State Certification or student in school psychology.

Membership Dues:
Regular: $35.
Student: $10.

Conferences:
March 1978   undecided
March 1979   San Diego, CA

Publications:
Monthly newsletter, *Communique,* which keeps school psychologists up to date on "what's going on" in the profession throughout the country. Quarterly *School Psychology Digest* which provides school

psychologists with condensed versions of articles, directly and indirectly related to their work, to be found through the constant surveillance of over 50 professional journals. Employment Service with listings exclusively for school psychologists resulting from a regular national survey of professional openings. Also many special publications are available concerning school psychology.

National Association of Social Workers, Inc. (NASW)
Executive Director: Chauncey A. Alexander, ACSW
Associate Executive Director: Len Stern, ACSW
Special Consultant: Mark Battle, ACSW
National Office: 1425 H St., N.W., Suite 600, Washington, DC
20005, (202) 628-6800
Founded: 1955

The National Association of Social Workers (NASW) has a professional membership of 69,000 persons who meet or exceed educational and experiential standards. NASW has chapters throughout the United States, in Puerto Rico, the Virgin Islands and in Europe. Its publications editorial office is in New York City, at 2 Park Ave.; and the NASW-Social Work Vocational Bureau is located at 386 Park Ave. South, New York City.

The Association's primary functions include:
—Professional development of members through Social Work practice studies, continuing education programs, professional journals and publications, research and demonstration projects.
—Creation and maintenance of professional standards of social work practice through a Code of Ethics, personnel standards, adjudication procedures, legal regulations, practice criteria, and the Academy of Certified Social Workers (ACSW), which accredits self-regulated Social Work practitioners.
—Advancement of sound social policies through technical analysis of social problems, expert public and professional testimony, and legislative and community action, most notably through its Educational Legislative Action Network (ELAN) in local chapters and headquartered at the national office.

NASW administers two major information services:
—Social Work Careers Information Service: to provide information and materials on opportunities and requirements for careers in Social Work.

—Social Work Vocational Bureau: to aid Social Workers in their search for employment by maintaining a permanent and fully authenticated personnel file which is made available to prospective employers.

Services:

Membership services, including books and publications; insurance program including life, disability income, hospital indemnity, and major medical; professional liability insurance for individuals and agencies; social work information service; national employment listing; and professional study travel programs.

Publications:

NASW *News* (including Personnel Information)—a free monthly tabloid sent to all members, keeps readers abreast of NASW programs and important professional issues.

Social Work—A free bi-monthly professional journal, available to all members.

Abstracts—A quarterly summary of key articles from 250 professional journals, at reduced rates for members.

Encyclopedia of Social Work—2 volumes, 1600 pages, the basic authoritative social work reference.

Plus an extensive publication program offering dozens of books and papers covering theory and practice, research and professional action issues as well as basic reference library needs.

Membership:

Regular: May vote and hold office and is entitled to all rights and privileges of membership.

Full: Have a Baccalaureate, Master's, or Doctoral in social work in a college accredited by the Council on Social Work Education (CSWE), or who hold a Doctorate in a related field and are working in the area of social work.

Student: Full-time in a CSWE accredited Master's or Doctoral program in social work.

Associate: All rights and privileges of membership except to vote and hold office.

Full: Holders of degrees, minimum Baccalaureate, in any field from colleges or universities accredited by an agency other than CSWE who are currently employed in a social work capacity.

Baccalaureate Student: Hold the same rights and privileges as Associate Members. Full-time students in Baccalaureate social work programs accredited by CSWE.

Dues:
Regular-Full: $60.
Regular-Student: Master's $15.; Doctoral $25.
Associate-Full: $35.
Baccalaureate Student: $12.

National Rehabilitation Counseling Association (NRCA)

President: James Gray, P.O. Box 7711, Longview, TX 75601
President-Elect: Phil Chase, Coliseum Plaza West, 720 Coliseum Dr., Winston-Salem, NC 27106
Executive Director: Fletcher Hall
National Office: 1522 K St., N.W., Washington, DC 20005, (202) 296-6080

The National Rehabilitation Counseling Association, a professional division of the National Rehabilitation Association and dedicated to elevating the professionality of rehabilitation counseling practice for serving disabled people, was established in October, 1958. It has maintained a national office since April, 1964, and operates with a structure of seven regional and an expanding number of state and campus affiliates called branches. It is the largest professional association in the field of rehabilitation counseling.

Membership:
Membership in NRCA includes persons qualified as rehabilitation counselors, counselor educators, counselor supervisors, researchers in rehabilitation counseling, students in training for rehabilitation practice, and support personnel to rehabilitation counseling.

(1) A Member of the Association must have a mimimum of a baccalaureate degree from an accredited college and be employed in a rehabilitation counseling setting and subscribe to the standards of practice set up by the Association. Dues are $15 annually plus NRA dues.

(2) A Professional Member of the Association must have a Master's degree in rehabilitation counseling with a minimum of one year's experience in a rehabilitation counseling setting and subscribe to standards of practice set forth by the Association. The designation of rehabilitation experience and rehabilitation counseling settings are determined by the Membership Classification Committee. Classification as a pro-

fessional member may be permanent and continuous with dues at $15 annually plus NRA dues.

(3) A Student Member of the Association is one enrolled in an accredited curriculum leading to a degree in rehabilitation counseling. Dues are $6 annually plus NRA dues.

(4) An Affiliate Member of the Association is any individual employed in a supporting, ancillary or helping capacity at a technical level in support of rehabilitation counseling practice. Dues are $6 annually plus NRA dues.

(5) Emeritus Member of the Association is a member who retires from professional practice and who applies for this status without further payment of dues.

All NRCA members must be members also of the National Rehabilitation Association.

Specific Membership Privileges:

(1) All members are entitled to become members of affiliated branches.

(2) All members are entitled to participate in national, regional, and local branch meetings of the Association.

(3) All members (except affiliate and student members) are entitled to be delegates to national meetings and vote in the Association's Delegate Assembly.

(4) Certified Rehabilitation Counselors are entitled to hold national office and be members of the national Board of Directors.

(5) A Professional Liability Insurance Program for all members providing $600,000 of professional liability, and $200,000 of personal liability insurance per year, at a minimum cost figure.

PSI CHI

Executive Director: Ruth Cousins (also *Psi Chi Newsletter* Editor)
National Office: APA Building, 1200 17th St., N.W., Washington, DC 20036, (202) 833-7600
Founded: 1929
Members: 94,134 people, 405 chapters

Psi Chi:

The National Honor Society in Psychology. An affiliate of the American Psychological Association and Member of the Association of College Honor Societies. Psi Chi is the national honor society in psychology. Most of its active members are students. About half of these are undergraduates majoring or minoring in psychology, and half are psychology graduate students and faculty members.

Membership:

Members do not pay dues, and the $15 national registration fee is the sole means of support of the organization. Membership is for life and no further financial demands are made of the members. Supplies are furnished to the chapters free of charge and a quarterly *Psi Chi Newsletter* is provided free to chapters for all their members. Members may transfer to other chapters without charge by the national organization. A record of membership is maintained at the national office which may be used as a reference by members at all times. A personal subscription to the *Newsletter* is available at only $3.50 a year, although members receive the issues when attending chapter functions.

Requirements for Psi Chi Membership:

Active members are men or women who are making the study of psychology one of their major interests and who are faculty members or students in an institution where a chapter is located, or who have been readmitted to active status by a chapter. All members are required to have high scholastic records in psychology. The national organization is a federation of local chapters located on campuses of accredited colleges and universities. The national convention is held at the time and place of the annual meeting of the American Psychological Association. Also six regions hold annual conferences jointly with the regional associations of APA. Each chapter elects its own officers from among its active members. Anyone interested in a charter affiliation to start a new chapter or anyone interested in a list of chapters and their addresses should contact the national office.

Western Association of Christians for Psychological Studies (WACPS)

Executive Director: Dr. Craig Ellison, Westmont College, 955 La Paz Rd., Santa Barbara, CA 93108, (805) 969-5051

Newsletter Editor: Dr. Gerald Frincke, 41 Grand Rio Circle, Sacramento, CA 95826

Managing Editor: Dr. Dene Simpson, Northwest Nazarene College, Nampa, ID 83651

Founded: 1974

Members: 425 (and growing rapidly)

Membership:

Regular Membership:

For those with an approved advanced degree or professional certification, who are or have been primarily engaged in psychology, psychiatry, social work, or the counseling professions. Dues are $15 per year.

Associate Membership:
For those with an approved Bachelor's degree who are actively pursuing a graduate-level degree in one of the disciplines indicated, or are professionally employed in one of those disciplines, or are engaged in pastoral ministries. Associate members have full benefits and privileges with the exception of holding membership on the Board of Directors. Dues are $15 per year. Full-time graduate students are eligible for $10 per year dues.

Nonmember Affiliates:
For those who do not meet membership criteria, including persons who do not have a Bachelor's degree. Receive *Newsletter,* reduced convention fees, and opportunity to be active in regional groups. Fee is $10 per year.

Member Benefits:
Bi-monthly *Newsletter:* Issues forum; member news; persons and programs of note; regional group news; referral services; association information; book reviews; employment notices. Informal communication with other Christians who share similar professional interests. Facilitated by regional meetings, sectional conferences, and the annual convention. Dialogue and exchange on issues of special interest to the Christian behavioral scientist and practitioner. Forms for presentation, exchange and education are available through regional activity, the annual convention, and the *Newsletter.* Identification of evangelicals in your field for personal and professional benefits. Professional resources at reduced rates. Tapes of convention presentations at cost. Convention registration fees reduced. Information about papers and other resources available from other members.

20 Service Organizations

Index to Service Organizations

National Center for the Prevention and Treatment of Child Abuse and
   Neglect (NCPTCAN)
National Clearinghouse for Alcohol Information (NCALI)
National Clearinghouse for Drug Abuse Information (NCDAI)
National Clearinghouse for Mental Health Information (NCMHI)
National Council on the Aging, Inc. (NCOA)
National Council on Alcoholism (NCA)
National Council on Family Relations (NCFR)
National Education Association (NEA)
National Institute of Mental Health (NIMH)
National Technical Information Service (NTIS)
Office of Human Development (OHD)
Overeaters Anonymous (OA)
Parents Anonymous (PA)
Patients' Rights Organization (PRO)
Rape Crisis Center (RCC)

List of Organizations

Action for Children's Television (ACT)
National Office: 46 Austin St., Newtonville, MA 02160, (617) 527-
   7870
President: Peggy Charren

ACT started out as an informal group of concerned parents, teachers,
and physicians who had a common bond: they didn't like what their
children were viewing on TV. Now ACT is a very powerful national
organization. Goals: to eliminate commercials for expensive toys and
for products that can be harmful to children (like highly sugared foods
that cause tooth decay); to eliminate sexual and racial stereotypes
from children's programming; to prepare resource handbooks for parents on specialized areas of children's programming, the arts, consumer education, science, and the handicapped child; to organize national conferences and workshops on children's television; to educate
and enlighten adults about the critical effect television has on children;
and to reduce depictions of violence in early evening when children
might be viewing.

Sustaining Member $ 50   Contributing Member $25

| Donor | $100 | Supporting Member | $15 |
| Benefactor | $500 | | |

All members will receive the *ACT Newsletter*. A copy of *The Family Guide to Children's Television* will be sent to all contributors of $25 or more.

Al-Anon Family Group Headquarters, Inc.

P.O. Box 182 Madison Square Station, New York, NY 10010, (212) 475-6110

The Al-Anon Family Groups are a fellowship of relatives and friends of alcoholics who share their experience, strength, and hope in order to solve their common problems and to help others do the same. Although an outgrowth of Alcoholics Anonymous with the same basic structure, it is a completely separate organization. Alcoholism is now recognized as a family disease which impairs the mental and often physical health of the family as well as that of the alcoholic. Al-Anon members help themselves by learning the facts about alcoholism and by working to improve their own attitudes and personalities through informal group discussions. Local groups are active in educational and public relations work within their communities, cooperating with all resources involved in treatment.

As of 1976, over 12,000 groups in the United States, Canada, and in 62 foreign countries had been added to the original 50. Although Al-Anon grew out of a need of the families of Alcoholics Anonymous, it now offers help to anyone whose life has been or is being deeply affected by a problem drinker. It is estimated that 50 percent or more of Al-Anon members are relatives of alcoholics who are still drinking.

The only requirement for membership is that there be a problem of alcoholism in a relative or friend. Members pay no dues; contributions are strictly voluntary.

Al-Anon is self-supporting and does not seek or accept contributions outside its membership.

Informative literature is available. It includes six books, over 40 pamphlets, 2 cartoon booklets and a monthly publication. There is also a growing selection of Al-Anon material available in foreign languages including French, Flemish, Spanish, Finnish, Swedish, German, and Japanese. Order forms describing each piece in detail are available on request.

People wanting more information on Al-Anon, or a speaker, may contact the local Al-Anon Information Service, Intergroup, or group.

The telephone number is generally listed under "Al-Anon Family Groups" or "Alcohol—Al-Anon." If there is no listing, the local Alcoholics Anonymous group or Alcoholism Information Center can usually supply a telephone number; or a letter of request may be sent directly to Al-Anon Family Group Headquarters in New York.

Alcoholics Anonymous, Inc. (AA)

National Office: P.O. Box 459, Grand Central Station, New York, NY 10017, (212) 686-1100

AA is a worldwide network of 28,000 local groups in 92 countries. AA is a fellowship of men and women who help each other stay sober, and is run by regular meetings at which members relate their experiences to each other. The usual format is the "Twelve Steps" and the "Twelve Traditions" based on established AA procedure that has proven successful. Meetings are open for anyone interested, and closed for alcoholics only. Local groups run themselves in a democratic way. You can find AA in almost any telephone book; if not, contact the national office. AA is totally self-supporting and does not accept outside contributions. Publications: many topics, write for catalog.

American Association for the Abolition of Involuntary Mental Hospitalization, Inc. (AAAIMH)

National Office: c/o Post Office, University of Santa Clara, Santa Clara, CA 95053, (408) 984-4361
Chairperson: George Alexander

Completely dedicated to stopping involuntary commitment of "mental patients." AAAIMH says that no group of professionals have ever rejected involuntary interventions, and this must be done to preserve the elementary principles of dignity, liberty, and morality.

Membership—Membership is open to all individuals who support the goals of the Association. Annual membership dues are $10 for regular members and $5 for student members. Dues are used to pay the operating expenses of the Association and to provide members with a subscription to the Association newsletter, *The Abolitionist,* a membership directory, and other information as requested.

American Association for the Advancement of Science (AAAS)

National Office: 1776 Massachusetts Ave., N.W., Washington, DC 20036, (202) 467-4400
Members: 115,000 individuals, 241 affiliated societies

Founded in 1848, The American Association for the Advancement of Science is the world's largest federation of scientific organizations. It is also an association of individual scientists and of other persons interested in supporting the aims and activities of the AAS. Despite its size and complexity, the AAAS is a scientific society in which members may take a strong personal interest. Its 21 sections embrace the principal fields of science; at sessions presented by the sections at the Association's annual meeting, members may participate in formal discussions and exchange views informally with their colleagues. There are also opportunities to attend or to take part in programs that involve several scientific disciplines, that explore relatively neglected areas, or that contribute toward the solution of problems that affect all scientists.

Membership:
Open to any interested individual ($25 per year). There are special requirements for "Fellow" and "Affiliated Organizations" membership.

Membership benefits include a subscription to *Science Magazine* (52 issues), annual meetings, discounts on audiotapes and books.

Some special publications:
AAAS Science Film Catalog.   1975. $16.95. A classified list of 5500 educational science films (16mm) currently available in the United States, for primary through college level. It includes brief descriptions provided by the distributors and information about rental or purchase.

AAAS Science Book List for Children (3rd edition).   1972. $8.95. (Member's cash price, $7.95.) A selected and annotated list of science and mathematics books for children in elementary schools and for children's collections in school, private, and public libraries.

The AAAS Science Book List (3rd edition).   1970. $10. (Member's cash price, $9.) An annotated and classified list of more than 2400 titles for secondary school and college undergraduate libraries.

AAAS Reprints: many subjects, very low prices. Write for free catalog.

American Council on Education (ACE)
National Office: One Dupont Circle, Washington, DC 20036, (202) 833-4700
President: Roger Heyns

Information Officer: Frank Skinner
Director of Publications: Clifford Fair

The American Council on Education exists to promote the public interest. Its mission lies in extending the range and quality of post-secondary education in the United States. The Council cooperates with all similarly committed institutions and associations, both here and abroad.

Publications include books, several authoritative guides and directories, a journal, a newsletter, monographs, and special reports, which provide a continuing flow of information to Council members, to the higher education community, and to the public. The backlist of studies and reports amply reflects the Council's broad-ranging interests and activities. More than 100 titles are currently in print; of these, a number have been published in cooperation with other higher education associations.

Two standard directories initiated by the Council are offered for sale. *American Universities and Colleges,* first issued in 1928, presents comprehensive information on accredited four-year colleges and universities and briefer descriptions of professional schools. A companion volume, *American Junior Colleges,* first issued in 1940, describes non-profit accredited two-year institutions and those recognized by state agencies.

The Council is the United States distributor of the *International Handbook of Universities.* A catalog of Council publications is available on request.

The American Humane Association (AHA)
P.O. Box 1266, Denver, CO 80201, (303) 779-1400

The American Humane Association, founded in 1877, is the nation's first and largest humane federation.

AHA is a nonprofit, tax-exempt organization with a single purpose: to prevent cruelty to children and animals. AHA programs, essentially educational, are designed to guide governmental agencies, organizations of related interest, local and regional child and animal welfare agencies, educators, school children, and the general public in the principles of humane care.

The Children's Division studies the causes of child abuse, trains workers to identify children needing help and assists in organizing child protective programs. The organization is becoming increasingly involved in research on innovative approaches to problems of child neglect, abuse and exploitation.

Considerable AHA staff time and funds are devoted to helping member and nonmember organizations provide efficient, effective, and humane animal shelter operations.

Services to approximately 1,200 animal agencies range from advising on administration and operating procedures to conducting workshops, staff conferences and training competent shelter personnel. Distribution of education materials and the support of needed local and national legislation are also significant AHA services.

The Association's animal protection work is concerned not only with inspection of animal performances, such as circuses and carnivals, but also includes the increasingly important areas of conservation of endangered species, care of native and exotic wildlife in captivity, of horses and livestock, and of laboratory animals used for medical research.

AHA is deeply concerned with animal population control through surgery and the development of chemosterilants and the latest methods of euthanasia.

American Humanist Association (AHA)

National Office: 602 Third St., San Francisco, CA 94107, (415) 543-3430
President: Bette Chambers
Membership: Open to all interested individuals
Dues: $15 for single, $22.50 for joint, for one year.

Local AHA chapters deal at the grassroots level with such issues as euthanasia, sexism, abortion, humanistic childbirth, humanizing factory work, and protecting the human rights of psychiatric patients and prisoners.

AHA uses TV, radio, press releases, lecture tours at colleges and clubs, workshops, and conferences to promote a humanist approach to contemporary problems facing American society.

Founded in 1940, AHA maintains continuous contact with lawmakers in Washington to insure a proper concern for human rights, environmental improvement, and moral values in current legislation. Members are notified in advance of important AHA meetings to be held in various parts of the country, and of international conferences organized in cooperation with humanist groups overseas. The AHA's Division of Humanist Counseling offers help to members facing social or personal problems. Counselors are also available for community action programs and to perform nontheistic wedding and funeral services. Publications: Newsletter *Free Mind,* and a bi-monthly journal *The Humanist.* Both are included as part of membership.

American Library Association (ALA)
National Office: 50 East Huron St., Chicago, IL 60611, (312) 944-6780
Executive Director: Robert Wedgeworth

The American Library Association is the oldest and largest library association in the world. ALA was founded in 1876. Since its first meeting, ALA membership has grown to nearly 36,000. Members include librarians, libraries, library trustees, publishers, information scientists, authors, business firms, and friends of libraries in the United States, Canada, and abroad.

The ALA believes it is the responsibility of libraries to make available material representing all points of view to all people regardless of race, religion, age, national origin, or social and political views. The philosophy is embodied in the Library Bill of Rights, the ALA's primary policy statement on intellectual freedom. The Bill of Rights was first adopted by ALA Council in 1939 and serves as librarians' interpretation of the First Amendment to the United States Constitution. It stresses that materials should not be restricted or removed from libraries because of partisan or doctrinal pressures and that censorship attempts should be challenged by libraries. In addition to the Library Bill of Rights, the ALA maintains a vigorous intellectual freedom program which includes the Freedom to Read Foundation, the Intellectual Freedom Committee, and the Office for Intellectual Freedom. The Office for Intellectual Freedom generates and distributes information related to censorship in a bi-monthly newsletter and in a monthly memorandum prepared for State Intellectual Freedom Committees. Advisory statements and position papers are also issued as the need arises. Among the magazines published by ALA are *American Libraries,* the official membership publication; *Booklist,* which reviews current books and nonprint materials for adults, young people, and children; and *Choice,* which reviews new books of importance to academic libraries.

Annual Conference Cities 1978–1979	*Year*	*Dates*
Chicago	1978	June 25–July 1
Dallas	1979	June 24–30

Each state has a library association.

There is also:

American Assn. of Law Libraries, 53 W. Jackson Blvd., Chicago, IL 60614

Association of Research Libraries, 1527 New Hampshire Ave., N.W., Washington, DC 20036

Canadian Library Assn., 151 Sparks St., Ottawa, Ont., Canada K1P 5E3

Catholic Library Assn., 461 W. Lancaster Ave., Haverford, PA 19041

Medical Library Assn., 919 No. Michigan Ave. (Suite 3208), Chicago, IL 60611

Music Library Assn., 343 S. Main St., (Rm. 205), Ann Arbor, MI 48108

Special Library Assn., 235 Park Ave., So., New York, NY 10003

Theatre Library Assn., 111 Amsterdam Ave., New York, NY 10023

Associated Councils of the Arts (ACA)
National Office: 570 Seventh Ave., New York, NY 10018, (212) 354-6655

The central purpose of ACA is to provide a united national voice in order to win for the arts a higher place among the priorities of our country. ACA works in partnership with more than 500 member state and community arts agencies and with a growing number of individual Advocates for the Arts. It places emphasis on developing the skills of arts councils, on research, and on an information and service lifeline.

Seminars:
Seminars are offered on a national and regional basis for ACA members.

Newsletters:
ACA Reports—A bi-monthly arts newsletter.
Word from Washington—Monthly news of the government's role in the arts.

Advocates for the Arts:
Launched as a program of ACA in 1974, Advocates for the Arts is the first national constituency of citizens engaged in economic, public, and legal action for the arts.

Membership is open to all interested people. *Individual:* $30. *Stu-*

dent: $20. *Library:* $35. Includes newsletters, membership mailings, etc.

Publications: Good list; write for descriptive account.

Association for Children with Learning Disabilities (ACLD)
National Office: 5225 Grace St., Pittsburgh, PA 15236, (412) 881-1191

A federated organization founded in 1964, ACLD has 47 state affiliates with over 600 local chapters, a total of more than 30,000 members, including parents, professionals, and concerned citizens.

Goals
Learning disabilities occur in many forms: visual, auditory, motor control, communication. Effective correction must include a total approach to the educational, psychological, and medical requirements of the individual child. ACLD believes in an interdiscipline approach. The major goals are to: encourage research, stimulate development of early detection programs and educational techniques, create a climate of public awareness and acceptance, disseminate information, and provide advocacy for the learning disabled.

Information and Referral: possibly the most important job of ACLD is to provide an initial contact for parents and professionals seeking help for a child they feel might have a learning disability.

School Program Development: ACLD and its state affiliates work directly with school systems on the planning and implementation of programs for early identification and diagnosis, as well as remediation in integrated and special classroom situations.

Advocacy: The Governmental Affairs Committee provides information and recommends action on all pending legislation which may affect learning disabled children.

Interdiscipline Communication: Annual international conferences bring together prominent specialists from all over.

Resource Center: ACLD National Headquarters makes avilable information on state and local affiliates and has for sale books, conference reports, pamphlets, and papers on a wide variety of related topics.

Newsbriefs: The official newsletter covers current developments in the field. Published monthly, it is available with state membership or on direct subscription.

Commitment

ACLD is a nonprofit organization. Financial support comes from dues, publication sales, grants, and donations. Membership is available through state affiliates. Where no state affiliate exists independent members may join National ACLD directly for annual dues of $5 which includes a subscription to *Newsbriefs*.

For a list of state affiliates and their addresses write to ACLD.

Center for Rape Concern (CRC)
Office: Philadelphia General Hospital, Mills Building C-16, 700 Civic
    Center Blvd., Philadelphia, PA 19104, (215) 823-7966
Director: Joseph Peters, M.D.
Research Director: Linda Meyer
Social Services: Maddi-June Stern

Since October 1970 the Center for Rape Concern (CRC) has provided crisis help to victims and their families and also started massive research in this area. CRC is evaluating victims and studying the effects on victims and their families. CRC is willing to be of service to all interested in their research. Write or call. CRC also has a number of publications available.

Child Welfare League of America, Inc. (CWLA)
Office: 67 Irving Place, New York, NY 10003, (212) 254-7410

The Child Welfare League of America, founded in 1920, is the North American voluntary agency serving the child welfare field. Through its program and services, the League seeks to protect and promote the welfare of children by helping child welfare agencies and communities provide essential social services for children and their families. The League has a membership of almost 400 agencies, distributed throughout 46 states, the District of Columbia, and six provinces in Canada. Though agencies in membership represent approximately 15 percent of the United States agencies providing services for children, they serve more than 50 percent of the children receiving services from agencies.

Program—The League uses every means to increase knowledge and promote better understanding of child welfare problems and to improve standards and methods in service programs for children, youth, and their families. It provides consultation; accredits agencies; conducts research; develops standards for services; sponsors educational conferences; works with national, international, and governmental organizations; maintains a reference library and information service; conducts agency or community surveys; administers special projects; and publishes a journal (*Child Welfare*), professional books and monographs, the *CWLA Newsletter,* and an annual directory of affiliated agencies. It serves child welfare agencies and the general public. Catalog on publications is available by request.

The Council for Exceptional Children (CEC)

Office: 1920 Association Dr., Reston, VA 22091
Toll free: (800) 336-3728 (United States)
Virginia residents call collect (703) 620-3660
Members: 60,000

Exceptional children are those who are both handicapped and/or gifted. The United States has nearly 9 million, of whom 7 million or more are handicapped. More than half of all 9 million, both handicapped and gifted, are not served by any special education program. One million are denied any education at all. Yet these children deserve an opportunity. CEC is trying to fill this gap.

CEC Center for Information, Technical Assistance, and Training on the Exceptional Person: Information services range from publications to customized searches and products. Technical assistance includes short and long term consultation and studies. Training activities range from self-instructional packages to speakers, conferences, workshops, and institutes. Services of the Center are available not only to all CEC members, but to all other persons concerned about exceptional people.

CEC Divisions

For CEC members with a particular interest. Divisions are completely autonomous, have their own membership dues, publications, and plan their own programs at CEC conventions. The divisions are: (1) Council of Administrators of Special Education, (2) Council for Educational Diagnostic Services, (3) Council for Children with Behavioral Disorders, (4) Division on Mental Retardation, (5) Division for Early Childhood, (6) Division for Children with Communication Disorders.

CEC Membership Dues:

Regular: $25. *Student:* $12.50. *Husband-Wife:* $37.50.

However, 15 states have different dues, write or call CEC for full information.

Educational Resources Information Center (Central ERIC)
National Institute of Education, Washington, DC 20208, (202) 254-5040

ERIC is a network of 16 clearinghouses around the country that catalog, index, and abstract documents on specialized areas and then send them to Central ERIC, where all documents are available to concerned citizens. Write to ERIC for full information on their services. The 16 areas are: (1) Career Education; (2) Counseling and Personnel Services; (3) Disadvantaged; (4) Early Childhood Education; (5) Educational Management; (6) Handicapped and Gifted Children; (7) Higher Education; (8) Information Resources; (9) Junior Colleges; (10) Languages and Linguistics; (11) Reading and Communication Skills; (12) Rural Education and Small Schools; (13) Science, Mathematics and Environmental Education; (14) Social Studies/Social Science Education; (15) Teacher Education; (16) Tests, Measurements and Evaluation.

Family Service Association of America (FSAA)
National Office: 44 East 23rd St., New York, NY 10010, (212) 674-6100
General Director: Keith Daugherty

FSAA is the national, accredited, standard-setting federation for more than 300 nonprofit, voluntary, family serving agencies throughout North America which was established in 1911. The FSAA national headquarters program spearheads a battery of services to strengthen family life and alleviate family stress by professional counseling, specialized help, and advocacy to improve social conditions that affect family life.

While family agencies vary in their range of services, all accredited by FSAA have a major program of family counseling for serious problems of marriage, child care, and personal adjustment, and all attempt to improve community conditions for family life. Many have programs of child adoption and foster care, homemaker service, information to enable people to find and use the right kind of help, and special projects. Both the national and the local agencies have Boards of Directors made up of experienced laymen who determine policy. More than 15,000 laymen participate in FSAA.

FSAA Services:
Sets professional standards for family social work, accredits Family Service agencies.

Directs pilot projects, special programs, and pioneering work related to mental and emotional health of the family, marriage breakup, problems of the aging, educating people for family living, and sponsors Plays for Living, an independently financed Division.

Strengthens local agencies by aiding them in administration, manpower, management, and counseling methods—through specialized departments, consultants, field staff, loan files, conferences, and other means.

Helps communities organize or develop efficient agencies and make voluntary Family Service available where needed.

Represents more than 340 Member Agencies by interpreting and providing valuable information to media, government, and private groups.

FSAA Publications:
Family Service Highlights, FSAA newsletter
Social Casework, FSAA Journal, 10 issues a year. $12 individual, $18 institution.
The FSAA Data Bank on the Family is a special collection of material containing information on all phases of family life. It now contains over 400 separate items and is still growing.

Federal Information Centers (FIC)
Many communities in the United States have Federal Information Centers (FIC). If you have a question about anything (contacts, publications, sources) concerning the federal government, then go to an FIC. If the Center cannot help you, it will put you in touch with an expert who can. If you need to talk to a federal agency, anywhere in the United States, you can call toll free from an FIC. If you are a professional or student doing research, or just interested in finding out information, an FIC can save you a lot of time and money by their toll free lines to federal agencies. To find the FIC nearest you just look in your telephone book, if not listed then check the major city nearest to you.

Feminist Therapy Collective
P.O. Box 442, Planetarium Station, New York, NY 10024, (212) 787-4600

The Feminist Therapy Collective grew out of the dissatisfaction with the current situation confronting individuals seeking therapeutic help. Individuals who call the Collective are encouraged to see two therapists for a consultation so that they may decide who best suits their needs. Your call will be returned by one of the members who will try to be of help to you. They have an internal newsletter and several members wrote an article published in *Love Magazine* (October, 1976, issue) on how to choose a therapist, etc. Although established for New York City, the implications of what the Collective have set up are tremendous for other communities or interested individuals. Should you want any more information they would be happy to respond.

Gam-Anon National Service Office
P.O. Box 4549, Downey, CA 90241, (213) 862-6014

Gam-Anon was formed in 1962 by wives of compulsive gamblers for spouses of compulsive gamblers. There are regularly scheduled group meetings where one is free to discuss problems and needs. "We learn to accept the fact that our spouse suffers from an emotional disturbance and although we cannot stop him or her from gambling, we can help ourselves if we so desire. In this process of sharing and caring we gather great strength to cope with our problems on a day at a time basis."

Gam-Anon is a self-supporting, nonprofit, international organization. Publications: variety, very inexpensive, write for list.

Mental Patients' Liberation Project (MPLP)
3407 Wessynton Way, Alexandria, VA 22309, (703) 360-7092

"We, of the Mental Patients' Liberation Project, are former mental patients. We've all been labeled schizophrenic, manic depressive, psychotic and neurotic—labels that have degraded us, made us feel inferior. Now we're beginning to get together—beginning to see that these labels are not true but have been thrown at us because we have refused to conform—refused to adjust to a society where to be normal is to be an unquestioning robot, without emotion or creativity. As ex-mental patients we know what it's like to be treated as an object—to be made to feel less of a person than 'normal' people on the outside. We've all felt the boredom, the regimentation, the inhumane physical and psychological abuses of institutional life—life on the inside. We are now beginning to realize that we are no longer alone in these feelings—that we are all brothers and sisters. Now for the first time we're beginning to fight for ourselves—fight for our personal liberty. We, of the Mental Patients' Liberation Project, want to work to change the conditions we have experienced. We have drawn up a Bill of Rights for Mental Patients—rights that we unquestioningly should have, but rights that have been refused to us. Because these rights are not now legally ours we are going to fight to make them a reality.

"Please contact us if there is any specific condition you would like us to work against."

The National Association for Creative Children and Adults (NACCA)
National Office: 8080 Springvalley Dr., Cincinnati, OH 45236, (513) 631-1777
Executive Officer: Ann Fabe Isaacs

Founded in 1974, the Headquarters of the NACCA offers:
1. A library for use of guests, students, children, and adults.
2. Creativity workshops for children and adults; spring and summer sessions are scheduled.
3. In-service teacher training.
4. Counseling for the creative child and adult.
5. Field term opportunities for children and adults. Credit is arranged with the individual's school or university. Individuals accepted work to advance the progress of the NACCA and their own individual talents.
6. Selected publications.

Membership provides a newsletter, discounts on publications and services, including: in-service teacher training; convention registration; annual visitation to schools for evaluation; field terms at NACCA Headquarters for children and adults; creativity workshops for children and adults, local chapter sponsors; question and answer service; *The Quarterly.*

Types of Membership:
Individual
$ 15—children under 18
$ 30—adults
$300—life, child or adult
Group and Organization
$ 50—local chapters (10 NACCA members min.)
$100—schools, junior colleges, libraries (1–499 persons)
$300—schools, universities, administrative offices, and businesses (over 500 persons)

The National Association for Mental Health, Inc. (NAMH)
National Office: 1800 N. Kent St., Arlington, VA 22209 (703) 528-6405
Executive Director: Brian O'Connell
Director of Information Services: Frances Bradley

Origin and Purpose:
The primary function of the National Association for Mental Health is to promote citizen interest and activity on behalf of the mentally ill and for the cause of mental health. The Association dates its origin from 1909 when Clifford Beers, an ex-mental patient and author of *A Mind That Found Itself* founded the National Committee for Mental Hygiene. In 1950 the Committee merged with two other organizations, The National Mental Health Foundation and The Psychiatric Foundation, to form a united front as The National Association for Mental Health.

The Association's original and continuing purposes are to:
—improve attitudes toward mental illness and the mentally ill;
—improve services for the mentally ill; and
—work for the prevention of mental illness and to promote mental health.

The Association is made up of volunteers who are sufficiently interested, informed and active to form a true special interest group. The organization functions at each level by involving several constellations of interested people studying and improving services for children, hospitalized patients, the discharged patient, and community mental health services. The Association is effective by having, at all three levels, knowledgeable and active volunteers with considerable influence on government, professional's organizations, and the general public so that prevention, identification, diagnosis, care, and rehabilitation of mental illness are achieved.

Structure: 809 chapters, 42 divisions, 5 committees, and a National Headquarters.
For a list of state affiliates write the National Office. Referrals, free extensive publications, and speakers come through the state affiliates.
Publications: quarterly magazine, pamphlets, leaflets, and films.

National Association for Retarded Citizens (NARC)
National Office: 2709 Avenue E East, P.O. Box 6109, Arlington, TX 76011, (817) 261-4961

Executive Director: Philip Roos, Ph.D.

NARC is the largest of the national associations comprising the International League of Societies for the Mentally Handicapped. NARC (formerly the National Association for Retarded Children) provides help to parents and other individuals, organizations, and communities in jointly solving the problems caused by retardation. Organized in 1950 by a handful of parents and friends of mentally retarded persons, by 1975 the Association had grown to more than 250,000 members affiliated with some 1,800 state and local member units located across the nation and in United States territories and military installations abroad. Youth NARC, the national volunteer youth movement organized in 1967 as a Division of NARC, includes in excess of 25,000 young persons between 13 and 15 years of age who are involved in providing services to mentally retarded persons, assisting in creating community awareness and understanding and acquiring firsthand knowledge of career opportunities in the field.

NARC is a nonprofit, voluntary organization.

Publications:
—*Action Together/Information Exchange:* Monthly newsletter. A roundup of items of interest in the ARC. $2.50 for one year.
—*Government Report.* Monthly. Review and analysis of the latest on national legislation and federal agency activities that affect the lives of retarded citizens. $15 one year.
—*Mental Retardation News.* Published 10 times a year. Devoted exclusively to the field of mental retardation. $3.50 for one year. $5.50 for two years.

Also, NARC has very low cost pamphlets on a wide variety of subjects concerned with retardation: general, architectural planning, community organizations, education, poverty, recreation, religion, research, residential services, social work, vocational rehabilitation, and youth.

National Center for the Prevention and Treatment of Child Abuse and Neglect (NCPTCAN)
Office: 1205 Oneida St., Denver, CO 80220, (303) 321-3963
Director: Henry Kempe, M.D.

The National Center for the Prevention and Treatment of Child Abuse and Neglect was established in the fall of 1972 to provide professionals working in the field of child abuse and neglect more extensive and up-to-date educational, research, and clinical material. The Center's staff includes pediatricians, psychiatrists, psychologists, social workers, educational coordinators, early-childhood education specialists, attorneys, research associates, adult- and child-care workers, and lay therapists. This staff has grown from members of the Child Protection Team which originated in 1958 in the Department of Pediatrics, University of Colorado Medical Center, under the direction of C. Henry Kempe, M.D., pediatrician, and with Brandt F. Steele, M.D., psychiatrist.

They originally became interested in children seen on hospital wards and in emergency rooms who had, what appeared to be, nonaccidental injuries. They felt the complexities of these situations required a multidisciplinary team approach for both diagnostic and treatment services to these families. Currently work includes education, consultation, and technical assistance, demonstration programs for treatment, program evaluation, and research. Since 1970 the staff has sponsored the Battered Child Symposium, which is open to all professionals throughout the nation and abroad. The National Child Protection *Newsletter* is produced quarterly and is sent without charge to a mailing list of approximately 6,000. Videotape and slide materials have been developed to help train professionals, and a free catalog which lists these may be obtained upon request. These materials are avilable for purchase or rental.

The staff has published numerous articles and books pertaining to medical, legal, and psychosocial aspects of child abuse and neglect— free list may be obtained by writing. Requests can be directed for bibliographies or the *Newsletter* at no charge. Persons interested in treatment in their own communities should contact the county department of social services, mental health clinic, Parents Anonymous, community crisis center, hospital, or private physician. Information regarding educational activities and special projects in a particular geographical area is available by contacting the Regional Director, Office of Child Development, for that area or the National Center on Child Abuse and Neglect (NCCAN), Children's Bureau, OCD, OHD, Department of HEW, P.O. Box 1182, Washington, DC 20013, (202) 755-0587.

It is NCCAN (Washington, DC) that is responsible for funding and monitoring Public Law 93-247 and the numerous resource and demonstration research projects. NCCAN also has available a national director of child abuse services and information. This book lists over 135 private and public child abuse treatment and prevention agencies across the United States, both research and practical, as well as ordering information. (Stock No. 100-74, $4.)

National Clearinghouse for Alcohol Information (NCALI)
Office: Box 2345, Rockville, MD 20852, (301) 948-4450

The National Institute on Alcohol Abuse and Alcoholism is charged with formulating and recommending national policies and goals regarding the prevention, control, and treatment of alcohol abuse and alcoholism, and with developing and conducting programs and activities aimed at these goals. The National Clearinghouse for Alcohol Information (NCALI), a service of the NIAAA, has been established as a supporting function to make widely available the current knowledge on alcohol-related subjects.

Information materials available from the NCALI are designed to satisfy the different needs of the many people concerned about alcohol problems, including the scientific and professional community as well as the general public. They cover a wide range of topics, from alcohol and highway safety to physiology of alcohol, psychological studies, and occupational alcoholism programs. Clearinghouse information services include: NIAAA Information and Feature Service, presenting articles on trends, opinions, and programs across the nation; *Alcohol Health and Research World,* a quarterly bulletin for those working in alcoholism prevention, treatment, and research; and a variety of books, pamphlets, and posters published by the National Institute on Alcohol Abuse and Alcoholism.

NCALI also offers a notification service to highlight current literature in the area of alcohol abuse. You can choose either of two formats: citation cards abstracting the latest articles and books in special interest areas, or bibliography booklets giving an overview of selected publications in each of 15 broad subject areas. In addition, NCALI replies to all individual requests, whether of a personal, technical, or research nature. To assure the most complete response, addresses of local treatment and counseling organizations are supplied, or manual and automated searches of NCALI files conducted.

There are a number of services you can receive at no charge from the National Clearinghouse for Alcohol Information. These include:

Reference Services:
Searches—Automated searches of NCALI computerized files for specific information regarding literature, statistics, studies, and papers.

Bibliographies—Preassembled bibliographies in commonly requested areas covering a broad range of topics.

Responses and Referrals—Answers to individual letters of a personal or technical nature and referrals to local treatment and counseling organizations.

Printed Materials:

Publications—Books, pamphlets, and directories are available in limited quantities.

Individual Notification—Citation cards abstracting the latest articles and books in specialized interest areas; issued monthly.

Grouped Interest Guides—Bibliography booklets giving an overview of selected publications in each of 15 broad subject areas.

NIAAA Information and Feature Service—Presents articles on trends, opinions, and programs across the nation; highlights the activities of the NIAAA and other alcoholism organizations; and spotlights topics of special interest. It is designed so that articles can be easily reproduced by other publications.

Alcohol Health and Research World—A quarterly bulletin for those engaged in research, prevention, or treatment of alcoholism; features survey articles, program reports, interviews, book reviews, and exchanges of opinion. This is a paid subscription magazine which may be ordered from the United States Government Printing Office.

National Clearinghouse for Drug Abuse Information (NCDAI)
Office: 11400 Rockville Pike, Rockville, MD 20852, (301) 443-6500

The National Clearinghouse for Drug Abuse Information, the focal point of all Federal information programs on drug abuse, is operated by the National Institute on Drug Abuse (NIDA). The major activities of the Clearinghouse include the publication and distribution of drug abuse information materials, the answering of inquiries, and the operation of a computer storage and retrieval file of drug abuse programs and literature.

National Clearinghouse for Mental Health Information (NCMHI)
Office: 5600 Fishers Lane, Rockville, MD 20852, (301) 443-4517

The National Clearinghouse for Mental Health Information was established to provide a central information resource on the many complex factors involved in mental illness and mental health. The computer data base is worldwide and includes journals, special published reports and documents from 40 different countries, written in 21 different languages. Routine scanning was extended to the Asian literature in 1972, and in 1973 the information base was enriched through input of multimedia materials. As of May, 1975, there were over 205,000 abstracts on-line in the system. More than 10,000 scientific inquiries are processed yearly, an active publication program is maintained, and the NCMHI provides technical consultation on the development and use of information services.

Research scientists, clinicians, professionals in many fields, agencies, students, and concerned citizens, all are part of the many audiences served by the Clearinghouse's mental health information base. Mental health professionals and advanced students may request from the Clearinghouse a computer printout of citations and abstracts on a specific topic. This is a free service offered to the professional community in the interest of speeding the research process, fostering innovation in practice and stimulating information exchange.

When requesting a Computer Search, be as precise as you can in defining the nature of your interest in the given subject. Give points or areas not to be included as well as identify what you want to use the information for. In response to the request you may expect to receive one or a combination of the following: a computer printout of literature citations and abstracts; publications; referrals to organizations or individuals that can give more complete information pertinent to the request.

Publications:

Current Ethical Issues in Mental Health.   Based on a workshop at the March 1970 Annual Meeting, American Orthopsychiatric Association, M.F. Shore, Ph.D. and S.E. Golann, Ph.D., (Eds.).

Latino Mental Health (publication date: October 1973) 2 publications: Bibliography and Abstracts. A Review of Literature.

Mental Health Directory.   A biennial listing of psychiatric (inpatient and community) treatment facilities in the United States.

Selected Sources of Inexpensive Mental Health Materials.   A listing of organizations that offer informational materials for mental health workers, teachers, and community leaders.

Bibliographies on the following topics:
Abstracts of the standard edition of Freud
Abstracts of the psychoanalytic study of the child, Vols. 1–25
Alcoholism treatment and rehabilitation: selected abstracts

Behavior modification in child and school mental health
Bibliography on racism
Early childhood psychosis
Epidemiology of mental disorders
Human intelligence
Pollution: Its impact on mental health
Psychological and social aspects of human tissue transplantation
Research in individual psychotherapy
Social aspects of alienation
Suicide and suicide prevention

For the General Public: Inquiries about mental health services, treatment, research, training, and other general areas should be sent to:
Public Inquiries Section, NCMHI, 5600 Fishers Lane, Rockville, MD 20852. Phone: (301) 443-4515

The Public Inquiries Section maintains and continually updates collections of publications, articles, and reference lists on many aspects of mental health and mental illness. These materials are available upon request from persons interested in learning more about mental health theory and practices.

The National Council on the Aging, Inc. (NCOA)
National Office: 1828 L St., N.W., Washington, DC 20036, (202) 223-6250
President: Mother M. Bernadette De Lourdes

The National Council on the Aging, a nonprofit organization, provides leadership and guidance in the development of services for older persons in hundreds of communities, in every state, Puerto Rico, Canada, and other parts of the world. Since its establishment in 1950, NCOA has worked to improve the lives of older Americans by eliminating the problems of aging and opening up opportunities for older people. NCOA is a membership organization of professionals, of organizations, and of the concerned public, drawn from every state in the nation. NCOA works with and through local, state, and national private and public agencies, private industry, union and national voluntary agencies.

NCOA derives its income from dues, sale of publications, contributions, contract services, and grants. NCOA administers research and demonstration projects and provides technical assistance to government agencies.

Publications

NCOA produces and publishes books and pamphlets dealing with a wide range of subjects related to the aging and services on their behalf. Some NCOA literature is published independently, while other literature stems from grant or contract requirements. Over 100 such publications, covering the broad aspects of aging as well as guidelines and how-to-do-it models for local planners and deliverers of specific services, are part of the technical assistance tools made available to the field of gerontology.

NCOA's regular periodicals include:

Perspective on Aging: a bimonthly magazine dealing with issues, research and programs on the aging and the aged;

Current Literature on Aging: issued quarterly, is an abstracting and indexing service covering the current journal and monograph literature in the field of aging;

Journal of Industrial Gerontology: a quarterly dealing with industrial and employment aspects of the elderly and containing original articles as well as summaries of significant articles appearing elsewhere;

MEMO from the National Institute of Senior Centers: issued monthly, includes practical suggestions for operation of Senior Centers, feature articles, program ideas, and legislative information;

The NVOILA *Newsletter:*   published monthly, provides a summary of current activities of major voluntary organizations involved in home support services.

A complete list of publications is available upon request.

National Council on Alcoholism (NCA)

National Office: 733 Third Ave., New York, NY 10017, (212) 986-4433
Executive Director: George Dimas

The National Council on Alcoholism is a national, voluntary health organization made up of local councils on alcoholism, State Alcoholism Associations, and national components, namely the American Medical Society on Alcoholism and the National Nurses' Society on Alcoholism. Though distinct organizationally, an interweaving of membership and program support among all of them assures the maximum in strength and innovativeness.

Assistance in the mobilization of concerned citizens, who have a deep and abiding interest in the problem of alcoholism, is furnished by the Department of Community Services and by the State Voluntary Alcoholism Associations Program. Both deal directly with the activation of community and state-wide voluntary citizens' organizations to plan and put into effect those kinds of programs which will lead toward the alleviation and control of alcoholism. Expertise in specific program areas is offered to Member Organizations of NCA through the Departments of Prevention and Education, Public Information, Medical, Labor and Management, Minority Program Development, Resource Development, and Publications, located at the national headquarters.

Publications:
NCA has a wide variety of publications, at very low cost, on many topics. The following are the areas covered: clergy, courts and the law, cultural patterns, general use, hospitals, labor and management, medical, nursing, psychiatry and psychology, social work, women, and youth education. Write for a free catalog or for further information.

National Council on Family Relations (NCFR)
National Office: 1219 University Ave., S.E., Minneapolis, MN 55414,
    (612) 331-2774
Executive Officer: Ruth Jewson

The NCFR was founded in 1938 as an interprofessional forum through which members of those disciplines interested in family life might think, work, and plan together for the strengthening of marriage and family life. Its objectives are to provide opportunities for individuals, organized groups, and agencies interested in family research, counseling, and education to plan and act together on matters relevant to marriage and family living, including establishment of professional standards, promotion, and coordination of educational efforts, encouragement of research, and extension of community services for families.

Publications include
Books, journals, newsletter, monographs, and directories. Write for free catalog.

Membership is open to all interested people:
Individual $30.
Husband/Wife $40.

Organizational $35.
Student $15.

Foreign and Canadian postage $2.

Members are entitled to two quarterly journals, a quarterly newsletter, and annual meetings.

National Education Association (NEA)

National Office: 1201 16th St., N.W., Washington, DC 20036, (202)
  833-4000
Executive Director: Terry Herndon
Members: 1,800,000

Founded in 1857, the purpose of the National Education Association is, "To elevate the character and advance the interests of the profession of teaching and to promote the cause of education in the United States." The NEA is the largest professional organization in the world.

Publications

All NEA members receive *Today's Education,* the journal of the NEA, and the *NEA Reporter,* a tabloid. All other NEA publications are listed in the NEA Catalog of Publication and Audiovisual Materials, which includes over 1000 titles. For a free copy of the catalog, write NEA Publishing or call (202) 833-4230.

School Counselors

Curriculum interests in counseling are fostered by the National Association of School Counselors, a nongovernance affiliate of NEA. Dues: $15. For further information contact NEA Executive Office, (202) 833-4303.

Sex Role Stereotyping

Sex role stereotyping or the differential treatment of boys and girls may be found throughout schools. NEA conducts conferences and workshops and develops materials dealing with the problems associated with sex role stereotyping. Contact Shirley McCune, (202) 833-4225.

Testing

Because of widespread misuse, the NEA advocates the elimination of group standardized intelligence, aptitude, and achievement tests to assess student potential or achievement until current testing programs are critically appraised and revised. Instruction and Professional Development (IPD) staff are assessing alternatives to standardized testing. For information, contact IPD, (202) 833-4117 or 4186.

Membership:

Active Membership—Active membership is open to any person who is engaged in or who is on a limited leave of absence from professional educational work. Active members shall hold or shall be eligible to hold a baccalaureate or higher degree or the regular teaching, vocational, or technical certificates required by their employment. Active membership is limited to persons who support the principles and goals of the Association and maintain membership in the local and state affiliates where eligible. Dues $30. The membership fee for persons eligible for Active membership who are regularly employed for less than 50 percent of the normal schedule is $15. NEA By-laws require that Active members must also be, and remain, members of local and state affiliated associations, if eligible. NEA does not accept Active membership applications directly. All Active membership applications will be processed by the local affiliated association, if available. If no local affiliate is available, then membership applications will be processed through state associations.

Paraprofessional—Paraprofessional membership is open to any person who works directly with educators in discharging their professional duties. Eligible members include teacher aides, teacher assistant, or the like, whose primary responsibility is to help the teacher with the teaching/learning process. A paraprofessional member receives all benefits and services, but may not vote or hold office. Dues $15.

Student—Student NEA membership is open to any student enrolled in or preparing for a program of study that qualifies the student for a career in education. Membership is available only through a local or state student chapter. Student members shall be eligible to be voting delegates at the Representative Assembly. Dues $3.50.

Educational Secretary—Educational secretary membership is open to any secretary or clerk in a school system, an institution of higher education, a private school, a state department of education, or local, state, and national organization affiliated with NEA in the United States or in United States schools abroad. Educational secretary members receive all benefits and services, but may not vote or hold office. Dues $15.

Associate—Associate membership is open to any person who is interested in advancing the cause of public education but who is not eligible for any other class of membership in the Association. Associate members receive all benefits and services, but may not vote or hold office. Dues $15.

National Institute of Mental Health (NIMH)
Office: 5600 Fishers Lane, Rockville, MD 20852, (301) 443-4513

The National Institute of Mental Health (NIMH) administers the Federal Government's major program of support for research in mental health. NIMH conducts and supports research into the etiology, treatment, and prevention of mental and emotional illnesses and research on a great number of public health problems related to mental health. The broad spectrum of biological, genetic, psychological, social, and environmental factors which affect and shape mental health and mental illness are studied through NIMH supported research in hospitals, universities, mental health centers, and community settings. Research on schizophrenia, the affective disorders, psychoneuroses and personality disorders, psychosomatic illnesses, organic brain disorders, and childhood mental illness accounts for a significant portion of the NIMH research support program. The development, testing, and dissemination of new knowledge of the epidemiology, etiology, diagnosis, typology, prevention, treatment, and rehabilitation of these conditions and many others is the primary research objective of the Institute.

Another portion of NIMH research support is addressed to studies of the mental health problems of children and youth, the family, the aged, and the effects of life events such as marriage, divorce, bereavement, and chronic illness. In addition, part of the research effort is devoted to studies of crime and delinquency, the impact and quality of urban life, and to special problems of minority groups. Emphasis is also given to research into the basic mechanisms of behavior in animals and man. Studies of the processes—biological, psychological, and social—underlying normal development and functioning form the core of the Institute's research program. Research designed to test models of mental health service delivery systems and studies of methods to improve existing programs for providing mental health care account for another portion of the Institute's research efforts. Extramural Research Grants are reviewed, funded, and monitored by 10 units contained in four divisions of NIMH: The Division of Extramural Research Programs; the Division of Special Mental Health Programs; the

Division of Mental Health Service Programs; and the Division of Biometry and Epidemiology.

NIMH professional staff represent all of the academic disciplines and specialized skills that comprise the mental health field. Psychiatry; social, developmental, physiological, experimental, and clinical psychology; neurochemistry; epidemiology; biostatistics; sociology; anthropology; and social work are among the disciplines represented, as well as expertise in substantive areas such as diagnosis, drug treatment in depression, etc. A significant part of staff work in science administration deals with research grant proposal review and the funding and monitoring of the over 1,000 research grants currently supported by the respective program units of the Institute. Staff responsibilities also include consultation and liaison with the scientific research community, other health agencies, and the Congress.

Publications: extensive list, literally hundreds, that are free. Write for free list. Services: answering letters, special searches, etc., free. Do not hesitate to write or call for information.

National Technical Information Service (NTIS)
Office: 5285 Port Royal Road, Springfield, VA 22161, (202) 724-3386

The National Technical Information Service of the U.S. Department of Commerce is the central source for the public sale of government-sponsored research, development and engineering reports and other analyses prepared by Federal agencies, their contractors or grantees, or by Special Technology Groups. NTIS also is a central source for Federally generated machine processable data files. NTIS ships about 19,000 information products daily as one of the world's leading processors of specialty information. It supplies its customers with about four million documents and microforms annually. The NTIS information collection exceeds 900,000 titles and all are available for sale. About 105,000 titles are stocked in multiple copies. Current lists of best selling reports describe those most in demand. NTIS is obligated by Title 15 of the United States Code to recover its cost from sales. The distribution of its information products and services is self-sustaining from the registration fees charged for information entering the system and from the sales of its products and services.

Customers may quickly locate summaries of interest from among some 420,000 Federally sponsored research reports completed and published from 1964 to date, using the agency's online computer search service (NTISearch) or more than 1000 Published Searches. About 60,000 new summaries and reports are added annually. An additional 180,000 descriptions of ongoing and recently terminated research projects, compiled by the Smithsonian Science Information Exchange, also are computer retrievable. Copies of the whole research reports, on which the summaries are based, are sold by NTIS in paper or microfiche. Write for a free catalog of services.

Office of Human Development (OHD)
Office: U.S. Department of Health, Education and Welfare, Washington, DC 20201, (202) 245-1605

The Office of Human Development was established by the Secretary of Health, Education, and Welfare in April 1973 to organize HEW's planning and resources more effectively for certain groups of "vulnerable" Americans with special needs: children and youth, the aged, physically and mentally disabled persons, Native Americans, and people living in rural areas. Programs serving these groups, formerly scattered throughout the Department, have now been consolidated in 13 OHD agencies and offices. Basically, OHD has been established to help these special groups of Americans develop their fullest human potential, to make the services they receive more effective and better coordinated, and to fulfill the Department's commitment to make the Federal government more responsive to their needs.

Six OHD agencies operate significant grant programs in addition to acting as advocates and coordinators of Departmental or government-wide services. They are: (1) Administration on Aging; (2) Office of Child Development; (3) Office of Developmental Disabilities; (4) Office of Native American Programs; (5) Office of Youth Development; (6) Rehabilitation Services Administration. The seven other OHD offices, committees, or boards do not operate grant programs but they do act as advocates for certain target groups and as coordinators of department-wide or government-wide services for those groups. They are: (1) Office for Handicapped Individuals; (2) President's Committee on Mental Retardation; (3) Office of Rural Development; (4) Office of Manpower; (5) Architectural and Transportation Barriers Compliance Board; (6) Office of Veterans Affairs; (7) Office of Volunteer Development.

Publications:
An extensive list is available from OHD for free. These cover all 13 sections of OHD on a wide variety of topics, write for a free catalog:

OHD, Publications Distribution Unit, Switzer Building, DHEW, Washington, DC 20201.

Overeaters Anonymous (OA)
World Service Office: 2190 190th St., Torrance, CA 90504, (213) 320-7911
Executive Director: Peter Beaman

Founded in 1960, Overeaters Anonymous is a fellowship of men and women who meet to share their experience, strength, and hope in order to recover from the disease of compulsive overeating. OA is not a diet club. It is a lifetime program of action which helps people resist their compulsion. Many have maintained large weight losses for several years and have learned to live life one day at a time without using excess food. They believe they have a progressive, three-fold illness affecting them physically, emotionally, and spiritually. Over a considerable length of time it gets worse, never better. There are no dues or fees for OA membership. They are self-supporting through their own contributions—the basket is passed during each meeting.

How does it work? They treat the emotional and spiritual portions of the problem by following the Twelve Steps, Twelve Traditions and Principles of the Alcoholics Anonymous program. "A person learns the tools to use, so that no matter what comes to us in life we do not have to eat to avoid our problems."

In responding to physical manifestations of this illness, many believe that they have a sensitivity to refined sugars and flour. One bite leads to another . . . and . . . another. Therefore, Overeaters Anonymous has two suggested eating plans for losing weight. Each is a disciplined manner of eating three weighed and measured meals a day with nothing in between except black coffee, tea, or sugarfree beverages—each calls for total abstinence from refined sugars and flours. They both work! They also have a plan for maintaining weight loss.

OA has several books and pamphlets available; write for a descriptive list. There are OA chapters in most cities; if you can not locate a local chapter then the National Office will put you in touch with the nearest available one or will help you to start one in your area.

Parents Anonymous (PA)
2810 Artesia Blvd., Redondo Beach, CA 90278, (213) 371-3501
Toll-Free Numbers: Outside California—(800) 421-0353
                     California—(800) 352-0386

PA members find that a once-a-week PA chapter meeting is helpful; at meetings they get together with other parents who have similar difficulties. Chapter members select a member to provide the active leadership. This member is then the chapter chairperson. To further enhance and strengthen the chairperson's role, the chairperson is aided and "backed up" by a sponsor, who is a professional person in one of the mental health fields. Together, as a group, they support and encourage each other in searching out positive alternatives to the abusive behavior in their lives. Members also share phone numbers and, occasionally, addresses so that during the week, should a crisis arise, they can call or visit one another for direct help. They also call other group members and share their successes in preventing a crisis or abusive incident.

PA is anonymous and no one needs to use other than their first name, although some members choose to use their full names. There are no membership fees, dues or other costs. No one has to openly "admit" their parenting problems, although many members do, and most find that "getting it off one's chest" is a great relief. PA is not a religious or spiritual belief program, therefore PA asks none of its members to change their individual religious or spiritual beliefs, or to believe in anything other than the human capacity for change and growth. Publications: newsletter, pamphlets, etc. Write for list.

Patients' Rights Organization (PRO)
Office: 2108 Payne Ave., #707, Cleveland, OH 44114
President: Fred Pierson

PRO was founded by a small group of people with similar feelings and opinions about injustices suffered by victims of the mental health system. These people formed a group under the guidance of Ms. Vonnie Rubin, a Vista worker. She and the Legal Aid Society helped pave the way for the group's formation in 1972. The Legal Aid Society offers PRO a meeting place and use of its facilities; however, they impose no restrictions upon the group.

PRO's work is concentrated in four main areas: living conditions of patients and housing for ex-patients; job discrimination against ex-patients; the general rights of ex-patients and patients; and community education regarding the public attitude toward the plight of emotional illness victims.

Rape Crisis Center (RCC)
P.O. Box 21005, Washington, DC 20009, (212) 333-RAPE

Will be happy to answer letters (self-addressed, stamped envelope) or telephone calls, on all areas of rape.

Publications:
How to Start a Rape Crisis Center, $3.50.
Bibliography, $1.50. A comprehensive, 10 page bibliography covering the following areas relating to rape: self-defense, medical, legal, psychology, other social sciences, and general.
Selected Articles, $1.50 for all, 25¢ each with self-addressed, stamped envelope.
—*Testimony of the Rape Crisis Center at the D.C. City Council Hearings on Rape & Follow-Up Testimony:* September 1973 (includes "Rights of Rape Victims")
  —*Counseling Guidelines*
  —*Politics of Rape*
  —*Effects of Self-Defense*
  —*Why Women Need Self-Defense*
  —*Note to Those Closest to the Rape Victim*
  —*What to Do If You Can't Start a Rape Crisis Center*
  —*Rape Prevention Tactics*

Feminist Alliance Against Rape Newsletter, $5 for one year subscription, $10 for institutions. Bi-monthly includes *National News Notes,* articles about organizing and operating a rape crisis center, political articles, and articles submitted by Centers, organizations or other individuals involved in antirape organizing.
All of the above mentioned publications, $10 for individuals; $15 for institutions.
The Rape Crisis Center is a nonprofit organization. It is the Center's policy to require payment before any material can be sent out. Please include a self-addressed, stamped envelope.

APPENDIX
Source List

AAAS
American Association for the
  Advancement of Science
1776 Massachusetts Ave., N.W.
Washington, DC 20036

Abingbow Press
201 Eighth Ave. S.
Nashville, TN 37202

Abelard-Schuman, Ltd.
666 Fifth Ave.
New York, NY 10019

Academic Press
111 Fifth Ave.
New York, NY 10003

The Academy Press, Ltd.
176 W. Adam St.
Chicago, IL 60603

Addictions (Journal)
Addiction Research Foundation of
  Ontario
33 Russell St.
Toronto, Canada M5S 2S1

Adolescence Journal
Libra Pub., Inc.
P.O. Box 165
391 Willets Rd.
Roslyn Heights, NY 11577

Aims Instructional Media, Inc.
626 Justin Ave.
Glendale, CA 91281

Alcohol and Drug Problems
  Association of North America
1101 15th St., N.W.
Washington, DC 20005

Aldine-Atherton, Inc.
529 South Wabash Ave.
Chicago, IL 60605

American Academy of
  Psychoanalysis
40 Gramercy Park N.
New York, NY 10010

The American Academy of
  Psychotherapists (AAP)
Tape Library
6420 City Lane Ave.
Philadelphia, PA 19151

*See also Professional Associations and Service Organizations.

American Council on Education
One Dupont Circle
Washington, DC 20036

American Humane Association
P.O. Box 1266
Denver, CO 80201

American Journal of Nursing
Education Services Division
American J. of Nursing Co.
10 Columbus Circle
New York, NY 10019

American Journal of Orthopsychiatry
1775 Broadway
New York, NY 10019

American Journal of Psychiatry
1700 18th St., N.W.
Washington, DC 20009

American Journal of Psychotherapy
119-21 Metropoliten Ave.
Jamaica, NY 11415

American Journal of Public Health
American Public Health Association
1015 18th St., N.W.
Washington, DC 20036

American Personnel & Guidance
Assn.
1607 New Hampshire Ave., N.W.
Washington, DC 20009

American Psychiatric Association
1700 18th St., N.W.
Washington, DC 20009

American Psychological Association
1200 17th St., N.W.
Washington, DC 20036

American Psychologist
American Psychological Assn., Inc.
1200 17th St., N.W.
Washington, DC 20036

AMS Press
56 E. 13th St.
New York, NY 10003

W. H. Anderson Co.
646 Main St.
Cincinnati, OH 45201

Annals of the New York Academy of
Sciences
2 E. 63rd St.
New York, NY 10021

Appleton-Century-Crofts
292 Madison Ave.
New York, NY 10017

Archives of the Foundation of
Thanathology
Alan R. Liss, Inc.
150 Fifth Ave.
New York, NY 10011

Arco Pub. Co., Inc.
10 E. 40th St.
New York, NY 10016

Aronson, Jason, Inc.
59 Fourth Ave.
New York, NY 10003

Association Press
291 Broadway
New York, NY 10007

Australian & New Zealand Journal
of Psychiatry
Australian & New Zealand College
of Psychiatrists

Maudsley House, 107 Rathdowne St.
Carlton, Victoria 3053
Australia

Avon Books
959 Eighth Ave.
New York, NY 10019

Ballantine Books, Inc.
101 Fifth Ave.
New York, NY 10003

Bantam Books Inc.
666 Fifth Ave.
New York, NY 10019

Baron's Education Series, Inc.
113 Crossways Park Dr.
Woodbury, NY 11797

Basic Books
404 Park Ave. South
New York, NY 10016

Beacon Press
25 Beacon St.
Boston, MA 02108

Behavior Research and Therapy
Pergamon Press, Inc.
Maxwell House
Fairview Park
Elmsford, NY 10523

Behavioral Sciences Tape Library
c/o Sigma Information, Inc.
545 Cedar Lane
Teaneck, NJ 07666

Big Sur Recordings
2015 Bridgeway
Sausalito, CA 94965

Bobbs-Merrill Co., Inc.
Subs. of Howard W. Sams & Co.
4 W. 58th St.
New York, NY 10019

Bookpeople
2940 17th St.
Berkeley, CA 94710

Brady, Robert J., Co.
Subs. of Prentice-Hall, Inc.
Rts. 197 & 450
Bowie, MD 20715

Brandon (Audio tapes)
Crowell-Collier Macmillan, Inc.
484 King St.
Littleton, MA 01460

Brigham Young University Press
205 University Press Building
Provo, UT 84602

British Journal of Addiction
Longman Group Ltd.
    Journals Division, Longman House
Burnt Mill, Harlow
Essex, England CM20 2FE

British Medical Journal
Churchill Livingstone
23 Ravelston Terrace
Edinburgh, England EH4 3TL

Brooks/Cole Pub. Co.
540 Abrego St.
Monterey, CA 93940

Brunner/Mazel, Inc.
64 University Place
New York, NY 10003

Bulletin of the Menninger Clinic
  Journal
Publications Division
The Menninger Foundation
Box 829
Topeka, KS 66601

Burgess Pub. Co.
7108 Ohms Lane
Minneapolis, MN 55435

CCM Films, Inc.
866 Third Ave.
New York, NY 10022

CRM Productions
9263 Third St.
Beverly Hills, CA 90210

California School of Professional
  Psychology, San Francisco
2450 17th St.
San Francisco, CA 94122

Canadian Psychiatric Association
  Journal
Canadian Psychiatric Association
Suite 103
225 Lisgar St.
Ottawa, Ontario
Canada K2P 0C6

Carterhouse Pub.
(Carter Craft Doll House)
5505 42nd Ave.
Hayattsville, MD 20781

Center for Cassette Studies
8110 Webb Ave.
N. Hollywood, CA 91605

Child Welfare League of America
44 E. 23rd St.
New York, NY 10010

Christopher D. Smithers Foundation,
  Inc.
41 E. 57th St.
New York, NY 10022

Churchill Livingstone
23 Ravelston Terrace
Edinburgh, England EH4 3TL

Claretian Publications
221 W. Madison St.
Chicago, IL 60606

Collier, P.F., Inc.
866 Third Ave.
New York, NY 10022

Columbia Cinematique
711 Fifth Ave.
New York, NY 10022

Columbia University Press
562 W. 113 St.
New York, NY 10025

Communications Through Cassettes,
  Inc.
4837 N.E. 18th Terrace
Fort Lauderdale, FL 33308

Community Mental Health Journal
2852 Broadway
New York, NY 10025

The Council on Foundations
Box 783
Old Chelsea Station
New York, NY 10011

Counseling Psychologist
Washington University
Box 1116
St. Louis, MO 63130

Cowan Pub. Co.
14 Vanderventer Ave.
Port Washington, NY 11050

Coward, McCann & Geoghegan,
Inc.
200 Madison Ave.
New York, NY 10016

Dell Pub. Co.
750 Third Ave.
New York, NY 10017

Do It Now Foundation
1301 E. McDowell
Phoenix, AZ 85006

Doubleday & Co., Inc.
245 Park Ave.
New York, NY 10017

Drug Abuse Council
1828 L St., N.W.
Washington, DC 20036

ETC, Inc.
15354 Weddington St.
Van Nuys, CA 91401

Elaine Lynn & Associates
1506 S. Bay Front
Balboa Island, CA 92662

Family Coordinator
The National Council on Family
  Relations
1219 University Ave., S.E.
Minneapolis, MN 55414

Family Process
The Nathan W. Ackerman Family
  Institute
140 E. 78th St.
New York, NY 10021

Fawcett Pub. Inc.
Fawcett Place
Greenwich, CT 06830

Film Library
Western Behavioral Sciences Institute
1150 Silverado
La Jolla, CA 92037

Film Library–Oregon
1633 S.W. Park
Portland, OR 97207

Films Incorporated
1144 Wilmette Ave.
Wilmette, IL 60091

Fordham University Press
University Box L
Bronx, NY 10458

Foundation of Thanatology
Columbia-Presbyterian Medical
  Center
622 W. 168th St.
New York, NY 10032

Free Press
866 Third Ave.
New York, NY 10022

W. H. Freeman — Co.
660 Market St.
San Francisco, CA 94104

Garland STPM Press
545 Madison Ave.
New York, NY 10022

Genetic Psychology Monographs
The Journal Press
Two Commercial St.
Provincetown, MA 02657

Gerontologist
Joseph Bourgholtzer, Inc.
The JBI Bldg.
Box 521
Mahwah, NJ 07430

Green, Warren H., Pub. Co.
10 S. Brentwood Blvd.
St. Louis, MO 63105

Grove Press, Inc.
53 E. 11th St.
New York, NY 10003

Grune and Stratton Pub. Co.
111 Fifth Ave.
New York, NY 10003

Hammond Pub. Co.
515 Valley St.
Maplewood, NJ 07040

Harcourt Brace Jovanovich, Inc.
757 Third Ave.
New York, NY 10017

Harper & Row
10 East 53rd St.
New York, NY 10022

Harvey, Miller & Medcalf, Ltd.
20 Marryat Road
London, England SW19 5BD

Health Sciences Pub. Corp.
451 Greenwich St.
New York, NY 10013

Holbrook Press
470 Atlantic Ave.
Boston, MA 02110

Holt, Rinehart & Winston
383 Madison Ave.
New York, NY 10017

Hospital Publications, Inc.
609 Fifth Ave.
New York, NY 10017

Houghton Mifflin Co.
110 Tremont St.
Boston, MA 02107

Humanities Press, Inc.
303 Park Ave. South
New York, NY 10010

Impact
P.O. Box 635
Ann Arbor, MI 48107

International Film Bureau, Inc.
332 S. Michigan Ave.
Chicago, IL 60604

International Journal of the
    Addictions
Marcel Dekker Journals
P.O. Box 11305
Church St. Sta.
New York, NY 10249

International Journal of Aging and
    Human Development
Baywood Pub. Co., Inc.
43 Central Dr.
Farmingdale, NY 11735

International Journal of Mental
    Health
International Arts & Sciences Press,
    Inc.
901 N. Broadway
White Plains, NY 10603

International University Press
239 Park Ave. South
New York, NY 10003

Inter-Varsity Press
Box F
Downers Grove, IL 60515

Joint Information Service
1700 18th St., N.W.
Washington, DC 20009

Journal of Abnormal Psychology
1200 17th St., N.W.
Washington, DC 20036

Journal of Alcoholism
Medical Council on Alcoholism
36 Eccleston Sq.
London, England SW1

Journal of the American Academy of
  Child Psychiatry
Journal Department
Yale University Press
92 A. Yale Sta.
New Haven, CT 06520

The Journal of the American Dental
  Assn.
211 E. Chicago Ave.
Chicago, IL 60611

Journal of the American Medical Assn.
535 N. Dearborn St.
Chicago, IL 60610

Journal of Applied Behavioral
  Analysis
University of Kansas
Department of Human Development
Lawrence, KS 66044

Journal of Clinical Psychology
Clinical Psychology Pub. Co., Inc.
4 Conant Sq.
Brandon, VT 05733

Journal of Consulting and Clinical
  Psychology
1200 17th St., N.W.
Washington, DC 20036

Journal of Contemporary
  Psychotherapy
APA, Inc.
1200 17th St., N.W.
Washington, DC 20036

Journal of Geriatric Psychiatry
International Universities Press, Inc.
239 Park Ave. South
New York, NY 10003

Journal of Jewish Communal Service
National Conference of Jewish
  Communical Service
15 E. 26th St.
New York, NY 10010

Journal of Orthomolecular
  Psychiatry (Regina)
Academy of Orthomolecular
  Psychiatry
2135 Albert St.
Regina, Saskatchewan
Canada

Journal of Pastoral Care
Association of Clinical Pastoral
  Education
475 Riverside Dr.
New York, NY 10027

Journal of Studies on Alcohol
Rutgers University
New Brunswick, NJ 08903

Journal of Thanatology
Alan R. Riss, Inc.
150 Fifth Ave.
New York, NY 10011

Karger, S.
c/o Albert J. Phiebig
P.O. Box 352
White Plains, NY 10602

Knopf, Inc., Alfred A.
201 E. 50th St.
New York, NY 10022

Know, Inc.
P.O. Box 86031
Pittsburgh, PA 15221

Lexington Library, Inc.
355 Lexington, Ave.
New York, NY 10017

Libra Publishers, Inc.
391 Willets Rd.
P.O. Box 165
Roslyn Heights, NY 11577

Lippincott Co., J. B.
E. Washington Sq.
Philadelphia, PA 19105

Little, Brown & Co.
34 Beacon St.
Boston, MA 02106

Liveright Pub. Co.
500 Fifth Ave.
New York, NY 10036

Longman Canada, Ltd.
55 Barber Green Rd.
Donsmills
Ontario, Canada

McGraw-Hill Book Co.
1221 Ave. of the Americas
New York, NY 10020

McGraw-Hill Films
330 W. 42nd St.
New York, NY 10036

Macmillan Co.
866 Third Ave.
New York, NY 10022

Marquis Academic Media
200 East Ohio St.
Chicago, IL 60011

Marriage and Family Living Journal
(formerly: Marriage and Family
   Counselors Quarterly)
The National Council on Family
   Relations
1219 University Ave., S.E.
Minneapolis, MN 55414

Medical Aspects of Human Sexuality
   (Journal)
Hospital Pub., Inc.
609 Fifth Ave.
New York, NY 10017

Medical Insight
Insight Pub. Co., Inc.
150 E. 58th St.
New York, NY 10022

Medical World News
1221 Ave. of the Americas
New York, NY 10020

The MIT Press
28 Carleton St.
Cambridge, MA 02142

William Morrow & Co., Inc.
105 Madison Ave.
New York, NY 10016

C. V. Mosby Co.
11830 Westline Industrial Dr.
St. Louis, MO 63141

MSS Information Corp.
655 Madison Ave.
New York, NY 10021

Nash Publishing Corp.
9255 Sunset Blvd.
Los Angeles, CA 90069

National Council on the Aging
1828 L St., N.W.
Washington, DC 20036

National Council on Family
  Relations
1219 University Ave., S.E.
Minneapolis, MN 55414

National Institute on Alcohol Abuse
  and Alcoholism
National Clearinghouse for Alcohol
  Information
P.O. Box 2345
Rockville, MD 20852

National Technical Information
  Service
5285 Port Royal Rd.
Springfield, VA 22151

New American Library
1301 Ave. of the Americas
New York, NY 10019

New Human Services Institute
184 Fifth Ave.
New York, NY 10010

NIMH
National Institute of Mental Health
5600 Fishers Lane
Rockville, MD 20852

Norton, W.W., & Co., Inc.
500 Fifth Ave.
New York, NY 10036

Omega: The Journal of Death and
  Dying
Baywood Pub. Co., Inc.
43 Central Dr.
Farmingdale, NY 11735

Oxford University Press, Inc.
200 Madison Ave.
New York, NY 10016

Pacifica Tape Library
5316 Venice Blvd.
Los Angeles, CA 90019

Panel Publications
14 Plaza Rd.
Greenvale, NY 11548

Pantheon Press
Division of Random House
201 E. 50th St.
New York, NY 10022

Peacock, F.E., Publishers, Inc.
401 W. Irving Park Rd.
Itasca, IL 60143

Penguin Books, Inc.
7110 Ambassador Rd.
Baltimore, MD 21207

Penn. State University
Psychology Cinema
17 Willard Bldg.
University Park, PA 16802

Pergamon Press, Inc.
Maxwell House
Fairview Park
Elmsford, NY 10523

Philosophical Library, Inc.
15 E. 40th St.
New York, NY 10016

Pitman Pub. Co.
6 Davis Drive
Belmont, CA 94002

Plenum Press
227 W. 17th St.
New York, NY 10011

Plume Books
1301 Ave. of the Americas
New York, NY 10019

Pocket Books
Rockefeller Center
630 Fifth Ave.
New York, NY 10020

Police Chief
International Assn. of Chiefs of
  Police
Eleven Firstfield Rd.
Gaithersburg, MD 20760

Prentice-Hall Film Library
Englewood Cliffs, NJ 07632

Professional Psychology Journal
American Psychological Assn., Inc.
1200 17th St., N.W.
Washington, DC 20036

Psychiatric Annals
Insight Communications, Inc.
150 E. 58th St.
New York, NY 10022

Psychiatric Opinion
Opinion Pub., Inc.
82 Cochituate Rd.
Framingham, MA 01701

Psychological Films, Inc.
110 N. Wheeler St.
Orange, CA 92669

Psychology Today
One Park Avenue
New York, NY 10016

Public Services Materials Center
104 E. 40th St.
New York, NY 10016

Putnam's Sons, G. P.
200 Madison Ave.
New York, NY 10016

Quadrangle/New York Times Book
Co.
10 E. 53rd St.
New York, NY 10022

Quarterly Journal of Studies on
  Alcohol
Rutgers University
New Brunswick, NJ 08903

Rand McNally
P.O. Box 7600
Chicago, IL 60680

Random House
201 E. 50th St.
New York, NY 10022

Raven Press
1140 Ave. of the Americas
New York, NY 10036

Real People Press
Box 542
Lafayette, CA 94549

Ronald Press Co.
79 Madison Ave.
New York, NY 10016

Roth, Leonard
53 Three Brooks
Freehold, NJ 07728

Sage Publications, Inc.
275 S. Beverly Dr.
Beverly Hills, CA 90212

San Francisco Newsreel
1232 Market St.
San Francisco, CA 94102

Shocken Brooks, Inc.
67 Park Ave.
New York, NY 10016

Scholastic Book Services
50 West 44th St.
New York, NY 10036

Science House, Inc.
59 Fourth Ave.
New York, NY 10003

Science Journal
IPC Business Press Ltd.
Dorset House
Stamford St.
London, England SE1

Science Research Assn., Inc.
259 E. Erie St.
Chicago, IL 60611

Scribner's Sons, Charles, Inc.
597 Fifth Ave.
New York, NY 10017

Seabury Pub. Co.
815 Second Ave.
New York, NY 10017

Serina Press
70 Kennedy St.
Alexandria, VA 22305

Sexual Behavior
1255 Portland Place
Boulder, CO 80302

Simon & Schuster
630 Fifth Ave.
New York, NY 10020

Smith College Studies in Social Work
    Journal
Northampton, MA 01063

Social Casework Journal
44 E. 23rd St.
New York, NY 10010

Social Worker
55 Parkdale Ave.
Ottawa, Canada K1Y 1E5

Spokeswoman
5464 South Shore Dr.
Chicago, IL 60615

Springer-Verlag New York, Inc.
175 Fifth Ave.
New York, NY 10010

Stanford University Press
Stanford University
Stanford, CA 94305

Stein & Day Publishers
7 E. 48th St.
New York, NY 10017

Straight Arrow Books
625 Third Ave.
San Francisco, CA 94107

Superintendent of Documents
U.S. Government
GPO–Washington
Washington, DC 20402

Tan Press
P.O. Box 424
Rockford, IL 61105

Tane Press
6778 Greenville Ave.
Dallas, TX 75231

Teachers College Press
1234 Amsterdam Ave.
New York, NY 10027

Thomas, Charles C
301 E. Lawrence Ave.
Springfield, IL 62703

Threshold
2025 Highland Ave.
Los Angeles, CA

Unitarian Universalist Association
78 Beacon St.
Boston, MA 02108

Universal Pub. & Distributing Corp.
235 E. 45th St.
New York, NY 10017

University of California
Extension Media Center
2233 Fulton St.
Berkeley, CA 94720

University of Chicago Press
5801 South Ellis Ave.
Chicago, IL 60637

University of London Press, Ltd.
Hodder & Stoughton Educational
P.O. Box 702
Mill Rd.
Dunton Green
Sevenoaks, Kent
England TN13 2YD

University of Miami Press
Drawer 9088
Coral Gables, FL 33124

University of Michigan Press
615 E. University
Ann Arbor, MI 48106

University of Michigan Television
Center
310 Maynard St.
Ann Arbor, MI 48108

U.S. Dept. of Health, Education and
Welfare
Washington, DC 20202

Wadsworth Pub. Co.
Ten Davis Dr.
Belmont, CA 94002

John Wiley & Sons, Inc.
605 Third Ave.
New York, NY 10016

World Health Organization
United Nations Headquarters
First Ave., 45th St.
New York, NY 10017

World Publishing Co.
110 E. 59th St.
New York, NY 10022

Yale University Press
92A Yale Sta.
New Haven, CT 06520

Peter H. Wyden Pub. Co.
McKay, David Co., Inc.
750 Third Ave.
New York, NY 10017